IDENTITY,
CONSCIOUSNESS
AND VALUE

IDENTITY, CONSCIOUSNESS AND VALUE

PETER UNGER

New York   Oxford

OXFORD UNIVERSITY PRESS

Oxford University Press

Oxford   New York   Toronto
Delhi   Bombay   Calcutta   Madras   Karachi
Kuala Lumpur   Singapore   Hong Kong   Tokyo
Nairobi   Dar es Salaam   Cape Town
Melbourne   Auckland

and associated companies in
Berlin   Ibadan

First published in 1990 by Oxford University Press, Inc.,
200 Madison Avenue, New York, New York 10016

First issued as an Oxford University Press paperback, 1992

Oxford is a registered trademark of Oxford University Press

Library of Congress Cataloging-in-Publication Data
Unger, Peter K.
Identity, consciousness, and value / Peter Unger.
p.   cm.
Includes bibliographical references.
ISBN 0-19-505401-6
ISBN 0-19-507917-5 (PBK.)
1. Identity.   2. Consciousness.   3. Values.
4. Mind and body   5. Self.
I. Title   BD450.U46   1990   126—dc20   89-28758

2 4 6 8 9 7 5 3 1

Printed in the United States of America
on acid-free paper

For Andrew

ACKNOWLEDGMENTS

Many philosophers are happy enough advocating what are, essentially, the same sorts of general views for all of their intellectual lives. As even a moderately full exploration of an ambitious view may well take several decades, this inertial tendency often works for the good of philosophy as a whole. But, for good or for ill, it appears that I am a more restless sort of person. I have a strong need, once in a while, to wipe the slate clean and to start over again. Six years in the writing, the present book represents a severe departure from most of my work during the previous dozen years. While the earlier writing was extremely radical, the present effort represents a philosophy that, both in method and in substance, is quite conservative.

It is no easy thing to attend seriously to someone who changes his direction so completely. Many people have done me the favor of making the necessary effort. Throughout the entire six years, two philosophers have been especially patient, serious and charitable. Both of them greatly influenced the work that you now hold in your hand.

More than any other single person, Derek Parfit inspired this enterprise. Even before their publication, his writings on personal identity and value brought an enormous excitement to the whole area. As was my good fortune, during five of the six years I was writing this book, Parfit spent considerable time as a visiting professor in my department at New York University. At these times, he discussed many ideas with me, offering lots of encouragement along with large doses of astute criticism. In addition, he read what amounted to two distinct drafts of this book: As regards the second of these drafts, he provided me with the most copious, detailed and helpful set of written comments that, on any of my work, I have ever received.

Through many hours of discussion, in each of the past six years, Mark Johnston was nearly as great an influence on the work. He also read what amounted to two drafts, including the draft just prior to the very last changes (all made in June 1989). From 1984 through 1987, he made quite a few day-trips from Princeton to New York, proving to be a bulwark of a very small discussion group on these topics that convened here in those years. In the academic year 1987–88, while on sabbatical from Princeton, Johnston was the philosopher in residence at NYU, perhaps a first for our department. In particular, the main theme of Chapter 7, the realistic compromise view of what matters in survival, is very similar to his view on that topic. It is largely through his forceful discussion that I was driven to adopt the view that, in that chapter, I now advocate.

A few other people also helped me greatly. Through sending me letters, papers and especially casettes, in which he espoused his own views, Arnold Zuboff showed me a whole universe of beautiful and important examples. These strongly influenced the sixth chapter, but also had an effect on the second chapter and on the appendix to Chapter 8.

During the first few years of the project, many discussions with my colleague, Thomas Nagel, were very important toward the formation of my views. Because his energies lately have gone almost entirely in the direction of ethics and political philosophy, in the past few years our interchanges have been few. But, in at the beginning, he was there when most needed.

In the past couple of years, two young members of my department took up the slack. Reading quite a lot of earlier material, but also reading the whole last draft—before the final June changes—John Carroll and Roy Sorensen provided me with astute criticisms, solid checks on my own intuitions, and friendly encouragement to push through to completion. It is a mark of their great versatility, and love for philosophy, that neither of their research interests overlaps much with the main themes of this book.

During his year here as a visiting assistant professor, Stephen White offered me many useful comments and, in this past year, provided more on the telephone. In every year, David Lewis gives me what I suppose are philosophy lessons on the phone, such is his brilliance and eloquence. Raymond Martin read the next-to-last draft, providing lengthy typed comments that, in many instances, directed my efforts and saved me from errors. Brian Garrett did much the same when he read the final draft.

Many others also supplied me with useful comments and criticisms. Some that come to mind are Susan Brison, Eric Brown, Mark Heller, Frances Kamm, Daniel Kolak, David Lewine, Geoffrey Madell, Colin McGinn, John

Richardson, John Robinson, David Rosenthal, Stephen Schiffer, Sydney Shoemaker, Michael Smith, Ernest Sosa, Jim Stone, Peter Van Inwagen, Bernard Williams, and Ben Zipursky.

Well before the book was completed, I wrote two papers that, in retrospect, were studies toward this larger work: A fair amount of the material in Chapter 2 originally saw print in "Consciousness and Self-Identity" and a fair amount of Chapter 6 was published in "Conscious Beings in a Gradual World." As both papers appeared in *Midwest Studies in Philosophy,* I thank the editors and the publisher of those volumes for permission to reprint.

Finally, during all too much of these past six years, the intensity of my work on this book has been almost obsessional. This behavior has placed a very great burden on my wife, Susan, and our son, Andrew. Now that the book is finished, they must feel as much relief as I. For their putting up with my lengthy withdrawals into the mazes of these esoteric ideas, and for loving me through it all, I am very grateful to them both.

New York   P.K.U.
July 1989

CONTENTS

IDENTITY,
CONSCIOUSNESS
AND VALUE

1

INVESTIGATING OUR
BELIEFS ABOUT OURSELVES:
AN INTRODUCTION

By the end of this book, if not before, you may come to have a fuller appreciation of some of your central beliefs about yourself, and some of your related attitudes. In particular, you may come to realize more fully that, even as you yourself most deeply believe, after several more decades at most, you will cease to exist, completely and forever. In the light of this awareness, and according to your deepest values, perhaps you will make the most of your quite limited existence.

1. Two Hypothetical Examples: A Clear Case of Survival and a Clear Failure of Survival

Sometime in the distant future, as we may imagine, wondrous technologies may become available that will work, not only on other sorts of things, but on people just like ourselves. One of these may be the process of *super freezing and super thawing*: A super freezing machine will stop a person's molecules in their tracks, so to say, almost perfectly preserving their relative arrangement for minutes, or for years. Almost instantaneously, it reduces the temperature of a person's body to within a very minute fraction of one degree Kelvin of absolute zero, and keeps it there until it operates in reverse. Later, the device may operate as a super thawing machine, raising the temperature of that body, virtually instantaneously, to normal body temperature.

As far as any technical matters are concerned, these devices work extremely well: Technically, the machines work even more reliably and proficiently than the best of our own very reliable electric light switches and, for the bodies that enter them, they are even safer than our own very safe elevators.

As we may further imagine, there may be only some small, even trivial differences between the person just after thawing and the person just before freezing. In all important respects, these differences may be noticeably less than the small differences, in actual fact, between you now and yourself just one minute ago, when you did not have your memories of this past minute. After the thawing, experience, thought and behavior will take up where, right before the freezing, they left off.

Will a person who enters this superbly reliable freezing and thawing process survive it? Or, will only the body survive while it becomes, toward the end, the body of an exactly similar, but numerically distinct, person? As we strongly respond, even the person himself will survive. At the end, there will not merely be some later person who is extremely like the earlier, and who is composed of the same matter arranged in the same way. No; there will be the very same identical person, existing both at earlier and at later times.

Regarding a person's strict survival, we make a very strong, positive response to the hypothetical example of freezing and thawing. Certain other hypothetical cases elicit equally strong responses, but in the negative direction. One of these concerns the process of *taping with physical temporal overlap*: Whether he is asleep or awake at the time, a person may enter this taping process quite directly. For dramatic emphasis, let us imagine a case where, at the outset, the person who enters is sound asleep, with no conscious thought or experience; he is, of course, asleep in a certain location, which we will say is "right here." In the taping process, a machine records the exact nature of, and the precise relative arrangement of, all of the person's atoms and molecules. Using this information and using a different batch of matter "over there," the device arranges, over there, exactly as many molecules, of just those sorts, in precisely that same arrangement. Exactly alike in all qualitative respects, there is a person sound asleep over there and a person sound asleep right here. After five minutes, there awakens right here a person who is, at the very least, just like the person who was right here before. There also awakens over there a person just like that. After another five minutes, there is an annihilating explosion right here, which disturbs nothing and nobody over there. From the moment of his awakening, right through and after the explosion, the person over there experiences, thinks and acts in just the expected ways.

Will the person who, right here, enters this temporal overlap process survive the whole thing, including the explosion, and end up as the sole person who emerges over there? Or, will he cease to exist, at the end there being, over there, only an exactly similar, but a numerically distinct, second person? As we strongly respond, someone who undergoes this second hypothetical process will not survive beyond the time of the explosion. The person who emerges from the process, over there, is a numerically distinct individual. Just as it is very clear that a person *will* survive the hypothetical process of super freezing, so it is very clear that a person will *not* survive this quite different hypothetical process of taping with physical temporal overlap.

Many of us believe that we have, or that we are, non-physical souls. This belief often encourages the further belief that we will survive the death and destruction of our brains and bodies. Without these beliefs, our earthly lives might seem absurd and unbearably hopeless. With them, we may live filled with hope: After someone's merely physical demise, it might be hoped, she may still enjoy much conscious experience.

Although many of us may have beliefs of this sort, these beliefs of ours are weak and, even by our own lights, they may be unreasonable. For we might have much stronger, deeper beliefs in the opposite direction. Our disparate responses to the case of freezing and thawing, on the one hand, and to the case of taping with overlap, on the other, begin to indicate that this is so. Do we really believe that we have souls that somehow will favor the first of these processes but, on the other hand, will so clearly fail to favor the second? That seems quite unlikely indeed. Nor is it much more likely that we harbor other beliefs that are very harmonious with a strong belief that a human person's essence, or his identity, resides in any immaterial soul that he has. Perhaps, then, none of us strongly believe, or believe with much confidence or conviction, that he may be saved by the saving of any immaterial soul that he has. With a bit more of an idea of where we may be going, we may repeat the idea with which we opened our discussion: By the end of this book, if not before, you should be well aware that, *even as you yourself most deeply believe*, after several more decades at most, you will cease to exist, completely and forever.

2. Three Main Topics: Personal Identity, Conscious Experience and Actual Values

As the discussion has indicated, the single most central topic of this book is the philosophy of our own strict survival or, to use a professionally popular label, *personal identity*. The main question of this area concerns what is involved when a person, like you or me, survives from the present time to some future time, like a hundred years from now. This main question should not be confused with certain other questions, all of which will be somewhat marginal to this present study.

In the first place, our leading question is future-oriented. As such it does not concern the conditions whereby we have survived up until now. As is at least arguable, there may have been a time when I was not a person, say, when I may have been a one week old fetus, quite newly conceived. At that point, I might not have had even a capacity for quite rudimentary feeling; perhaps, I then had only the disposition to develop into a being with psychological attributes.[1] But none of this is directly relevant to the question of my focus. For now, I am a person; I am a being with a very complex psychology. For me to continue on from this point, it might be necessary that some of this psychology be causally furthered.

In the second place, our question must not be confused with the quite different question, "What is a person?" Many philosophers who have professed a wish to focus on a question like ours have gotten side-tracked, I think, by concentrating on this other interesting query.[2] As should be obvious, you might learn a great deal, for example, both about the conditions of your dog's survival and also about the conditions of your cat's survival. Indeed, in all their main lines, the two accounts might run in parallel. Even so, all of these three things may remain true: First, you may have no articulate idea as to what a dog is; second, you may have no articulate idea as to what a cat is; and, third, you may be quite sure that a good account of what a dog is will be materially different from any good account of what a cat is.

For us, the distinction between these questions is quite important: As I suspect, a good account of your survival will run closely parallel to a good account of your dog's survival. But I do not suspect, for one minute, that your dog is a person. Moreover, I am also quite sure that there are all sorts of important differences between your psychology and his. Both of these points may be important, for example, to various ethical questions. At the same time, they both may be rather marginal to the question of your dog's survival and, at the center of our present focus, to the question of your own survival. Despite those two points, in giving an account of your survival, the best strategy may be to focus on the parallels between your survival and your dog's survival.

In the third place, and in line with this, I distinguish between the question of what are the conditions of my survival and, on the other hand, what are the conditions for me to remain a person. Now, if I am essentially a person, then these two questions will receive answers that are essentially the same. But, as we remember, it is at least arguable that I once was a very young fetus and not a person. Especially with this in mind, we should not be certain that

---

1. For an interesting discussion of these matters, see Jim Stone, "Why Potentiality Matters," *Canadian Journal of Philosophy*, 1987.

2. One very recent example of this, as it appears to me, is Kathleen V. Wilkes, *Real People*, Oxford University Press, 1988.

if I ever should cease being a person, then, for that reason, I will cease to exist altogether. Not overly impressed with the label "personal identity," our main question concerns only the conditions of our survival itself.

A second important topic for this book is the philosophy of our consciousness, or of *conscious experience*. While I will say little positive about the nature of conscious experience, I will try first to uncover and then to refute some influential positive ideas. In so doing, I hope to promote a more objective approach to our conscious experiences. This objective approach will encourage and support the thought, although it will not establish the conclusion, that each conscious experience is a physical process. At all events, insofar as we may promote an objective approach to our consciousness, we may promote an objective approach, as well, to our survival. As we will begin to make clear in Chapter 2, any serious philosophical study of personal identity will concern itself with the topic of consciousness.

While we would be delighted to be around a hundred years from now, delight in such a prospect is not unconditional. Given our actual values, there is no good, for us, in being alive many years in a wholly non-conscious state, as may happen to some people in deep coma. By itself, time alive is of precious little value, if any at all, to us who are alive. For my life to be of much value to me, I must enjoy conscious experience during much of my life. As would you, I would far prefer twenty more years of normal life, replete with much conscious experience, to sixty more years alive only in wholly non-conscious states. Now, having much conscious experience will not guarantee that my life will be worthwhile for me, of course, as my life might be painful, pointless or inadequate in other ways. But, given the values we actually do have, a person's enjoying much conscious experience is a precondition of her life being of much value for her.

Of the main areas of philosophy, both personal identity and conscious experience are most appropriately considered topics of *metaphysics*. As we noted, although questions of conscious experience are metaphysical matters, consciousness is a main focal point of our values. As may be somewhat less obvious, our strict survival is also deeply intertwined with our basic values or norms. In line with this, the third main topic of this book is the *appreciation of our actual values*. It is my hope that, as will certain of my thoughts about conscious experience, my investigation of personal identity will cast some light on some of these important normative questions.

3. Toward a Sensibly Balanced Methodology

The account of our survival that I shall seek is not meant to apply to all logically possible situations. More modestly, it is intended to hold for those situations the obtaining of which is consistent with the main lines of our accepted world view.

The limitation that we place on our ambitious project sits well with the sensibly balanced methodology that we mean to employ. On our methodical approach, we give great weight to our responses to examples, not only actual cases and those hypothetical situations permitted by a correct science, but also quite a few scientifically impossible scenarios as well. For all I know, the two hypothetical cases presented in our first section are, from the perspective of the correct science, themselves impossible examples. Still, in relevant ways, those cases are not so wild but that they may instruct us with regard to our beliefs about the general conditions of our survival.[3]

Although it allows great weight for a wide variety of examples, our methodical approach is to be balanced in at least two ways. First, the weight given our responses to examples can be offset, and even overridden, by the weight given to plausible philosophical hypotheses. When an exotic case, or even a special group of examples, appears to refute a highly credible description of our beliefs, sometimes we may explain away, as misleading, the force those examples have with us. Balancing plausibilities all the while, we work back and forth between apparently relevant cases on the one hand and, on the other, apparently reasonable generalities that they may seem to confirm or to deny. While the favorable presumption may initially reside mainly with the particular cases, that is just the first step in an appropriately searching exploration.

Second, even beyond their conformity or discord with plausible philosophical hypotheses, we want a balanced approach regarding the question of how seriously we are to treat the various examples that we may encounter. When an example's suppositions clash severely with our central beliefs about what is possible, we have one sign that the case may not be highly relevant to our study. When an example's description is extremely sparse and incomplete, we have another sign. For the most part, we treat most seriously only those cases that both have adequately rich descriptions and also conform well enough with what we most strongly believe. All of this wants some discussion.

The descriptions of our examples should be in at least rough conformity with the main outlines of our world view: This is not conformity with some basic scientific principles, which may be known only to some few scientists; but, rather, it is conformity with propositions that are central to our common fabric of belief. When an example asks you to suppose a central belief of

3. A protracted, and a very interesting, discussion of many bizarre hypothetical examples is found in Roy Sorensen's *Thought Experiments*, forthcoming. Sorensen displays many similarities between the philosophical employments of these examples and their scientific employments: in particular, he discusses the utility of many scientifically impossible scenarios in, and for, science itself.

yours to be false, or otherwise to be abandoned, various of your other beliefs will be dragged in its wake. Then, relative to the context of the exercise, you might not be left with a firm basis of belief from which to respond to the example. In that situation, your attendant responses, insofar as they are available at all, are liable to be rather weak, conflicting and indecisive. At all events, they will provide no good guide to what really are your beliefs regarding those questions that the example is meant to concern. Often enough, and happily, hypothetical examples don't clash so severely with our central beliefs. Concerning the question of personal survival, this happens in a positive direction with the case of freezing and thawing. In a negative direction, it happens with the case of taping with physical temporal overlap.

The descriptions of our examples should be reasonably rich in those details that are relevant to answering questions that we pose about the cases: Without these helpful indications, we may again be left up in the air, with no firm attitudinal basis for responding.[4] Then various ambiguities may involve us in irrelevant, and even misleading, guessing games. To illustrate, here is a case presented without adequate indication of relevant details: While you are sound asleep, enjoying no conscious experience at all, a certain parrot starts to speak in a way that seems to express thoughts that only you could have, to express memories of your early school days, and so on. After the parrot has spoken for a while, and without anything ever again awakening where you fell asleep before, your brain and body die and decompose. Do you yourself survive, nonetheless, now in the body of a parrot and with a smaller brain? Or, have you ceased to exist, and are succeeded by a parrot that now thinks so very similarly to how you used to do?

Given the sparse description, we don't know what to think about the example as presented. On the one hand, there is some tendency to think that the example is meant to present some evidence that our world view is, and has been, quite badly mistaken: Contrary to entrenched belief, perhaps some of us might have immaterial souls that enter into intimate association with human brains and bodies at certain times, but that, at other times, break off their relations with these human tissues and, instead, enter into similarly intimate association with bird brains and bird bodies. That is one main course for the guessing game encouraged. On the other hand, there is a tendency to hold firm the main lines of accepted belief while filling in further details: Perhaps the parrot's brain somehow was wonderfully restructured in such a way that, owing to its new neural structures, the bird brain somehow realized

4. These matters are discussed, to good effect, in my opinion, by Charles Daniels in "Personal Identity," in P. French and C. Brown, eds., *Puzzles, Paradoxes and Problems*, St. Martin's Press, 1987.

a dispositional psychology just like yours. For example, perhaps by employing a suitable taping device, some super scientists somehow managed to do this. That is another main course for the guessing game.

On the first line of thought, our response is that I will survive; I will be reincarnated as a certain parrot. On the second line of thought, by contrast, our main response is that I will not survive; I will just be succeeded by an amazing parrot who thinks very much like I used to do. Given only the very bare description of the proposed example itself, we are left to guess the intended contours of the case's details. Consequently, few make any strong, clear-cut response to this baldly described case of the amazing parrot, while the weak responses that many make in one direction conflict with the weak opposite reactions of many others.

Perhaps all imaginative examples leave respondents with at least a bit of guesswork about the intended details. In many cases, however, the degree of guesswork required may be slight. Or, the details remaining to be guessed may prove largely irrelevant for the main direction of response. For example, with thought taking a positive direction for survival, a sufficiently rich indicative description was provided with the case of super freezing. And, with response taking a negative turn, that happened with the offered case of taping with physical temporal overlap. Because this is so, we may treat those cases quite seriously. In the sparsely described case of the amazing parrot, by contrast, there is no rich indicative description. Because there is not, we may treat this case much less seriously. Of course, there is no formula for separating the good cases from the much less worthwhile examples. But, informally using our good judgment, we might often be quite successful in making appropriate selections.

Even when our selected cases are most appropriate, and even when our responses have a fairly direct bearing on our main topics, these reactions cannot give us direct access to what are the main facts of our existence and survival. Our largely a priori method can be no substitute for the hard labors of empirical inquiry concerning the nature and limits of us human people, and concerning our relations to a complex world in which we find our place. But educated people, like ourselves, have been much affected by the main course that, over the last few centuries, scientific investigation has taken. In a general way, we have had our beliefs about ourselves shaped by the results of this inquiry. Our responses to examples can help us better appreciate the character of these culturally acquired beliefs about ourselves.

We want to provide an account of our strongest beliefs about the conditions of our survival and, in all likelihood and indirectly, an account of those conditions themselves. Now, as noted, if we try to shape our account to cover even the weakest responses to the wildest examples, then we are apt to produce a distorted representation of what we really think. Well, why not resolve, then, to stay away from almost all imaginative efforts; why not stick only to actual cases, or to those extremely mild hypothetical cases that even the most precise details of true science will sanction?[5] The reason is that this extremely conservative methodology is apt to incur great costs: If we confine our survey to that narrow range of cases, then we may deprive ourselves of a great deal of data relevant to ascertaining what are some of our most interesting beliefs. Indeed, we might well do even worse than that: In attempting to ascribe beliefs to ourselves on the basis of quite limited data, we might wrongly describe our own attitudes. On the other hand, with more data, we have more points of reference to confirm, or disconfirm, our ascriptions of belief. With the data from many imaginative examples included in our corpus, we will have a better chance at a more accurate understanding of our attitudes.

To be sure, a loss may be incurred on either side: On the one side, for fearing to face fairly farfetched examples, we may forgo the help of what might be genuine data. On the other, for being overly zealous about canvassing all cases, we might wrongly rely on responses for which our actual concepts and beliefs really give us no sound basis. In any particular instance, we cannot tell in advance where the greater risk lies. But the risk of zealotry may be hedged far better than that of passivity. For, with vigilance, the errors of zealotry may be corrected readily enough. But how can one ever correct passivity's errors of omission?

When it is part of a sensibly balanced methodology, a reliance on imaginative cases may be instructive. But, for true instruction to be gained, and as that methodical approach directs, the canvass of cases must proceed with caution. Along with the problems already noted, there are two dangers that may be worth special emphasis. By providing this emphasis, we may increase the likelihood that, with a balanced methodology, we will usually circumvent, or overcome, the traps that these dangers otherwise may impose.

First, unlike the case of freezing and thawing, which is pretty resistant to contextual pressure and distortion, many cases that are appropriate for inquiry into a particular topic area may easily be presented in such a context, or in such a fashion, that responses to the examples are misleading, rather than informative, regarding the main questions of interest. However, if we

5. As I read her, this very extreme view is propounded by Kathleen Wilkes in *Real People*. Especially as concerns questions of personal identity, a view only slightly less extreme has been suggested by no less illustrious a figure than W. V. Quine, in his review of Milton K. Munitz, ed., *Identity and Individuation*, in *The Journal of Philosophy*, 1972. Very recently, views that are, in turn, only slightly less extreme than Quine's have been propounded by Mark Johnston, in his "Human Beings," *The Journal of Philosophy*, 1987, and by John Robinson, in his "Personal Identity and Survival," *The Journal of Philosophy*, 1988.

are sensibly artful about the matter, dangerously distorting contexts might be recognized for what they are. The susceptible examples may then be presented in appropriately different contexts, where distorting tendencies are, if not eliminated altogether, significantly decreased.

A good example of this is the presentation of a case in the context of viewing or reading a science fiction story. In such a context, almost all of us may respond to a case as though it is perfectly possible for a given person to go backward in time and, at a certain particular past time, perform an action that is *other than* what, before, she herself did at that very time. Of course, the belief that this response appears to indicate is obviously inconsistent. It is doubtful that so many of us believe that a particular person both does, and also does not do, a particular thing at a particular time. It is more likely that the explanation of our response lies elsewhere.

Often enough, we may discount features of stories that make them entertaining enough to be worth the telling, such as the continuity of main characters throughout much of the plot. Providing it with a proper discounting, we may rethink the alleged case of a person going back and changing her past life. We may then respond to the case by giving it quite a different description. For just one way of doing that—there are others—we may say that another person, exactly similar to the first, went back to the past time and then performed an action that was the opposite of what, before, the first person did at that past time.

There is a second main danger. Even in favorable, revealing contexts, not all examples will elicit responses indicative of philosophically interesting attitudes in the area at which the case may be aimed. Dominant responses to these potentially dangerous examples may indicate, instead, certain rather general psychological tendencies that we have. Although sometimes useful to us in other ways, for purposes of philosophical inquiry these tendencies will be distorting. In other words, beyond contextually generated distortions, there is the danger of distortions generated by long-standing aspects of our psychological makeup.

In several earlier writings, I have discussed a certain class of these distorting tendencies.[6] Prominent in the class is our tendency to interpret examples so that our own social group comes out right about the categories of the things we believe ourselves commonly to have encountered. For example, if feline animals were replaced by look-alike Martian robots a hundred years ago, then, for the past century, we respond, there will *still have been many cats*

---

6. This is done in my paper, "The Causal Theory of Reference," *Philosophical Studies*, 1981, and in my "Toward a Psychology of Common Sense," *American Philosophical Quarterly*, 1982. Part of the first paper is slightly reworked in Chapter 5 of my *Philosophical Relativity*, University of Minnesota Press, 1984. Along somewhat different lines, Mark Johnston makes some interesting observations on these matters in his "Human Beings."

around that we have encountered; they will just be cats of a second, robotic kind. By contrast, if there was this replacement only for a century that ended two thousand years ago, then *those ancients will have just been fooled*: They will *not have encountered robotic cats*, but, instead, will have lived through a time when there were only feline, or felinistic, robots on earth. In short and in rough, we respond so as to "protect" our own belief that we have seen many cats, even while we do not similarly protect the similar belief of those who are socially far removed. In the area of our present study, in much of the next chapter we will encounter examples that, owing to another distorting tendency, are systematically misleading. But, even all taken together, the compass of these tendencies appears to be limited. As it is most reasonable to suppose, misleading cases will be exceptions rather than the rule.

When using a sensibly balanced method, where the plausibility of more general statements is also given weight, often these exemplary culprits may be spotted. Indeed, the very fact that they promote conflict with highly plausible principles may be a signal that, somewhat exceptionally, certain examples are systematically misleading. At all events, in a sensibly artful way, we may usually see the exceptional cases for what they are and, in our philosophical inquiries, we may discount them accordingly. So, although we cannot be lazy or complacent, we need not be intimidated, either, by this other main danger of our reliance on imaginative examples.

Finally, a few words about whom to trust as respondents: To begin, each of us should, of course, take stock of our own intuitions, both on particular cases and on proposed generalities. In relation to a given subject area, however, some of us have intellectual investments that can strongly influence our responses. Indeed, just by having read a lot on a topic, one may become attached to a certain approach. Instead of responding in a way revelatory of one's untutored attitudes, one may then respond so as to favor an approach that, even if perhaps only temporarily, is conspicuously endorsed. Respondents who are so inclined are not to be much trusted. At the same time, a most useful respondent will rather fully understand even the more intricate offerings that she encounters. Putting these two considerations together, our preferred respondents are those colleagues, and those students, who are as detached as they are astute.

4. Method and Substance

In the final analysis, the acceptability of a method must be judged not only by its own plausibility, but also by that of the substantive results to which its application most naturally, or most directly, leads. At the same time, of course, substantive theses also will be assessed both by their own plausibility and by that of the methodical reasoning by means of which those theses are reached. Method and substance together form a whole package, which we may either accept or reject. The acceptability of any part of the package depends on what we may think of the other parts, and thus on how we assess the whole.

Our assessment of any package of method and ensuing substantive views will, realistically, be made by comparison with those other whole packages that, at the time, also are available. By my lights, the package offered in these pages compares very favorably with the available alternatives. Of course, that is a question on which the reader must reserve final judgment, to be rendered only upon the completion of her reading.

In the meantime, it will be useful for me to outline the main contours of the package of method and substance that I aim to exhibit: As is already apparent, one main aim of this introduction is to present, to clarify and, in some degree, to justify the balanced method that I mean to employ. A second main aim is to provide an overview of my claims about our single most central topic, the general conditions of our survival. My approach is metaphysically objective and, beyond that, is heavily physical in its orientation: Briefly and roughly, as part of his total (dispositional) psychology, each of us has a core, or a basic, psychology that, as a matter of fact, he has in common with all normal, and with most subnormal, human beings. Then, also briefly and roughly, one of us will survive from an earlier to a later time when whatever physically realizes that person's core psychology continuously (enough) real-izes that core of basic psychological capacities from the earlier to the later time. In some later sections of this chapter, and of course in some later chap-ters, we will become clearer about the import of this position and about the plausibility that it may have.

Very roughly described, that is my heavily physical approach to our survival or, at any rate, the heart of my view. For an approach like that to seem more than crude, two things are required. First, we must plausibly explain away temptations toward other views. Second, we must admit many qualifications into our physically oriented view of ourselves. In the course of the book, we will do both of these things.

To a fair extent, my methodological and substantive aims should be accom-plished together. Otherwise there would be justification for the charge that, however good the method was in other areas of philosophy, it might be inad-equate for, and perhaps even irrelevant to, the furtherance of understanding in the area of personal identity. To some extent, however, the method should receive independent motivation. Otherwise there would be justification for the opposite charge that, as though it were tailor-made for my purposes, the method might deceptively appear to confirm just my substantive views in just this area.

In at least a tentative way, I want to generate some confidence that there is not much justification for either of these charges. This will require a brief consideration of a fair number of leading examples, some of which will be treated at much greater length in later chapters, where they will be placed in a context of appropriately related cases. This will also require the presentation of some proposals without much qualification or much argument, with a fuller presentation to be supplied later. At all events, in the next section, there will be an illustration of how imaginative examples can help us to understand what, according to our actual standards, are the important conditions for our survival. And, then, in the section right after this next one, there will be an illustration of how such examples can illuminate questions from very different philosophical subject areas.

5. Two Cartesian Views of Our Survival

We are prone to a certain amount of confusion about what are our deeper beliefs and values. Usually, this is because we tend both to oversimplify and to overgeneralize. We may then subscribe to philosophical proposals that are somewhat in error. The force of well-chosen examples can help us to avoid these errors. Although this also happens in areas far removed from personal identity, first I will consider a couple of related proposals that concern our central topic.

On the Traditional Cartesian View, a particular person will exist just so long as she consciously thinks. But, as it seems, we might endure periods of deep sleep, between dreams, when we are not conscious at all. According to Descartes, the reason we survive each night is that, despite appearances, we do have conscious experiences all night through: Regarding the experiences we have between dreams, we just forget them, completely and forever, directly upon our having them.[7] Of course, to most of us, this appears to be a rather desperate expedient. Still, we may wish to assure ourselves that, according to our firmest beliefs, this Cartesian move fails to locate any deeply important condition of our survival. How can we best do that?

Further, arising from the Cartesian move, there is a related question that we should consider: Even if we might all agree that the Traditional View is erroneous, some contemporary philosophers might think to borrow a page from Descartes' book, without accepting the whole volume. First, in the spirit

---

7. As I understand it, Descartes essays his position on this issue in his *Reply to the Fifth Set of Objections*. This is available in Haldane and Ross, eds. *Philosophical Works of Descartes*, Dover Publications, 1955. At all events, as far as Cartesian scholarship goes, I hope that my remarks are neither very controversial nor, even, very interesting.

of these times, they may recognize, in addition to conscious thought, non-conscious thinking as well. Perhaps they will find that, in doing justice to their own strong beliefs about themselves, they need to retreat from the Traditional View. Then they may adopt this less ambitious Modified Cartesian View concerning our survival: A person will exist just as long as she is continuously involved in thinking, or mental activity, whether conscious or non-conscious. How can we assure ourselves that this Modified View similarly fails?

An appropriate imaginative example may help us with both of these questions at once, both giving us more confidence that the Traditional View does miss the mark and also showing us that the more cautious Modified View fares no better. We need only recall our case of super freezing and super thawing. To this example, we very strongly respond that a person who is put through the process will survive. We also strongly respond that there is here a person who, after clearly having conscious mental activity, went through a period when she had no mental activity at all, neither conscious nor even non-conscious. We are quite confident that, in this sort of case, the person has no mental activity during the indicated period. Why are we so confident?

In the most extreme version of the case, there is no physical change at all. This is very different from anything like mere sleep, wherein a person undergoes many systematic physical changes. Now, as we very deeply believe, without any physical change on her part, a person will enjoy no mental activity at all. Even in less extreme versions of this super freezing case, wherein there is some slight motion of small particles, once she is frozen the person will be involved only in physical changes that, by any ordinary reckoning, are extremely small. More to the point, it is our strong belief that, relative to the production of any mental processes on the person's part, such changes as do occur will be random.

Our confident responses to cases of super freezing and super thawing are generated by strong beliefs of ours about ourselves. As we can come to realize, the Traditional Cartesian View does not locate something that, according to our strong beliefs, is a deeply important requirement of our survival. And, as we also can appreicate, we no more strongly believe in the Modified Cartesian View than in the Traditional View.

In addition to this clear negative lesson, we may learn a vague positive lesson from our strong response to this example: One thing that is important for a person's survival is that her main mental *capacities* be preserved. Ordinarily, this will happen only if the person continues to have some mental activity, even if that is wholly non-conscious mental activity. But, as the case of super freezing persuades us, there may be continuity of mental capacity even when there is no continuity of mental activity. The weaker condition of continuously realized capacity, it seems, might be the one that, as we believe, is the more deeply important for a person's survival.

6. Experience Inducers

Among the plenitude of only fairly wild examples, there are many that are philosophically useful. Here is one that, while it clearly concerns questions basic to philosophy, does *not* much concern questions of our identity over time. Beyond confirming the idea that our cautious methodology of cases has a wide application in philosophy, this example will prove useful for specific reference quite a few times in later chapters.

At least at first encounter, it may seem that an active life is of value only because it contributes, directly or more indirectly, to pleasant or interestingly varied conscious states, in the agent herself or in other conscious beings. But although many people may unreflectively think that this is so, they may all be in error. This initially appealing View of the Exclusive Value of Conscious States may be false. Perhaps a suitable hypothetical example may bring those who espouse it to see their error and to correct, not their values themselves, but their somewhat superficial belief about what is, and has been all along, their pattern of deep values and concerns. Even for those people, that View may be convincingly challenged by the example of the *experience inducers*. Perhaps in this way these people may recognize that, contradicting their somewhat superficial belief, there is a deeper and more accurate belief they have about their values.[8]

Each of us might have all, or almost all, of her experience caused by electrodes suitably attached to her brain. While she is on a table or bed, these electrodes may directly stimulate her brain in such a way that it seems to her that she is living an active, happy and worthwhile life. What I have in mind is a far cry from the mere stimulation of any "pleasure" center, though, somewhat indirectly, it may possibly involve that. Rather, we may acknowledge that different sorts of experiences may be more interesting, and more enjoyable, for different sorts of people. Just so, the stimulating impulses that come in to a particular person's brain may be generated by a computer program designed for someone with just that person's sort of psychology and neurology. For example, if the person has a considerable aptitude for and interest in music, she may seem to experience a life of great musical success, composing many fine musical works, playing many of these with excellent bands or orchestras, receiving great critical acclaim, popularity and financial reward for her composing and for her performing, and so on. The rest of her life

---

8. The conspicuous occurrence of these machines in the literature is in Robert Nozick's stimulating work, *Anarchy, State and Utopia*, Basic Books, 1974. Indeed, for all I know, that is the first mention in the literature. But in oral communication, since at least the late 1960s, these meager generators of value have loomed large in my introductory philosophy classes and, in all likelihood, they cropped up orally, in other venues, far earlier still.

might also seem wonderful, and be filled with many years of artificially induced experience well tailored for her. Her life in the inducer, and her time awake in this condition, might be about two years longer than the life she would have outside. Finally, based on mountains of evidence, we might be more confident in the technical proficiency and safety of these inducers than in our reliable present-day cruise ships.

Though our lives would be filled with more conscious experience, and more interestingly varied and pleasant conscious experience, few of us would choose a life in an inducer. We would not choose it for ourselves, nor for others. Is this owing to a worry about some psychological conflict we may experience when inside an inducer? Consideration of additional suppositions shows that such a worry can be only a small part of the reason for our aversion: Upon learning of the inducers in a most convincing fashion, we might convincingly (and correctly) learn as well that, once in the inducers, we would forget about there being inducers. Though we would have all of the rest of our personal memories, we would not have these memories from our last few days outside. Only the few volunteers who remained, each for a certain period, outside of the inducers, would have knowledge of people being in inducers. And a volunteer custodian would have this knowledge only during the period of her custodial service, a relatively small portion of the rest of her life.

Most of us feel the impact of this thought experiment quite forcefully. Largely because of this, we may be rationally convinced that there is something seriously wrong with the view that certain conscious states are all that matter to us. As did the example of freezing and thawing, the case of the experience inducers may show us, even if only very roughly, the character of the serious flaw in the View it challenges. By so doing, it may, in a rough way, provide positive instruction: Quite beyond their causal efficacy to produce experiences, each of us values, deeply and rationally, many of her realistic involvements with many parts of the world beyond her own mind. We value reasonably veridical perception of things and of people beyond ourselves; we value effective action with respect to many of these things and people, including acts of communication with some of the people; we value reasonably veridical perception of the effects of these various actions on these people and on other entities, including the acts of others aimed at affecting us, and so on and so forth.

7. Two Attempts at Transporting Some Inanimate Objects

Although we are mainly interested in the conditions of our own survival, we have some interest, too, in the transtemporal identity of ordinary inanimate entities, like rocks and shirts, many of which we also readily perceive. Part of this interest is due to the hope that, as we learn something about the survival of these relevantly simpler things, we might indirectly shed some light on the conditions of our own survival. But another part of the interest is due to sheer curiosity about the familiar things in the world around us, and about how we may most logically think about them. Some hypothetical examples involving exotically advanced technologies may help us to satisfy our interest in learning something about the possible careers of these familiar inanimate individuals.

Without begging any questions, we may refer to each of these technologies as forms of *teleconstruction*. An individual rock, for example, may be caused to undergo any of these technological processes. In the middle period of each process, there will not be any molecules arranged in the manner customary for, and most appropriate to, a rock. At the end of each process, there will be a rock that is, at the very least, precisely like the one that was there at the process's beginning. Now, perhaps the rock at the end might be the very same one that first entered the technological process; in such an event, we can say that, in its last phases, the technology *re*constructed a particular rock. Or, perhaps, the rock at the end, although qualitatively just like the original, is numerically distinct from the original rock; in such an event, it will be more appropriate for us to say, instead, that the technology *newly* constructed a particular rock, perhaps a rock that never before existed.

The first teleconstruction technology is *purely informational*. As a device records the exact relative arrangements of the molecules in a certain rock, it separates all of these original molecules one from the other and casts them to the winds. Later, utilizing the information about molecular arrangement that it has recorded and stored, the device may operate on an entirely new batch of matter, near to hand. Out of this new matter, the device constructs a rock that has the exact same sort of molecular composition as was first recorded, but a rock whose matter is all distinct from that of the rock at the beginning.

We strongly respond that the rock at the end is newly constructed, rather than the original rock reconstructed. The device has made an exact duplicate of the original rock, instead of preserving, in a purely informational way, the original specimen.

A second technology involves complete *molecular restoration*. The device of this technology does not cast the molecules to the winds when it records their arrangements and breaks their bonds. Rather, it stores them for future use and, what's more, keeps track of which molecule is which. During the interim period, these molecules are not used to compose anything else of much interest, let alone any rocks. Later on, the device combines these stored molecules in just the way in which they were arranged in the original rock.

Almost all of us have a dominant reaction to this effect: The process with molecular restoration reconstructs the original rock; by way of this technology, the original rock survives, and does exist at the later time. As regards the preservation of rocks, or of shirts, for that matter, this technology is utterly different from the purely informational procedure.

There are some lessons that we may learn from these cases. Some of these lessons may be quite substantive. Here are some that are primarily methodological.

These teleconstruction cases may be presented to us in any of a great variety of contexts. Most of the contexts will be far less antiseptic than the one we implicitly established just a couple of paragraphs back. Certain of these more loaded contexts will more readily call forth psychological factors that may distort judgment about the cases. This happens with the contexts in which, typically, we read or view science fiction.

As embedded in a science-fiction scenario, either of these technologies of teleconstruction may likely be offered as a form of teletransportation. In such cases, the story has the object at the end appear at a location somewhat distant from that of the original object, not in the same location (relative to the most salient planet) as the original object had. Accordingly, these technologies would be offered as forms of transporting objects from one location to another, typically with great speed; with distances that are not enormous, the period of time involved will be very brief.

Now, we are apt to play along with almost any story; we are apt to interpret the story in a way that will make it more entertaining. This is manifest, as we noted, in our generosity toward tales that have a given person go backwards in time and do the opposite of what, before, she herself did at that very time. In a quite similar vein, almost all entertaining stories where the characters intend routinely to transport rocks and shirts are treated as stories where those rocks and shirts do get transported, by a means that, although exotic for us, is routine for the story's characters. We don't suppose that, contrary to the intentions of the highly confused characters, the rocks and shirts routinely get destroyed in favor of distant duplicates of them. We are not so stupid that we cannot recognize that the former, not the latter, provides the appropriate interpretation. Just so, when the context calls on our sensibilities as an audience, we may respond to the purely informational technology just as we would to the technology of molecular restoration: They are both perfectly fine ways of transporting, and so of preserving, shirts and rocks.

It is a logically possible option, of course, to think that the contexts of these stories are the most philosophically illuminating ones. Then we will think that, by becoming engrossed in such stories, we will learn interesting things about the survival conditions of shirts and rocks: Contrary to what at first seems appealing, it is easy for them, all of a sudden, to leave all of their matter behind. But few will think this option a wise one. It is far more reasonable to suppose that, when we view or read these stories, we typically help create contexts where distorting factors come to the fore.

Indeed, insofar as our initial response to the purely informational teleconstruction might have been less than fully clear-cut, the slight conflict may well have been due, in part, to our familiarity with science fiction. When reading about any of the technologies proposed above, almost all of us were, more or less strongly, reminded of just such stories. The stronger the connection made in the reader, the less clear-cut the difference in her responses to the cases. Once made aware of this distorting tendency, however, we may discount it. Then we may place greater stock in our responses.

When we try to think seriously about cases, we will take pains to discount such distorting psychological tendencies as may be operative: You may care a lot about a particular rock, or shirt, perhaps because of its historical or its sentimental value. Many of us Americans care about Plymouth Rock; you may care a lot about your deceased grandfather's favorite shirt. When such objects are involved, you will be careful in evaluating various offers of teletransportation, quite beyond making sure of the mere technical proficiency of the offers involved. Rationally, even when transporting your grandpa's shirt, you would spurn an offer to involve the garment in a process of purely informational teleconstruction. By contrast, in preference to "old-fashioned" moving methods that are more expensive, slower and technically less reliable, you might well accept an offer of the process with molecular restoration.

8. Three Attempts at Getting Human People to Survive

Even many centuries from now, it is likely that there will be fatal diseases which, for a while, have no cure. As medicine learns ways to kill existing viruses and other "germs," these tiny beings evolve in ways that make further medical research necessary. Now, for example, we are faced with a growing epidemic of fatal AIDS, a disease whose viral agents did not exist on earth only a few decades ago. Eventually, as we hope, a cure for AIDS will be found. But, even if only indirectly, many people will die from the disease before such a cure is made available. Evolution being what it is, even in the forty-first century A.D., there will be diseases for humans as fatal and incurable then as AIDS is now. But, at that late date, there might be ways of trying to preserve a person until a cure is found for her particular affliction. Let us imagine some of the technologies that might then be available.

We have already mentioned one such advanced technology: the process of super freezing and super thawing. Supposing that the technology was more reliable even than our present-day radios, this would be a fine procedure. An afflicted person might be almost instantaneously frozen into virtually complete stasis; years later, after a cure for her affliction had been discovered and proven effective, she would be almost instantaneously thawed to a normal body temperature. Then the cure might be applied to her. It is the very same person, we may be quite sure, who is later cured and made healthy. Instead of living for just two more years long ago, when she had the then incurable disease, the same person would, typically, now go on to live healthily for at least twenty years. In the case of many afflicted people, this would be a great benefit.

Two cheaper technologies, parallel to our procedures of teleconstruction, may also be available. The cheapest might be a purely informational taping process. In this taping process, a person's brain and body are quickly decomposed as detailed information concerning their molecular arrangement is recorded and stored on tape for as long as needs be. The tiny bits of matter that composed her are cast to the winds. Perhaps ten years later a cure is found. Then the device uses the stored information to make, out of a new batch of appropriate matter, a person who is, at the least, almost precisely like the original person last was. Qualitatively, this lately constructed person is more like the original, overall and in all important respects, than you now are like you were just a minute ago. The cure is applied to this constructed person, who then goes on healthily to live for at least another twenty years.

Intuitively, most of us strongly respond that this offer is not genuine: The person who goes into the process does not survive it, but is destroyed and, years later, she is replaced by a duplicate. This may be of some instrumental value to the original person, as that duplicate may, for example, complete a book that the original person did not have time and strength enough to finish. But, outside of such instrumental value, this process offers the person little more, or nothing more, than does ordinary sudden and painless death. The original person is destroyed completely; she will never again have any thoughts or experiences.

Most of the strength of our response is due to rational causes that are extremely direct. Some is due to more indirect implicit reasoning. For one thing, the time gap of ten years is very substantial and, largely for that reason, very salient. We reason that, during that period, the person is nowhere, and does not exist at all: She is not on the tape, nor is she the tape, nor is she some larger combination of things. Further, we reason that, given the general correctness of our world view, a particular person cannot fail to exist for such a significant period and, after that, exist again. It is a new individual, qualitatively just like the original person, who exists at the later period.

For another thing, we are strengthened by our discussion, in the previous section, of our tendency to be generous to anticipated science-fiction scenarios. We may then be successful in blocking this tendency: Thought of the

taping process will remind us of stories involving the alleged teletransportation of people. Unprepared, we might be as generous to the taping, as
regards judgments of survival, as we were to such teletransportation processes. But, as we saw, we are willing to go along even for cases involving
rocks. Having been prepared, we blunt the force of this distorting tendency.
Strongly and rationally, we respond that the purely informational taping process is not a way of getting someone to survive.

Another technology may be a little more expensive, but not so expensive
as the process of freezing and thawing. This is the process of *taping with molecular restoration*. In this process, a person's separated molecules are not only
stored, but are tracked in the storage chambers. By employing this information appropriately, years later all of the molecules are again arranged in just
their "original" relative order.

Will a person survive this more conservative taping procedure? Again, my
dominant response is negative. But, unlike with the purely informational taping case, there is significant conflict in my responsive thought to this present
example. Others may respond somewhat differently.

Perhaps in this case, although there is a right answer, it is just very hard to
tell what the right answer is, even given the assumed truth of our detailed
factual beliefs. Or perhaps given the correctness and completeness of our
detailed descriptions, it is indeterminate whether a person would survive such
a conservative taping process. Perhaps an adequate account of our identity
will eventually decide which alternative holds sway. But it is not important for
us that this issue soon be decided.

What an adequate account must do, we may be confident, is to reflect the
idea that this case is a difficult one. As an account of our survival should
reflect, this case of taping with molecular restoration has more going for it,
toward being a case of personal survival, than does the purely informational
case. As the account should also reflect, it has less going for it, toward being
such a case, than does the case of freezing and thawing.

9. The Idea that Our Survival Requires
Much Physical Continuity

The thought that we may not survive taping with molecular restoration will
be quite interesting to attentive readers. To those of them who are acquainted
with the contemporary philosophical literature of identity over time, it will
also be a bit surprising.

As we responded before, a rock and a shirt, in contrast, *will* survive taping,
or teleconstruction, with molecular restoration. Trying to explain all of this
data most plausibly, we attribute to ourselves a belief, possibly deep and

unobvious, to this effect: Unlike these unthinking things, we might require temporal processes that, in a certain physical respect, are quite conservative: In a central sense of "physical continuity," we thinking beings, with our capacity for conscious experience, might require more physical continuity than do such non-thinking physical entities as shirts and rocks.

According to much of the philosophical literature, we require much less in way of physical continuity, and certainly not more, than do unthinking, non-conscious entities of ordinary kinds. Our intuitive responses, then, suggest an idea that is opposed to much of the literature. Because much of this literature has been produced by very able philosophers, this new idea is a bit surprising.

How might we rationally advocate the idea that, in comparison with rocks, we might require much physical continuity? We should seek an explanation of why, according to our system of attitudes, this might be so. Understood in this light, the wanted explanation comprises two main parts.

The First Part: In our thought about reality, what are, for us, the most important concrete things to think about are, next to ourselves, such others as are natural and easy for us to perceive, or to employ, or to control, or even to think about. By and large, these are entities that belong to *ordinary concrete kinds*, like rocks, shirts, roses, planets, mice, and computers. These ordinary entities, which may be called ordinary things or *individuals*, may be contrasted with ordinary events or processes, such as trials and naps.

Whatever general view of reality we form, perhaps we will wish to interpret it in such a way that, as much as consistency permits, it comports with a general proposition about the survival of these ordinary individuals. The proposition may be to some such effect as this: Regarding any such ordinary concrete entities, for example, a rock, there will not be a time when the thing exists, and then, later, a period when it does not exist, and then, later still, a time when that very thing exists once again. Especially for thinking, experiencing concrete individuals, like me, for example, perhaps some such proposition should be respected. Thus, I will be inclined to interpret situations in such a way that, in them all, there is not first a time when I exist, and then, later, a time when I do not exist, and then, still later, a time when I myself exist once again.

As noted, in regards to events and process, we are not set to impose any such requirement. Additionally, as regards such ordinary more abstract things as social clubs, which are neither events nor individuals, we are lenient about allowing for temporal gaps. Accordingly, it is easy for us to allow that there may be a temporal gap in my nap, that there may be many significant gaps in your protracted trial, and that our organization may have survived a period during which it did not exist. By contrast, we shall be loathe to allow that there is any interruption of our own existence.

We may take this point further. On the most relevant description of a process that involves an ordinary concrete entity, a process that involves the entity's surviving *cannot allow for it to be accidental*, relative to the entity's involvement in the process, that there is no time gap in the individual's history. Let us suppose that, on a particular occasion, a purely informational teleconstruction process involving a particular rock might proceed instantaneously. Even so, on any description of this process most relevant to issues of a rock's survival, it is not essential to the process that the envisaged occurrence be instantaneous. By a relevant standard for individuating processes that involve a rock's history, that same teleconstruction process might have obtained somewhat differently: It might have obtained without being instantaneous. Then there would have been a time gap between the decomposition of the original rock and the construction of the rock at the end. Consequently, even if the teleconstruction process should happen to be instantaneous, it will fail to preserve a rock, a shirt, and, especially, you or me. As I am suggesting, we are most strongly inclined to describe situations in this way.

The Second Part: In our thought about reality, what are, for us, the most important distinctions all belong to a certain family. The salient members of this group include the distinction between the mental and the non-mental, and that between the conscious and the non-conscious. In line with this leading idea, our principles for individuating concrete entities in the objective world order, not only as regards space but also as concerns time, may reflect the great importance of these distinctions. Accordingly, a particular person's basic mental capacities, like her capacity for consciousness and her capacity for simple reasoning, may be more central to her survival than any comparable property, be it a capacity or a disposition, of any shirt or any rock. By contrast, the survival of a shirt, or a rock, may be more closely tied to the matter that, over time, constitutes it.

We may combine the two parts of our explanation: For you to survive from now until some future time, there cannot be, in between, a time when you do not exist. Perhaps this much is also required of rocks. But for you to exist, at any time, there must then be realized certain particular capacities. At any time that you exist, there must be realized, not just mental capacities exactly like yours, but *your very own particular mental capacities*.

How are your particular mental capacities distinguished even from others that are precisely like them? If you had an immaterial soul, your capacities might be realized in just that particular soul, while anyone else's might be realized in something else. But, given the general truth of our view of the world, there is no such soul for you to have, nor anything remotely like that. Now, without a soul or something else non-physical to realize your mental capacities throughout a given stretch of time, you need something physical to do that. So, throughout any given period, your mental capacities must be realized in some physical entity, or at least in some succession of physical entities. Finally, for your very own mental capacities to be realized by a process that ensures there will be no time gap in their realization, throughout the period there must be, as a matter of fact, physical continuity of whatever physical entity, or whatever succession of such entities, then realizes those particular mental capacities.

In the case of freezing and thawing, during the freeze your mental capacities are realized in your completely frozen brain. So you exist during the middle period and thus, also, at the end. In the case of purely informational taping, during the years between decomposition and construction, your mental capacities are nowhere realized. So you do not exist at that time, nor at any time thereafter. In the case of taping with molecular restoration, the matter is more difficult. Let me try to characterize, roughly, wherein the difficulty lies.

There are two alternative approaches to take to this example, each of which has at least some appeal. On the one hand, and perhaps somewhat less attractively, we may take this lenient approach: During the middle period, it might be that your mental capacities are realized in the stored molecules. They are realized there because of the real causal relations between these molecules and the devices that track them and that, in restorative construction, can systematically arrange them. If there is this realization, then, even so, your mental capacities will be terribly far from being exercised. For that to happen, much more needs be done than any mere thawing. The device must reconstruct, in human form, a person from the tracked materials in the containers. In this form, when awakened, the person consciously thinks and feels.

For me, a more stringent approach is more compelling: What the device does is far too ambitious properly to count as bringing about the exercise of already existing mental capacities. On the contrary, it might be that, in the middle period, there is no entity with mental capacities, but there are only entities with other capacities. Most fittingly, perhaps, we may think of the tracking and construction device as an entity with certain interesting capacities: It has the capacity to produce, out of certain materials, a human person with mental capacities exactly similar to those of the original person. The newly constructed person would, of course, have mental capacities that are not far from being exercised. (Some might prefer a more exotic description along the same lines. Here is one: There is a complex, somewhat scattered entity consisting of the technical device and the stored molecules. This entity might have the capacity to so structure part of itself, the part in the containers, that the part thus structured will then have mental capacities.)

There is a consequence of the more stringent approach that some may find a bit surprising, but that does not much lessen, for me, the greater appeal of that treatment over the more lenient one: On the stringent approach, although my brain and body will make it through teleconstruction with molecular restoration, I myself will not. At the end of this process, that brain and body will no longer be my brain and body, but, instead, they will be the brain and body of an entirely new person. Qualitatively just like I was, but numerically distinct, this new person is a causal descendant of me. It is he, not me, who now has the healthy brain and body that before were mine.

This is one way—there are others—in which my view about our survival differs from any view that, without very much exaggeration, can be characterized as maintaining that wherever there is a certain brain in an appropriately healthy condition, there I will be. In Chapter 4, and especially in Chapter 5, these differences will become clearer.

As many will agree, there is a great deal of vagueness in our talk and thought about entities and their capacities. This vagueness might make it indeterminate whether a human person, as we believe her to be, would survive the taping process with molecular restoration. Or, as seems more likely to me, it might just make it very difficult for us to know whether she would.

At any rate, if the foregoing explanation is on the right track, we may have located, roughly but to good purpose, the main contours of some important vagueness. If that is so, then, rough as it is, this explanation may contain the main elements of an adequate account of our identity over time.

10. The Avoidance of Future Great Pain Test

There is no conclusive test to tell us, even in those cases where it delivers a vivid verdict, whether an interesting hypothetical example presents, as we most deeply believe, a genuine case of personal identity over time. But there are two *strongly presumptive* tests for personal survival. In cases where they vividly deliver a verdict, these tests will, in general, rationally prevail. And, in those cases, unless other considerations strongly indicate otherwise, they will always prevail. As subsequent discussion will make clear enough, the two tests will always, or very nearly always, deliver highly similar verdicts. Accordingly, there will be no great advantage in our applying them both. [To calm the most sophisticated sort of reader, let me offer this note of anticipation: In Chapter 7, we will notice that, most directly, these are tests for (our beliefs about) *what matters in our survival*, in the prudential use of those terms that will be noted in Chapter 3. But, then, less directly, they will remain good presumptive tests for our beliefs about our survival itself. Moreover, later in that seventh chapter, we will show how, as tests for our beliefs about survival itself, these tests may be refined and improved.]

As we will soon enough observe, one of the two tests is extremely gruesome and, in addition, is fairly complex and roundabout. By contrast, although it is no bundle of joy, either, the other test is rather less gruesome and, in addition, is relatively simple and straightforward. This second test, which will be a main tool of ours throughout this book, is the *avoidance of future great pain test*.

Like its more complicated cousin, this test is not really an independent source of evidence about our attitudes concerning our survival. Rather, in applying the test, you just establish a context wherein the conditions are highly conducive to your making a very serious and pointed judgment, rather than a casual and quite possibly distorted judgment, regarding the question of whether you will survive an imagined process. To be sure, I may speak of my original intuition about a case being confirmed by the avoidance of future pain test. All this means, however, is that my more serious judgment about the case, elicited by the context of these pain considerations, is the same judgment that, in a more casual context, I first made.

When you apply this test, in your thinking about an example, it is usually best to imagine yourself as the person who is to undergo the interesting hypothetical process that is the case's core. When you apply the test to the case of freezing and thawing, for example, it is best for you to imagine yourself as undergoing that futuristic process. The next best thing is to imagine a person about whom you care deeply, such as your child, undergoing the process. In advance, you will have to make choices concerning the person at the beginning of the process and also the person at the end.

As most will find easy to do, when you apply the test to yourself, you suppose yourself not to be an extreme masochist. On the contrary you suppose yourself to be a person who intensely dislikes being in very severe pain; the more severe the pain, the more you abhor the experience. Further, you are to suppose that the person emerging from the process also will abhor some form of pain: Even if the forms of experience might be different in important respects, there will be certain experiences that will be much more painful to, and much more disliked by, the emerging being than, before the process, rather mild pain is disliked by you. At all events, there is nothing subtle about any of the pain involved; as with the sort of pain typically produced by strong electric shock to sensitive areas, it takes no great intellect, or emotional depth, to appreciate it fully.

Further still, in applying the test to yourself, successful application requires that, in contemplating the person before the process and the person after, your main basic attitude will be one of self-concern. As it does to most people, the prominence of such an attitude comes very easily to me; causally, the direction I give myself is very nearly superfluous.

When I imagine myself as undergoing a possibly problematic process, for example, the process of super freezing and thawing, there must be made the supposition that I have no choice but to undergo that process. But I do have a choice between just these two options: I may elect to experience, before the process, very considerable pain and, as I know full well, thus ensure that the being who emerges will, after awakening to consciousness, feel no pain. Alternatively, I may elect to endure no pain before the process begins and, as I also know full well, thus ensure that the being who emerges from the process will, after awakening, undergo really excruciating tortures for quite a long time.

In a case where there is just an ordinary process of daily human life, such as occurs with my eating a bowl of tomato soup, I will most certainly endure the early pain. The explanation is simple: First, I would rather endure much lesser pain soon than much greater pain somewhat later. And second, as I strongly believe, it will be *me* at the end of that ordinary process, who rises from the lunch table. The test thus establishes a strong presumption that, according to our confident beliefs, we do survive from day to day, notwithstanding the professed doubts of some brilliant historical philosophers.[9] Regarding the hypothetical case of freezing and thawing, I will also elect to endure the very considerable pain beforehand. This strongly suggests that, as I believe, I will indeed survive that process as well. It will be me, I reason, who will get that terrible torture otherwise, and, insofar as I am concerned for myself, I certainly want to avoid that great future pain.

There are, as I have found, some frequent objections to this test for determining (our strongest beliefs about) our identity over time. Fortunately, none of these is a serious objection: It may be objected that, in regards to any hypothetical process, we may be conflating uncertainty over the details of the outcome with a proper judgment as to the status of the outcome. Or, it may be objected that, in regards to a process that takes much time, we may be conflating a discount rate toward the future with a judgment about whose welfare it is that is at stake in the future. Or, other objections concerning peripheral issues may be made. There are several complementary ways to meet such objections. The most direct is just this: We specify such enormous differences in pain experience, for the future as against the earlier time, as will totally swamp any such uncertainties, discount rates, and whatever. This may be done by making the future torture very much more intense, and very much lengthier, than whatever the objector may have had in mind. A second point of reply bids us to remember that this test is not meant to be a conclu-

9. On one plausible interpretation of him, David Hume is modern philosophy's most famous skeptical nihilist on these matters. In ancient times, and in different ways, honors are earned by Heraclitus and, under the leadership of Parmenides, by the Eleatics. After the Eleatics, we find the Megarians, with honors for the most dazzling argumentation going to the great Eubulides.

sive one: Rather, it is offered as a procedure that, where it does deliver a vivid verdict, establishes only a strong presumption, one way or the other, concerning particular judgments of personal identity.

On a brighter note, the greatest advantage of this test is that it separates the issue of survival from certain questions that are often conflated with it. One is the question of how a person might now feel about the (sort of) person that, after undergoing a certain process, he might become. Another is the related question of how the person now might feel about the (sort of) life that, in some such altered state, he may lead. As compared with the avoidance of great pain test, just about any other tests for our survival beliefs do less well at this task of separating the issues. To appreciate the importance of this difference, a somewhat extended discussion may be helpful.

The avoidance of great pain test is an instance of a quite general sort of test: *sacrifice for future well-being tests.* In that it involves the avoidance of pain, rather than the procurement of positive goods, it is a *negative form* of these well-being tests. In that the pain to be avoided is extremely great, this pain avoidance test is of an *extreme* negative form. At the other extreme, there are very positive forms of future well-being tests. For example, there is this very positive test question: Will I sacrifice much now so that, after I undergo a certain process, the emerging person will have, instead of only a moderately long and pleasant life, an extremely long and pleasant life? Because I am not forced to confront the prospect of great future pain, such a more positive test may provide rather unreliable indications about my survival beliefs.

As a case in point, let us imagine that a horrid surgeon tampers with my brain so that she reduces the intellect supported by that brain to the level of a typical moron's, but always higher than that of your standard imbecile. In addition, she causes the irreversible loss of all of my personal past memories. Finally, removing virtually all of my more distinctive personality traits, there emerges a person with a personality that is about as dull, and as undistinctive, as is imaginable. Will the person who emerges from this surgical process be me? My dominant response is that this unfortunate will be me.

With regard to this case, let us now apply two contrasting forms of well-being tests. First, a positive form may well yield a result that might seem to discomfirm the indication of the original response that favored survival: I will *not* sacrifice much, in advance, so that, later, the amnesiac cretin will have a long life with much pleasure, rather than a shorter life with less pleasure. By contrast, the avoidance of great pain test strongly confirms my original response: I *will indeed* sacrifice much now so that, later, the amnesiac cretin will not suffer so many horribly painful tortures. The extreme negative test, as we see, gets me clearly to focus on the question of whether that cretin will be me.

With the positive form of the test, my focus may have been distorted.

Rather than resting on any of my deep beliefs about survival, my refusal to make the early sacrifice might be grounded in other thoughts: An amnesiac cretin may seem so repugnant to me that, whether he is me or is only someone else, I might not greatly care that he get much pleasure rather than only moderate pleasure. Moreover, the sort of life that such a dull cretin can lead may strike me as so vacuous that, even if that cretin is me, I don't care very much whether that life be very long or not so long. As we reflect on these future well-being tests, it becomes clear that the positive forms often will be positively misleading, that any "mixed" forms might often mix us up, and that the extreme negative form, alone, will provide us with our strongest relevant presumptions.

As I said, there are two sorts of strongly presumptive tests concerning our (deep beliefs about) our survival. In addition to the extremely negative form of the future well-being tests, that is, the avoidance of great pain test, there is the extremely negative form of *process selection tests*. Unfortunately, although many writers on personal identity employ process selection tests, at least implicitly, they (almost) invariably use positive forms of these tests. But, with regard to questions of our survival itself, when used in a positive form, process selection tests will confuse us even more than do positively oriented future well-being tests.

In process selection tests, whatever their form, the question is whether I will make a certain early sacrifice in order that I may select one process, say, whatever goes on during normal resting on my bed for an hour, over another, say, the horrible surgery lately described. Generally, as I suggested, a positive assumption is made regarding the quality of life for whoever may emerge from the processes. The emerging person will, in either case, have at least a pretty good life. Given such an assumption, will I now endure much pain so that, shortly, I will undergo mere resting on my bed rather than the rather badly incapacitating processes of that dastardly surgery? You bet I will. Does this result establish a strong presumption that, although I will survive that bedrest, I will not survive the harmful operation? In other words, does this result do much to disconfirm the intuition that, even if I undergo the operation, I will still be around? No, it does not.

The fact that I will endure much pain to be spared going through a certain procedure provides only a very weak presumption that I will not survive that procedure. For I might survive but be in such a terrible state that my life will be of very little value to me, or no value at all, from then on. Indeed, although quite certainly surviving that process, I might even be in a state that, given my present values, is much worse that death itself. In point of fact, this is just what will happen, surely, even in many cases that require little imagination: A surgeon might not touch my brain, but might cut off my arms and legs, and cut out my eyes and ears, providing me with no replacements but making sure that my wounds all healed. Although I would most certainly survive this procedure, my life would then be horrible; I would much prefer a swift and painless death to that.

One might think to devise a more suitable positive process selection test. For example, it might be specified that, even by your own present standards of what is a good life for a person, the being who emerges from the (more) problematic process will then live a life that is a very good one for her. Although it seems promising, such a strategy ultimately will disappoint. Consider a process whereby you come to have complete personal amnesia, but no loss of intellect or personality. Even according to your own values, the intelligent, kindly, witty person who emerges may go on to lead a very worthwhile life. At the same time, however, you may endure great pain so that you may select innocuously eating a bowl of soup, for example, over the process that gives you this amnesia. Does that choice provide a strong presumption, then, that you will not survive the amnesia? No; it does not. For there is another pervasive consideration that should be separated from the question of your survival: You may care very much that there *be certain connections between the good life you are leading now and a good life you might live later.* You may care enough about this that you are willing to endure much pain now if the alternative is undergoing a process that will prevent your life from having many of these connections. For example, even if it is you happily going along later on, you may abhor the prospect of your doing that with no memories of the earlier parts of your life, or with none of your interest in philosophy.

To get a process selection test that compares well with our avoidance of great pain test, we must have the selection test, like that pain test, be of an extreme negative form. Instead of the standard positive assumption, we make an extremely negative supposition about the life of the emerging person: From both of the compared processes, the person emerging will have a life filled only with many terribly painful tortures, year after year, until the person finally expires. As I intimated, this means a test that is both extremely gruesome and also quite complex: The idea is that you will endure much early pain to select a certain process if, and only if, as you deeply believe, the person emerging from *that* process is *not* you, while the person emerging from the *other* process *is* you. As your only reward for enduring the bad early pain, you will die shortly thereafter. In that way, you will avoid for yourself, and force onto the person emerging from the other process, all of those future tortures.

Return to consider the operation that not only removes my personal memories, but also greatly reduces my intellect and my personality. By way of comparison, also consider the processes that occur in my ordinarily eating a bowl of tomato soup. For whoever emerges from either process, there will be, starting next week, relentless and excruciating physical torture. This torture will be so severe that, although I might clearly enough imagine how it might go on even longer, I cannot imagine how, in any other way, the horror might be any worse for the emerging person. We pose our extremely negative selection test question: Will I endure very great pain during this present week so that I may select undergoing the surgery, at the end of this week, rather than the eating of the soup? No; I will not. This indicates my deep belief that, just as I will survive that soup eating, so also will I survive that operation. In either case, I am quite sure, the person to whom this horrible life will occur really will be me. And, in either case, the future life will be so utterly horrible that, in the other case, the future life will be no worse. Consequently, there is no good reason for me to make this present week a terrible time as well.

As I promised, this is an extremely gruesome sort of test and, in addition, one that is confusingly complex. Some readers, no doubt, will see further problems with this test, leading them to question its reliability as well: Perhaps I should actually choose to undergo the operation, not because of any questions of identity, but because, contrary to the test's assumption, when I am in a cretinous amnesiac state, those terrible tortures really will not be as bad for me as any tortures ever can be. Although I do not find them very compelling, I am not entirely unmoved by such doubts. In any case, such doubts cannot alter what is our preferred tool of investigation. Rather, at the most, they can only add to the reasons for shying away from this extremely gruesome and complex test and stressing, instead, the avoidance of future great pain test.

At any rate, as compared with any test that is not extremely negative in form, this test of avoiding future pain has the advantage that it all but forces us to be most serious in judging questions of personal identity and, in that way, the test helps us to discount such distorting tendencies as might otherwise be more effective. It might seem so tempting to have medically available taping processes. But, when in an egoistic frame of mind, would you endure severe pain beforehand so that the person emerging from these processes be spared much greater pain later? Few of us will make that painful choice. As we believe, the people emerging from these processes are not us, but are only duplicates of us; and we will not endure much pain just so they may be spared afterward.

With a taping process that stores, tracks and restores matter, a real risk appears to be involved. A fair amount of early pain now may seem a prudent sacrifice; for you cannot be sure that, even as your deepest beliefs go, the person emerging from this more conservative process will not be you. But the apparent risk, or whatever it is, cannot be terribly great. After all, you are not willing to endure, in advance, a very great deal of pain. So, it does not appear clear, either, that your deep belief is that this emerging person will be you. In sum, when applied to this case, the avoidance of great pain test delivers no very vivid verdict. That is not, however, any fault of the test. On the contrary, there is here just a further indication that this case is, indeed, a difficult one.

11. Some Evidence About Some Strong Beliefs

Especially after we apply the test of avoiding future great pain, we may be confident that we have uncovered some evidence about what, most strongly, we believe to be conditions of our survival. This is also evidence about what, most strongly, we believe ourselves to be.

Perhaps I might believe that I am not a physical being, or any being in the objective world order, but, instead, I am a pure transcendental subject of conscious thought and experience. Or, perhaps less radically, I might believe that, although I am in the objective order of things, I am essentially an immaterial soul. But, if I do believe any of these things, then I will have stronger beliefs about myself that are opposed to them. Most strongly, I believe myself to be an entity who is wholly or largely physical, and whose survival requires rather a lot in the way of physical continuity. This is indicated by our responses to several of the foregoing examples.

As Quine has famously emphasized, a person may consistently maintain just about any of her beliefs providing that she subscribes to other beliefs that are appropriately related. Thus, in particular, I may maintain that, despite what my responses to our examples show, my strongest beliefs about myself and my survival are not those that most directly appear to be indicated. With a stab at consistency, what might I say?

Going as far away from a physical conception as is possible, I might say that I most strongly believe myself to be a purely subjective being, with no real existence in objective space and time. What then explains my strong egoistic aversion to great pain for people emerging from certain physical processes, but not for people emerging from other physical processes? I may say, I suppose, that, in addition to this, I have very strong beliefs about the highly contingent relationships that, from one objective time to another, I will enter with various parts of physical reality. For instance, I may say that I very strongly believe that I will stay attached to a certain beloved body through super freezing and super thawing, but not through ordinary freezing and thawing. I may say, as well, that I strongly believe that I will not enter such attachments with human brains and bodies produced by purely informational taping processes. I may say that, although I strongly believe that negative proposition, I have no very strong belief, one way or the other, about whether I will enter such attachments with the product of a physically more conservative taping process, such as the taping process with molecular restoration.

To be sure, I may *say* all of these things, and more; and so may you. But, for most of us, these words will ring hollow.

Just as matters look very bad for the idea that our strong beliefs are that we are transcendental subjects, so too do they look bad for somewhat less heady ideas about ourselves. We may say, of course, that we strongly believe ourselves to have immortal immaterial souls that, unlike our brains, are our really essential parts. To be comprehensive and consistent, we will then have to say, as well, that we have all sorts of strong beliefs about the behavior of these souls and, in particular, about which technologically exotic physical processes they favor and which they reject. With any sincerity, few will find this an easy thing to do.

By way of suitably employing an appropriate methodology, we have begun to build a convincing case for ourselves about what, as we most strongly believe, is our nature: We are wholly objective beings and, at the least, we are largely physical beings. And we have some pretty good evidence about what, according to our strongest beliefs, are the conditions of our existence and our survival: One of us will survive just so long as enough of her very own basic psychology is continuously enough realized in the physical matter that constitutes her. Although we have begun to build a convincing case for these propositions, we have much to do before that case is even remotely close to being complete.

2

CONSCIOUS EXPERIENCES AND SUBJECTS OF CONSCIOUSNESS: SIX METAPHYSICAL DOCTRINES

Each of us is, in fact, a complex physical being, occupying a region of space for a period of time. For one of us to survive into the future, there must be, in fact, significant physical continuity, from now until that future time, of whatever physically realizes, from now until then, that person's basic dispositional psychology. We are not purely subjective, transcendental beings that might have much better prospects for indefinitely great future existence. Nor are we even immaterial souls that might be quite immune from eventual physical deterioration and decay. Nor is any of us a simple, indivisible physical entity, such as a certain electron may be, or some particular quark. Against all of these conceptions and more, each of us is a complex physical being. As the introductory chapter made fairly convincing, this is our most deeply believed view of ourselves.

It is the task of the present chapter, and of several of the chapters to follow, to convince us much more strongly that this really is, by far, our most confident view in these matters. Now, one thing that makes this task difficult is the undoubted fact of *consciousness* in each of our lives. When I focus on the conscious experience that I am having, it can seem impossible to believe that I am a physical being, or even that I am part of any objective order of space and time. In our discussion so far, this difficulty was placed aside.

We may recall the exotic cases involving people that were presented in the introductory chapter. During the crucial middle period of each case, when exotic processes were occurring, there was never a candidate person having conscious thought, or experience. Now, before that period, as we supposed, the original person was conscious. And, after that period, the person at the end was conscious, too. But if there was a person around in the middle period, then, as we supposed or inferred, he was not conscious at that time.

Those who would deny a fully objective view of ourselves might cite this as a great fault in all of those examples. With consciousness absent at an example's crucial juncture, they might say, a case may well be quite irrelevant to the most central issues of our existence. After outlining our objective view, we shall begin to examine this perplexing challenge.

1. The Objective View of Ourselves

In our culture, we try to understand all of concrete reality as belonging to a single system of things. Each of us is, of course, himself part of concrete reality, in no wise a mere abstraction. In particular, then, we try to understand ourselves as each belonging to that unifying system.

The system we employ is a system of things in objective time and, many or all of them, in objective space as well. By some route through space and time, everything in the system is related to everything else in the system. Here is a box, for example, an object in the system that is fairly substantial spatially and that has existed for a moderate period of time. This plastic box, here before us now, is related in the system to Julius Caesar's first conscious thought of his crossing the Rubicon, which thought occurred long before this box first existed. Indeed, as we ordinarily conceive of these matters, the relation is uniquely appropriate, so that it takes us from this present box through space and time to just that ancient thought: First, we go from the box here and now to the there and then of Caesar's body and brain. Further, as we understand these matters, there is a single conscious Caesarian thought with the appropriate content that is then most intimately associated with that imperial organism. And, as is also our understanding, the inverse relation takes us from that particular thought to just this box now. So both the ancient conscious thought and the present plastic box will each find its own unique place in the system that is our objective space-time order. In our natural sciences, we strive to gain an understanding of everything concrete in terms of this unifying objective system.[1]

Much as is a box, or a tree, so also is a person objectively understood in this way. Through the influence of scientific inquiry, we form a view of what distinguishes us not only from such enduring objective things as lifeless plas-

---

1. A nearly classical presentation of our objective world view occurs in Peter Strawson's *Individuals*, Methuen, 1959.

tic boxes, but even from healthy blueberry bushes: We form a view of our-selves as living human beings, each of us in fact a somewhat distinctive mem-ber of our particular biological species. It is characteristic of members of this species that each can have conscious experience, and that this capacity is real-ized mainly in the brains of its members, when those organs are appropriately functioning. As compared with other species with which we are familiar, what ours is best at is thinking, and at achieving a higher level, or a greater degree, of consciousness. Given all of this, we take our brains as the natural parts of us that realize our most conspicuously distinctive capacities. So we take our brains to be, in fact, much more *important* parts of ourselves than any of our other parts, beyond our brains, more important than our hearts, our lungs, and our limbs. Indeed, our brains are more central to our existence than all of those other parts taken together.

Insofar as it is appropriate, we treat other conscious beings along the same general lines. Because the analogous capacities of a dog are, in fact, most directly realized in its brain, we take this organ of the dog as, in fact, more central to its existence than all the rest of the dog, external to the brain, taken together. This might not be much reflected in linguistic usage. But suppose that your pet collie's brain is placed in the body of an exact duplicate dog and the duplicate brain of that other collie is placed in the (head of the) body of your pet. Regarding an impending future torture for one or else the other of these two resultant animals, a forced choice between the two animals is an easy one: You will rightly choose for the dog with your pet's brain to be spared the torture, while the other canine will, as a consequence of your choice, be caused severe pain. This choice is just about as easy as a choice between the two animals that were there before any brain and body switch. As you believe, in both cases your dog will be just the animal with its original brain, well structured for the support of canine thought and experience. When our thoughts about canine identity are most serious, those thoughts focus on the whereabouts of a particular healthy canine brain.

By contrast, we may imagine a worm that is conscious, but whose capacity for consciousness is not centered in any of its parts. As regards survival, we treat that worm as a whole, no part favored over any other, much as with a presumably non-conscious rock. Perhaps the worm may be severed so that both the long part, four-fifths of the original, and also the short part, support consciousness. Then perhaps the original worm is only four-fifths of its for-mer length, while a short new worm is made of protoplasm that, before the slicing, composed part of the original worm. Or, although it seems a bit less felicitous, perhaps the original worm ceased to exist, and was succeeded by two extremely intimate descendants, one a good deal longer and more mas-sive than the other. At any rate, as regards judgments of their identity, different sorts of conscious beings might be treated differently. But all of them will be treated wholly objectively: the human, the dog, and the worm.

2. Conscious Experience and Subjects of Consciousness: Three Metaphysical Doctrines Concerning Each

Although it is also true of dogs, and probably even true of frogs, the fact that we have *conscious experience* can often seem to be the most amazing fact of our existence. In each of our lives, this apparently amazing phenomenon is very pervasive. Now, as I am using the expression, conscious experience is to include "inner experience," that is, conscious thoughts, mental images, dreams, and so on, as much as the "outer experience," or sensory experience, associated with ordinary conscious perception of things beyond our minds or brains. If we may term various sensations of our bodies "middle experience," as may occur in kinesthetic perception and in the vivid registering of various internal pressures, then middle experience, too, will be included. But, however we classify them more specifically, conscious experience is to include any of the conscious mental states that anyone ever has.

For the purpose of this study, I stipulate this usage for the term 'experience': Any experience that is ever had is conscious experience. On this usage, it is inconsistent, or nonsensical, to speak of unconscious, and non-conscious, experience. And it is redundant, although often appropriately emphatic, to speak of conscious experience. In this way, my stipulated use of 'experience' differs from my ordinary use of 'thought', 'belief', 'wish' and 'desire'.

When one reflects on one's own conscious experience, certain propositions become very appealing. These propositions then can seem not only to be necessarily true, but to be deep metaphysical truths. These apparent metaphysical truths will seem to be far deeper than any quite trivial semantic truths, than any propositions whose necessary truth is primarily due to linguistic conventions we maintain.

The appearance of there being such deep propositions can affect what view of ourselves we favor: It may get us to look more favorably on Descartes' view of ourselves, for example, or to favor certain other views of ourselves that conflict with our objective view. In order to defend our objective view against potential challenges by these conflicting views, it is important for us to examine this situation. We begin by noticing the appeal of three metaphysical doctrines concerning conscious experience.

Absoluteness of Experience: *Conscious experience is all-or-none.* Conscious experience is metaphysically determinate; it is in no way a matter of degree. The intensity of, or the level of, a subject's experience may be a matter of degree, as may be certain other *features of* his conscious experience. But, at any particular time, either a subject actually is conscious, however low the intensity or level of his experience may be, or else he then is completely lacking in conscious experience.

Privacy of Experience: *Conscious experience is completely private to a single subject.* When he is having conscious experience, a subject and his experience are deeply and seamlessly unified. Just so, the subject's absolute intimacy with his own experience is itself absolutely inviolable: Except for that particular subject himself, nobody else and nothing else can *have* that conscious experience that he has. As another gloss on this idea, nobody else, and nothing else, can be *directly conscious of* the experience of that particular subject.

There are some related thoughts that are often mistakenly conflated with the appealing doctrine just presented. As it often appears, they might be less certain than the idea in focus: First, there is the merely related idea that (the most salient aspect of) a subject's conscious experience is *completely evident to*, or is *transparent to*, that subject himself: When he has conscious experience, a subject must have a correct idea of, and must even know, (the most salient aspect of) the qualitative character of his current experience. Can that subject *also* have an *incorrect* idea of his present experience's (most salient) character, then having *conflicting* ideas about the matter? Perhaps there is much truth in the further, still different related idea that a subject's present moment experience judgment is *incorrigible*. If so, then, at the least, there can never be any substantial conflict here, or any significant error: Although he might be wrong about other aspects of reality in substantial ways, if there is any possibility for error at all in the matter, a person can be wrong about (the most salient aspect of) his own present experience only in ways that are quite trivial, or superficial, such as may occur in careless misclassification. At all events, these other ideas are to be distinguished from the doctrine of the privacy of experience.

Indivisibility of Experience: *Conscious experience is absolutely indivisible.* Whether it is physical or whether otherwise, *what* a subject is conscious *of* might divide. For example, the keyboard that I consciously see and feel may divide. But my conscious visual experience itself cannot possibly divide, nor can my tactile experience, which appears to be seamlessly of one piece with my visual experience. If we employ the term 'part' in a sufficiently strict use, we may say that a *subject's total present conscious experience* is without any real *parts*: If my tactile experience alone should suddenly cease, then my total experience will *not come apart*; rather, it will suddenly shrink, so to say, or will suddenly become impoverished in a certain way. By the same token, that tactile experience of mine *cannot exist independently of* that total experience of mine: If the rest of my present experience—all of it except my tactile experience—should cease, then, for all that loss, my total experience will certainly *not* cease. Instead, my tactile experience will then serve wholly to constitute that total experience of mine.

It seems that, especially for one's own case, the absolute necessity of these truths is *revealed to one simply by reflecting on the phenomenology of one's own present experience*. When I think about the total conscious experience that I have right now, the experience itself seems to reveal to me the absolute necessity of these three features that it has. When reflecting on my experience, it also seems that these truths about it are extremely *certain*.

The three doctrines about experience find close parallels in three appealing doctrines about the metaphysics of people or, more generally, the metaphysics of *subjects of consciousness*. Although the doctrines about subjects do not ever seem to be quite as certain as the doctrines about experiences themselves, often they may seem to be nearly as certain. Especially when we think of ourselves *as we are when we are conscious*, these three parallel doctrines will seem quite compelling.

Absoluteness of Subjects: *A subject is all-or-none.* A subject is in no way a matter of degree. The level or intensity of a subject's mental life may be a matter of degree. The presence or absence of certain psychological states of the subject, and of certain relations involving the subject, may be a matter of degree. And what causally supports or influences a subject and his experiences may also be a matter of degree. With all of these other things, there may be a middle ground where, if anything does, mere conventions may decide the matters. But quite beyond any conventions, at any particular time, the subject himself either exists in full or else he fails to exist completely.

Separateness of Subjects: *A subject is completely separate.* A subject is separate and distinct from every other subject, as well as from everything else that is not one of his own conscious states. A subject's body may be organically joined to another subject's body. As a result of some suitable fusion or merger, perhaps two subjects might even share the same brain. But, just as no subject can share conscious experience with any other, so no subject can himself merge, fuse or conjoin with any other subject, nor with anything else, for that matter. In an alleged fusion of two subjects, something else really happens instead: Perhaps one subject ceases to exist while the other suddenly gains all, or part, of what was previously the brain of the one. Or, perhaps both of the subjects of experience cease to exist, their brains, or brain-parts, then suddenly serving to support the consciousness of an utterly new person. Or, perhaps something else happens that involves the fusing of one thing with another. But no subject himself ever merges or fuses.

Indivisibility of Subjects: *A subject is absolutely indivisible.* A subject's body and brain certainly may be divided. And perhaps a subject's phenomenal field might also be divided. But the subject himself cannot possibly be divided. If a problematic physical or phenomenal division occurs, the possibilities for him will still be limited: Either he will go in one direction, or he will go in another, or he will cease to exist, completely, just when that division occurs.

It is plausible that the three doctrines about conscious experience help to foster, and even to ground, the appeal of these doctrines about subjects of experience. For it is only *as we are at those times when we are conscious* that we seem most invulnerable to gradual fade-out, to division and to merging, in contrast with simple abrupt termination. As should be noticed, when we suppose ourselves to be without conscious experience, perhaps thinking of ourselves as being in deep sleep between dreams, there is less appeal to ideas that we are so invulnerable to fade-out, fission and fusion. Moreover, as remarked before, even at their best, the doctrines about subjects seem a bit less certain than the parallel doctrines about their experiences. At all events, for a most illuminating counter to the doctrines about subjects, and to the challenge that they might pose to our objective view of ourselves, we should dispel the notion that there are those deep necessary truths about conscious experiences. In some later chapters, a serious effort will be made to dispel that compelling but misleading notion.[2]

To be frank, I confess that I am at least agnostic about, and perhaps incline toward being skeptical about, whether there are any properly metaphysical necessities at all. I do accept that there are plenty of necessary truths, all right, but those I accept are of less controversial sorts. On the one side, I accept the rather "unworldly" necessities that are logical, and mathematical, and conceptual, and so on. On the other side, I accept the more worldly, but less "strict," necessities of natural law and causation. Unlike quite a few brilliant philosophers, from Aristotle to Kripke, I am less sanguine that there are any necessary truths that go quite beyond these two broad classes. But, to forestall any misunderstanding, let us notice that what I am now suggesting neither requires, nor does it exclude, my more general agnosticism. For my

---

2. As I read them, there are some able contemporary philosophers who might endorse some, or all, of these doctrines. The doctrine of the absoluteness of subjects, perhaps the most central of the group for our main topic, may be endorsed by Geoffrey Madell in *The Identity of the Self*, Edinburgh University Press, 1981, by Colin McGinn in *The Character of Mind*, Oxford University Press, 1982, and by Richard Swinburne in "Personal Identity," *Proceedings of the Aristotelian Society*, 1973–74. Presumably, these authors also endorse the companion doctrine of the absoluteness of experiences. Perhaps in addition to endorsing those propositions, in his *Person and Object*, George Allen & Unwin, 1976, Roderick Chisholm befriends the doctrine of the indivisibility of subjects and, with it, he might also endorse its companion, the doctrine of the indivisibility of experiences.

For reasons whose propriety will emerge, I will not mount a sustained argument against the six doctrines until my sixth chapter.

present suggestion amounts to no more than this: *Even if there are many metaphysically necessary truths, these six doctrines are not among them.*

As our "robust sense of reality" appears to tell us, the foregoing six (groups of) sentences do not express deep metaphysical truths. Rather, either those sentences express no necessary truths at all or else they express propositions true largely by convention. But what is this robust sense of reality? Part of it is a healthy epistemological realism: It cannot be nearly so easy as this to uncover deep truths about main aspects of concrete reality. As with other psychological phenomena, an adequate understanding of conscious experience requires experiment, observation and theorizing that is both protracted and painstaking. And an understanding of our own nature should require no less. Another part of this robust sense may be a certain metaphysical conviction, one that might be more deeply held than we realize: We may have a strong belief in the wholly physical nature of concrete reality. This deep belief may here be coupled with the thought, doubtlessly correct, that those six groups of sentences express no deep metaphysical truths about anything that is wholly physical.

On the most plausible development of our objective view of ourselves, each of us is a complex physical being, composed of very many simpler physical things. Because these simpler things can combine in ever so many ways, the conditions of our existence, our experience and our survival are, in a variety of ways, relevantly gradual conditions. So, there is notable conflict between the six metaphysical doctrines and, on the other side, our objective view.

Because of this clash, the appeal of these doctrines engenders turbulence. Perhaps this is one of the main reasons why, for so many years, so many philosophers have found the mind-body problem to be so exciting. Directing attention to our present main topic, perhaps this is one of the main reasons why, for so many years, so many philosophers have found problems of personal identity to be so exciting.

We may notice a contrast that supports this last surmise: In the first chapter, when considering our examples of freezing and thawing, of teleconstruction and of other technological exotica, we may also have felt a certain excitement. But, in comparison with thinking about questions where consciousness is salient, that interest seems superficial. Other contrasts also support the conjecture: Questions about the identity of non-conscious physical objects, like rocks and shirts, and even living non-conscious bushes, by comparison seem dull matters of uncovering linguistic conventions.

At all events, because the six appealing doctrines clash with our objective view, at certain times we may be drawn to competing views of ourselves, with which the doctrines better accord. We turn to examine some of these alternative positions.

3. Three Competing Views of Ourselves

While we can never really abandon our objective view of ourselves, to which our commitment is enormously strong and deep, we may, in our more philosophical moments, find certain alternatives to be appealing. While all of these alternatives must conflict with the objective view in at least some significant respect, some of them present a greater conflict, a more radical departure, than do others. We may best begin, I imagine, by considering an alternative that is historically most influential. This is Descartes' view of ourselves or, if not precisely the view of the historical Descartes, an appealing and influential *Cartesian view of ourselves.*

The Cartesian view posits an extremely close and direct relation between each person, or subject, and conscious experience: Required by the very conditions for his survival, a person is conscious at every moment of his existence. Because there is so much appeal in the doctrine that conscious experience itself is all-or-none, on the Cartesian view, where experience and the experiencing subject's existence are so directly related, there is a nice explanation for the appeal of the doctrine that our own existence is an all-or-none matter. Thus we might have a certain good feeling toward the Cartesian view.

In addition to having such a strong requirement of consciousness as a condition on our survival, the other most conspicuous feature of the Cartesian view concerns our relation to objective space. As regards space, the Cartesian view clearly requires that a person not occupy any finite or infinite volume of space; a conscious being must have *no spatial extension.* This doctrine effectively blocks any thought that subjects may be divisible, even in principle. For, although it leaves open the bare logical possibility of a self that divides nonspatially, we haven't the slightest inkling of how that possibly might occur nor, then, any tendency to allow for any process answering to such a description. Thus the doctrine of the self's indivisibility, like that of its absolute existence, is well served by this approach.

Even though it would not affect the question of the self's divisibility, on the Cartesian view, at least on a suitably pure version of it, a person has no spatial location, either; no person can be at a pure point in objective space. This accords with the appeal of the third attractive doctrine about ourselves, namely, that we are absolutely separate. By disallowing a person even any spatial location, the view discourages strongly the idea that two people can ever merge or fuse, even if it may not remove all room for such a possibility. For, quite literally, there is *no point at which* they can ever come together. If selves are to merge, on this view, they must do so in a way that does not concern space at all. While we may not be certain that this is impossible, we haven't the least understanding of how such a confluence of conscious beings might occur. Insofar as we are under the influence of the Cartesian view, then, thoughts of fusion will be quite effectively blocked.

As regards spatial involvement for people, what *does* the Cartesian view allow? On this view, a person *can be intimately related to* various points in space, but *need not* ever be so related to any. The relations to these spatial locations, and to such bodies as may there be located, will be contingent in the extreme. Accordingly, my relation to my brain and body is highly contingent; possibly without much harm to me, this relation might be terminated when those entities die, or become very unsuitably structured.

As all the world knows, Descartes' view has its attractions. When contemplating our six appealing metaphysical doctrines, it can seem very attractive indeed. When in a more worldly frame of mind, there appear to be significant disadvantages. As we noticed in section 5 of the previous chapter, one of these might be rather considerable: With respect to time, nobody can endure any gap in his conscious experience. This apparently repugnant claim is not an unmotivated, gratuitous burden of the Cartesian view. On the contrary, we should view this claim as following from more basic metaphysical requirements imposed by that view: First, in whatever is the time in which he exists, anyone must be conscious at every moment of his existence and, second, everyone must exist only in objective time.

As it seems to us all, this constraint is indeed a very strong one: For Descartes, we cannot be unconscious in a period of deep sleep, or when under a powerful general anesthetic, and possibly survive the objective episode. Now, we all believe we do survive periods of deep sleep, say, such sleep as occurs between our dreams. Quite rightly, Descartes wished to respect this belief of ours. To do this, he required an auxiliary hypothesis: In objective periods of deep sleep, although it *appears* that there is no consciousness, one really is conscious nonetheless; each of us just *completely forgets* all of his conscious thoughts and experiences *almost directly upon* his having them.[3]

Now, right off, this auxiliary hypothesis strikes one as highly implausible. But this initial implausibility is not by itself a sure sign of a deep disadvantage. A somewhat surer sign is the conflict between the hypothesis and what we believe about the case of super freezing and super thawing, as noticed in the brief investigation of section 5 of the first chapter. For a still surer sign, let us investigate still further.

Suppose we were confronted with scientific findings that strongly suggested Descartes was actually right about most of the main actual facts of our conditions of sleep and waking life: Under an impressive variety of relevant

---

3. As remarked in the notes to the previous chapter, this hypothesis occurs in Descartes' Reply to the Fifth Set of Objections.

circumstances, certain esoteric brain activity is discovered to be associated with much nearly immediate, and quite complete, forgetting of one's experience. And it is found that this activity is most intense, and is continuously present, whenever we are in periods of deepest sleep, under powerful general anesthetic, and so on. Moreover, a second sort of esoteric brain activity is discovered to correlate positively with intensity of consciousness, whatever exactly we take the latter to involve. Interestingly enough, during both key transition periods between full sleep and complete wakefulness, there is only a very low degree of this second sort of brain activity: There is a low degree just before a person falls off to sleep and, again, just while he is awakening. But, at least to some degree, this activity is found to be present in every human brain at all times, from before birth until death. Pointedly, such activity is found often to obtain to a very high degree, not only when we are fully awake, but also when we are in deepest natural sleep, between remembered dreams, and when we are under very powerful general anesthetic. Thinking of the possibility of them now, what is our reaction to such supposed findings?

These imagined findings would indeed help to confirm Descartes' view about our actual situation. At the same time, we do not take them to involve any matter about which we are urgently concerned. Now, if continuous consciousness through objective time was an important requirement for our survival, then this would be, we might presume, a matter of very urgent concern. We might even feel some distinct *relief* associated with the contemplation of such findings.

The fact that we are rather blasé about the possible prospect of such findings is not, however, as sure a sign as it may seem that Descartes has gotten things wrong in this matter. For, as I have argued in previous works, we may have long-standing psychological mechanisms that will get us to think that we have been right about our *past existence* relative to the great majority of possible scenarios.[4] When we are presented with this case of imagined scientific findings, perhaps it is just this mechanism that is blocking us from appreciating the correctness of Descartes' requirement.

A surer sign requires only a fairly small extension of our imaginative inquiry. We now suppose that, in addition to the interesting findings, a special drug is discovered. When this drug is applied to someone, then in periods of deep sleep his brain will, for the first time, support no conscious experience. All of the evidence would indicate that most strongly. Relative to such an imagined *future-oriented* situation, do we regard taking that drug as tantamount to poisoning oneself fatally? Clearly, we do not. Although no known

---

4. As I said in a note to the previous chapter, I first presented these ideas in "The Causal Theory of Reference" and in "Toward a Psychology of Common Sense."

suspicious psychological mechanism is inducing us to do so, we still make a strong negative response. Now, it may possibly be that, even so, Descartes is still right in his requirement of continuous consciousness. For there may be an as yet unknown mechanism blocking us from appreciating its correctness even in such light as this imagined future-oriented case may provide. That is an epistemic possibility for us still. But we may now responsibly think that, although possible, this idea is quite improbable. In all likelihood, Descartes' requirement is nothing that any of us do deeply believe, or ever will have much reason to believe. Still impressed with the appeal of our six propositions, this may lead us to seek a less demanding alternative to our objective view of ourselves.

On one pretty plausible interpretation of their writings, Joseph Butler and Thomas Reid offer a philosophical view of ourselves that is in some ways like Descartes', but that differs in such a way as to avoid the distasteful Cartesian consequence just discussed.[5] These thinkers might be taken to line up with the Cartesian view regarding the self and matters spatial: A person has no spatial extension and, presumably, not even location at a point in objective space. On the temporal question, like both Descartes and our objective view, this *Butlerian view of ourselves* has every person exist in objective time.

As for Descartes, for these philosophers, too, a conscious subject must exist in objective time without any interruption. Butler and Reid avoided Descartes' "problem of the apparent gap" by requiring a less stringent, and less pure, relation between the self and conscious experience. A person need not actually be conscious at every moment, but need only have the *capacity* for consciousness at every moment he exists. In other words, while it must always exist, and while, perhaps, it will always be realized in some entity or other, the person's capacity for experience need not always be exercised.

With this step toward our psychologically powerful objective view, these philosophers can offer us a position that does not have such a glaring appearance of unnaturalness. But the decrease in discomfort is dearly bought. There are two parts to the price. First, although it seems very clear that consciousness itself is all-or-none, it seems much less clear that the capacity for anything, even the capacity for consciousness, is in no way a matter of degree. On the Butlerian view, then, the appeal of the doctrine of the subject's absoluteness is left wholly unexplained and, in any case, is not connected very closely with the greatly attractive doctrine of the absoluteness of conscious experience. Second, we feel that this Butlerian position is not a view of which we can make much sense: When a person is *not* exercising his capacity for consciousness, *what*, in any *positive* terms, is this nonspatial self supposed to

5. I claim no scholarly expertise at all regarding these thinkers. Indeed, my sources are only the short selections in John Perry's anthology, *Personal Identity*, as cited in the Bibliography.

be? When this capacity is not being exercised, what *is* it that *realizes*, or grounds, this merely dispositional property that the non-spatial self so essentially possesses? There appear to be no credible answers to these questions, and to indefinitely many related questions. At the same time, it appears that there should be some good answers. So this Butlerian view also seems to have some serious disadvantages.

Dissatisfied with the Cartesian and the Butlerian views, we may seek still another alternative to our objective view of things. We may then consider an alternative that, among competing positions that are intuitively somewhat appealing, might present the greatest possible departure from our objective view of the self. For that reason, we might call this position the *subjective view of ourselves*.

The subjective view defines each person as being just the bare, transcendental subject of his own experiences, existing whenever, and only whenever, just those experiences occur. Claiming that we transcend the objective world order, the subjective view of ourselves will have each of us be subjects of consciousness *as opposed to* objects in the world. This statement is suggestive. But what does it suggest? The view has major implications regarding the self in relation both to space and to time.

On the subjective view, we exist neither in objective space nor even in objective time. A conscious being cannot exist in objective time, not even for a moment. Rather, each self, on this view, has his own *subjective time*, which is the only appropriate temporal framework for considerations of his existence. Existing only in his own subjective time, how might a person be related to things in objective time? The matter is treated similarly to the way that all three of these considered alternatives consider the question of the relations between subjects and objective space: If all goes well, a subject of consciousness may be intimately, but highly contingently, related to points, or periods, of objective time. Thus he may be related to those worldly things that exist at those objective times.

As does the Cartesian view, the subjective view requires that a person always have conscious experience: According to the view, someone must actually be conscious at every moment of his existence. For Descartes, with his commitment to objective time for our existence, such a requirement seems extraordinarily difficult. But the subjective view gives an interpretation to the requirement that leaves it very much less imposing than it first appears. For, on this subjective view, the only time to consider, in determining someone's existence or survival, is that subject's own subjective time order. But then the moments in question are not instants of objective time. In his own subjective time order, there will be no temporal gap between the moments of a subject's existence, and he may have experience at every last one of these times when he exists. Because it provides this extremely favorable temporal interpretation, the subjective view can have a requirement regarding experience and time that is not so enormously demanding.

The obvious disadvantages of the subjective view are those that concern this very notion of a person's own subjective time. Not only is there no independent reason for accepting the existence of all of these conveniently gap-dispensing private time orders, there seem many mysteries about how anything in its own subjective time might interact with what is in objective time.

Ordinarily, my reaction to the subjective view is that it is ridiculously unrealistic. But, then, ordinarily I do not focus on thoughts much like the six appealing metaphysical doctrines. When we contemplate those doctrines, the subjective view, like the other alternative positions, can appear much less ridiculous.

Now, all of these alternatives, and especially this most radical subjective view, might be deeply incoherent. But there may be great appeal to a view even if there is deep incoherence or inconsistency in the position. Although the reason for this is rather evident, it might be worth emphasizing now: As long as the incoherence of a view is sufficiently *unobvious*, as deep incoherences often are, there is no bar to our finding the view to be an appealing one.

Because it is such a radical departure from our objective view, this purely subjective view may be a helpful landmark, useful in locating other alternative views. Each in a different way, they might all lie between the objective view and this extreme subjective position. Indeed, we may regard them in this light: They may each be obtained by replacing certain features of the subjective view with correlative features of the objective view. By so doing, we may obtain different *compromise* views, or *hybrid* views of ourselves. In particular, the Cartesian view and the Butlerian view may be regarded as compromises between the pure subjective view and the objective view of ourselves.

Because they sharply conflict with our confident objective view of ourselves, in the final analysis, we find these competing views quite incredible. Each of the alternatives noted is, to my mind, philosophically interesting. But it is hard to see any of them argued, or developed, to a point where they should receive rational acceptance. There appear to be great problems, for example, as to how these selves, none of them in objective space, will be able to interact with what is in objective space. How are they to learn anything about the world around them? How are they to learn anything about each other, or communicate in any way? We can posit special faculties they have that somehow enable them to do these things, but few of us can believe that this will be more than so much empty hand-waving. As far as I can see, none of these views will provide a framework for, or will even be an important part of, a satisfactory understanding of what we are.

Suppose that this is correct. Then these particular alternative views should not be adopted. But might not there be some other metaphysical alternative that is much more satisfactory than any of these? Although this is a logically possible option, I cannot see that it is a likely prospect. If I am right about this more general point, then we forgo any attempt at seeking an alternative to our objective view. As the present book argues, perhaps we should, not only in our deepest beliefs but also in our explicit philosophy, endorse a wholly objective approach to ourselves.

4. The Continuity of Consciousness and Physical Division

There are some examples concerning conscious experience and personal identity that are useful for us to consider. In the most intriguing of these examples, conscious experience itself, as opposed to underlying causes of experience, is highly salient. For each of us, these most intriguing examples will prove most forceful just when the person supposes that it is he himself who enters the central process of the case. In this way, these examples parallel the ego-centrically framed passages of Descartes' most famous, and most forceful, writing. But, as may be somewhat surprising, the examples will still be quite intriguing even when another, not oneself, is imagined as the protagonist.

By any reasonable reckoning, our responses to these examples are puzzling. To the cases where consciousness is salient, we respond *as though* we maintained an alternative to the objective view: Perhaps we look like either implicit adherents of the subjective view or adherents of the pure Cartesian view. Whether we actually do implicitly maintain any such view, in conflict with our strong objective view, is a difficult question that we need not consider.[6] At all events, our responses to these examples can make these alternative views look good to us and, correlatively, make the objective view look not so good. For it may appear that these alternatives allow for a better explanation of our responses than any credible form of the objective view provides. As I am quite sure, this appearance is misleading. Later in the chapter, we will explain our perplexing responses in a way that dispels this appearance. In that way, we will provide some indirect support both for our sensibly balanced methodology and for our objective view of ourselves.

By my standards at least, these examples are pretty wildly hypothetical. This

---

6. In "Consciousness and Self-Identity," *Midwest Studies in Philosophy*, 1986, I conjectured that, in an uneasy balance, we actually hold conflicting views of the self. Not at all confident of the conjecture even at the time, I am now still less enamored of it. At any rate, in the present text, there are presented only very much less ambitious psychological hypotheses about the matters in that neighborhood.

considerable degree of wildness is a sign that, even as they ask us to suppose to be false certain beliefs that ordinarily help provide us with a firm basis for response, the examples may prompt the operation of misleading, or distorting, psychological dispositions. Still, by itself, that wildness can be only a rather small and uncertain sign of any such unwanted connection. On the other hand, in that we will alertly notice that the examples are rather wild, we might be prepared for a need to discount our dominant responses to the examples. For that reason, the fact that the cases are pretty wildly hypothetical will present no significant danger for our inquiry.

Cases of surgical division have figured prominently in the recent literature on personal identity. I would like to consider a new case of this general type, one where a "stream of conscious experience" figures about as conspicuously as can be.

In this new example an anesthetic is applied to the major portion of someone's brain, say, to an appropriate two-thirds of it, but no anesthetic is applied to the remaining part of the brain. As a result, only the remaining third continues to support consciousness; at this time, none is supported by the rest of the patient's brain or body. Then the active one-third is severed from the rest of the brain and is surgically removed from the body. Still supporting consciousness, this significant minor portion is kept viable elsewhere. Perhaps it is placed in a sustaining and stimulating vat. Alternatively, it might be placed in (the head of) a duplicate of the original patient's body. In any case, a while after the minor portion is safely ensconced, the anesthetic wears off in the major portion and conscious experience is again intimately associated with what is there, too. At the end of the procedure, there are two people, both of them conscious: There are no more direct mental connections between them then than there now are between, say, you and me. And, if it is possible to do so at all, it is only through the most radical physical reconstructions that the smallish brains of these two people might ever be joined in such a way that, as mere parts of a resulting whole brain, they will together support anything like a single unified mental life.

Suppose that I undergo such an operation. The resultant person with the third of my original brain will be, we naturally may suppose, only moderately like I was at the start as regards relevant dispositional psychology: There will be only a moderate overlap of ostensible memories—many will be lost; there will be only moderate similarity of personality, and so on. These great changes will have occurred rather suddenly, the direct result of a quick surgical slicing.

We are explicit in our supposition regarding the dispositional psychology of the person (eventually emerging or becoming conscious) on the other side. We will stipulate that this person, with two-thirds of my original brain, will be, in all these psychological respects, extremely similar to me at the start, before the surgical slicing. The psychological similarity will be as great as, say, that which ordinarily obtains in my life from one day to the very next day.

Will I survive this operation? And, if so, who will I be? Although there is some conflict, my dominant response is, first, that I *will* survive and, moreover, that I will be nobody but the patient who was conscious throughout. Even if it is, perhaps, no accurate guide about (our strong beliefs about) the conditions of our survival, this response appears to be rather typical.

What does the response indicate? First, in making judgments about our survival, generally we do *not have high standards* for (what counts as) *continuous* conscious experience. In the present case, what happens between the original patient and the non-anesthetized third of his brain is taken, quite spontaneously and quite comfortably, to involve the support of consciousness that is continuous. Second, in making judgments about our survival, the *continuity of consciousness may outweigh so many other factors all weighted together against it*. (Although we do seem to be disposed to accept this extreme weighting, good sense may direct us, in the end, to discount this tendency of ours.)

To see the interest of these indications, we consider the obvious variant of our perplexing case of surgical division. By itself, this comparatively dull version is not at all perplexing. Everything is the same as in the first version except for this key difference: In the variant, although my brain supports conscious experience before the surgery and I then am conscious, throughout the surgical procedure all of my brain and body are fully exposed to the potent anesthetic. As we are now supposing, in the middle period when the surgery occurs, there is no consciousness associated with me at all, nor with any part of me. Only at the end, well after the smaller brain portion has been separated from the two-thirds of the brain and from the body, is the anesthetic lifted from any of my original parts. Simultaneously, it is then completely lifted from both of the separated salient parts. At that time, but not in the middle period before, conscious experience is supported on both sides. At the end, there are two conscious people.

In this variant version of the case, will I survive? And, if so, who will I be? For most of us, the dominant response again is that I will indeed survive. But this time, for those of us whose response is favorable to the idea of my survival, I will be nobody but the person with *two*-thirds of my original brain, with all of my original body, and with just about all of my original (precise sort of) dispositional psychology. Now, for some few of us, the dominant response may be that I will not survive. And, for another few, there may be the dominant response that I somehow survive as, and am perhaps constituted of, both of the people at the example's end. But, for our inquiry, the main point surely is this: Nobody thinks that I will survive just as the person who has only one-third of my original brain.

When support of consciousness is uninterrupted just with the smaller portion, most of us respond that I survive as just that person there. By contrast, when conscious experience is, significantly and simultaneously, interrupted all around, none of us responds that I survive only as the person on that side. As far as intuitions go, there is a striking difference.

5. Continuity of Consciousness Through Rapidly Radical Change

The variant cases just considered presented a kind of "branching." Let's now look for an example that shows the great weight we may give to consciousness but that has no branching. If we are successful, then the weight intuitively given to consciousness in making judgments of personal identity will be a rather general phenomenon, present both with branching and without.

Modifying a suggestion from Mark Johnston, we consider two versions of a case of *rapid radical cellular changeover*.[7] In the first version, conscious experience is supported throughout. While there is this continuous consciousness, my cells are replaced, gradually but rapidly, by organic duplicates of the cells of somebody else. A different one percent of them removed at each stage, my original cells are progressively replaced by duplicates of Albert Einstein's cells as they were on his forty-fifth birthday. (Once any of my cells is replaced, it is thrown in the garbage.) Now, although this sequence of replacements is quite gradual, comprising, as it does, one hundred equal steps, it may proceed very rapidly. The whole operation may be over within, say, less than an hour. At every stage, we suppose rather unrealistically, the cells then in place, whether Ungerian or Einsteinian, all work well together. At the end of the sequence, and with conscious experience still supported, there is a man with the body and the brain and, thus, with the psychology of an Einstein. Will I survive this operation? Most of us respond quite affirmatively: That conscious man will be me. Always conscious, I simply will have undergone some very remarkable, and fairly sudden, changes. Although it is typical, perhaps this response also is no very accurate guide.

In the second version, everything is the same as in the first except for this conspicuous difference: Owing to the work of a powerful anesthetic, there is

7. Just as in the present text, on Johnston's original suggestion, my cells are replaced in a gradual but rapid sequence. But, on his suggestion, they are replaced not with any other cells, but with "mentally productive" bionic structures that, made of metal and suchlike, might not even be alive. I see nothing amiss with that additional flourish. At the same time, although the total suggestion is most intriguing, there is nothing particularly new in the business about the brain-part replacers being bionic; that much comes from old stories of the philosophical underground. The truly novel features of Johnston's suggestion are, I believe, preserved in the somewhat less radical, and somewhat more realistic, suggestion in the text. Of course, I realize that there is no great advantage in my present presentation.

no conscious experience supported during the period of the imagined cellular replacements. Only after all the replacements have been made is there again a man who is conscious. Will this conscious man be me? To this alternative version, most of us respond that I will *not* survive. By the end of the rapid and radical cellular changeover, the single person in this case will no more be me than he will be, say, Charlie Chaplin.

Although there is no branching, there is a striking difference in our responses to the two versions of this example. Both with branching and equally without, when it appears that conscious experience is continuously present in a case, then, as is our tendency, we give that appearance great weight in making judgments about survival. As I have been suggesting, perhaps we give that appearance far more weight than we should.

6. The Explanation of Our Responses to These Examples

To the version of our examples where conscious experience was interrupted, our responses are not at all surprising. As we respond, the subject then fails to survive the operation. We can begin to explain our response that there is this failure by attributing to ourselves a strong commitment to the objective view of ourselves. We can go further with these explanations by attributing further deep beliefs, within the compass of that general approach, that we have about ourselves. While the details of the explanations may be interesting, the explanatory task is not urgent. It is hard to have such a relaxed attitude, however, toward our responses to the version where conscious experience was supported throughout.

To this version of the examples, we respond that the patient will survive. This is surprising. After all, on any plausible form of the objective approach, survival will be very clearly denied. Does this mean that we have found a flaw in our objective view of ourselves? Does it mean that we are not really so deeply committed to that view?

In terms of alternative views that give a special place to actual experience, such as the subjective view and the Cartesian view, here are some neat little explanations of our responses to the perplexing versions. First, we give an explanation for the case with branching: When the anesthetic is selectively applied to his brain and body, certain intimate contingent relations between the patient and the active one-third of his brain are maintained. But, because of all this, and because no experience itself can divide, the relevantly similar relations between the patient and the rest of his brain and body are not maintained. Further, when the one-third is severed from the rest, any remaining intimate relations with the major portion are broken, but all of the intimate relations with the minor portion are still maintained. So, the patient goes the way of just that minor portion. As we may then appropriately say, the patient survives only as the person whose brain is the minor portion of his original brain.

Next, we give an explanation for the case without branching: Through each small change, the conscious subject maintains his relations with the biggish brainy mass causally effective in supporting experiences for him to enjoy. No small change will upset these relations. Because the patient does, in this way, survive *each* small change in conscious association with the brain, he survives *all of the changes* in such association. Accordingly, at the end, the patient not only survives, but he survives precisely as that conscious being specially related to that particular supportive brainy mass.

Because these explanations are nice and neat, they make these alternative views look good. Because no plausible form of our objective view can provide such nice explanations here, the objective view may not look good. But although the offered explanations are nice and neat, they are, after all, very difficult to believe. When we are honest with ourselves, we admit that, to us, they might be quite incredible.

We are moved to seek more pointedly psychological explanations of our responses, which may have little or no metaphysical import. We begin with an attempt to explain our response to the first, or branching, case in this more modest way. There are two main points of origin for our explanation: First, the salient feature of this case is conscious experience itself, as distinguished from any cause of the experience. Now, in certain other cases, there may be factors at work that bring the causal basis to the forefront of our thinking. But, whatever those factors may be, they are not strongly operative here. Second, with conscious experience most salient, and also with the causal support of experience continuing only on the minor side, we directly are moved to think that conscious experience itself continued on just this side.

From these two points, our explanation proceeds as follows: When our focus is so concentrated on conscious experience, we are apt to think in ways that are quite unusual. Much more than otherwise, we may then be influenced by the appeal of the six metaphysical doctrines. In particular, we are apt to be much influenced by the idea of the *privacy of experience*. If we think that a particular conscious experience is continuous in a certain way, then we will tend to think that the subject of that experience must continue along that same path. For any particular experience must be had by, or must be an experience of, *some particular* subject of experience. And, according to the privacy of experience, no *other* subject can ever have that particular experience: No more than he can share an experience of his at the moments that he has it, a person cannot, either, literally pass his conscious experience to someone else, whose experience it then becomes. (Rather than any such impossibility ever occurring, the first person will have his one experience and, perhaps directly caused by the fact of his then having it, immediately after that the second person may have his other, perhaps precisely similar, conscious experience.) Now, in the case at hand, the experience in question began by being an experience of the original patient. So, it is always just that person, and nobody else, who is having that continuous experience. So, our implicit reasoning gets us to respond, the original patient survives on the side of the active minor portion of the brain.

Furthermore, we are also apt to be much influenced by the idea of the *indivisibility of subjects*. Now, according to this idea, just as with any other subject of experience, the original patient cannot divide. In particular, in a case where the patient's physical basis is divided, that subject himself will not divide. But, as our reasoning has already directed, the original patient survives on the side of the minor portion. So he is not, as well, on the side of the sometimes unconscious major portion. Putting the pieces together, implicit reasoning issues in our full response: The patient survives on, and only on, the side of the active minor portion.

We turn to examine our response to the non-branching case. Here, a sequence of many small changes, both physical and psychological, befell our original subject. Because the changes occurred so gradually, their occurrence was not salient. Again, the salient feature of the case is the conscious experience that was continuously supported through all of this change. A second starting point of our explanation is this. Because there was, in the case, complete continuity in the causal support of conscious experience, we are spontaneously moved to believe that the experience itself was continuous. The experience at the end was the same particular experience as began before the sequence of changes.

As we agreed before, when conscious experience itself is so salient, then, much more than is usual, we are apt to be influenced by the six metaphysical doctrines. In particular, we are apt to find the idea of *privacy of experience* to be very persuasive. Inasmuch as the original experience is continuous throughout the case, the experience at the beginning is the same particular experience as that at the end. Now, this experience must always be the experience of some subject. As it begins as the experience of the original patient, and by the privacy of experience cannot ever be had by any other person, it must end as the experience of just that original patient. So, even at the end of the sequence, it is the original patient, and nobody else, who has that experience. Consequently, as our implicit reasoning directs us, the patient does survive.

The idea of *absoluteness of subjects* works to strengthen this response. Whether physical or psychological, each of the changes that occurs in the sequence is a rather small and trivial one. It is very hard to believe that, as a matter of fact, one of them can mean the difference between the conscious subject existing and his completely failing to exist. But, by the absoluteness of subjects, there really is no middle ground. So, with each small change, the subject still does clearly and fully exist. So, after all of the small changes, he clearly and fully exists.

7. Methodology, Continuous Consciousness and Personal Identity

In the introductory chapter, I noted two main dangers of the method of using responses to hypothetical cases as a means toward uncovering our deep attitudes. One danger is that even an example that often is quite instructive may be presented to us in a distorting context. Then our responses to the case will provide us with more confusion than instruction. In the present chapter, however, with its rather austere and antiseptic contexts, this danger scarcely mattered.

The other danger is that certain examples, presented in even the most innocuous contexts, may fail to connect strongly, in us, with deep beliefs in the philosophic area that appears to be their aim. Instead, they may connect more strongly with certain long-standing aspects of our psychological makeup. These connections may issue in responses that are philosophically misleading. In the present chapter, this second danger befell us markedly and repeatedly.

An example where continuous consciousness is made most salient, and where nothing is very notable about the causal ground of the conscious experience, may connect with tendencies toward belief in certain propositions that are not necessarily true. Then we may respond to the example, either dominantly or at least with a disturbingly strong dominated reaction, in a manner encouraged by the misleading tendencies. The offending tendencies may include a proclivity to believe in one, or in more than one, of the six metaphysical doctrines. To examples that allow these tendencies to be so influential, often our responses will be philosophically misleading.

Our discussion of them strongly suggests that just this situation obtains with the perplexing versions of this chapter's two most intriguing examples. Confronted with this suggestion, it is rational for us to do three things. First, we should seek small variants of the apparently dangerous cases that, although the same in all essentials, may have features that block the operation of the suspected tendencies. Upon encountering variants that appear promising in this regard, we notice our responses to the variant examples. If we notice quite different responses, reactions that accord much better with most of our strong beliefs about things, we may reasonably conclude that the suspicious cases really did mislead us in the manner suggested. Second, with the suspicions about our prereflective responses to the original examples being confirmed, we may conclude that those responses really were misleading: The correct description of those cases really does lie in quite an opposite direction. Third, in further inquiry into the topic of personal identity, when seeking valid clues from exotic examples, we should look toward cases that, as is clear, lack those features perceived to be so readily misleading.

How might we appropriately vary our perplexing examples? In our sequential case without branching, rather small and insignificant changes were made at each stage of the sequence while, as we assumed, conscious experience kept flowing. As is well known, in ever so many sorts of cases, when such small changes occur, we tend to overlook or ignore the large changes that, eventually, result from the accumulation of the small changes. In philosophy and logic, this shows up in the ancient, famous and still unresolved *sorites paradox*. In psychology, this shows up all over the place. That may occur with our example of continuous consciousness through rapidly *gradual* radical change: By specifying that only quite small changes are surgically produced in the causal ground of the conscious experience, in the brain, we make this causal source, along with the large changes that eventually occur, comparatively inconspicuous. In particular, the experientially productive brain may then be much less salient than the flowing consciousness that it causally generates. The discrepancy may be sufficiently great that we respond mainly on the basis of the assumed continuity of conscious experience itself, paying little notice to its most direct source and cause.

To test this plausible conjecture, we need only alter the causal ground, the brain, in a few large and significant surgical steps, and note our responses to this simple variation. The fewer the steps of change, the more dramatic will be each step; and, the more dramatic each step, the more dramatic will be the result. Among simple variants, the fewest steps will occur when we change half of the original brain at each step: While I remain conscious, half of my brain is destroyed and then removed. With conscious experience continuing in the remaining half, a minute later, there is joined an anesthetized duplicate of the corresponding half of Einstein's brain, as it was in his prime. After a minute, the anesthetic is lifted from the Einsteinian half, and the whole brain, not just the original half, supports conscious experience. After another minute, with consciousness still continuing, the other half of my original brain is destroyed and removed. After yet another minute, that half is replaced by an anesthetized duplicate of the other half of Einstein's brain. A minute later, the whole Einsteinian brain supports conscious experience. A single conscious person is in place at the example's end, a man who now is just like Albert Einstein once was. In this case, will I survive these enormous, and enormously abrupt, changes? Will that conscious Einsteinian person be *me*?

The strong intuitive response is that I will certainly *not* survive. The single person, at the end of these few minutes, will not be me. He will be a duplicate of the late Albert Einstein, a duplicate whose causal history is, during my last few minutes, briefly and marginally intertwined with mine.

When we notice our response to this example, we confirm the suspicion that our example of much more gradual change did fool us: When hundredths of my brain are very rapidly replaced with continuing consciousness, I no more survive than when halves are so rapidly replaced. Although it might sometimes exert great psychological influence on our judgments of personal identity, the phenomenon of continuing conscious experience, we should be convinced, has little or no weight in the truth of these judgments: When hundredths of my brain are replaced with continuing consciousness, I no more survive than when hundredths are replaced under a powerful anesthetic, without any consciousness supported until the drug is lifted at the example's end. Although our prereflective responses to the case may favor survival, on reflection, these intuitions should be discounted.

In our branching case with continuing consciousness, we may have stacked the deck in another way that fooled us. Throughout, there was enough on the minor side so that not only was experience always supported, but a person always was there as well. This being may have been very dull, but, as was stipulated, he had enough intelligence, personality and whatever to be a person. And, by certain relevant standards, that much may be quite a lot. In contrast, let us imagine this variant of our branching example: We will suppose that, not a fairly potent one third, but only a very much smaller, and psychologically very much less effective, brain piece goes onto the minor side. On the major side, just as there will be left even more than in the previous variant, so, as we suppose, my dispositional psychology will there be continued very well indeed. Returning to consider the minor side, and most important for us now to contemplate, although a conscious being is there, that being has a mentality about on the level of a normal mouse.

If such a surgical slicing as this is performed on me, then, quite clearly, although some conscious experience always may be there, I will not survive on the minor side. Any conscious being who is there will, by a very great deal, fail to be a person. And, failing to be a person by so very much, that being will, quite clearly, not be anyone at all. In particular, that being, constituted of material structures extracted from my brain, will not be me.

Perhaps owing to an interruption of conscious experience on the major side, will I fail to survive this operation altogether? Just as it appears, that suggestion is quite absurd. I will quite definitely survive this operation: Not only will the being on the side with so much of my original brain and all of my body always be someone, but, quite clearly, exactly one person will be there throughout the entire procedure. That one person will be, of course, nobody but me.

When we make the causal ground of experience so very much more paltry on the minor side, then, for the entire example, we make the factor of the causal ground quite conspicuous. Correlatively, conscious experience itself becomes a less salient feature than before. Now, the salience of experience relative to that of other features may vary considerably from case to case. As a consequence, the psychological influence of thoughts about continuous experience may, from one example to the next, vary quite considerably. But it is very hard to believe that, as a factor in the *truth of judgments of personal identity*, the weight of continuous experience will vary so substantially. On reflection, in making these judgments we should give exceedingly little weight, or perhaps no weight at all, to what, as it appears, is a continuous flow of experience. So, prereflective responses that give much weight to this appearance should be heavily discounted. So, on reflection, in our case where, with one-third of my brain, there is a strangely dull but conscious person on the minor side, that person will not be me.

As a general rule that may be treated with some flexibility, in looking for cases that might help us toward an adequate view of the main conditions of our survival, we had best avoid examples where continuous consciousness is a salient factor. And, when not avoiding these cases, we must be extremely careful in assessing what it is that generates our responses. For the topic of personal identity, this is an important part of a sensibly balanced methodology.

8. The Spectrum of Decomposition Versus The Absoluteness of Subjects

In order most convincingly to deny alternatives to our objective view, we must convince ourselves that the six metaphysical doctrines really are not any deep metaphysical truths. This is a difficult task. To be done well, the task requires the presentation of many arguments and examples. And some of these demand a formulation that is rather lengthy and elaborate. We will not be in a position to see the need for such elaborate formulations, however, until a fair amount of groundwork has been laid. For this reason, I postpone, until the sixth chapter, anything like a full-blown argument against the alternative views. Even without much preparation, however, a surprisingly persuasive argument can be mounted against one of these doctrines, and in a way that gives us some sense, at least, that all of them may be in jeopardy. The *argument from the spectrum of congenial decomposition*, which is nearly as brief as it is easy to appreciate, is a strong initial thrust toward a reasoned, articulate endorsement of our objective view of ourselves.

Of the six metaphysical doctrines, perhaps it is the *absoluteness of subjects* that is most influential in fostering dissatisfaction with the objective view, and in attracting philosophers to alternative views of ourselves. According to this influential doctrine, in any situation whatsoever, the question "Am *I* in that situation; does that situation contain *me*?" will have a perfectly definite answer, either "Yes" or else "No." And further, in no situation at all will the fact of this definite answer be primarily, or even largely, a matter of any mere conventions of linguistic usage. Rather, the definite answer is always due to my metaphysical nature: Simply because of what I am, in any situation whatever, either it is fully and clearly true that I exist or else it is definitely and completely false.

The argument from the spectrum of congenial decomposition persuasively challenges this influential doctrine of the absoluteness of subjects. The spectrum at the core of this argument consists of an appropriately selected sequence of cases. Drawing on both points of method observed in the previous chapter as well as those noted in this present one, there are at least four conditions that guide the selection of a sequence that is suitable.

First, unlike most of the examples treated in earlier sections of the chapter, all of the cases in this sequence will be only quite mildly hypothetical and, beyond that, will give reasonably rich indications of those detailed suppositions most needed for us to make relevant responses. The reason for this is clear: We are now arguing about what it is that we most deeply believe about the actual conditions of our existence. Do we most deeply believe in the absoluteness of subjects; or is our deepest belief along quite different lines? To avoid guessing games that are only of rather tangential psychological interest, we want a rather firm basis for response.

As a second important argumentative guideline, we will impose a condition of consciousness, and perhaps also a condition of ego-centricity, on the selection and presentation of the cases in our spectrum. After all, we want this spectrum to join issue with the doctrine of our absoluteness quite directly, dramatically and persuasively. For that to happen, each reader should suppose the salient entity, at the center of the spectrum's cases, is the reader himself or, if that is not possible, a being that is most directly derived from himself. Thus, for example, as I myself now reread this section, I will have the central figure of each case be me, or if that is not possible, a salient candidate for being me. Further, as far as is possible, and whenever there occurs anything of philosophic interest regarding questions of my existence and identity, this candidate for being me should always be conscious.

A third important part of the spectrum's persuasive power is owing to the fact that, by relevant measures, there will be very many adjacent cases in this spectrum, and each will differ from its nearest neighbors only to a very small degree. To be sure, regarding the question of my survival and existence, cases near either end of the spectrum will admit of easy determinations, at one end positive and at the other negative. So these opposed cases will not prove instructive in the matter. But near the middle of the spectrum, there will be many other cases. Because they may admit of no easy, or very clear-cut, determination, it is these intermediate cases that may prove to be instructive.

Even with the satisfaction of all three of these guidelines, there might still be no clear instruction about what are our deepest beliefs on the question of whether we are metaphysically all-or-none. For, as we saw in the previous section, the occurrence of many small differences can easily fool us. Worse still, when conscious experience is present in all of the many small steps, as will happen in this spectrum, we may be fooled all the more easily.

These considerations mean that, for us, a fourth point will also be an important guideline: In constructing our spectrum, I will make the causal ground very highly salient indeed. In cases near the spectrum's far end, the best candidate for being an effective causal ground of experience will be a group of only four or five active nerve cells! By highlighting experience's causal ground, we may take care that our reaction to the spectrum is not heavily influenced by distorting factors. So much for our general guidelines; now, we turn to sketch the rather specific way in which they are followed.

The first case in the spectrum, or sequence, involves a certain person as he is at a certain time, say, me as I am when writing this very sentence. Each further case is produced from the one just preceding by the *net removal* of a very small and unimportant part of that previous case's best candidate for being me. The parts might be as small and insignificant as, say, water molecules. But, for simple and yet graphic exposition, we may let them be my biological cells. Because no removed part is ever replaced, each case includes a very slightly smaller and, beyond certain points, a very slightly "less well qualified" best candidate for being me than did the case just before.

As regards what counts toward my still existing, some cells are more important than others; neurons of my brain are more important than muscle cells of my arms. Before any more important cell is removed, a less important cell must be removed. Where there is a tie, as may very often occur, we arbitrarily remove one of the tied least important cells, perhaps one of many millions, to get to the next case. Thus early cases in the sequence will differ by, say, a fat cell from my leg or by, say, a skin cell from my nose. Not until we are well along in the sequence will we find adjacent cases that differ by a nerve cell from my brain.

In this spectrum, there is no danger posed to my existence from either death nor any lesser biological breakdown. That is part of what I meant when I called the imagined decomposition *congenial*. Matters are always made most congenial, or most conducive, for the candidate to be functioning optimally: They are most conducive, first, for the candidate entity to be alive and well, second, for that healthy living candidate to be thinking and experiencing and, third, for that living, thinking, experiencing candidate to be me. So, for example, well before any biologically dangerous situation might develop, life-support systems are brought in to prevent the danger from developing. And, well before any unwanted blackout of experience might develop, stimulatory systems are brought in to keep experience well supported. Pretty well along in the sequence, then, I have been reduced to being a brain that is in a vat, or reduced to being constituted by such a brain. Floating in a nutrient bath, supplied with oxygenated blood, stimulated by electrodes, and so on, the existence of this highly functioning brain means that I, too, quite clearly exist. Quite certainly, I did not cease to exist before this, the difference between me and no me being, say, a few cells from my spleen, or from my stomach!

Very far along in the sequence, probably when there is a good deal less than a third of a brain floating in the vat, there will be conscious experience supported still. After all, even mice, and probably even frogs, have experience. That is good; we want experience to persist through this sequence as far as may be really possible. As we observed in remarking on our second guideline, for our argument against the absoluteness of subjects to be maximally persuasive to us, this is important. But then a certain question naturally arises: With a sequence that might be very long in the number of its steps, we may have a sequence that, as well, takes a long time. But, with any semblance of realism, how can any reasonably realistic candidate being stay awake for so long, through all of this relentless reduction? With much realism wanted, this may seem to create a problem for our argument.

The problem is easily treated. Indeed, we may do that in two ways. First, we may enormously shorten the sequence during which actual removal will occur, it being granted by all parties that, with most of a brain, I will survive. Further, we may let anyone who champions our absoluteness select what, to him, might be a most promising sequence of a thousand removals, during which the occurrence of something metaphysically significant is more likely to occur than during any other sequence of a thousand adjacent cases. As may be imagined, in much less than an hour, quite rapid removals may be made for just these thousand steps, the "patient" then being awake all the while.

Second, we may allow the sequentially reduced person to have periods of deep, restful sleep, when he may not be conscious. We may allow that as long as we adhere to this provision: No removals will be made during any of these non-conscious periods. Removals are made; a deep nap is taken; only after the nap is completely over are more removals made.

Down and down we go. Eventually, there may be five neurons floating on the surface of the nutrient bath, possibly firing back and forth. Now, scarcely anyone believes that, in such a circumstance as that, I will exist. Indeed, very few believe that, in such a situation, there will be any subject of experience at all. But, then, when did the finite sequence of cases stop containing me?

No doubt, it happened much earlier in the sequence. With the removal of just a few nerve cells out of many millions still remaining, or possibly with the removal of just one of them, there will occur a case where, for the first time in the sequence, it is *not true* that I exist.

At the very least, that much earlier removal of a very few cells, or perhaps even just one, must have meant *some* sort of crucial *conventional* difference. The removal of just one (tied) least unimportant cell, or at most only a very few such cells, meant the difference between a case in which it was clearly, definitely, and completely *true* that I exist and a case in which the matter was *otherwise*. Now, perhaps this otherwise might be best characterized as involving some sort of indeterminacy as regards my existence. Or, perhaps it might simply be false that then I still exist. Or, perhaps some other option might be most appropriate. Although it is of some logical and linguistic interest, in the present context, the specific characterization of a best alternative, of an otherwise, is of no importance.

We have no idea precisely where in this sequence these adjacent, or nearby, cases are located and, in all likelihood, we will never know. But, whether or not we will ever know where it occurs, there must be some place where some such division occurs. For the present issue, it is also of no importance that we may forever be ignorant of the precise location of the division.

Is there occasioned by the removal of just one of these millions of tied neurons, or even by the removal of only a few of them, a *metaphysically significant* difference? It certainly doesn't seem so. Most notably, after the removal, there was *something* in the situation that *had conscious experience*. After all, *mice* quite certainly have conscious experience and, probably, even frogs do, for goodness sakes! By comparison, a being who so very *barely* fails to be me should have little trouble. Indeed as it certainly appears, no sudden, non-conventional break occurred as regards any metaphysically significant processes at all.

At certain points in the spectrum, there was enough of a brain to support conscious experience and many other mental processes, all right, but just a little too little for it, clearly and definitely, to support *me*. It certainly seems, then, that the difference between the two nearby cases amounts to just this: In the finite sequence of the imagined spectrum, that is where our implicit conventions, governing the semantics of 'I' and 'me' and related terms, just happen to draw a certain line. That is where those conventions may draw the line, say, between what is with absolute clarity properly called *me* and, on the other side, whatever the favorite alternative to that may be.

While our logic and our language may, or perhaps may not, be all-or-none, we ourselves are not deeply absolute. Although perhaps not as notably so as clouds, or even bricks, we are *gradual* beings. Even as matters of our existence and survival are, of course, heavily substantive questions, dependent on *non*-conventional considerations, at the same time, these matters are *also* largely *conventional* questions. In sum, the metaphysical doctrine of the absoluteness of subjects represents no deep truth.

While not absolutely conclusive, even at this early stage of our inquiry the argument from the spectrum of congenial decomposition creates a powerful presumption in favor of the objective view. In the sixth chapter, we will make a concerted, and protracted, effort to develop this powerful presumption. For the meanwhile we may see that, in the light of this present argument, our objective view of ourselves looks good, whereas its less worldly competitors look not so good.

3

THE PSYCHOLOGICAL APPROACH
TO OUR SURVIVAL

Nowadays, many leading writers give their endorsement, in one form or another, to our objective view of ourselves. In so doing, they reject the purely subjective view of the self, as well as hybrid views like the Cartesian view and the Butlerian view. But our objective view may itself take various forms. Indeed, there may be several competing objective approaches, each of which is initially plausible. Any of these plausible approaches will treat questions of our existence and identity as being, in large measure, conventional matters. However, each will differently locate the conventions that shape answers to these questions.

The most influential of these objective views can be usefully divided into two groups: Slightly altering the use of a couple of fashionable labels, we may say that one group of views follows, or clusters around, the *psychological approach* to personal identity and, in contrast, the other follows the *physical approach*. For the most part, the present chapter will be a discussion of the psychological approach, while the next chapter will examine the physical approach to our identity.

There are very able philosophers who advocate views within, or very nearby to, the psychological approach. Nonetheless, I will argue that a correct view will be much closer to the physical approach. As has long been my suspicion, most of the plausibility of a psychological view may be only apparent, perhaps withering away in the light of searching reflection. To be confident that we understand our subject, however, we must give an explanation of why, despite its substantial errors, able philosophers are so persistently attracted to the psychological approach. By citing a number of complementary factors, we will try to explain how this may occur.

1. Core Psychology and Distinctive Psychology

On any plausible form of objective view, certain appropriate connective relations, not mere relations of similarity and difference, will play a central role in determining whether I survive. Playing a sort of dual role, these connections will secure my survival as distinguished from my mere duplication later and they also will accommodate not every conceivable change that I might undergo, but just those changes that I really will survive. As many philosophers do, perhaps we may allow ourselves to talk, fairly freely, in terms of the stages of, or the phases of, people's lives. These life stages may be exceedingly brief, perhaps even momentary. In these terms, it may be said that, in order for me to survive, there must obtain, between this present stage of my life and a future stage of someone's life, connections that play this dual role. Only in that case will there be a future someone who is me.

First, perhaps we may venture a few words about why these connections must rule out mere duplication: Entities in objective space and time may be qualitatively identical to, but numerically different from, other objective entities in space and time. In other words, if I am an objective entity, there may be some others exactly like me at earlier and at later times, and elsewhere even right now. These others will not be me, but will be mere "duplicates" of me, just as I will be a mere duplicate of each of them. Now, without an appropriate real connection between this stage of my life now and, a moment later, a stage of someone's life who is right here, there will be, a moment later, here in this very place that I now occupy, not me myself, but, instead, only a mere duplicate of me.

In addition, perhaps we may also venture a few words about why these connections must accommodate certain changes involving me, but not all such changes: First, each of us may lose some of his physical parts, or may have his structure altered. If I lose very few parts, or only rather unimportant parts, or if my structure is altered rather trivially, then I will survive the physical changes. So, these relevantly small changes need to be accommodated. On the other hand, if I lose too many of the more important parts, or if my structure is altered too radically, then I will not survive. So, these relevantly greater physical changes should not be accommodated. Second, relevantly similar things might happen as regards the "parts" of, and the "structure" of, my psychology. Older memory states may be lost even as new ones, concerning more recent experiences or events, may be gained or formed. So, too, with personality traits, desires, and so on. By obtaining in the face of all but the most severe gains or losses, perhaps certain psychological connections may obtain between this present stage of my life now and a stage of someone's life in the future. When that happens, then I will be that future person.

Understanding the term, *causality*, in a suitably loose and inclusive way, these required connections will be appropriate causal relations. On any very plausible approach, for a particular person to survive, at least some of that person's present psychology must be causally carried into the future as the psychology of a single future person. As long as there is an *appropriate* causal dependency of just that future person's psychology on the present person's psychological states, then the present person may be the future person. Different plausible objective approaches will differ as regards which sorts of psychologically furthering causal relations will be sufficiently appropriate to secure, or to play a major role in securing, a particular person's survival.

To provide a description of the psychological approach, and also of the contrasting physical approach, it will be useful for us to make an explicit distinction between two aspects of a person's *dispositional psychology*: We distinguish between her *core psychology* and her *distinctive psychology*. Among the mental capacities that it comprises, my dispositional psychology includes those that I share with all other normal human beings, notably my capacity for conscious experience, my capacity to reason at least in a rudimentary way, and my capacity to form some simple intentions. These capabilities are shared, too, with many humans who are markedly below the psychological norms. We may call this group of capacities my *core* psychology, with the understanding that this term may be highly, and perhaps irremediably, vague. Certain other aspects of my psychology I share with some normal humans but do not share with others, for example, my (ostensible) memory of having tasted butter pecan ice cream. Still other aspects distinguish me from all other actual human beings, for example, my (ostensible) memory of having written the preceding chapter. Let us say that my *distinctive* psychology comprises both of these other aspects of my psychology. So part of my distinctive psychology I share with some, but not all, other normal human beings, and the rest I share with none.

Far from being analytic definitions, the characterizations of core and of distinctive psychology are what may be called *ostensive indications*. So perhaps it might happen, for example, that all human beings somehow lose their capacity for conscious experience, and live in an adaptive and even creative "trance" from then on. Even if that should ever be so, the capacity for consciousness will remain a component of core psychology. Or, shades of the old epistemological problem of other minds, perhaps it might be that, beyond myself, all along no normal humans, nor any other human beings, have had that capacity. Still, even under such a circumstance as that, the capacity for conscious experience will be part of the core psychology that I have; other things equal, the others will lack the full complement of a core psychology.

Although these ideas are vague ones, the notions of core psychology and distinctive psychology may be philosophically useful ideas. Unless we are very badly wrong about ourselves, the distinction that these vague terms make is, with respect to every normal human person, both exhaustive and exclusive: Every normal human person has a core psychology and, in addition to that, a distinctive psychology, which together entirely compose her dispositional psychology. As you and I are normal human people, our psychologies may be exhaustively categorized by these terms. At all events, what happens to us as regards our survival may depend on what happens to these aspects of our psychology, and it might depend, as well, on what happens to *what realizes* these two aspects.

On the psychological approach, the key to my existing at a future time is that much of my present psychology be causally carried forward in time and, thus, be much of a single future person's psychology. To be me, the person at the later time should have, not only all of my core psychology, but much of my distinctive psychology as well. It may be indeterminate how many of, and which ones of, the distinctive dispositions the future person is required to have. But, to be me, he must have rather many of my (ostensible) personal memories or, lacking that, he must at least have rather many of my present character and personality traits.

It is interesting to note that this psychological approach is quite demanding in a certain way while being quite lenient in a related respect: On this approach, a lot is demanded regarding how much of a person's psychology must be causally preserved for me to survive. But very little is demanded regarding how this causal preservation must take place. It will be useful to illustrate this disparity.

An alleged teletransporter may destroy my brain and body in the processes of extracting information as to my innermost constitution. It may then send this information to a companion device that, out of new matter, constructs a new brain and body, qualitatively the same as the old. Owing to these causal connections, the new brain may realize a psychology just like that last realized by the old one. On the psychological approach, I will, in such an event, succeed in making the trip, even though I suddenly have a new brain and body at my destination. To be sure, the causal route by way of which my psychology is carried forward is quite abnormal, not merely in marginal ways, but in ways that are very substantial. In particular, this causal route involves little or none of the physical continuity ordinarily present in cases of our survival. Further, the causal route will allow that, in a possibly brief middle period, I do not exist at all. On the psychological approach, that makes no difference: Roughly, but usefully enough, because there is a causal thrust into the future of, and thus a later realization of, so much of the psychology that was mine, I will survive.

On a physical approach to personal identity, by contrast, much more is demanded of the ways that a person's psychology is causally carried forward. For purposes of exposition, I stipulate that, as regards the more general features, we are right about the causal structure of our lives. Given this stipulation, we may say that, on the physical approach, for a person to survive, some of her psychology, her core psychology, must be carried forward in ways that are, on the whole, not terribly different from the ways that psychological continuity is achieved in ordinary cases. Most importantly, this will require a fair amount of physical continuity between the past person and the future one. In the case of the alleged teletransporter, there is virtually nothing in way of physical continuity in the causal process. So, on the physical approach, I don't survive that exotic procedure.

An important point bears special emphasis: In outlining the contrasts between these two approaches, my use of 'normal' and 'ordinary' only helps to provide useful ostensive indications. Just so, in trying to understand the import of these approaches, it is a mistake to focus on what is, or even on what has been at least until now, most usual for us. Various examples can contribute to making this point clear, one of which follows: Suppose that, as has been true since the dawn of mankind, every year each human being loses the distinctive psychology that he has developed over the course of that year. Perhaps due to a naturally occurring annual restructuring of living human brains, at the end of each year all of us lose not only our personal memories of the year, but all of our distinctive personality traits as well. These losses are quite irrevocable and, in any case, they are never reversed.

In such a circumstance, even though it is usual for distinctive psychology to last at most a year, that fact won't lower the psychological approaches' standards for how much psychology must be carried forward for survival. Rather, that standard remains constant. Instead of the standard flexibly changing, the approach reckons much shorter lives for all of us human people. Although most of our healthy brains and bodies may last over seventy years, each human person will last only one year. Accordingly, a particular brain and body will be "occupied" by about seventy distinct people, one after the next. By contrast, on the physical approach each person lives through these annual psychic changes. The losses of distinctive psychology may make their lives much less desirable, of course, but they will not make their lives any shorter.

Although they are in keeping with the contemporary philosophic literature, there remains some danger, I suppose, that our labels for these two views may be misleading. The danger is not great, but it would be well to reduce it. To a fair extent, we can lessen the danger by explicitly noting that the labels we employ have no bearing on the traditional problem of mind and body. What we have called the psychological approach is completely compatible with materialism, or physicalism, and may be consistently advocated by philosophers who hold that all mental events are physical events. And what we have called the physical approach is compatible with certain forms of dualism about the mental and the physical. The physical approach to personal identity, as here understood, may be consistently maintained by a philosopher who holds that there are mental events, such as conscious pains, that are not physical. When we bear these points in mind, it is harder for our labels to mislead us.

We can further reduce the danger by noting that even the physical approach is aimed at certain psychological factors, namely, those of core psychology. A person's physical parts and structures are important to her survival *only insofar as they continue to support, and to realize, her basic psychological capacities.* If I am made into living meat, with no mental capacities, I do not survive. If, a day later, a person is configured from this living meat, that person is not me.

2. A Formulation of the Psychological Approach

At this point, we should have a pretty good idea of the import of the psychological approach. Guided by this informal understanding, it may now be useful to provide a brief characterization of the psychological approach. Toward this end, we will discuss some technical terms that, largely due to Parfit, have become entrenched in the literature.[1]

There is a technical distinction between psychological continuity and, more strictly, psychological connectedness. Psychological connectedness involves the holding of a particular direct causal connection between a mental state in a person at a certain time and a suitably associated mental state in a person, the same or another, at another time. A good example would be my now remembering some particular experience that I had yesterday: the experience that I had then is directly causally connected with the memory-state I have now as of having such an experience. Another is my current interest in philosophical inquiry causally derived from the interest in such inquiry that I had yesterday. But the nature of the causal connections, or of what is responsible for their holding, need not be so normal as in the everyday cases just cited.

We may suppose that the taping machines provide an extremely effective way of generating future mental states just like mine on the causal basis of my present mental states. Then there will be ever so much psychological con-

---

1. Derek Parfit, *Reasons and Persons*, Oxford University Press, 1984, section 78.

nectedness between me now and each of ten people who, via the taping process, may be simultaneously produced from me. Indeed, in each of these ten
instances, there will be considerably more psychological connectedness than
there is, in the ordinary case, between me now and myself a week from now.

In the literature, psychological continuity is a technical notion defined, or
understood, in terms of this notion of psychological connectedness. So
understood, psychological continuity need not involve the continued existence of any entity that realizes mental capacities, but need involve only the
holding of certain overlapping chains of psychological connectedness. Further, on these technical definitions, although connectedness will be a matter
of degree, continuity will not be a matter of degree. Now, because people
change psychologically from day to day, there will be very little psychological
connectedness between myself now and myself thirty years ago. Even so,
there may well be (full) psychological continuity between me now and me
then. A sufficient, and a quite common, overlap of direct connections will
ensure this continuity over the thirty years.

For the treatment of certain issues, it may be useful to keep clearly in mind
the distinction between this connectedness and this continuity. But it is not
important for us to do so now. Because this is unimportant for our inquiry,
I will feel free to use the single term 'psychological continuity' to cover the
stronger as well as the weaker relation. Accordingly, I will use this term as
admitting of degrees: On my use, for example, there may be very great psychological continuity, or, alternatively, only a little continuity, between a person now and a person in the future.

In effect, I am collapsing and rejecting the distinction between this connectedness and this continuity. This allows me to express myself in a much
simpler and much more understandable idiom. By the same token, as the
reader may verify, none of my arguments crucially turns on my conflation of
these technical terms.

With this convenient simplification, we may provide a schema for how the
psychological approach attempts to demarcate the conditions of our survival.
A formulation of the approach that is at once both vague and abstract, our
schema might, nonetheless, serve to indicate manageably useful terms in
which the psychological approach may be discussed:

> The person X now is one and the same as the person Y at some time in the
> future if, and only if, (1) there is sufficient psychological continuity between X
> now and Y at that time in the future, and [probably] (2) {some clause suitable
> for ruling out unwanted cases of branching}.

Although it is done vaguely, the heart of this approach is expressed in (1), the
formulation's first defining clause. Because our interest is in the main themes

of these issues, not the logical niceties, we have little concern about how such a first clause might be best formulated.[2]

The second clause, which I have left unspecified, need not concern us much, either. It is there only to rule out identity, if there should be a need for so doing, in sufficiently severe cases of psychological branching. (The bracketed 'probably' is placed before this clause to acknowledge the thoughts of those few philosophers who hold that branching does not affect questions of our identity over time, but to indicate, at the same time, that I cautiously disagree with those thoughts.) Now, questions of fission and fusion are not peculiar to the psychological approach; indeed, parallel questions of physical branching attend the physical approach. Moreover, we will not discuss issues of branching until much later in the book, mainly in the eighth chapter, at which point we will have laid the groundwork for a tolerably clear discussion of those matters.

For the most part, at any rate, on this psychological approach matters of survival are relatively straightforward. Accordingly, the psychological approach directs that, even with a middle period of a hundred years, the purely informational taping process will provide for your survival. First, you will exist, composed of your present brain and body. Then, for a hundred years, you will not exist at all; none of the people then in existence will be you. Still later, you will once again exist, this time with an utterly new brain and body, suddenly constructed from an utterly new batch of matter. For most of us, this perfectly straightforward consequence of the psychological approach is counter-intuitive. As seems quite clear, and as the avoidance of future pain test appears to clarify still further, this is out of line with our actual beliefs and attitudes about ourselves.

There are able philosophers, however, who do not seem to mind this discord. Even in the face of it, able philosophers endorse the psychological approach to our survival. Or, at the least, they advocate mild variants of this view, positions that have the same disturbing consequence for the example just described. I disagree strongly with these able philosophers. As I see it, although there may be some grains of truth in the view, the psychological approach not only is false, but is quite badly false. So, in developing an account of our survival, we should look for most of the truth in a quite opposite direction. In order that we be most rational in this conviction, we should explain why, despite its being badly false, the able philosophers find them-

---

2. In the very imperfect formulation of the psychological approach, significant improvements, beyond earlier versions, have been effected by John Carroll. Much the same goes for the semi-formal statement of the physical approach in Chapter 4 and for that of the slightly modified physical approach in Chapter 5.

selves holding to a view that, at the least, is very close to the psychological approach.

3. Three Salient Motivations Toward This Approach

What attracts philosophers to this approach to personal identity? There are many specific factors, interacting variously on various people. In the present section, we will consider three that are rather conspicuous. We will argue that these motivations provide no good reason for accepting any view much like the psychological approach.

First, what is perhaps the most obvious factor is an *epistemological* one. Stemming from Locke, early psychological views of our survival focused on *memory*. One reason for this focus derives from thoughts of how each of us, when she awakens in the morning, knows that she is the same person as someone who had certain experiences on previous days. In brief, the answer is, of course, that we have certain mental states that, quite directly, inform us of these earlier experiences of ours. These are our memories: I have a memory of my drinking beer yesterday that informs me, quite directly, that I consciously drank beer some time before I went to sleep last night. I do not know about my drinking beer by having someone watch my body overnight, much less my brain, and by having him assure me that they were the body and brain involved both in yesterday's beer drinking as well as in today's waking and judging.

Philosophers are attracted to views of things that make our knowledge of these things appear direct, easy and unproblematic. Because of this tendency, philosophers may think that *what makes* a past experience one of *my* past experiences is a certain causal effect of the experience that, quite directly, gives me knowledge of that past experience's occurrence. So this proclivity draws philosophers toward the psychological approach.

The tendency is to be avoided. After all, it is this same disposition that, some decades ago, moved many able philosophers to consider ordinary physical objects, such as tables and rocks, to be complexes of quasi-mental entities, that is, to be complexes of sense-data. If a table is a complex of potentially directly available data, then, by perceiving some of its parts as directly as can be, you might perceive the table itself at least pretty directly. This fairly direct perception will, in turn, allow your knowledge of the table to be pretty direct, easy, and unproblematic. In the philosophical climate of fifty years ago, this view of tables and rocks had very great appeal. Although it is not now at all fashionable, even today this idea has a certain attraction. But, for more than reasons of fashion, few actually believe tables to be complexes of quasi-mental entities. Rather, as we strongly believe, insofar as typical tables are complexes, they are complexes of their legs and tops. At a much deeper level, tables are complexes of the ordinarily imperceptible particles that compose them.

Epistemological considerations give no better reason for a psychological approach to personal identity than for a sense-data approach to tables and rocks. In both cases, the best response is to think that we have an overly simple idea of how our knowledge of the relevant matters is obtained and retained; in the bargain, we have overly simple ideas of what is involved in memory and in perception. For an adequate total philosophy, we will do well to improve our understanding of these epistemological topics. Whether they concern mere tables or whether, more fashionably, they concern us knowers ourselves, we will not do well to embrace such metaphysical creations as our epistemological preconceptions may appear to encourage.[3]

A *second* motivating factor concerns our thoughts about how others are to treat us, and we them. These ideas are quite general, but their greatest impact may be in the area of *reward* and, especially, that of *punishment*. If a man willfully commits heinous crimes against others, then our immediate reaction is that he should be punished for his deeds. This is most obviously true if he harms someone that we love.

Suppose that, as a result of despotic governmental policy, deranged divine intervention, or whatever, a certain murderer has had his distinctive psychology irreversibly eradicated. In particular, he has neither any of the memories of his past acts nor any of the distinctive character traits that may have issued in the deeds. It then seems pointless to kill the man, to jail him, or even to inflict any harm upon him at all. In the first place, since he has no memories of his past life, the whole point of any conceivable punishment will be completely lost on the man, or entirely beyond him. Moreover, with so little in the way of any psychology, the man does not seem accountable even for his present actions, let alone for the past deeds forever lost to memory. Even from a more utilitarian point of view, the matter is quite the same: Since the man's distinctive character traits are all gone, in particular, his bad traits are gone; thus, there is no need to protect society from this newly docile man. Nor is there now any need to reform him, even while there is little that may now make much of an impression upon his dim wit and docile nature.

Finally, let us consider deterrence. As this murderer is in the pitiful state of having no personal memories, and scarcely any personality at all, he is an

3. In these matters, I have profited from discussion with John Carroll. In his paper, "The Humean Tradition," *The Philosophical Review*, forthcoming, he briefly makes a similar point regarding issues of natural law and, by implication, causality: It is tempting to interpret causal propositions in such a way as will appear to let our knowledge of them arise in a comfortably simple fashion. But, in all likelihood, that temptation will lead to a distorted treatment of causality and natural law. In Carroll's forthcoming *Laws of Nature*, there is a more developed discussion.

example of an evildoer who might deter anyone. Where there is known to be a very strong positive correlation between harming others and irreversibly losing one's distinctive psychology soon after, I certainly would watch my step! Few indeed will find this a low price to pay for wrongdoing. From a moral point of view, and from a social point of view, we may best no longer regard this pitiful evildoer as one who needs to be considered in terms of anything that he allegedly has done. It seems that, instead of the murderer, we have a quite different person before us now. Thus, there is some pretty effective motivation toward the psychological approach.

Although thoughts like these may provide motivation toward the psychological approach to personal identity, they provide little reason for such a view. Let us reflect on a rather ghoulish and unrealistic, but perhaps a relevantly telling, example: Under a fully effective general anesthetic, you may be operated on so that your brain is restructured to be ever so like that of a known kidnapper. This felon might be your long lost identical twin. As we may suppose, the neural restructuring is causally based on information about her brain's constitution. This information is obtained by a special taping process, which has a somewhat delayed effect on her. Before that delayed effect sets in, however, for just one day of overlap, there are two people who each have the precise sort of psychology that your twin so laboriously acquired. She, the criminal, is where her original brain and body are while you, the innocent, are where your quite distinct brain and body are.

A day after your brain is restructured, the delayed effect sets in: Processes already set in motion suddenly result in a rather different restructuring of your twin's brain, making her a terribly dim and docile dullard. Forever after, this previously malevolent twin is without any of the personal memories and the character traits that she had acquired over the many years.

Because of the day of overlap, it appears very clear that, two days later, the person who was anesthetized and operated on in the middle of that fateful night is still around. Is it right, or even morally permissible, to harm this one existing person? Although this is the only person then around with the relevant criminal mentality, harmful treatment of this individual is not all right. No, it is utterly wrong. Quite clearly, this person still is you; and, quite clearly, you are completely innocent of any wrongdoing. It is terrible that you have been deprived of your memories and have been given a different, and presumably a much worse, personality. Should you be harmed on top of that? You have done nothing to deserve the painful treatment. We would then just be heaping one wrong upon another.

The lesson to be learned from the motivating thoughts about how to treat people is not that we should adopt a psychological approach to our identity. Rather, it is that we have conceptions of reward and punishment that do not cohere well with each other, and which thus must be revised. Our conception in terms of desert does not accord well with our conception in terms of consequences of our treatment. My recommendation in these matters is to play down the former conception and to build upon the latter, perhaps in a highly modified form. But that is a further issue. Indeed, it is an issue that should not affect what we take to be the proper treatment of personal identity.

A *third* motivating factor concerns our aims and intentions, our goals and ambitions, in a fashionable word, our *projects*. For example, I very much want this particular book, the one that I am now writing, to be completed. And, who will be able to work on these unfinished pages most effectively, and most in line with my particular aims? Why, me, of course. Now, if there is someone tomorrow with just the same, or very much the same, psychology as I have now, that person will, under ordinary and likely circumstances, manage to do this well. Even if he has an entirely distinct brain made out of a completely distinct batch of matter, one that is not at all physically continuous with my current brain, he will do this well. For example, if he is produced by the taping machine, with my brain and body destroyed in the process, he may be very effective. If no other person is similarly produced, then, in all likelihood, he will be the only person around with a mentality precisely like, or even very much like, mine now is. When there is only one person with that psychology around tomorrow, there will be no others to compete for working on these particular pages with him, no potentially interfering duplicate. Then the well-motivated person may proceed most effectively indeed.

This psychologically continuous person will do well at achieving my aims, the simplest explanation runs, because *he is me*. On the other hand, if there is someone tomorrow whose brain is the very one that I now have, but who lacks my personal memories, aims and personality traits, then he will not do well by the projects I now have. Indeed, he will not even be moved to attempt them. The simplest explanation of this related fact, and so the best one, is that *this* person will *not* be me, but will be someone else with quite different beliefs, traits and ambitions.

Although it is not obvious, there are certain projects of mine that involve me necessarily, and which thus require absolutely my continued existence for their completion: I do not just want this book to be completed, I also want for it to be completed *by me*. And, to take another sort of example, I do not just want my son to be brought up well and happily, I want him to be brought up well and happily by my wife, who is his mother, together *with me*. These *self-involving* projects, as we may call them, have been noted by various philosophers.

On the psychological approach, the unique psychologically suitable person tomorrow, who can do well at working on this very book, and at raising my own son, *will be me*. If we accept this approach to identity, but perhaps not otherwise, the people who emerge from technically effective teletransporters, taping machines and the like, will fulfill our self-involving projects just as well as they do our related aims that are not necessarily self-involving. The recognition of this point adds to the motivation provided by the factor of our aims and projects.

Reflection suggests that this factor, too, provides no good reason for the psychological approach. We should not think that, in every possible case, the people who will best fulfill our projects will be ourselves. Just as a person without my beliefs and goals will do poorly by my projects, so will one without my arms and ears and eyes. But just as I myself may exist without my arms and ears and eyes, I may also exist without most of the beliefs and goals that I have, and without any of those that are, in fact, distinctive of me. Ordinarily, I will indeed be the best person around as regards furthering those projects that I now have. But, in certain bizarre cases, someone else may be much better.

Psychologically oriented cases confirm this point: I may know that, beginning tomorrow, I may have much less in the way of my intellectual powers as well as my personal memories. This may be the result of a delayed-action drug given to me just minutes ago. In addition, just before being given that drug, I may have been forced to undergo the *process of taping with physical temporal overlap*, whereby a person with just my present psychology, but without the bad drug, will soon be produced. In this process with overlap, my brain and body need never be destroyed. At the least, for a goodly while they remain the brain and the body of a living, thinking person. In the present example, after brief observation of the other person, I may be locked in a room for many years, until, eventually, I die from the natural causes associated with old age.

Because he does not have the drug in him, the exotically generated person will retain intellectual powers and personal memories like my present ones, tomorrow and well beyond. Because I am locked up in the room, there will be no one to interfere with his attempts at completing my projects. Because he will be psychologically well equipped and well motivated, and because he can engage in the tasks without anyone else getting in the way, the exotically generated person will be in an excellent position to complete my projects, just as good as my own position under more ordinary circumstances. On the psychological approach, he, and not the person in the room, will be me. For once the drug has had its effect, the person in the room has much less mental continuity with me, the author and the father. So, *on that approach*, the exotically generated man, and only he, will be in an excellent position to fulfill *even my self-involving projects*. But, on sincere reflection, few will think that this unique excellent executor really will be me. Quite correctly, most will agree that I am nobody but that unfortunate person who is locked up in the room.[4]

4. Three Subtler Motivations

Having canvassed three relatively straightforward motivations, we now turn to examine three others that are less easily noticed. Although somewhat subtler, these factors provide no more of a rational ground.

A *fourth* motivating factor begins with the idea that, for me, *my survival is very desirable*. And it is not just desirable because it will allow for the fulfillment of my projects. More to the central point, my survival is of value to me because it provides the only chance for me to experience what the world might offer. Philosophers may want a view of our identity to account for this value that our survival has for us.

A natural question now arises: If I retain none of my personal memories, and none of my personality traits, to boot, how much value for me will there be in my survival? As it would seem, not very much. Now, on the physical approach, for example, the value of my survival is left unaccounted: Without much value for me, I may survive with no personal memories or distinctive traits. Indeed, unless there are substantial constraints regarding distinctive psychology, even on the view that I am an immaterial soul, this value is left unexplained. If my soul goes to heaven, but with never any memories of my past, nor with my desires, beliefs or habits of thought, how much benefit for me is there in that?

On the psychological approach, in contrast, there is built right into my survival itself a lot of what makes survival desirable for me—a lot of continuity of my distinctive psychology. In that way, the value for me of my own survival is quite directly explained. There is only the illusion of a possibility, but no real possibility, of my surviving without such personal memories and character traits as are needed to make my survival worthwhile.

This fourth motivating factor also provides little in the way of good reason. On a bit of reflection, we must realize that there are, in fact, very many instances where a human person's survival will be of no value to her at all. We may imagine, for example, that something has removed my arms and legs, my eyes and ears, and that I never get any replacements, natural or pros-

4. Along the lines of the psychological approach, there are accounts of our survival that would deny these last points, such as the treatment offered by David Lewis in "Survival and Identity," A. O. Rorty, ed., *The Identities of Persons*, University of California Press, 1976. Aware of their existence, in these pages I am arguing that, despite their great ingenuity, such accounts are, at the least, enormously implausible. On these matters, I have benefited from discussion with Mark Johnston.

thetic. With no electrodes in my head or anything of the like, even my immediate experience will be, forever after, impoverished and painfully frustrating. Unless we irrelevantly include negative value, my survival in this condition is of no value to me at all.

As a matter of fact, my arms and legs, my eyes and ears, are very important for me to have a good life, for me to survive in a way that is of much value to me. But they may still be quite peripheral parts of me, not central to my existence or identity. Somewhat similarly, my memories and personality traits also may be very important for my having desirable survival. But these psychological factors, like the physical or biological factors just mentioned, are quite peripheral aspects of my existence itself. Even if some small part of the value of our survival typically should be explained by an account of our survival itself, almost all of that value must be located elsewhere. Whatever little an account of our survival might contribute here, that might be accomplished plenty well enough by a psychologically sensitive physical approach to our identity.

A *fifth* source of motivation concerns *predictions of our behavior in strange futuristic scenarios*. It will usually be conceded that we would at first avoid devices that causally continued our psychology in radically abnormal ways, such as alleged teletransporters. But, if you were forced once to undergo the process promoted by such a device, then on future occasions you would go along. We would not then deprive ourselves of the great convenience, the great economic savings, and so on.

Perhaps this source of motivation for the psychological approach is pretty influential. Nonetheless, these ideas provide no good reason to accept the approach. For one thing, if I do not really survive the alleged teletransportation, then, after I have been subjected to the procedure, the person who later emerges will not be me. In such an event, it will not be me, but perhaps only a person quite like me, who is there, after the procedure, to have any preference, whether for or against any further application of that procedure. To suppose that I myself will then be in a position to choose, as should be clear, begs any question now at issue.

For another thing, questions of accurate prediction may have little to do with the relevant questions of rationality. To make the point clear to myself, it will be helpful for me to make an horrific supposition: In a few hours I might somehow come to discover that, a few months ago, I emerged from just such a purely informational alleged teletransport process. Among other things, I will then discover, I suggest, that I am only a few months old. Now, in the face of such an unsettling discovery, and quite apart from any considerations of rationality, many of my beliefs and other attitudes might change quite radically. Notably, I may come to be much less concerned about my strict survival. That jolting discovery might have that effect. Now, because there really is so little basis for doing so, nobody can make an intelligently informed prediction as to what psychological effect on me such a cause in fact will have. But, for the sake of instruction and argument, let us assume that the offered prediction is absolutely correct.

What follows? Well, given the attitudes about personal identity that I may have after the horrific imagined discovery, it might well be rational for me to submit myself to such an alleged teletransport procedure. But that does not mean that now, before any such alteration and with just those attitudes that I actually do have, it is rational for me to submit to any such thing. On the contrary, it will be nearly as irrational for me now to undergo these processes, should they be available, as it is for me to leap in the path of a fast moving freight train.

Recall the experience inducers, each run by a program that, to the person inside it, seems to give her a highly successful and very pleasant life. We may notice an instructive parallel between these machines, which are rather bad options for us, and the teletransporters, which are, in other ways, bad options: It may be conceded that, at first, we will avoid the inducers even at great cost, even if we are completely convinced of their technical effectiveness. But if you once have been placed in an inducer for a while, it may be said, or even if you just firmly believe that, your fears will vanish. If you are then taken out of the inducer, or believe yourself to be, and if you are offered much pleasant experience by a return to the inducer, you will choose the inducer. And perhaps it will be rational for you to make that choice. So, despite our fearful squeamishness, it might be argued in parallel, the inducers really would be a great benefit to us, even as we are right now.

We should notice that these remarks, although some of them might be true, are all irrelevant to the question of what is rational for us now with regard to inducer offerings. If I become convinced that I have spent the past three years in an inducer, what seemed the happiest years of my life, this may have a great effect on my beliefs and values. We may suppose that it does. Given the new configuration of attitudes that I may have after that great alteration, it might be rational for me then to choose many very pleasant future years in the inducer. But, given the quite different attitudes that I actually now do have, this choice is irrational.

A *sixth* factor is closely related to the fifth. This is the thought that the conception of survival embodied in the psychological approach is a *more rational conception of survival* than any that is very different from it. Those who maintain this conception will usually fare better, in terms of that selfsame conception, than those who hold, say, the physical criterion, will fare by the standards that the physical notion holds to be relevant. Taking the point further, we will, collectively and perhaps unconsciously, have recognized this superiority. Owing to our recognition of the advantage, we will have already shaped our thinking so as to capture it. Even if, in ages gone by, humanity started with a more mundane conception of survival, those days are long gone. Nowadays, in the rationally liberating spirit of the psychological approach, we maintain a much more rational idea of the matter.

Why will it be thought that the psychological approach is so advantageous? Well, folks who have integrated this conception of their survival into their system of thought will, with consistency and reason, be in a position to avail themselves of the conveniences of teletransportation. Better still, they may be able to use a purely informational taping process greatly to prolong their lives: Rationally, by their own superior lights, they may put themselves on hold while awaiting life-saving medical breakthroughs. In sum: Those who maintain such a notion will, in terms of their very notion of survival, have better chances for securing their survival and, as well, better prospects for enjoying the time that they have. Smart as we collectively are, we will not have missed out on these chances.

This line of reasoning is, however, as confused as it is seductive. The confusion is much the same as with the factor considered just before. One way to expose this present confusion is to ask a simple question: For whom is it, precisely, that the psychological conception is a more rational way of thinking about people over time? It is *not* more rational for people with beliefs and values much like *ours*. For us, who can be rather clear about what are our actual conceptions and attitudes, such a conception is quite an irrational one, fitting badly with many of our deep beliefs and values while fitting well with few or none. By acting on it, we will, even by our own deepest beliefs and values, bring about our termination, completely and forever. By endorsing the conception, we will, even if indirectly, encourage the formation of practices that, if they are engaged in, will mean our absolute termination.

As happened with the previous motivating factor, regarding predictions of changes in preference, the main point concerning this present one can be driven home well by thoughts about experience inducers. Now, there may be those who really do place intrinsic value on only the conscious states of sentient beings. As we are supposing, that is the true description of their deepest value. Well, for people with that attitude, perhaps it may be true that, even at a very deep level, life in an inducer will be the rational choice. According to their own deepest values, that choice may make their lives go very well indeed.

Some philosophers may seek to compare us unfavorably with those people: In their own terms, their lives are better for them than, according to our quite different terms, our lives are for us. Now, as it sometimes seems to me, there really may be no coherent basis for such a comparison. For the sake of argument and instruction, however, let us suppose that there is. Supposing that to be so, there will still not be, in any such comparison, any point that is

relevant to the question of what conception of life, or of happiness, or anything else of great importance, is the most rational conception for us to have.
Given our deep values, we would be irrational to endorse any such conception. By endorsing the conception, we will, even if indirectly, encourage the
formation of practices that, if they are engaged in, will mean that our lives
will largely be wasted.

5. From Science Fiction to Philosophical Investigation

When reading or viewing science fiction, we often confront examples that, in
the context of the narrative offering, are readily taken to be cases where a
person survives. Many of these are alleged cases of teletransportation, examples whose general form is a frequent feature of these pages. As may be worth
noticing, these cases vary in how radical they are: In the most radical sort of
teletransport case, only information about the detailed constitution of a person, or of another entity to be transported, is sent from the starting place to
the intended destination. No constituting matter is ever transported. In a
somewhat less radical case, the constituting matter is sent, presumably in a
narrow stream, along with information about how the matter is to be
employed; but the relevantly tiny and interchangeable bits of matter, say, the
atoms or the elementary particles, are not kept track of throughout. For
example, (almost) any carbon atom may fill the spot in the final arrangement
that (almost) any *other* carbon atom had in the original arrangement. In a still
less radical case, the small physical components are all kept track of and,
largely because of this, each small bit occupies the same relative position in
the whole at the far end as it did, at the start, in the original constituted entity.

Many stories may leave it ambiguous, or vague, how radical are the cases
in which its characters are involved. But even should the most radical sort of
cases be specified, there is little doubt but that we readers will be easily
enough satisfied that true transportation occurs. As Robert Nozick notes,
"the readers of such stories, and the many viewers of such television programs, calmly accept this as a mode of travel. They do not view it as a killing
of one person with the production of another very similar person elsewhere."[5] What are we philosophers to make of all this public approval?

A response that the person really travels, and is not killed and replaced
elsewhere by a duplicate, seems to give support to the psychological
approach. Along with apparently acceptable auxiliary hypotheses, the
hypothesis that we implicitly maintain a psychological conception of our sur-

5. The quote is from page 41 of Nozick's *Philosophical Explanations*, Harvard University Press,
1981.

vival predicts this ready response. By contrast, an approach along noted physical lines predicts an opposite reaction, a response of death and replacement.
The fact that the psychological approach wins these science fiction contests
is a *seventh* motivational force toward its acceptance by philosophers. As Nozick does, many philosophers may uncritically take our calm responses at face
value. Because they place considerable weight on these widespread intuitions,
able philosophers are drawn to views, like Nozick's, that depart from the psychological approach more in letter than in spirit or substance.

A more critical and reflective use of hypothetical examples may show this
motivation to be poorly founded. In the bargain, it may allow us to observe
some points of independent interest. So, in greater earnest and at greater
length, we now take up a theme that was introduced in our first chapter.

Why is it that, in attending to science fiction, we so readily interpret the
examples as involving survival rather than duplication? Is it really just a matter, or even mostly a matter, of our manifesting an implicitly maintained conception of our survival? As I believe, the explanation lies with some very different factors.

In part, the ease of this interpretation may be due to the author's instruc-
tions: The author may, for example, actually say that the person quickly *trav-
elled* somewhere. In part, linguistic conventions may guide us, such as using
the same name for the same person. In large measure, however, we do not
even need any of these cues: We have a tendency to be very generous to sto-
rytellers, ourselves included. Related to this, we have a sense of what makes
for an interesting story. For instance, in a good story, usually the same characters should be present throughout many significant episodes; and even particular inanimate objects, such as swords, guns or spaceships, should persist.
Knowing this, when thinking of examples that resemble little scenes from science fiction, we treat the salient objects and people in ways that help such
stories move along.

In responding to many of these examples, we have other tendencies, too,
which may be philosophically more important. Sometimes the general bias
toward better stories will prevail over a philosophically more significant tendency. For purposes of philosophical inquiry, that will be very unfortunate.
Sometimes, although it will not prevail, that bias will still blunt the force of
the more significant tendency. For philosophical inquiry, even that will be
unfortunate.

We do well to expose misleading tendencies. The best exposure will be by
way of several different sources of illumination. When rationally convinced
of the distorting power of a particular proclivity, we may then discount the
responses that it promotes.

A first way to expose the tendency conjectured is to note how it might operate, just as effectively, to produce favorable responses for a person's survival

even in examples that are *far more extreme* than any of the typical cases of teletransportation. As we did before, we consider some extreme stories of time travel: A person getting into a booth at a certain place and time, we may respond, is the same adventurer as the qualitatively identical person finding herself outside of that booth, perhaps in what is relevantly the same place, twenty years ago. That much is not so bad. But we continue with this response even if, as it is specified, that very person immediately proceeds to do *otherwise* than what, before, *she herself did at that very same past time*. For the sake of stories about time travel and defying fate, many viewers or readers, myself included, calmly allow actual contradictions to pass as assumed fact. We do this because we are not so mechanically stupid as to focus on any trouble with a good story's premises: We do not, for instance, make the logically more consistent but much sillier response that, say, the original person was annihilated and, at the past time mentioned just after in the story, a qualitatively identical but numerically distinct person, in a relevantly similar environment, performed a contrary action.

For similarly literary reasons, it is all that much easier for us to allow as assumed fact the logically consistent, even if entirely false, premise to the effect that radical teletransportation, not killing and replacement, has occurred: As we may very readily respond, a person getting into a certain nearby booth, perhaps one of a different sort from that used in time travel, is the same explorer as the qualitatively identical, but physically discontinuous, person getting out of another booth a little later. Very much as we should certainly discount the happy time-travel response as of no philosophic utility, so we should almost certainly discount the quick response concerning teletransport.

A second way to expose the tendency is to examine putative teletransport examples themselves, but to look at radical cases where the intended cargo is about as far from being personal as concrete reality affords: Consider a story that features putative teletransport of a quite radical sort, with only information and not any matter, sent from one location to another. Suppose that there is, in this story, a conspicuous *hunk of mud*, dense with a rare mineral. Perhaps held in a space explorer's gloved hand, the hunk, as well as what is holding it, may be exposed to an information-extracting machine. As a side-effect, this device casts the hunk's material bits to the wind, along with the bits of anything holding the hunk. On the other side, owing to the transmission of suitable information, numerically different electrons, protons and neutrons are caused to assume certain appropriate arrangements. On this other side, there thus appears just the right sort of hunk of mud, constituted of new matter, held in just the right sort of gloved hand.

When reading a story in which a scene like this occurs, we're perfectly willing to allow that a hunk of mud will be transported from the machine on the alien planet to the machine in the space lab. As assumed fact, we allow that, suddenly formed of entirely different matter, the hunk in the space lab is the *very same hunk of mud* that, several seconds ago, was on the alien planet! To allow the story to develop in the best narrative manner, we assume as fact what, on the least bit of more sober reflection, almost all will find a clearly false proposition. For the same reason, we are similarly willing to suppose that the glove, as well as the hand and the explorer herself, will be transported from one place to a second place distant, not that they will be destroyed and will be duplicated elsewhere. We do all of this, I hypothesize, to get on with a suitably engaging story.

At any rate, and as I submit, our more serious thought is to the contrary: That is no way to transport a hunk of mud, but is only a way to destroy a hunk of mud and to create an exact duplicate of it elsewhere. The same thing is true, our serious thought continues, for gloves, for hands and also for explorers.

A third way to expose the distorting tendency is to juxtapose the straightforward case of alleged transport with a few very similar cases that, for obvious reasons, are much less suitable for most fictional works. With an eye toward ready adaptation, we recall the process of taping with physical temporal overlap. Conveniently supposing that the alleged teletransporter uses a taping mechanism, we may call this following example the *case of singular taping with physical temporal overlap*: You are exposed to the taping process, but you do not expire upon the information regarding your molecular arrangement being recorded for future use. Rather, you remain alive for several days. At the same time, at the beginning of these days, a constructive device makes a person qualitatively just like you out of entirely new matter. During the few days, you may observe this other person, clearly a duplicate of yourself. Only after this do you die. The duplicate, by contrast, will live on for many years.

Intuitively, it is clear that, if only for a few days, you survive the operation of these devices, and that you do so only in the person of the moribund observer. As is clear, the person with the newly constructed brain and body is not you, never was and never will be. On the pure psychological approach, however, this person has just as much claim toward being you as the person who also has so much nice physical continuity. And, if the first of the two devices, in addition, should even slightly upset the psychology realized in the original brain, then the moribund observer will be a *worse* candidate! As almost all conclude, so much the worse for the psychological approach.

Various able philosophers, like Shoemaker and Nozick, nonetheless stay quite close to the psychological approach. From the perspective of logic alone, one cannot fault their moving to make certain rather limited adjustments. But, intuitively, it seems that cannot be right.

A *case of multiple simultaneous taping* provides, from a very different direction, a consideration that is almost as unsettling: After destroying your brain and body while taping you, the taping device sends the information to fifty different constructive devices. Exactly five minutes after the information has been received by all, out of fifty new batches of matter, each machine constructs a precisely similar person. As we all intuitively respond, not only is none of these fifty individuals you, but you expire, completely and forever, at the original location.

Without a clause to deal with cases of branching, the psychological approach would count this as a case of your survival. "Not to worry," the psychological theorist might say, "we may provide for this by an appropriately phrased clause in the characterization of our survival, by a suitable specification of clause (2) in the rough schema provided earlier." As with the previous difficulty, from a purely logical point of view, the present reply is perfectly in order. But, intuitively, the brisk reply seems to miss the point of what is going on with the obviously disturbing situation. Again, there is a strong suggestion that, for all of the cases in the neighborhood, a completely different sort of approach is wanted.[6]

6. First-Order Intuitions and Second-Order Intuitions

We may call an intuition about whether you will survive a particular process, say, the process in the case of singular taping with physical overlap, a *first-order* intuition about cases concerning our survival. We also may have an intuition that, as concerns the question of survival, the straightforward taping case is essentially the same as that case with physical overlap: Whether the cases stand or whether the cases fall, they stand or fall together. This additional reaction is one of our *second-order* intuitions about cases concerning our survival. We have a similar second-order intuition concerning the aforementioned two cases and another example that was recently described, the case of multiple simultaneous taping. As far as a person's survival is concerned, all of these cases, we respond, really are in the same boat.

Not only do we have reliable first-order intuitions about many hypothetical cases, and reliable second-order intuitions about which cases are, in relevant respects, the same as which other cases, but, in addition, we have reliable

6. Although some might think of it as overkill, there are some nice extensions of these examples suggested by Mark Johnston in his "Reasons and Reductionism," *The Philosophical Review*, forthcoming. In particular, there is the case where, without ever destroying the original person, a taping device makes, one after another, fifty precisely similar people. As Johnston notes, that device will work, at a more complex level, very much like a machine from Xerox. Also, there may be a deluxe time-saving model, which makes fifty such people simultaneously. With either model, there will still be only one original person at the end; all of the rest are mere copies of him.

second-order comparative intuitions. As an example of this, we respond that, as far as survival is concerned, each of the three cases recently described is very much more like the other two than it is like ordinary cases of survival. Judiciously treated, such comparative intuitions may help justify us in being more confident about our more straightforward second-order intuitions.

Although they have their exceptions, these generalizations may prove true on the whole. Moreover, the domain of these generalities might not be confined to the topic of personal identity, but may include other areas of philosophic interest. Indeed, it would be rather surprising, for example, if these ideas had little bearing on the proper treatment of examples in moral philosophy.

We may apply these general ideas to the cases at hand: Almost all of us respond that, as concerns matters of survival, the straightforward taping case is very much more like the case of taping with physical overlap than it is like the cases of everyday life. This helps to justify our more absolute second-order intuition: As concerns whether the central person in each of them survives to the example's end, these cases stand, or they fall, together. We combine this with our first-order intuition that, in the case with temporal overlap, the original person does not survive. In this way, we justifiably strengthen our first-order intuition about the simpler, more familiar case: In straightforward taping, the original person does not survive.

Even when considered all by itself, the straightforward taping case will appear to some of us, myself included, as not really presenting anybody's survival. Even so, and even to me, this case does *not* seem to involve an *enormously clear* failure of survival. But we do get that impressive appearance from the case of taping with physical overlap. In this slightly more elaborate case, the failure of survival is about as clear as can be. Now, almost anyone will admit that there is *some* discrepancy between these two hypothetical cases. But, then, exactly what sort of difference is it?

As I surmise, the discrepancy is purely psychological, with no import at all for the philosophy of personal identity: The straightforward case arouses a long-standing tendency we have to be generous about matters of survival, a proclivity in part instilled by, and often aroused by, science fiction. The duplication variants introduce psychologically effective elements, as powerful as they are salient, that impede the operation of the misleading tendency. In a case with physical temporal overlap, one such element is, of course, the presence of a person who, even if there should be some mental detriment that occurred to him, will continue, in what is very much a normal way, to live out what may remain of his life. The effect of noticing this man is to block the formation in us of the aforementioned generous frame of mind. The formation is blocked not just for judging those cases themselves, but also for judging cases perceived as relevantly similar. Or, if we already are in the generous frame of mind, the effect is to take us away from that into a more strict and sober mental set.

7. Other Societies, Other Statements, Other Conditions of Survival

Certain thoughts about *language* can provide still another motivation toward the psychological approach. As with the other motivating factors, this *eighth* one, too, provides no good reason for moving anywhere close to this approach. But when ingeniously presented, arguments concerning language can be, literally, quite stunning. Rather than be stunned, we may freely move to a vantage point where sober reason prevails.

Consider this proposal from Shoemaker concerning the *brain-state transfer device*.[7] In most important ways, this device differs only marginally from a purely informational taping device. But, owing to its prominence in Shoemaker's discussion, as well as in the philosophic literature, I will provide a brief description of it: The machine is supposed to "transfer" a brain state from the brain of a living person, whose brain it then destroys, to a blank recipient brain, which then becomes the brain of a person. It does this by recording constitutional information from the first brain and imposing this information on the second. Stored in a biological bank, the recipient brain may have been cloned from part of the original person quite a while ago. But before the transfer, the recipient brain is totally incapable of generating any thought and, thus, is not yet the brain of any person. Finally, because the device operates according to causal laws that have the happy effect, there never is any outcome that might encourage any puzzle either of temporal overlap or of branching.

Some philosophers, Nozick is again an example, think that they would survive the operation of this device.[8] My own response is to think that this device will provide only a way of killing me and making another person, who is my duplicate. Shoemaker agrees that this response is the intuitive one.[9] But he thinks the plausibility of the response may be overridden without much trou-

7. See Sydney Shoemaker and Richard Swinburne, *Personal Identity*, Basil Blackwell, 1984, pp. 108–111. A slightly more complex device appears in Bernard Williams' paper, "The Self and the Future," *The Philosophical Review*, 1970. For all I know, although devices like these might long have been used in science fiction, Williams provides them with their first employment in the philosophical literature.

8. *Philosophical Explanations*, p. 39.

9. *Personal Identity*, p. 108.

ble. How is this to be done? Chiefly, it is to be accomplished by enlarging upon the case in an appropriate manner.[10]

We are to imagine a whole society living in a land with much unhealthy radiation all about. Every few years, each of the society's members goes in for a brain-and-body change, as they see it, before the old brain and body are fatally damaged by prolonged exposure. This procedure is quite routine for these people. They take it for granted that, each with a suddenly new physical realization, they survive the work of the brain-state transfer device. They take this for granted even though, as is specified, the facts of their world, and so the metaphysics of their situation, are just as we take ours to be. Recognizing all of this, there is relatively little difference, overall, between their system of beliefs and ours.

Despite their different principles for and practices of individuating people, Shoemaker contends that their word 'person' is synonymous with our 'person.' Further, he believes that those people are right in thinking that the procedure of brain-state transfer allows for their personal survival. Finally, he holds that, if they are right, then we will be right only if we agree that this procedure prolongs a person's existence. Not much of this is acceptable.

Shoemaker says that the people in radiation-land have a word 'person' that means the same thing as does our word 'person.' Given his story, the claim that they have a word 'person' cannot be questioned. But, even if expressed by the same sort of marks and sounds, it is at least somewhat questionable whether our 'person' means the same as a word employed by people whose practices of individuating themselves are so markedly different from our own.

Shoemaker appears to assume that because both societies will agree about which entities are persons, and which are not, there will be agreement on all substantive questions that might ground a difference in meaning for their 'person' and for our 'person.' But we will disagree with them about when a certain situation contains the *same person* as does a later, or an earlier, situation. These substantive differences are not to be ignored.

While it is not the only way to interpret these differences in our judgments, one plausible interpretation will have the two societies have different meanings for such compound expressions as 'same person.' By having at least some respect for the ideal of compositional semantics, such an interpretation will go on to have the two communities have at least slightly different meanings for the constituent word, 'person.'

On this approach, although their word means *very much* the same thing as our word does, it will *not* mean *exactly* the same thing. And the difference in meaning, even if it might be comparatively slight overall, may make for large

10. *Ibid.*, pp. 109–111.

differences in certain areas of discourse. Perhaps when one of them says "People can think better than elephants, even though they are not as big or strong," the meaning of his utterance differs only trivially from the meaning of homophonic words of ours. And perhaps the same goes with "People should be treated with respect" and with "All the people I know have brains." But perhaps things go otherwise with "That person will survive the procedure of the brain-state transfer device," and, by extension, with "That person was just informationally teletransported." Perhaps, for what it means, their 'person' allows them to utter truths with these last two sentences. Perhaps, for its somewhat different meaning, our 'person' would have us utter falsehoods with such sentences, or with our homophonic counterparts of them. This approach may be extended, of course, so that, along with small differences in meaning for 'person' and kindred common nouns, there will be small semantic differences for certain pronouns and for certain proper names.[11]

There are other ways of consistently replying that also explain how we might be entirely rational in our beliefs and attitudes about personal identity, complete with their involvements with physical continuity. These alternative responses may allow that the people of radiation-land mean *exactly* the same thing by their 'person' as we do by ours. To put the point differently, these reactions allow that the two societies have exactly the same word. According to one alternative of this sort, the word 'person' will have a rather peculiar *indexical aspect* to its semantics.[12] On this approach, each society will have the same semantics not only for 'person' and close cousins, but for all of their terms. According to another alternative reaction, although there is a slight difference in meaning between certain expressions, none of those expressions are the ones standardly used in reference to people. Instead of there being any difference in the meaning of 'person,' all of the semantic difference in 'People will survive the procedure of the brain-state transfer device' may be due to, for example, a difference in the meaning of 'will survive.'[13] On this

11. A similar line is offered by Mark Johnston in his review of Shoemaker and Swinburne's *Personal Identity*, in *The Philosophical Review*, 1987.

12. In a greatly compressed form, the idea is this: The term 'person' is standardly used to express just those criteria that, among the objectively proper criteria for the term's application, are ranked high by the then current user of that very term or, perhaps, by a certain social group to which the user belongs. Well, just as they have a location that is different from ours, so the people of radiation-land have a ranking of these proper criteria that is different from ours. So, perhaps, they may speak the truth when they utter "That person survived the brain-state transfer procedure," even while we will not speak the truth when we utter, in the very same sense, precisely this same sentence. For, on this account of things, the *proposition* that *they* express with this sentence will concern, in a relevant way, those of the objectively proper criteria that are ranked high *by them*, while the *different proposition* that *we* express will concern the (different) proper criteria ranked high *by us*.

13. The approach was floated by John Carroll.

approach, while the radiation-landers mean one thing by 'survive' and cognate predicates, for us those expressions have a somewhat stricter semantics.

Which of these replies ought we to prefer? For my part, I prefer the first sort of reply. But, as I see it, the main point now really is this: In the present context, the question is out of place. For all such replies are outlines of theories about how our language interacts with our beliefs and values. And, we do not need much confidence now in either one or else another of these theories.

Whichever sort of theory is best, we may be reasonably confident that it will endorse most of our deepest beliefs about matters less abstruse. In particular, whichever sort of theory is best, we may be confident of this: It will be a serious mistake for any of us to undergo the procedure of the brain-state transfer device, just as it will be a serious mistake to accept the offer of the purely informational taping process.

When we are guided by our actual linguistic usage, we are not likely to make these seriously erroneous choices, if ever we should be faced with the options. Were we, instead, to let ourselves be guided by the noticeably different usage of an alien linguistic community, it is more likely that we would err. None of this is very surprising.

8. Three Uses of "What Matters in Survival"

Very probably, the following sentence expresses a fact about how the world is at a time later than the writing of this very sentence itself: One of the people who will exist ten years from now is me. Contemplating the probable truth of the sentence makes me happy. Should I think there was much chance of its being false, I would be despondent.

But *what is it that matters* so much, at least to me, in the fact that one of the future people will be *me*, that is, in the fact that *I* will survive for at least another ten years? What is so important, to me at least, about *my* existing ten years from now, in contrast to there existing in ten year's time someone, other than myself, who is exceedingly like me in ever so many ways and who is causally descended from me? These questions can be strangely puzzling. To many philosophers, their puzzling character makes the topic of personal identity all the more intriguing.

In asking these questions, however, philosophers may not all be using the key motivational terms, 'important' and 'what matters,' in the same way. Instead, we might be using them in several identifiably different ways. Perhaps our differing uses cluster around a few different paradigms of use, some of us gathering around one of the paradigms, others around another.

As I will argue shortly, many philosophers may focus on a use of these terms that connects closely with matters of psychological continuity. By virtue of this focus, these thinkers will favor a *psychological approach to what matters in our survival*. It will then be but a short step to favoring, as well, the psychological approach to our survival itself, or at least a view quite close to that position. This tendency may be a *ninth* motivating factor toward the psychological approach to our survival.

The question then arises: What are the philosophically prevalent uses of 'what matters in survival'? In this connection, it is instructive to inspect an influential passage from David Lewis, an advocate of the psychological approach to our survival itself:

> What is it that matters in survival? . . . What do I really care about? If it can happen that some features of ordinary everyday survival are present but others are missing, then what would it take to make the difference between something practically as good as commonplace survival and something practically as bad as commonplace death?
>
> I answer, along with many others: *what matters in survival is mental continuity and connectedness*. When I consider various cases in between commonplace survival and commonplace death, I find that what I mostly want in wanting survival is that my mental life should flow on. My present experiences, thoughts, beliefs, desires, and traits of character should have appropriate future successors. My total present mental state should be but one momentary stage in a continuing succession of mental states. The successive states should be interconnected in two ways. First, by bonds of similarity. Change should be gradual rather than sudden, and (at least in some respects) there should not be too much change overall. Second, by bonds of lawful causal dependence. Such change as there is should conform, for the most part, to lawful regularities concerning the succession of mental states—regularities, moreover, that are exemplified in everyday cases of survival. And this should be so not by accident . . . but rather because each succeeding mental state causally depends for its character on the states immediately before it.[14]

As do other friends of the psychological approach, perhaps Lewis is using 'what matters in survival' in a way that is not highly relevant to questions of our survival.

In trying to understand how philosophers may be employing the term, we should begin by distinguishing between two uses: On the use that Lewis apparently favors, which I will call the *desirability use*, 'what matters in survival' will mean much the same as this: what it is that one gets out of survival that makes continued survival a desirable thing for one, a better thing, at least, than is utter cessation. On this desirability use, if one has what matters

---

14. "Survival and Identity," in *The Identities of Persons*, p. 17.

in survival, then, from a self-interested perspective, one has reason to continue rather than opt for sudden painless termination.

On this use, the expression's range may threaten to become so expansive
as to be virtually the same as that of 'what matters in life': If this use is taken
to the extreme, we will employ the expression so that its range may come to
include the having of varied and pleasant experiences, the performance of
worthwhile actions, the enjoyment of interpersonal relationships, and so on.
Of course, even friends of the psychological approach never do get very near
this extreme: With artful good sense, this expansive tendency may be firmly
held in check by a concern to stick at least fairly close to considerations of
survival itself.

Although this desirability use may have its advantages, philosophical illumination of personal identity is not one of them. On the contrary, in trying
to stick close to the topic of personal identity, we want to avoid this use about
as much as we can. As our discussion proceeds, the reasons for this will
become increasingly clearer.

A second use is much more appropriate for questions of personal identity.
On the use I have in mind, which I will call the *prudential use* of 'what matters
in survival,' the expression will be glossed in some such rough way as this:
From the perspective of a person's concern for herself, or from a slight and
rational extension of that perspective, what future being there is or, possibly,
which future beings there are, for whom the person rationally should be
"intrinsically" concerned. Saying that this rational concern is "intrinsic"
means, roughly, that, even apart from questions of whether or not he might
advance the present person's projects, there is this rational concern for the
welfare of the future being. So, in particular, this prudential use is to connect
directly with our favorite sacrifice for future well-being test, namely, the
avoidance of future great pain test.

Tomorrow, I might become a complete amnesiac with regard to all of my
past life. Even as Lewis will agree, it is quite clear that I will survive this terribly unfortunate incident. On the desirability use, in this case there will be
quite a lot less of what matters in my survival than there is in the ordinary
case, where I will have a rich store of personal memories. On the prudential
use, by contrast, even in this sad amnesia case, there may be all of what matters in my survival. For example, to spare myself from great electric shocks
in two days time, I will rationally undergo just as many slight shocks now on
the confident belief that I will become highly amnesiac, or at least very nearly
as many, as I would on the equally confident belief that I will not become
amnesiac.

Among the rational choices to which this prudential use alludes, the most
conspicuous will be those that involve the avoidance of future pain. But not
all "intrinsic" choices regarding future well-being are as gloomy as the most

conspicuous one. So you may choose to accept a slight decrease, for just one day, in your impending great pleasure. Your prudential concern may be for a great increase in your pleasure, for many years, beginning right after an impending operation that will render you highly amnesiac.

To anticipate the discussion of some later chapters, we may observe that, as indicated by our phrase, 'or from a slight and rational extension of that perspective,' this prudential use might be appropriate not only in cases of strict survival, but also in certain closely related cases. For an illustration of this suggestion, we might look to our spectrum of congenial decomposition, focusing on a case that is just beyond the last few where, as our conventions have it, I myself will be. From a very slight extension of my familiar egoistical perspective, I might be rationally concerned for my terribly intimate descendant who, for want of a nerve cell or two, just barely fails as a candidate for being me. On the prudential use of the term, when there is just that descendant being, there may be, not all of what matters in my survival, but not none of what matters, either. Instead of either of those "extreme" alternatives, there may be quite a lot of what matters. On the desirability use, by contrast, in such a sad case as this there will be rather little of what matters in my survival.

Very roughly, the desirability use aims at just those situations that we should most like to encounter, whereas the prudential use aims at all those that, somewhere or other in logical space, must be faced. Because any serious inquiry into personal identity means facing some sour music along with the sweet, this prudential use is, I think, so important for our topic area that, if it did not already exist, we should invent it. But I do not think that this use needs to be invented. Indeed, it is just this prudential use that I find consistently dominant in my own employment of 'what matters in survival.' Partly because I incline in their direction, I suggest that, when they may consider questions of rational self-concern, it is this use that will dominate the thought of philosophers who favor the physical approach to personal identity.

There is a third main use of the expression, 'what matters in survival,' which I will call the *constitutive use*.[15] Here the leading idea is that we focus on what it is about a case that *counts toward* the case being one that involves a person who does survive. For this constitutive use to have much philosophical interest, there must be some truth to at least one of two related underlying assumptions: First, it should be true that there are a number of different factors each of which may count toward personal survival. Second, it should

15. In the "Importance of Being Identical," in *The Identities of Persons*, on pp. 85–86, John Perry distinguishes between two "senses" of 'what matters in survival.' More or less, he distinguishes between what I am calling the constitutive use and what I call the desirability use. So far, so good. But it is not nearly far enough. Accordingly, as I see it, Perry falls into many of the same errors as Lewis, whom he is criticizing, and Parfit, with whom he is largely in agreement.

be true that at least some of these factors are largely matters of degree. For example, on the psychological approach, perhaps a future person must have *enough* of a certain present person's distinctive psychology, if that future person is that present one. Or, for example, on the physical approach, perhaps there must be a *sufficiently* continuous physical realization, from now until some future time, of that present person's core psychology. Whatever sort of objective approach we favor, most of us deeply believe that at least one of those underlying assumptions is correct. Because this is our belief, we may also believe that this constitutive use is of some interest.

As is obvious, like the prudential use, but perhaps unlike the desirability use, in trying to be relevant to questions about personal identity, the constitutive employment is a use that we may exploit to the full. As also is obvious, this constitutive use does not directly concern the evaluative, or the motivational, matters that surround the topic of our survival. For that straightforward reason, this use has no direct connection with questions of rational concern for oneself in the future.[16]

The consideration of an appropriate example may help us to see how these three different uses may variously influence our thinking: Suppose that a surgical procedure is applied to you with these following effects: Very little of your distinctive mental life flows on, but all of your core psychology flows on by the normal route of realization in your brain. You will thus be left with your capacity for consciousness, with a capacity for a fair variety of experience, and with what we might call a modicum of intelligence or reasoning ability, perhaps as much as is typically present with a person with an IQ of about 30. But few or none of your personal memories will be realized in your brain now, or flow on in any way at all; few or none of your distinctive personality or character traits will flow on; few or none of your even moderately distinctive capacities, views, or interests will be continued; and so on, and so forth. For good measure, we may further suppose that the effects of this procedure are never reversed. Now we may ask: After such surgery is applied to you, how much of what matters in survival will there be?

We may employ the expression 'what matters in survival' in accord with the desirability use, as Lewis apparently does in the cited passage. If we use the expression in this way, we will mean, close enough, how much value is there for you in the life of the resultant being. Then the answer to our question will be just the answer Lewis would find: not much at all. For you to undergo this procedure is practically as bad as commonplace death. Quite rationally, given your values, you would undergo great sacrifices now to prevent this from happening. Given your values, how good can it be for you to have the life of such an extremely dull and disoriented person? Indeed, for many peo-

16. In formulating the descriptions of these three uses, I have been saved from some errors by helpful comments from Derek Parfit and from Mark Johnston.

ple, this prospect has *negative* value. If one of them had the chance before-hand, he would, perhaps quite rationally, arrange for the swift, sudden and painless death of the person, perhaps himself, who emerged from this surgical operation. He might do so even if the process of making these arrangements was one that, in advance, involved considerable pain.

Alternatively, we may employ the expression 'what matters in survival' in accord with the prudential use. Using the expression in this alternative way, we will mean, in effect, something like this: Is there anyone left from such an operation for whom you may have a rational egoistic concern and, if so, how great will this concern be? To this quite different question, we find a quite different answer: Yes; there is someone left, namely, the unfortunate amnesiac imbecile who will be you; and, for yourself, the strength of your rational self-centered concern will be very great. Suppose that, unless you choose to undergo considerable pain beforehand, just that particular imbecile will be mercilessly tortured soon after the operation. From a self-interested perspective, it is rational for you now to undergo the lesser pain, so that this amnesiac imbecile will not then suffer that very much greater pain. And it is very clear why this is rational for you: It is bad enough, indeed much worse than bad enough, that you will then be devoid of almost all of your personal memories and distinctive mental characteristics, not to mention so much of your reasoning ability. But, bad as that may be, it will still be you who is in such a sorry and pathetic state. And, bad as that may be, it will be far worse still if, on top of all that, you will be tortured severely.

It should be clear that this prudential use of 'what matters' *is not* the one most operative with Lewis and like-minded thinkers. It should also be clear that this prudential use *is* the motivational use that is most closely related to questions of personal identity. It is the prudential use, not the desirability use, that is the motivationally relevant counterpart of the constitutive use.

The prudential use fits well with a physical approach to what matters in survival and, by extension, with the physical approach to our survival itself. Partly for this reason, philosophers who are moved to favor a view of our survival that is close to the physical approach are, I suggest, quite close to the truth.

9. Three Other Objective Approaches

Among the many philosophers who accept our objective view of ourselves, views of our survival cluster around two polar paradigms: the psychological approach and the physical approach. In order better to understand these two views that dominate the literature, it will be useful to compare them with three other objective approaches to personal identity: These are an approach that I call the Demanding view, one that I call the Lenient view and, finally, a Substantial Compromise between the psychological and the physical approaches. We may then be encouraged to ask why these three views are, in fact, largely passed over by leading writers in the field.

As we have defined these two leading paradigms, the sort of demand made by the physical approach is just the reverse of that made by the psychological approach to personal identity: The physical approach is very demanding as regards the sorts of causal routes that may properly take *any* of my psychology from me now to a person in the future who will be me. But it is very lenient in another way. On this approach, very little is required in the way of how much of my psychology must be causally carried forward: My core psychology will be enough. A surgeon may work on my brain so as to remove, without even the slightest trace, virtually all of my (ostensible) memories of personal experience and virtually all of my character and personality traits. She may leave little beyond a capacity for conscious experience and a capacity for rudimentary reasoning. On the physical approach, that disoriented cretin will still be me. For my core psychology is carried forward by a causal route that involves a substantial enough degree of relevant physical continuity.

On the psychological approach, by contrast, this unfortunate will not be me. That is because not enough of my psychology is carried forward and realized in him; more specifically, little or none of my distinctive psychology is thus carried forward. True enough, the operative causes satisfy pretty strict demands on causal routing. But, according to the psychological approach, that is not the right place to make our demands. So long as some genuine causal continuation is present, that is enough on that score. The serious demand is to be made elsewhere: Not just core psychology, but a lot of my distinctive psychology must be preserved in order for me to survive. Since that demand is not satisfied in the case of this terrible surgery, the pathetic person emerging from the operation clearly is not me.

Both the psychological approach and the physical approach are pretty demanding, but neither is terribly demanding: As noted, one of them makes demands of one sort, while the other makes demands of a quite different sort. With this contrast made conspicuous, we may easily notice two other objective approaches.

On the first of these, which I will call the *Demanding approach* to personal identity, demands of *both* sorts are made at once: A lot of the past person's psychology must be carried forward *and also* this must be done by a causal routing that involves enough relevant physical continuity. Few philosophers take this Demanding approach.[17]

In stark contrast, on the *Lenient approach* to personal identity, *neither* sort

---

17. In *Reasons and Persons*, Parfit floats, among other approaches, a view he calls the Narrow Version of the Psychological Criterion. For example, see page 208. As far as I can tell, this is the same thing, or very nearly the same thing, as what I am here calling the Demanding approach.

of forceful demand is made. As long as a minimal core is carried forward, that is enough psychology. And, as long as there is any genuine causality doing this, matters of causal routing are satisfied well enough. On this approach, I will survive dastardly brain surgery directly followed by purely informational teletransportation: I will be a very distant and disoriented cretin. Very few philosophers, indeed, want much to do with this Lenient approach to personal identity.

Why do so many philosophers take one or the other of the two leading approaches, or at least take a view very like one of them, while so few take the Demanding approach and so few the Lenient approach? This is a question worth asking. It is rather puzzling, after all, that their views should cluster around the two polar approaches. I proceed to offer only a partial explanation.

From any objective view of our survival, we may want each of two competing ideas to be pretty well satisfied: On the one hand, we may want the conditions on our survival to be *not too terribly demanding*. In other words, we may want not to exclude in advance, for ourselves and for our descendants, too many possible processes that, otherwise, might be considered ways of securing survival. Perhaps this is part of the explanation of why few philosophers advocate the Demanding view.

On the other hand, although we want survival to be pretty easy for us, we also want survival to be meaningful, to amount to something that we believe to be of some significance. But, if the satisfaction of virtually any conditions will do, and if we have any inkling of this great largesse, then there will not be the appearance of much significance.[18] Accordingly, we also want the con-

---

Even if, perhaps, it might not be done by any other salient author, does Parfit, at least, endorse this Narrow Version as the most accurate approach to our survival? It is very hard for me to tell. Perhaps he does not actually endorse *any* view on this subject, thinking, as he does, that the whole issue is not one of any great importance. For Parfit, of course, the key issue is what matters in survival. Perhaps because he might be embroiled with the desirability use of the terms, on this latter issue his position is what would be expected from one who endorses, on the question of survival itself, (something much like) the psychological approach.

18. This ties in with a point I stress in my paper, "Toward A Psychology of Common Sense." As I say there, although we might let cats turn out to be robots, we won't let them turn out to be a certain feature of a vast hallucination. If, as we might discover, all of our experience to date has been induced in us by a Cartesian demon, and the world beyond our experience contains no entities that are even remotely feline, then there just won't ever have been any cats. In other words, according to our currently actual attitudes, we do not allow that, in such a case, there still will have been cats (and they will always have been just certain experiential features). Why not? Well, we can't do that and, at the same time, have it still appear, even to ourselves, that our term, 'cat', has much meaning at all. Almost the same, and also true, we can't pull the trick and let it still appear, even to ourselves, that the existence of cats ever amounted to anything much. As I am suggesting in the present text, much the same thing may be going on with our own existence, not just in relation to what past there might have been, but also in relation to what future there might be.

ditions on our survival to be *not too terribly lenient*. Perhaps this is part of the explanation of why so few philosophers advocate the Lenient view.

In contrast to these two neglected approaches, both the psychological approach and the physical approach impose nicely moderate constraints on our survival. But, there is another sort of approach that does this, too. We may adopt a Substantial Compromise approach, a view that appropriately combines aspects of the two leading paradigms by giving substantial weight to each. For example, we may take an approach that requires there to be carried forward, perhaps in addition to her core psychology, not a great deal of, but at least a moderate amount of, a person's distinctive psychology. As the approach is a substantial compromise between the leading paradigms, it will make demands, as well, on the sorts of causal routes that may carry forward at least this much of a person's psychology. But these demands will be only moderately constraining: For example, perhaps the allowable routes are those that, overall, are at least moderately similar to the routes that are most typical or, for other reasons, are most preferred. In particular, perhaps a quite modest sort of, or a quite moderate amount of, physical continuity will do. For example, on a Substantial Compromise a person might clearly survive, not purely informational taping, but taping with molecular restoration. Further, she might immediately go on to survive, quite clearly, surgery that removed much of, but that also left a fair amount of, her distinctive psychology.

Why do philosophers, in fact, seldom give no more than lip service to a Substantial Compromise? After all, in the abstract, it would seem to be a rather attractive sort of view. I offer two partial explanations, each complementing the other.

The first explanation itself has several parts, all closely related to each other: Because the polar paradigms are more extreme, they are more salient than, and they also are more easily characterized than, a Substantial Compromise. Now, first, as a person is apt to judge cases in terms of a view that is salient for her, she is the more likely to find a more salient view to be confirmed by her responses to examples. Second, one is apt to judge cases in terms of a view that will encourage easily articulated justifications. This is another reason why the two more extreme views will be the more likely to appear confirmed by the cases. Third, and finally, part of the reason may be as simple as this: People have a tendency to think in extremes, or in ways that are quite close to the extremes. Much of the time, this allows us to avoid uncomfortably puzzling areas of vagueness and ambiguity. Going to one extreme or another, one has no truck with a potentially unsettling compromise between them.

The second partial explanation makes reference to two of the uses of 'what matters' distinguished in the previous section. In thinking about questions of rational concern, philosophers tend to focus on one or else the other of the two motivationally relevant uses of 'what matters in survival,' and of related terms. Some philosophers focus on the desirability use. This focus tends to feed on itself and, increasingly, may involve the thinkers in what we may call an *expansive frame of mind* toward these questions of concern. Then they may strongly persist in a psychological approach to what matters in survival. Finally, because of this, and because they rightly think the two questions to be closely related, they may also persist in the psychological approach to survival itself, or in views that are very similar.

Other philosophers focus on the prudential use. More and more, they will come to be in what we may call a *conservative frame of mind* toward questions of rational concern about themselves. Once someone is in this frame of mind, it, too, grows on the thinker. So, philosophers in this conservative mind set may persist in a physical approach to what matters in survival and, thus, to the question of our survival itself.

All of these partial explanations are very far indeed from being complete accounts. Indeed, at times, when mulling over the discussion of this section, I think that the only thing of much value in it is my raising of the question in the first place: Within the overall objective view of ourselves, why do the views of active authors cluster around the psychological approach and, on the other side, around the physical approach to our survival? As our discussion indicates, it is not easy to answer this intriguing question in a very satisfactory manner.

For our main purposes here, the great incompleteness of our answer does not much matter. For, as this book argues, those authors whose views cluster around the physical approach are pretty close to the truth. At any rate, their views are much closer to the truth than are the views that cluster around the psychological approach to our survival.

4

THE PHYSICAL APPROACH
TO OUR SURVIVAL

The physical approach to our survival is the best *basis* for an adequate treatment of our identity over time: Any better approach will more likely result from a modification of this approach than from a rejection of it. For this reason, it is important that we understand the import of the physical approach.

In keeping with the spirit of this book, the physical approach is not offered as any sort of analytic or conceptual truth. For one thing, I see no conceptual necessity about our being physical at all. Rather, subject to whatever qualifications may be required, the view is offered as adequate relative to the proposition that, in broad outline, our view of the world is correct.

Even if it is quite rough, an attempt at a suitably phrased formulation of the approach may be a useful first step toward understanding the view. A main task of the chapter's first two sections is to provide a usefully schematic characterization. Key expressions used to formulate this characterization will be, at once, both technical and vague. Since there appears to be much vagueness attending questions of our survival, at least the fact that these expressions are vague looks to be a positive feature of them. Their technical aspect, by contrast, needs to be justified. At any rate, as the chapter develops, a discussion of a variety of issues will help to clarify the intended use of these expressions. And, as I hope, there will then emerge considerations that warrant my trafficking in some technicalities.

We do not only want to understand the import of this approach, of course, but also want to assess how much truth there may be in it. In much of our discussion, we will be working on these two main tasks at once: Even as we try to clarify the treatment's import, we will be looking to see how much truth it may contain. To some extent, this might bias our investigation in favor of our vague, technically formulated approach. But the extent of the bias may not be so great as to deprive our efforts of their point.

1. Two Formulations of the Physical Approach

The physical approach, as here understood, places infinitely more weight on the brain, or the central nervous system, than it does on all the rest of a person's body. Much of our discussion has already indicated the propriety of this, but a few thoughts about a very simple example will confirm the point dramatically: Improving on a famous case of Shoemaker's, we imagine two people who are qualitatively identical.[1] One may be you, the other your absolute twin. Under a powerful anesthetic, the two brains are taken from the heads of the two bodies. Then each brain is put back in the head of the other body. Two people awaken. One has your original brain and your twin's old body; the other has your original body and the twin's old brain. Shortly after awakening one of these two people will get excruciating pain and the other will get no pain at all. You can do nothing about that. But you do have this much choice: Before the operations are performed, you may choose which of the two will be tortured and which spared. With little doubt indeed, you will choose the person with your original brain to be spared, the torture going to the other. Your reasoning is simple: This person is you and you want very much not to be tortured, whether or not you have the same body.

The physical approach does not insist that there is any logical or analytic connection between anything physical, let alone a particular brain, and the survival of a person from an earlier to a later time. Rather, the reasoning behind the approach may proceed along these lines, offered by Thomas Nagel, who holds a view of our identity that is rather close to what I call the physical approach:

> Let me repeat that this is not offered as an analysis of the concept of the self but as an empirical hypothesis about its true nature. My concept of myself contains the blank space for such an objective completion, but does not fill it in. I

---

1. Shoemaker presents his by now classic example in *Self-Knowledge and Self-Identity*, Cornell University Press, 1963. Unlike my two men here, his two have quite different distinctive psychologies, as well as various other qualitative differences. By eliminating this feature of these qualitative differences, perhaps we may allow the case to be a bit more illuminating. On either version, at all events, the intuition is that each man ends up where his brain goes.

am whatever persisting individual in the objective order underlies the subjective continuities of that mental life that I call mine. But a type of objective entity can settle questions about the identity of the self only if the thing in question is both the bearer of mental states and the cause of their continuity when there is continuity. If my brain meets these conditions then *the core of the self—what is essential to my existence—is my functioning brain.* . . . But the brain is the only part of me whose destruction I could not possibly survive. The brain, but not the rest of the animal, is essential to the self.[2]

Less friendly to the physical approach, but also understanding it as empirically motivated, Derek Parfit offers this formulation:

> *The Physical Criterion*: (1) What is necessary is not the continued existence of the whole body, but the continued existence of *enough* of the brain to be the brain of a living person. X today is one and the same person as Y at some past time if and only if (2) enough of Y's brain continued to exist, and is now X's brain, and (3) this continuity has not taken a 'branching' form.[3]

For focusing on the brain as contrasted with the rest of a person's body, and also for being offered as empirically motivated, both of these statements of a physical view are on the right track. When we think about things critically, however, they both may be found wanting. Somewhat ironically, the main error in Nagel's formulation is, in a certain sense, exactly the opposite of Parfit's: As concerns what is needed from a person's brain, Nagel goes too far even while Parfit fails to go far enough.

Parfit notwithstanding, it is clearly not sufficient for much, or even for all, of the earlier person's brain to continue to be alive until the time that the later person needs a properly structured brain. There must be a stronger requirement to the effect that, in the interim period, the brain in question continues to realize certain features of the original person's dispositional psychology. In any ordinary case, of course, the brain will do this by being, throughout the period, suitably structured.

Without this requirement there might be, in the interim, just a brain that is little more than living meat, a brain that is not the brain of any person at all, let alone the brain of Y or of X. There may then be *enough* of a whole brain for it to be the brain of a living person, all right, but it may be structured very unsuitably for supporting mental life. Once Y's brain becomes the

2. *The View from Nowhere*, Oxford University Press, 1986, p.40. The indicated emphasis is my own, not Nagel's.

3. *Reasons and Persons*, p. 204. (In the first few printings of the book, including the initial 1984 printing cited, clause (3) reads somewhat differently. Parfit has assured me, in written communication, that the latest printing is as above. At any rate, for our discussion, this clause is unimportant.)

brain of no being with a capacity for a significant mental life, and with Y presumed not to have any other physical realization of her psychology, then Y ceases to exist. Whatever the later person X may be, she will not be Y.

For the ordinary cases, we might clarify the point by speaking of different levels of physical structure. Appropriate gross physical structure is enough to ensure the existence of a brain, whether living or not. Appropriate structure that is somewhat finer may be needed to ensure that this brain is composed of living tissue. But much finer structure still is needed, as a matter of fact, for the realization of psychological capacities by that brain. At least in any of the more ordinary cases, in order for someone to survive, there must be continuity of these very fine structures, not just the grosser ones.

Nagel, as I said, goes too far in the other direction. As he says or implies, the brain must be *functioning* properly throughout. But recall the process of super freezing and super thawing. In the middle period of that process, the brain is not functioning at all. Still, the person clearly survives. She survives because enough of her brain, although not then functioning, is suitably structured so that it realizes her psychology.

Perhaps Nagel may be assuming the Modified Cartesian View: For survival, there must be continuity of the subject's mental life, where this implies continuity of her mental activity, although not necessarily her conscious mental activity. But, at least relative to any plausible physical view, this assumption is incorrect. For survival, there need only be continuity of certain psychological *capacities*; there need *not* be continuity of any psychological *activities*, whether conscious or non-conscious.

Alternatively, and perhaps more likely, Nagel may assume that, for the continuity of someone's mental capacities, there must be the continuity of the functioning of her brain. But, even if there must be some continuity involving her brain, that will not be the one required. As a matter of fact, appropriate physical *functioning* is needed only for psychological activity. Continuity of adequate physical *structure*, by contrast, will suffice for the capacity for that activity. When there is continuity of appropriate structure of someone's brain, then the person whose brain that is may survive.

So much for our discussion of Parfit and Nagel on brains. With the need for two significant clarifications duly appreciated, we turn to see some of the great appeal of the physical approach.

In the normal course of events, my brain realizes both my core psychology and my distinctive psychology. On the physical approach, it is owing to its realization of my core psychology that my brain is so important for my survival; by contrast, my brain's realization of my distinctive psychology is completely incidental. An appropriate example helps us to see that this central claim is, at the least, quite close to the truth.

We may imagine that a maniacal surgeon records on tape precise information as to your brain's constitution. Then she tampers with your brain so as to remove all of your distinctive psychology, leaving you only with your core. A week later, she may use the recorded information to restructure your brain, again, thus restoring the distinctive psychology that, for the week, was missing.

On the physical approach to personal identity, the surgeon's patient will be you throughout the week. This is certainly our intuitive response. By employing a pain avoidance test, we may confirm our intuition. Ahead of time and from your natural perspective of self-interest, you must choose when the surgeon will impose what pain. You have precisely two options. On the one hand, you may choose for her to impose some fairly slight, but significant, pain before this week (and never any other pain.) Alternatively, you may choose for her to impose very much greater pain during the week, when there is someone with that brain realizing only core psychology (and never any other pain.) On the belief that you will get much less pain, you will choose for her to impose the much lesser pain before the operation and, thus, before the week in question. Indeed, you will choose for her to impose the much lesser earlier pain *whether or not*, at the end of the week, the surgeon restores your distinctive psychology. For, as you may deeply believe, in either case, as long as your brain is continuously structured to realize core psychology and, thus, as long as it always is the brain of a person, you will still exist.

2. A Better Formulation

The physical approach has enough plausibility and power to be worth characterizing reasonably well. When suitably modified, formulations in terms of the brain, like Nagel's and Parfit's, are pretty good expressions of the spirit of this pure approach. But they are not optimal expressions of it. This is true for two reasons.

First, even given the assumption that a physical approach is in general correct, it may not be true that the survival of a person's brain is necessary for the person herself to survive. Second, it is because the physical approach is sensitive only to core psychology that this treatment is the appealing analogue of traditional views of ourselves as immaterial seats of consciousness and reasoning power. This appeal is not reflected well just by a reference to the brain, or even to the entire central nervous system. For, as a matter of fact, a person's brain, or that system of hers, realizes her distinctive psychology as much as it does her psychological core. While little more needs to be said about the second of these reasons, some elaborate but useful remarks may be made regarding the first. As all of the main points may be made by a simple reference to the brain, in offering these remarks I shall, for the most part, omit the lengthier reference to the central nervous system.

Taking it as given that a physical approach is in general correct, it may be impossible clearly to refute the claim that, in order to survive, a person needs a brain, at least some brain or other. Indeed, it is difficult enough to refute the claim that, in order to survive, a person needs the brain with which she begins life as a person. Even as regards this weaker claim, most apparently promising attempts quickly fall apart. For example, in certain cases, you may survive even though you and your brain are scattered into quite a few pieces, or are gradually changed into an entity that is made mainly of metal. But, then, your brain may also survive in these cases, with you coming to have a scattered brain, or a metallic brain. Your brain is merely *transformed*; it is not replaced or made superfluous. It is not very easy, then, to undermine the idea that, within the physical approach, the survival of one's brain is crucial to one's own survival. But, with the appropriate material before us, some disturbing doubts may emerge.

Certain examples suggest that, by way of a suitably gradual process, a person might come to have, instead of her original brain, a new brain that then realizes her mentality.[4] But the raising of doubts along these lines, where we always stay rather clearly within the category of brains, is not central to these present issues. Rather, we should focus on the more modest claim that, even if your original brain may not be required for your survival, you might always need some brain or other in order to survive. For, if that claim is correct, then, in our formulation of the physical approach, we may want at least a rather general sort of reference to brains.

The following sort of example appears to undermine even the idea that, in our formulation, we should have this quite general, and more cautious, reference to brains: Sequentially and gradually, the work of my brain is taken over by structures that are not bunched together as in a typical animal organ, but are spread quite evenly throughout the whole organism. In the less ambitious version of the case, as the nerve cells of my brain are killed, newly inserted nerve cells, much more widely dispersed, may take up their contributory roles. In the more ambitious version, my central nerve cells are replaced not by any new nerve cells, or even by any organic matter at all, but by complex bionic circuitry that is strung throughout most of my body. In either version, rather than being placed near each other in my head, the new structures may be strung throughout my body so that, in late stages, my psychology is as much realized in my arms and legs as in my torso and buttocks, but in my head least of all. In either version, of course, the process may be

---

4. In section 5 of the next chapter, I describe some of these cases.

both slow and gradual, occurring in small steps spread out over much lived time. After sufficient time, there will be, in my brain pan, only a dead brain that is, for the realization of psychology, completely unsuitable and ineffective. Finally, that dead brain may be removed and placed in a frying pan.

In this sort of case, I will survive. But, at the step before the end, will I have, in addition to the dead brain in my head, a second brain that is spread throughout almost all of my body? Apparently not. The only brain I then have is in my head, suitable for little but a meal for a cannibal. At the last step, when the dead brain is on the fire, will there be a *brain* there in my body that is then realizing my psychology? Apparently, no more so than in the step just before.

Now we may, I suppose, use 'brain' in such a way that anything physical that ever realizes any person's psychology will count as a brain. If we use the term in this extremely lenient way, then, in this case, I will have two brains near the end: One of my brains, in my head, will then be good for nothing psychologically; the other, spread throughout my body, will realize my psychology. But it may be that, in thus speaking of a second brain, both enormously diffuse and possibly inorganic to boot, we are not fully respecting the meaning of our term, 'brain.' We do not want our formulation to verge on any such possible semantic violations, nor to traffic in confusing ambiguities.

Similar remarks apply to a parallel formulation in terms of the central nervous system rather than the brain: First, unless we use 'central' only to mean *important for realizing psychology*, in the case imagined there is nothing central about the system of physical realization that, by the end, is operative. And that use of the term is not just controversial, but is liable to be confusing. Second, in the version where it is bionic circuits that are spread far and wide, there is no clearly relevant sense of 'nerve' or 'nervous,' either, that happily describes what is realizing psychology.[5]

To achieve a reasonably clear statement, as well as an appropriately general one, it will be best for us to make no mention of brains, or of central nervous systems, in our formulation of the physical approach. Instead, let us talk of whatever physical entity realizes a person's core psychology, calling it the *physical realizer of the person's core psychology*. In these terms, we may charac-

---

5. In a recent paper, "Johnston on Human Beings," *The Journal of Philosophy*, 1989, David Oderberg warns that, for all we really know, "*on its own*" a brain may not be able to support any mental life. Beyond the usual situation for it in a human body, perhaps the actual universe will allow for no supporting systems that will permit an extracted brain to support any mental life. Extending this idea, we may surmise that the same might hold true even for the whole nervous system. While I do not think there is much reason to be skeptical in these matters, these suggestions do, it seems to me, mean still more reason to avoid formulations that make any reference at all, however general, to a brain, or to a nervous system.

terize the physical approach in a way that, although vague, is not objection-
ably unclear:

> The person X now is one and the same as the person Y at some time in the
> future if, and only if, (1) there is sufficiently continuous physical realization of
> a core psychology between the physical realizer of X's core psychology and the
> physical realizer of Y's core psychology, and [probably] (2) {some clause suitable
> for ruling out unwanted cases of branching}.

Because fission and fusion are as much side-issues on the physical approach
as on the psychological treatment, we again place to the side any thoughts
about (2), the second clause.

There are a number of points to emphasize about the physical approach as
just characterized. First, this formulation is no more offered as a conceptual,
or logical, or analytical truth than are any of the formulations that make reference to brains. To the contrary, even as now characterized, the adequacy
of the physical approach is only *relative to* the correctness of a certain view of
reality as a whole. This is a view of the world as being, at the least, very largely
a physical world. On this view, this physical world is reasonably stable, regular
and well behaved: For example, like rocks, and trees, and cats, people do not,
along with their matter, pop out of existence, or pop into existence. Rather,
people begin, continue, or end, as a consequence of changes in the mutual
arrangements of certain comparatively simple physical things.

Second, this formulation has the physical approach focus squarely on *core
psychology*, giving no importance to distinctive psychology. There is some
vagueness here, of course, but vagueness that may be suitable for a useful
formulation. For example, this may well capture the vague idea of a person
as a center of rational reflection.

Third, suitably vague and general but explicit nonetheless, there is the
focus on a *physical realizer* of that core psychology. The physical realizer need
not be a contiguous object and, up to certain points, it may fail to be physically well behaved in a great variety of ways. Further, there may even be some
cases where the physical realizer of Y's psychology is not the same physical
entity as the realizer of X's mentality; perhaps there may be an appropriate
physically continuous succession of realizing entities. But, in any case, the
realizer of X's psychology must be physically continuous with the realizer of
Y's and, further, this continuity must be of such a sort that it allows us to say,
correctly, that there is the physically continuous realization of X's core psychology from the present until that future time, when that psychology is Y's.
Now, having taken precautions with our terminology for psychological realization, we need not be overbearing in the employment of our terms. For, as
a matter of fact, most of what may be said about a person's physical realizer

also may be said about her well-structured brain. Because this is so, we may often use 'brain' as a familiar shorthand term for 'physical realizer.' Since context will serve to make matters clear enough, that may improve exposition.

Finally, there is the reference to *sufficient physical continuity*. This reference should not be understood, of course, in a way that turns the formulation into a pointless tautology. Rather, the idea is that sometimes there is, and sometimes there is not, appropriate physical continuity. Within this physical approach, inquiry aims at discerning when there is sufficient continuity between an earlier and a later brain for this physical continuity to ensure that there is realized, at different times, the psychology of one and the same person. On the appropriate conception of it, this physical continuity may involve *various matters of degree*: Not only are matters of material composition and replacement important, so, too, are matters involving the operation of various forces, fields, binding processes, whatever.

3. Wide Physical Continuity and Contextual Flexibility

Certain sorts of cases may get some to think that the physical approach must be quite wrong even in general conception. At a certain moment, all of the elementary particles that just before composed you cease to exist. A moment later their vacated regions may once again be full of matter. About this situation, some may offer thoughts like these: "With an exceedingly brief period when the regions are empty of matter, will you not survive the episode? Surely, you will survive. But, on the physical approach, you will not survive. So much for the physical approach to our survival."

In several ways, these thoughts are too quick. In the first place, unless there is reason to think that the case has some basis in reality, it cannot begin to pose a threat to the physical approach. For this approach, it will be remembered, is offered as adequate only relative to the general truth of our world view. And perhaps this case is not, in any relevant way, a realistically possible example. If not, then citing it may provide no real challenge. Although worth noticing, this first point of reply might not be a very strong one. And, in any case, it is not very illuminating.

Fortunately, a second point appears to be better on both counts. Usually, when we think of an ordinary thing's physical continuity, we think only in terms of the continuity of its constituting matter through ordinary space with respect to time. Usually, we may say, we think only in terms of *narrow physical continuity*. But, perhaps there may be more to an ordinary individual's physical continuity. For example, in addition to ordinary space, there may be other physical dimensions in which, during a certain interval, the individual's matter exists. When there is this more exotic continuity for that matter, just as much as when there is the more ordinary kind, we may say that both the matter itself, and also any ordinary object constituted of that matter, has *wide physical continuity*.

Especially when thinking in terms of this wide continuity, we have a highly liberal, or very wide, understanding of matter itself. On narrower conceptions, matter may pertain to a portion of physical reality only when it is in certain states. On our wide conception, however, some matter will be any portion of physical reality, regardless of state, that is suitable for constituting (wholly or largely) physical individuals.

In relation to this notion of wide physical continuity, the problematic example is left largely unspecified. If it is specified in certain ways, then the original matter, or least a goodly portion of it, will exist throughout the brief episode. On one favorable specification, for example, that matter, always in some suitable form, may go on a trip into some further physical dimensions, even while not, in any ordinary spatial way, moving from the salient spatial region. On such a favorable specification, the person constituted of that matter may also exist throughout. In such a specified circumstance, you will survive the episode.

The problematic example may also be specified in other ways. On certain other specifications, it will be clear that, at the end of the brief episode, none of the original matter is there. Quite abruptly, there will be present only some precisely similar, but numerically distinct, matter. For example, as an absolute physical miracle, the original matter may simply cease to exist, completely and forever. Just a bit later, as another absolute miracle, there may begin to exist, *ex nihilo*, some completely new matter that is, as it happens, just like the old and just where the old was last located. In this quite different specific circumstance, you will not survive the episode.

We do not need to go into these matters in very much detail. Rather, for us, it is enough to explain the main *differences* between our own survival, on the one hand, and, on the other, the survival of other sorts of ordinary concrete individuals, like bushes, ships and rocks. Now, as far as the continuity of a person's constituent matter goes, the cited case finds close parallels in cases concerning these other individuals. Insofar as any of these cases shows any need for continuity of matter, or of physical parts, the whole group of cases will show an equal need across the board. Any such widespread need is of little consequence to our investigation. For us, the only interruptions of much consequence will be those that, although they let bushes and rocks survive, terminate us people. In other words, we are properly interested only in those physical interruptions that are appropriately *selective*. Because an interruption of matter relative to ordinary space is wholly *unselective*, in an inquiry like ours it can be discounted. By a standard of reckoning most relevant to present inquiry, the widely continuous presence of matter will provide us, as well as bushes, ships, and rocks, with physical continuity that is adequate for us to survive. Because this is so, there is nothing in the offered example that means a defect in the physical approach to our survival.

A certain flexibility may attach to the physical account that might be well worth noting: When engaged in theoretical studies we tend to overlook the fact that often we treat continuity as a matter of degree. For, when thinking of continuity theoretically, its ideal cases are salient. But, like many other ideals, in concrete reality this one, too, is rarely if ever realized. We readily adjust our thinking to the pervasive circumstance: What we count as continuous is, in the case at hand, what we count as being sufficiently close to the ideal case for the dominant interests of that context.[6]

A physicist, for example, may accept a theory of light according to which light is emitted from a source in discrete units. In a context where he most wants to express the theory clearly, he may deny that there is a signal continuously coming from a certain source. In a different context, by contrast, he may affirm that the signal was continuous: Without interruption, the signal was indicating that it was unsafe to open a certain door during a certain period. What is close enough to the ideal case for (the main interests of) the second context is not close enough for the different (main interests of the) first context.

Harsh reality may all but force us to adopt lower standards than we might otherwise like. Up to certain points, which ones depending on context, we go along with what reality dictates. In the physicist's second context, that went on with the treatment of the light signal. This may go on, as well, with questions regarding the continuity of ordinary individuals and their constituting matter, ourselves included.[7] Accordingly, even while we might insist on our survival requiring the physical continuity of our physical realizers, we may, at the same time, create contexts where the standards for this physical continuity are obligingly low. In ever so many contexts, then, we may understand the physical approach as allowing for our survival.

---

6. For philosophers, the locus classicus for considerations like these is David Lewis, "Scorekeeping in a Language Game," *Journal of Philosophical Logic*, 1979. In my *Philosophical Relativity*, University of Minnesota Press, 1984, there is an extended treatment of these matters.

7. An especially intriguing example of this sort is offered by Eddy Zemach on page 212 of his marvelously provocative paper, "Looking Out for Number One," *Philosophy and Phenomenological Research*, 1987: "Let us say that an elementary particle "flashes" in and out of existence, on the average, a million times a second. Given the number of elementary particles in the brain we can calculate how often all its particles go out of existence simultaneously. Suppose that this happens once a year. I therefore get a wholly new brain every year." Being charitable to this

4. The Derivative but Great Importance of Physical Continuity

To you, at least, your existence at future times is a matter of considerable importance. Moreover, the importance of your future existence seems to be quite basic, not dependent upon some other fact being an important one. That there should be much physical continuity of whatever realizes your psychology, by contrast, may seem to be a very unimportant fact. Why should you, or anyone, care about *that*? This sort of thinking may get one to believe that physical continuity must have little to do with our survival.

For our survival, whatever importance physical continuity may have is not basic. Or, if it is best to treat these questions as matters of degree, then such importance is not basic to even a moderately high degree. All of this must be admitted. In other words, it must be admitted that, as far as personal survival is concerned, whatever importance physical continuity may have is derivative. But although this importance may be highly derivative, it might, at the same time, be very great.

All of this may seem paradoxical. This apparent paradox might get some to overlook, or to deny, the importance of physical continuity. To remove the air of paradox, we want a derivation of how it is that, as a matter of fact, physical continuity is crucial to our survival. There follows a derivation consisting of two main parts. Especially as regards the second of these parts, there are propositions that are to be taken, not as true in any wholly *a priori*, entirely universal, or purely conceptual way, but only as true relative to the general truth of our view of the world. Consequently, the derivation as a whole should be taken only in this rather modest way.

.The first part of our relativized derivation concerns our existence at different times: It will never be true that someone exists, and then later does not exist, and then still later exists again. This condition of "no interruption" applies across all plausible metaphysical conceptions in which we may find a place. Even on wholly subjective conceptions, where each of us exists only in his own time, nobody will survive an interruption with respect to time. Perhaps this condition is not absolute. But, if it is not, then, at the least, the

---

passage, we ban ourselves from asking many sensible questions. Even so, contextual features serve to block Zemach's conclusion, as well as any relevantly similar conclusions.

Treating "continuous" as sensitive to context, we may say that, just as I may draw a continuous line with a pencil, despite microscopic areas where there are no particles of carbon, so, even in such a circumstance, there may be the physically continuous realization of my psychology. Just as there are not interruptions in the pencil line every trillionth of a millimeter, so there will not be interruptions in my organs, or in my life, every year.

condition provides a very strong guideline for any adequate account of our survival.

There is more to this point than the claim that, as a condition on our existence, none of us will ever happen to have a temporal interruption. Further, the condition of no temporal gap itself must be grounded in *real processes* that, as most naturally and relevantly described, *ensure that* there will be no interruption.[8] To help clarify this strong condition, it may be useful to consider a quite hypothetical example: Consider a process whereby all of the matter of a person suddenly was annihilated. Causally unconnected with this first process, there might be another process that caused a material person, one of just the same sort, to be in just the place where that matter was annihilated. The new matter may be imposed on this place *immediately* upon the annihilation of the old matter. Fantastic as it seems, all of this is a complete coincidence. In such a situation, there will be two people, one there immediately after the other. This is very clear.

When properly developed in this strong way, our condition of no interruption yields that clear result: If, contrary to the condition, there was one person throughout, then the main process involving her would be a total process consisting of the two processes mentioned above. Because there is no causal connection between those two processes, the total process consisting of them both is one that, as most naturally and relevantly described, *will allow for an interruption* in the existence of any person that might be there throughout the period. On our offered condition, however, no process can work in so fortuitous a way if it is to involve the survival of a person.[9] So there must be two people in this situation, not one person throughout.

Similar propositions appear true, as well, about many other ordinary concrete individuals, like rocks, shirts, trees, and mice. In this way, ordinary concrete individuals differ from ordinary events. For example, unlike a rock itself, the erosion of a rock may be discontinuous: There may be times when the rock is being eroded, later times when it is not, and still later the erosion may occur again. And, unlike a student herself, the education of a stu-

8. I failed to see this very important point until forced to observe it by comments from David Lewine, who opened my eyes.

9. Compare this with a parallel point about factual knowledge: In knowing that something is so, it cannot be accidental, or coincidental, that I am right about its being so. Further, in order for there to be no undermining accident, in the case of many sorts of propositions, there should be the right sort of real (causal) connections between the thing that is so and me, the putative knower. As I have been given to understand, the first of these two related points was made long ago by George Santayana. Not then knowing anything of Santayana, I made heavy use of the idea, possibly a bit too heavy, in my paper, "An Analysis of Factual Knowledge," *The Journal of Philosophy*, 1968. Regarding the second point, in the contemporary literature a seminal paper is Alvin Goldman's "A Causal Theory of Knowing," *The Journal of Philosophy*, 1967.

dent may have temporal interruptions. In this way, ordinary concrete individuals may differ, too, from ordinary entities that are more abstract: Unlike a soldier himself, a platoon of soldiers may exist, then may be disbanded and not exist and, then, perhaps called into existence by some order, may exist again.

However intuitive this proposition may seem concerning various other sorts of ordinary concrete individuals, it seems most forceful in the case of us subjects of experience. However clear it may seem for us people, that will never be as clear as one might like. For this initial proposal is both so strong and so general that one must always suspect that it might be untrue. This suspicion need not unsettle us: Even if there is some failure of the proposition offered, the idea behind it may be on the right track. In our derivation, we may substitute for the claim now offered a weaker proposition along the same general lines. Already acknowledged and now repeated, the strong generality offered is meant only as a guideline with which more specific, more guarded proposals should be in general agreement.

The second part of the relativized derivation begins with this observation. There is no single occurrent mental phenomenon, such as a conscious self-referential thought, that any of us has at every moment of her existence. What we may say, more weakly, is that, at every moment of her existence, each of us has some basic *mental capacities*. How might a person's mental capacities importantly figure in her survival?

In our thought about ordinary individuals, we employ many common distinctions concerning their properties. But, in our scheme of things, certain of these distinctions are more important than others. Paramount among these are a family of dichotomies whose conspicuous members include the distinction between the conscious and the non-conscious and that between the mental and the non-mental. The key positive properties thus distinguished—mentality, consciousness, and their ilk—have a special place in our thought about ordinary concrete individuals. In line with this, our common principles for individuating ordinary entities may reflect the importance of the noted distinctions: A person's mental capacities may be more central to her survival than any even remotely comparable property of a rock, be it a capacity or a disposition, is to the survival of that rock. And they may be more important to her survival, even, than any comparable properties of a (living) tree, or a (living) brain, are to that tree, or to that brain. Accordingly, what is needed for your survival is the future existence not just of basic mental capacities that are precisely like yours, but of your own particular basic mental capacities.

How are a particular person's basic mental capacities to exist throughout a certain period of time? This takes some doing. After all, each of our core psychologies is exactly the same; all of my basic mental capacities are precisely similar to all of yours.

My basic mental capacities will exist from now until a future time only if, from now until then, they are continuously realized in some physical entity or, at the least, in an appropriate succession of physical entities. In largest measure, this is just a brute fact about the relations between myself, mentality and the objective world order. Now, while both of us are similarly objective physical beings, and while both of us have precisely similar basic mental capacities, you and I are different people. So, at least during some of the time that you exist, and perhaps during all of it, your mental capacities must be realized in one physical entity, or one succession of them, while my mental capacities are realized in another.

Moreover, if my basic mental capacities are to be realized at a future time, as contrasted with capacities just like mine, then there must be sufficient physical continuity between the physical realizer of them now and the physical realizer of them at that future time. In line with this, there must be the continuous physical realization of them by this present physical realizer or, at the least, by a physically continuous succession of realizers beginning with this present one now.

Now we put the parts together: For you to exist at a future time, you must exist, continuously, from now until then. For that to be so, there must be the continuous existence, from now until then, of your particular basic mental capacities. For there to be the continuous existence of just those capacities, there must be, in this wholly or largely physical world of ours, the continuous physical realization of them in a physically continuous realizer or, at the least, in a physically continuous succession of physical realizers. Consequently, for you to exist at a future time, there must be appropriate physical continuity.

The importance of physical continuity for our survival is, thus, derivative rather than basic. Indeed, it is derivative in two ways. First, the importance of physical continuity is *indirect*. Physical continuity *provides for* what is more directly important: the future existence of an individual person's basic mental capacities and, more directly important still, the future existence of that person herself. Second, the great importance of physical continuity is *relative*: It is only relative to the general truth of our view of the world that physical continuity has any importance for our survival. Because we may be confident that, in broad outline, this view is correct, we may believe that physical continuity is of very great importance to our survival, however derivative, indirect and relative that importance may be.

At times, it is hard to believe that anything so crucial to our survival should be of such derivative importance. Then it may be thought that, for this reason, physical continuity cannot really be so very important. Some may thus be moved completely to reject the physical approach. Perhaps this is yet another motivating factor toward the psychological approach to our survival, the salient alternative. But, like other factors, this one, too, provides no good reason.

5. Survival and the Realization of Psychological Capacities

The physical approach to our survival must make very heavy use, and perhaps rather subtle use, of the notion of a mental *capacity*. Without an appropriate treatment of capacities, the physical approach is little better than a bad joke. This wants some discussion.

In our common thought, we make some important distinctions concerning the capacity to think: First, there is the very obvious distinction between having the capacity to think and, in contrast, having the capacity to *create or produce something that has* the capacity to think. Some entities have both of these capacities: A super scientist of the future may have, not only the capacity for thought, but the capacity to create something with that capacity. By using materials in her laboratory, she may, for example, produce a duplicate of herself. Other entities have only one of these capacities: Especially if she is biologically sterile, a scientist of the present day has only the capacity to think, not the capacity to create a thinker. Other entities may have only the latter capacity. The unthinking devices that engage in the taping processes will be of this sort.

Second, there is the slightly less obvious distinction between an entity having the capacity to think and, in contrast, an entity having *the potential to have* that capacity.[10] A fertilized egg has the potential to have the capacity to rea-

---

10. As Roy Sorensen points out, these ideas relate to the distinction drawn by C. D. Broad among levels of "higher order dispositions." So, going beyond the zygote, still another thing may lack the potential to have, or to develop, mental capacities, but it may have the potential to have, or to develop, *that* potential. And so it goes.

In the free spirit of pure inquiry, try this thought on for size: Paralleling what I am calling the physical approach to our survival, there may be an infinite hierarchy of nicely ordered physical approaches. (And, then, too, one might mention the "infinite, all-encompassing" approach that, at once, puts forth the entire hierarchy.) Now, noticing that I already am a person, I see no need, in giving an account of my survival, to go any higher than the possession of the psychological capacities themselves. But I am open to the possibility that ascent might be required. At any rate, the guiding spirit of all of the hierarchically ordered treatments is the same: Whatever level a given approach favors, it focuses on the physically continuous realization of the level's dispositions that are directed at, or that concern, (core) psychology.

Applicable to all sorts of capacities, not just psychological ones, Broad puts forth the kernel idea in his *Examination of McTaggart's Philosophy*, Volume I, Cambridge University Press, 1933, pp. 266–7.

son, but does not have the capacity itself. A person in deep sleep, by contrast, has the capacity to think, not merely the potential to have that capacity.

Although it is not so readily recognized, a third distinction may be equally important. Concerning certain matters of degree, this is the distinction between reckoning mental capacities according to strict standards and, by contrast, reckoning by lenient standards. To see the importance of this distinction, we consider actual cases of very deep and prolonged coma. As is obvious, these cases are well endowed with biological continuity. But is there much continuous realization of psychological capacities as well? At first glance, it may seem that there is not: Relative to *everyday standards* for reckoning capacities, when she is in a deep coma, a person will not have the capacity for much of, or perhaps even for any of, a mental life. However, this appearance might be deceptive. Although it may sound paradoxical to say so, in these matters, our ordinary standards for having mental capacities may be very demanding standards.

If these strict everyday standards are employed in evaluating judgments of personal survival, we might make incorrect judgments. We might hold, incorrectly, that a person may exist even while she has no mental capacities. Or, perhaps even worse, we might hold that, when a person's brain and body are in a deeply comatose state, that person does not exist. Such incorrect contentions may prove especially embarrassing in those few cases where, beyond all expectations, a person comes out of a very deep and prolonged coma, awakening to enjoy much complex conscious thought.

There are other ways of reckoning a person's mental capacities that are very much more lenient. When we reckon our capacities in these ways, the lenient standards we employ may be more relevant to questions of strict survival. Judgments made in accordance with these standards may conflict with what we say in everyday discourse. But perhaps there is no serious conflict between our more pragmatic assertions and our more reflective statements.

A person who is in what we ordinarily call an *irreversible coma* has a highly structured living brain that may not be all that different from your brain now. Do we believe that a person with such a brain is completely without psychological capacities? Only relative to a practical but possibly superficial way of reckoning such capacities can we confidently give a positive answer.

Then what do we mean when, in everyday life, we speak of a person going into an irreversible coma? For the most part, what we mean is this: Unfortunately, things have happened to this person so that, without the aid of appropriate intervention—be it surgical, electrical, chemical, a combination thereof, or whatever—she will never again think or experience; at the very least, she will never again do so in a conscious manner. Our present medical science cannot provide a helpful intervention and, in typical cases, we are nowhere near being able to do so. Relative to both the course impersonal nature will take and to any course that our society can soon provide, the person in this coma will never be conscious again.

When making common assertions about people in very deep coma, we mean little more than that mental capacities are to be reckoned in this pragmatic way. Inasmuch as the medical resources of the near future look to be quite limited, and particular human beings do not last for centuries, this evaluation may be highly appropriate. In many cases, I suggest, it is only relative to some such quick but severe reckoning that a coma is confidently regarded as irreversible. It is only relative to such a standard that we confidently consider a person to have lost all mental capacities and, thus, to have ceased to exist.

Compare the victim of deep coma with a hypothetical unfortunate whose brain has been turned into a "lump of live jelly," perhaps by some powerfully destructive radiation. In this other case, there is now entirely lacking such internal structure as is relevant to the support of any thought or experience. There is only the persistence of a living mass of flesh of typical brain weight with typical gross brain structure. Now, in virtually any context for their use and in virtually any sense that the terms might reasonably be assigned, perhaps it will be true to say that this person has *lost all of her mental capacities*. If this is so, then the person with the jelly brain will be importantly different from many people said to be in irreversible coma.

In these matters, we might be dealing with large differences in the logical space of possible interventions that alter the brain. With the person who is in the deep coma, there might be certain *comparatively* minor alterations of her brain whose occurrence would have her mental capacities brought to a point where they may be quite readily exercised. With the person whose brain has been turned to jelly, by contrast, the only processes that will do that involve enormously major alterations. As far as reckoning the presence of mental capacities, these enormously altering processes might be more like the construction of a new working brain, out of otherwise useless matter at hand, than they are like the alterations required for the person in a deep coma.

If these considerations are well taken, then, as far as having mental capacities is concerned, a person whose brain has been turned to jelly is more like a person whose brain has been annihilated altogether than she is like a person in a deeply comatose state. In such an eventuality, for the lack of mental capacities, the person whose brain was jellied will no longer exist, while, for having such capacities, the person in a deep coma will still exist. What is very unfortunate is that, given the limitations of science in the present and the not very distant future, the coma patient does not have these capacities to a high enough degree to be of any use or value to her.

6. How Important for My Survival Is My Capacity for Life?

Much of the import of the physical approach may be brought out by a few futuristic examples. While some of these have already been presented, they may be usefully juxtaposed now with others not yet encountered. For drama, we may think of these cases as offers that doctors might make to their badly diseased patients.

Taking up the thread of the just previous section, we begin with a case of *coma induction*: According to this first offer, a diseased patient, who would otherwise die within a couple of years, is placed in a state of *total coma*. When the organism is in this complete comatose state, the progress of the disease is effectively halted. As well, with the onset of this coma, all mental activity ceases. With all of the required materials supplied as needed, the brain serves only to direct the lower life functions: respiration of air, circulation of blood, and so on. This may continue for years. During this time, a cure for the disease is found. After the cure is found, the completely comatose organism is made comatose no more: thought and experience once again are supported by that organism's brain. There certainly is *a* person now, one with the original patient's brain and body, a person who is ever so like the original patient. The cure is immediately applied to him. Consequently, he leads a rather normal life, not for only a couple of years, but for twenty years or more.

Will a person survive this process of coma induction; is the person at the end the very same individual as the person in whom total coma was induced? It is quite clear indeed that a person will survive the process just described. Why is that? Most of the answer is rather obvious, and can be succinctly stated: Especially as regards factors deemed important for survival, the case is only marginally different from actual cases of coma followed by recovery.

This case abounds with factors important for a person's survival. What appear as the most important of these may usefully be divided into two salient groups: There are the factors concerning the continuity of the *life processes* of the being in question and, in contrast, there are those concerning the continuity of his *mental capacities*. For a person's survival, might one sort of factor really be much more important than the other?

We recall the case of super freezing and thawing. In this process, the endangered person is instantaneously and completely frozen, or very nearly so. All of her molecules, we may imagine, remain in the same relative arrangement for years. When an adequate cure for the illness is discovered, the person's body, including her brain, is instantaneously unfrozen, or thawed; it is thus returned to its state when last alive. As a result of the thaw, there emerges a person who is, all told, at least as much like the person who was frozen as you now are like you were an hour ago. The cure is then effectively applied to her. Is the offer of this procedure a genuine offer of survival?

Indeed, it is; the person who emerges from this process is nobody but the original person. This positive response is very nearly as strong as our response to coma induction. There is only a very slight difference.

Why is there this difference? Most of the answer is relatively simple: The case of coma induction involves the continuity of life, in much the same way and to much the same degree as do certain actual cases of survival; by contrast, the case of freezing and thawing does not. To be sure, when he is super frozen, it is *not true* that the person is *dead*. Still, it might be that there is no determinate truth, one way or the other, as to whether the person then is living. But, if it is not determinately true that the person is not living, then, in such a state of complete stasis, it is not (determinately) true, either, that the person is living. Nonetheless, we confidently judge that freezing and thawing allows for our survival. Apparently, we are prepared to forgo a certain feature of normal survival that, antecedently, we may have thought was crucial for us determinately to survive from an earlier to a later time: We are prepared to forgo its being determinately true that, from the earlier until the later time, the person in question is living, or is alive.

For our survival, the continuous realization of mental capacities is more important than continuously being alive. But another comparison also should be made and judged: When super frozen, although I might not be determinately alive, I then may yet have the *capacity to be alive*, or the *capacity for life*. Let us not, then, compare any occurrent processes with some mere capacities. Rather, perhaps more fairly and more instructively, let us compare one capacity, or one group of capacities, with another: As compared with my basic mental capacities, how important for my survival is my capacity to be alive?

Perhaps there is some sense of 'living,' or of 'being alive,' according to which it is logically sufficient for an entity to be living, or to be alive, that the entity have some mental capacities. If so, then, when understood as involving such a sense, our question will not be a very interesting one. Accordingly, in what follows, I will understand these expressions in a sense that yields no such tight logical relation between being alive and having a psychology.

Although it is notorious that there is no very clear distinction between the two that is entirely general, in this particular instance, as in some others, perhaps a useful attempt might be made to consider the conceptual aspects of the present question apart from the more "worldly" aspects. To do that, we will simply assume that there are certain non-organic bionic structures that, with an impressive dual effect, may be joined with various parts of my living human brain: On the one hand, the metallic complexes will do nothing to sustain a judgment that I am alive; to the contrary, the more of me that is composed of the structures, the less of me will then be alive. On the other hand, for any significant portion of my brain, there is a certain bionic structure that may replace it, with the result that the very same dispositional psychology realized organically before will, right after the replacement, be realized by an integrated structure. And, after a suitable sequence of such replacements has been completed, we are supposing, all of my psychology will be realized in an entirely bionic inorganic structure. Perhaps most notably, the capacity for conscious experience will be so realized.

Suppose that, very gradually and over much time, thousandths of my brain are sequentially replaced by suitable bionic structures. The parts replaced are killed. Originally there will be a brain that is entirely organic; finally, there will be only a brain that is entirely bionic. During the brief periods when replacements are made, there will be 99.9% of a brain. Between replacements, of course, there will be 100% of a brain. Except at the first and the last steps, it will be an integrated brain. When there is only 99.9% present, the least there ever is, there will be a slight loss as regards my distinctive psychology. But, even at those times, there will be no loss of core psychology. Moreover, as I, the patient, can quite directly tell, at any stage when there is not deep sleep induced, there is a rich variety of conscious experience.

At the end of a year, with all replacements made, there is a person with an entirely bionic brain. This brain then may be removed from my body and kept functioning well in some other way. The body may be killed. The person may then be given a suitable bionic body. Unless we consider there to be a life process of mentation, not a good idea in the present context, this person is not involved in, nor can he then partake in, any of the main processes of life. Indeed, reckoned by any but the most lenient sort of standard, this person does not even have the capacity for life.

Given the truth of these strong "worldly" assumptions, will I survive this bionic replacement process? It seems very clear that I will indeed survive. Although I will still exist, I will not then have even the capacity for life. At the very least, it will not be determinately true that I then have such a capacity. Fair enough, I may then be a person who, through a long and precisely integrated series of further "opposite" replacements, may be *converted* so that I will (again) have this capacity. But that is a very different thing from actually having the capacity to be alive.

If fatally ill, a person may be made an offer of such mentally supportive bionic transformation. For some people, this may not be a very attractive or desirable offer. Nonetheless, as a pain avoidance test confirms, this would be a genuine offer of survival. Moreover, if there is a later conversion back to being normally organic, and if the interlude of being bionic is pretty short, most of us may find the offer not only genuine but even quite desirable. At any rate, in such a case as this, it is determinately true that I will continue to exist.

In our positive judgments of our survival, we are prepared to forgo quite a lot of what obtains in the ordinary cases. As even coma induction indicates, we will do without any occurrent thought processes, non-conscious as well as conscious. Freezing and thawing makes that clearer. Moreover, as that freezing process indicates, we will do without its being (determinately) true that we remain living. Lastly, as the recent case of bionic replacements indicates, providing that the structure of the world is cooperative, we will even do without (its being determinately true that we have) the capacity for life.

These thoughts reflect well on our formulation of the physical approach to our survival. As formulated, this approach requires only physically continuous realization of basic mental capacities. It does not require, for our survival, that there continue to be realized any (logically independent) capacity to be alive. As our discussion indicates, a proper formulation will make only the first, and not the second, of these requirements.[11]

7. Physical Continuity and the Gradual Replacement of Matter

As I am using it, "physical continuity" is a technical term. Although certain previous remarks help show the meaning I wish the expression to have, a lot more is needed in that direction. Thus I now will try to indicate some *main aspects* of what counts toward an ordinary individual's having much physical continuity. The *first aspect* concerns the *gradual replacement of an object's matter*.

In actuality, except for my nerve cells, all of my cells, with almost all the matter they ever contain, are replaced every several years. Moreover, while many nerve cells in my brain stay with me from birth until death, the matter of these cells itself is constantly changing. Eventually, almost all the matter of each cell is replaced. Despite all this replacement, there is a certain continuity of my matter. For there is a fairly evenly gradual replacement of old matter by new. As regards the replacement of matter, both me and my brain have enjoyed quite a lot of physical continuity.

What would happen to me if I became involved with replacements much more rapid, or much more abrupt, than the ordinary ones? Perhaps a certain abruptness of replacement will do me in. But the rapidity of replacement is not in itself an important factor: As long as they are relevantly even and gradual rather than uneven and abrupt, I can survive the most rapid of complete serial replacements.

11. As I see it, considerations like these provide one of the best reasons for abandoning biologically oriented approaches to our survival. In the contemporary literature, perhaps the leading exponent of a biological treatment is David Wiggins, *Sameness and Substance*, Harvard University Press, 1980. A far more radical approach along biological lines, brilliantly provocative even if literally incredible, is offered in Peter van Inwagen, *Material Beings*, Cornell University Press, forthcoming.

Let us suppose that an exotic procedure is applied to me so that all of my matter, including all the matter of my brain, is replaced in a tenth of a second. In order that the example appear more realistic, perhaps we might suppose that I am first super frozen; only then is the replacement of matter imposed in a suitably inclusive spiral; finally, the person composed of the new matter is super thawed. Anyway, at any very brief time during the crucial tenth of a second, such as a millionth of a second, almost all of the matter present was also present just before, during the just previous millionth. So there is a very rapid, but nonetheless quite gradual, replacement of matter.

Will I survive this rapid procedure; will the matter really flow through *me*? Or, on the contrary, will I expire when exposed to this process; after a certain amount of matter has been replaced, will further matter flow, not through me, but only through a region that, before much of the flow occurred, I will have occupied? Our dominant response is quite strong: I will survive; the matter will indeed be flowing through *me* and not only through a region once occupied by me. Applying our test of future pain avoidance confirms this idea: Because the person at the end of this rapid material changeover is me, in advance, I will do much to protect this person from future torture.

In the case just considered, the replacement of a person's matter was very rapid, but the material changeover occurred in an even and a gradual way. In other cases the changeover is much more uneven and abrupt. As is important to note, this abruptness may include the matter of my brain: First, I may be extremely well frozen. Then, every fifteen minutes, a different quarter of my brain is replaced with a newly made duplicate, as may also occur with my body. At the end of this hour, a person is successfully unfrozen. This person will have a brain and a body that is, if not identical with, then at least enormously like, the original brain and body. At the very least, this person will be just like I was right before the procedure began.

Will I survive this replacement procedure? No, I will not exist at the end. Vaguely and briefly, the reason for the failure is that too *much* relevant matter is replaced too *abruptly*: There is too large and abrupt a replacement of the matter that, most directly, realizes my core psychology. Because of this, there is *not sufficient physical continuity* of an entity that might continuously realize *my* basic mental capacities. Thus, my core psychology ceases to exist and, so too, do I.

How might other sorts of ordinary entities fare: a brain, a tree, a ship, and a rock? Just as I will not, none of these things will survive rapid replacement of material parts anywhere near as large as quarters. What about the very rapid replacement of billionths? Unlike me, a typical anonymous rock will not survive this changeover. Having no particular function, either in humanly social terms or in more natural ones, the identity of a rock may be tied too closely to the matter that composes it. Very slow changeovers might perhaps be all right, as may occur in certain geological processes. But physical continuity, however great, will not make up for a great increase in speed over the natural norms.[12]

With a ship, a tree, and a brain, it seems that they will make it through. The first is of a sort members of which have a characteristic use or function. The second is of a sort living members of which partake of characteristic processes of life. The third is of a sort living members of which typically have characteristic functions and also partake of certain of the life processes. In these somewhat different ways, these features apparently serve them in good stead in these matters. Because they have more of a tie to function and process, these entities are less closely tied to their constituent matter than are rocks.

8. Physical Continuity and Constitutional Cohesion

For an ordinary physical entity, a *second aspect* of physical continuity concerns *constitutional cohesion*. Looking at the aspect negatively, it concerns the separation of an ordinary physical entity's matter, or the separation of its physical parts. When I speak of this separation, I mean it to be quite complete: When the parts are separated, there are no distinctive causal forces, or anything of the kind, continuing to maintain any relationship between them. A good example may be the separation of a wooden ship into its planks, then widely dispersed. Except for forces like universal gravitation, which are wholly indiscriminate, nothing physical then serves to unite those planks into any relevant physical whole. Another good example is the grinding of a plank into sawdust, and the scattering of the tiny bits to the winds. In both the case of the ship and the case of the plank, there is a loss of constitutional cohesion and, thus, of physical continuity.

Other things equal, the more constitutional cohesion there is for the parts of a physical entity, the more constitutional cohesion there is for the whole entity. And, other things equal, the larger the parts for which there is much constitutional cohesion, the more constitutional cohesion there is for the whole entity that the parts compose. An example illustrates our suggested usage: A certain solid ball may be broken into two roughly equal parts, even while there is a very high degree of physical continuity, throughout the epi-

---

12. Although I strongly disagree with much that it contains, I strongly recommend the stimulating discussion in Chapter 7 of Eli Hirsch's book, *The Concept of Identity*, Oxford University Press, 1982. Also very well worth reading and, by my lights, very far from the truth, there is Daniel Kolak and Raymond Martin's provocative "Personal Identity and Causality: Becoming Unglued," *American Philosophical Quarterly*, 1987. On the other side of these issues, see Chris Swoyer's refreshingly sensible "Causation and Identity," *Midwest Studies in Philosophy*, 1984.

sode, for each of these two parts. By contrast, a second, precisely similar ball may be broken into a thousand roughly equal, much smaller parts. In every way logically compatible with this stipulated contrast, the situation of the two balls is precisely the same. Then there will be greater constitutional cohesion, and so greater physical continuity, for the first of these two balls than there is for the second.

For ordinary corporeal entities that are more "specifically" structured than balls, including ships, clocks, trees, mice and human people, there is more to their survival than their having sufficiently large parts that each has a high enough degree of physical continuity: Certain parts of a clock, for example, may be more central to that clock's survival than other parts are. Even so, constitutional cohesion and physical continuity may be just as important for the survival of these objects as they are for balls: Other things equal, and below the very clear cases of survival, the more constitutional cohesion there is for the more central parts of a certain clock, the more there is that counts toward that clock's surviving a process of physical change.

From a purely logical point of view, however small the parts of any ordinary physical entity, be it ball, ship, clock or tree, those parts may later be joined together. As with these other sorts of ordinary concrete entities, there are ever so many ways in which a person's parts may be separated for awhile and then be joined together as before. For questions of personal identity, however, ever so many of these ways will be uninteresting: Uninterestingly, provided that the rest is kept going all right in the interim period, I will survive the separation of my lungs and heart from the rest of me followed by their rejoining. By contrast, certain other ways of separating and joining my parts will be of greater interest. The most conspicuous among these will involve the separation of my brain into parts that are roughly equal in their contribution to the realization of mentality.

Suppose my brain is removed from my head and that, all at once, it is then divided into four roughly equivalent quarters. For a goodly while, the quarters may each be nurtured in separate vats. About equal in size, each quarter did about as much as any of the others toward realizing my psychology. But as we may suppose, by itself, none of the quarters will come close to realizing the core psychology of even a dog, let alone the core of a person. After a while, my brain-quarters may be rejoined and put back in my head.

The most vivid way to imagine these operations is with the brain tissue alive and functioning well throughout. But for somewhat increased realism, we might want to hold things still, so that the brain-parts don't lose any needed synchronization. We may do this by, first, super freezing the patient. Only then will the separating operations be performed. Each brain-part may be placed in its own chamber. Later, the frozen parts are suitably rejoined, and suitably placed in the still frozen head. Finally, when all of the tissue is almost instantly thawed, a person ever so like the original awakens.

Will I survive this operation? It is clear that I will. From a perspective of self-concern, I will do much to protect the person at the end who, with the brain quarters joined, can fully feel great pain.

Appropriately understood, the physical approach yields my survival in this case. For one thing, my brain survives the process. So there exists throughout that which was, when it was whole, the realizer of my core psychology. But, more than this, we may best think of my quartered brain *as continuing to realize my mental capacities*. For these capacities to be exercised, the quarters need only be rejoined. But the proper placement of just four heavily contributive, and highly distinctive, pieces requires no terribly complex or difficult process; it is not much like constructing a new brain out of my present brain's matter. On all but the most bizarrely severe standard for reckoning when entities realize capacities, my quartered brain realizes my mental capacities. Because this is so, I will exist when my brain is in separated quarters.

There is a spectrum of cases here, which we may call *the spectrum of separating and joining*. At one end, we may place the case of the brain quartering. Partly because it is clear that this is not a case of fission, it is clear that this example has not more than only one person in its middle period. Partly for that reason, this is a good choice for the spectrum's topmost case. For our operative procedures, we then apply this general directive: Going beyond any given case, in the next example a brain part envisioned as one of the largest for the just previous case will be divided into roughly equal parts. So, in the second case from the top, there are three separated quarters and also two separated eighths. In the case after that, there are two quarters and four eighths; and so it goes. Eventually, by the time we have a bit over ten billion salient little brain-parts, we have my brain separated into all of its component neurons, or nerve cells, each with a group of glia, or support cells.

My response to this case of cellular scattering is that I will not survive. This response of mine is not a very confident one. This seems to be the typical reaction. Before proceeding to further cases in the spectrum, I would like to consider what may lie behind the unconfident response to this case.

When we respond that there is no personal survival, we may reckon that the scattered neurons do not realize my basic mental capacities. Accordingly, we think of the rejoining of these little bits as a quite special, complex and refined process. We think of the rejoining more in this way than as a confluence of parts that are naturally suited to working together. We play down the complexity and the distinctiveness of the individual neurons, even as we emphasize the complexity and distinctiveness of their mutual arrangement in the whole brain. When we do this, we think of the rejoining as being much like the creation of a brain from scratch. In thinking of the situation in this way, we may be applying a pretty high standard for judging when there is an entity that realizes a person's mental capacities. In most contexts, such a standard may be the correct one.

Although all of that may be true, we may not always feel comfortable applying such a high standard. After all, just as there are upwards of ten billion neurons in the normal adult human brain, many of which are quite distinctively arranged, so there are upwards of ten billion atoms in the normal developed human neuron, many of which are also quite distinctively arranged. So this case is really very far from one where a brain is created from undistinctive atoms. True enough, we usually look at the case negatively, as when we think that, alas, a certain glass is about half empty. But we may also look at it more positively, as when we think that, all right, the glass is about half full. Apparently, sometimes we want to do just that.

As just implied, there are many cases further down in our spectrum. Over ten billion further cases each involve the halving of each of the (frozen glia and) neurons. Twenty billion cases beyond those involve the halving of each of the frozen neuron halves. Eventually we get to a case where my brain is separated into millions of billions of potentially constituent molecules. Very large molecules, such as those of DNA, may each be decomposed into many smaller molecules. After a great deal of complex construction, all of these small molecules may be later rejoined to have their original places in the final arrangement. In almost all contexts, very few will think that, even when they are widely separated, the small molecules jointly, and continuously, realize my capacity for thought and for experience. Just so, few will think that I will survive this more radical scattering procedure.

Where are we to draw the line here, between survival and failure to survive? Or, not much easier, where are we to draw a line between fully determinate survival and indeterminacy in the matter? There is a truly enormous area of uncertainty here; there is an ocean of ignorance. Even as it discloses great ignorance on our part, this spectrum may be philosophically useful. It may remind us of our deep belief that, as gradual beings in a gradual world, we must be demarcated by our own conventions. For our survival, physical continuity for larger and more central parts is better than continuity only for smaller and less central parts. Since nothing else can do it, and something must, it is just our conventions that decide, well enough, when there is enough of this continuity for one of us to survive.

As regards the aspect of constitutional cohesion, how does our own situation compare with that of ships, of trees and, perhaps most interestingly, with that of particular brains? We may best understand this issue in conjunction with our noticing two further main aspects of physical continuity.

9. Physical Continuity and Systemic Energy

A *third aspect* of physical continuity is what I call *systemic energy*. Other aspects equal, the more systemic energy involved with an ordinary entity during a period of time, the greater the physical continuity of that entity during that time.

Recall the process of taping with molecular restoration. During the middle period of that process, there is continuous physical tracking of the separated molecules. This tracking process involves considerable systemic energy. For that reason, a ship, or a bush, or a person involved in that process will, even during that middle period, enjoy a certain degree of physical continuity. This may well be enough for the ship, or the bush, to survive the process.

We may think of the physical energy by means of which the device continuously tracks each molecule as being tantamount to so many electronic strings by means of which the device can control the molecules. When there is restoration, it is as though the device pulls appropriately on all of these strings and, by so doing, pulls all of the molecules back into their original places in the initial arrangement. In the interim, the presence of the electronic strings provides a certain degree of physical continuity.

Certain other processes may involve less systemic energy: If the separated molecules are each placed in differently tagged containers, then continuous tracking is not necessary for precisely accurate restoration. The later assembly may accurately proceed by following an order given by the tags. After the tags are put on, but before they are read, there might be a period where there is not very much systemic energy. For example, if the rearrangement from this condition back into the original form is much slower and more difficult than with constant tracking, then this tagging procedure may involve much less systemic energy and, so, much less physical continuity.

It is hard to think of there being anything in this tagging set-up that has quite the place of the imaginatively posited electronic strings in the previous procedure. By contrast, here there appears to be a much less direct relation between the physical realization of the information needed for full restoration on the one hand and, on the other, the small particles whose precise relative arrangement is, in the end, to be restored.

Still other processes will involve still less systemic energy: If the separated molecules are in no way individually distinguished by a real physical system, then a later reassembly can only make sure that a molecule of a certain precise kind finds a place in the final arrangement occupied by a molecule of just that kind in the original arrangement. Within any such kind, the particular molecules are treated as no more than interchangeable parts. A taping device that operates in this less constrained way may be said to engage in a process of *taping with random molecular shuffling*. With this shuffling process, there appears to be no encouragement at all for thoughts along the lines of our little electronic strings.

Now, on a very rare occasion, a bush, or a person, may be put through this random shuffling process and, by fantastic luck, at the end there may be a bush, or a person, with *exactly* the same arrangement of the same particular molecules. But, because there is so little systemic energy involved, the bush at the end may not be the very same bush as the one that first entered the process. And, in the parallel case, the person will not be the same one who first entered.

The limiting case of these processes involves no systemic energy: A bush's molecules, or a person's, are scattered widely. Wholly by chance, they later come together in just the arrangement they had before. This may be a few minutes later or, perhaps more likely, the statistical miracle may happen only after the passage of many millions of years. At any rate, as there is here complete randomness above the molecular level, there is, above that level, no systemic energy at all. Accordingly, there is terribly little physical continuity involving the original bush, or the original person. According to our intuitions, there is a numerically different bush at the end. In the parallel case, where I myself enter such a "miraculous" sequence of events, the intuition is very strong: At the end, I will not exist. Instead, there will be someone who, with just the same matter in just the same arrangement as before, is just like I once was.

At least roughly, this may be the implicit reasoning behind this strong response of ours: If it really is me, then one of two options will hold. On the one hand, there is the option that I have radically interrupted existence; in the middle period, perhaps for many millions of years, I simply did not exist. As it appears, this option is not very credible. On the other hand, there is the option that I existed throughout the middle period with my molecules meandering, perhaps for millions of years, in a completely random fashion. This option also is not very credible. So, as is more credible, it is not me who is there at the end of the statistically miraculous sequence of events.[13]

13. Among what I class as ordinary concrete individuals, the likes of rocks present perhaps the most puzzling case in regard to these present considerations. (As I am using the term, hunks of mud, and lumps of bronze, don't count as ordinary individuals.) We ask: With random paths for its erstwhile particles, will a rock make it through the sort of multimillion year saga just depicted? In personal correspondence, John Robinson proposed that, simply because there are just the same particles in just the same arrangement at the end, it will indeed be the very same rock millions of years later. And he also proposed that this may be a clear counter-example to the general claim that ordinary individuals will never have interruptions in their existence. These intriguing proposals merit a response.

Perhaps the best thought notices a divide. On the one side, we have no strong intuition, either way, about whether the rock at the end is numerically the same rock as the rock at the beginning.

10. Thinking Beings and Unthinking Entities:
A Contrast Concerning Survival

When there is little going for it in way of other aspects of physical continuity, if it is to survive, even a nail needs at least a fair amount of systemic energy. But, at all events, when a nail undergoes the process of taping with molecular restoration, the unthinking object does survive. By contrast, when you undergo the process, you do *not* survive. Especially when we effectively discount distorting tendencies, in most contexts that is our dominant response. What explains the difference?

Typically and rationally, we employ pretty much the same standards for the continuous realization of our most central capacities as we do for those of a nail, or a tree, or a brain. For individuals of all these ordinary kinds, ourselves included, in almost all contexts, most of us employ at least a moderately demanding standard for the realization of capacities by entities. Little doubt but that this is rational.

According to such standards, in the middle of the conservative taping process, the tracked molecules of a nail do not realize the nail's hardness or, much the same, they don't realize its capacity to withstand penetration by other biggish objects. Nor does anything else realize this rather central, or characteristic, property of the nail. How does this affect the question of a nail's survival? Whether or not the nail has that capacity, or any other of its characteristic properties, does not much matter: The nail still exists. Nor will similar gaps in characteristic properties matter much for the survival of a tree, or even a brain. For you and me, and for a dog, the situation is quite different.

According to closely parallel standards, when your molecules have been dispersed, then, even if they are constantly tracked, there is no entity that

---

Rather, we have only weak responses in both directions. Perhaps, then, it is indeterminate whether there is, at the end, numerically the same rock. If so, then there is no very damaging counter-example.

On the other side, and perhaps more important, suppose that we (resolve to) favor the idea that it is the very same rock at the end. Given this supposition, or stipulation, what is then the most plausible description of the lengthy middle period? Is it that, for millions of years, the rock did not exist and, then, at the end of the eons, it once again existed? Even if not better by miles, perhaps a somewhat better description is that, in the great interim, the rock will have existed, not only in a greatly scattered way, but also in a highly chaotic way.

Collecting these ideas together, what still seems a very unattractive approach is this: It is definitely true that the rock at the end is the very same rock as the rock at the beginning and, as well, it is definitely true that, in the lengthy middle period, that rock wasn't anywhere at all.

However interesting these interchanges may be, they concern matters that, for our present study, are side issues: After all, you and I are not inanimate, unthinking rocks, but are thinking subjects of experience. And, concerning the likes of us, Robinson's proposals have very much less force.

then realizes your capacity for consciousness, or your capacity for rudimentary reasoning. How does this affect the question of your survival? For you, the continuous realization of your most central capacities matters much more: You will not survive.

For beings with mental capacities, their most characteristic properties are certain of these capacities. If they are ordinary concrete individuals, then, in order to survive, these beings require some of these most characteristic properties continuously to be realized. Now, ordinary concrete individuals that lack mental capacities may have other capacities among their most characteristic properties. But these unthinking entities may survive without the continuous realization of their most characteristic features. In our common system of thought, this idea represents a fundamental contrast. No matter how demanding or how lenient are the standards used for reckoning capacities and dispositions, this basic contrast holds true.

In our thought about nails, we might sometimes employ enormously liberal standards. If we did, then we might say that, in the middle period, a particular nail was still hard, in particular, that it still had its capacity to withstand ordinary attempts at penetration. How might such liberal standards operate to such an effect? In rough, the answer may run like this: In virtue of their continuous tracking by the restorative device, the nail's molecules provided for this hardness. Owing to this continuous relationship, at any time and with great speed, the device might combine the molecules in their original arrangement: Ordinary attempts at penetrating the apparently vulnerable powder would be thwarted.

We might sometimes employ similar enormously liberal standards for us people. If we did, then we might say that, in the middle period, there was a scattered entity that did have a capacity to think; in your case, it would be an entity with just your own capacity to think. In virtue of their continuous tracking by the restorative device, your molecules provided for the realization of this very mental capacity. Owing to this continuous relationship, at any time and with great speed, the device might combine your molecules in their original arrangement: Almost as soon as a question was asked of what was in the storage containers, appropriately responsive thoughts would be generated.

Whether our standards for capacity attribution are so liberal or are not so liberal, it is important to notice that matters of capacity attribution are different from, even if related to, questions of physical continuity. The process of taping with random molecular shuffling provides a telling example. For simplicity's sake, we consider only the case of a hard nail that undergoes this process. Now, as we will assume, in the middle of the process, the restorative device can very quickly, and very easily, arrange the available particles in the form of a nail just like the original nail. Further, the enormous quickness and ease of achieving such an arrangement is due precisely to the fact that, first, the shuffling restorer does not have to keep track of each molecule's position and, second, that restorer may freely insert any handy particle of any given sort wherever something of that sort might be needed. Impressed by this great ease and speed, and employing very liberal standards for capacity attribution, we may be moved to attribute the capacity to resist penetration to something that, even in the problematic middle period, remains present in the situation.

Because there is not much physical continuity, however, it will not be the original nail whose hardness is then exemplified. But, then, to what might we be attributing these capacities? Without necessarily excluding each other, various candidates may serve well to take on these attributions. For one thing, we might attribute the capacities to the matter that, even in the middle period, surely still was there: The matter that was once the nail's, we may say, not only still does exist, but still has the capacity to resist penetration.

Although questions of physical continuity dominate this chapter as a whole, it is matters of capacity that are the focus of this one section and, so, it is to these that we return. With regard to matters of capacity and questions of survival, the main point transcends the complex considerations of contexts, standards and attributions. That main point remains just this: For future existence, you in fact require the continuous physical realization of certain (mental) capacities; in contrast to what you require, a nail, a tree, and even a brain, do not require anything comparable for their surviving into the future. The possible variety of appropriate standards serves only to indicate that there may be a certain contextual aspect to all this. If that is so, then, it is just our survival that requires there to obtain something that has this contextual aspect. By contrast, the survival of a nail, a tree, or a brain does not require that there obtain any comparable capacity, with a similar contextual aspect.

The positive side of this contrast is not confined to us people. The same holds for any beings, like dogs and mice, that think and experience. For us to insist upon this point, we must allow for a certain qualification: As common usage has it, just as a dead brain is still the same brain as used to be alive, so a dead dog is still the same dog that used to think and feel. Even after he becomes rottenly decomposed, and has no mental capacity, we may properly say that the dog is still there. Going by this usage, a dog's mental capacities are not so important to its continued existence. This usage may be misleading.[14]

---

14. And what of our everyday talk of people? Not only do we often say of a person recently dead that he no longer exists, but, in other moods, we say that he is in the funeral parlor. Whatever the linguistic analysis of these utterances, the former sort of discourse is, by far, the better expression of our more serious, and our more accurate, thought about ourselves.

Just as we may place aside some of our talk about ourselves, so, too, we may place aside much of our talk about ever so many animals.

My suggestion is that we need not adhere closely to every nicety of ordinary usage. A small infidelity, if it comes to that, may be a small price to pay for a clear and consistent statement of our deeper beliefs: A being capable of thought and experience will exist just so long as that being's own core psychology continues to be realized. As soon as your core psychology is not realized, you will cease to exist. As soon your dog's lesser core psychology is not realized, she will no longer exist. Although a dead human brain and a dead canine brain may still exist, and although a dead human body and a dead canine body may still exist, in a recognizably serious sense of the terms, both you and your dog will no longer exist.

At this juncture, it is perhaps worth recalling a point first essayed in Chapter 1. It is plausible that, in taping with molecular restoration, although my brain and body will get through, I myself will not survive. Let us suppose that, on the standards most germane for reckoning these matters, all of that really will be so. Then, after such a process, as will my body, my brain will be the brain of another person, a duplicate successor of myself. This may be one way, then, for my brain and body not only to exist in the future, but to support personal experience and activity, even while I myself have ceased. In any case, as we shall see in the next chapter, there are other ways.

11. Physical Continuity and Physical Complementarity

When there is a very low degree of constitutional cohesion, then, other things equal, there will be little physical continuity. To some degree, a severe lack of cohesion can be offset by a high degree of systemic energy. But it is somewhat doubtful that this sort of compensation will ever provide a great deal of physical continuity and, in particular, that it will provide enough to secure our own survival. Perhaps, though, there is still another aspect of physical continuity that might do more for us in situations where there is a severe lack of constitutional cohesion.

A *fourth aspect* of physical continuity is what I shall call *physical complementarity*. Over a period of time, this complementarity may occur when an ordinary physical entity is first subjected to one gross physical process and is then subjected to a second gross process that, being the physical inverse of the first process, leaves the entity in very much the same state that it was in just before the first process occurred. Even when there is hardly any constitutional cohesion at crucial middle times, if I am involved in a sequence of physically complementary processes, then there may be, throughout this involvement, sufficient physical continuity for me to survive the entire sequence. As I hypothesize, for the physical continuity I need to survive when constitutional cohesion is lacking, physical complementarity may do more than systemic energy.

In order to assess this hypothesis, we must, of course, first understand what is meant by this physical complementarity. In order to foster the wanted understanding, it may be best to begin with a familiar example that, although it also does involve much constitutional cohesion throughout, will quite clearly exhibit the main features of this new aspect of physical continuity. Accordingly, we again recall the processes of super freezing and super thawing.

Because super thawing is a relevantly restorative physical inverse of super freezing, the total process composed of their familiar sequence may provide much physical complementarity, and thus much physical continuity, for the entities that are subjected to it. Why might that be so? To begin with, although physical grossness is a matter of degree, it should be clear that both this freezing and this thawing are physically gross to a very high degree and, as such, may be appropriately termed gross physical processes. In ways that are as obviously important as they are difficult to specify, these processes are very different from the refined physical events that typify the functioning of complex machines. Although it is very hard precisely to specify the relevant differences, there is a world of difference between the grossness of freezing and thawing, on the one hand, and, on the other, the physical delicacy involved in the process of taping with molecular restoration.

One important difference may be this: In super freezing, the physical entity involved loses much of a certain rather basic physical property that, at the outset, it has to a considerable degree, namely, its heat. In the physically complementary process of super thawing, the frozen entity regains that highly quantifiable property to very nearly the exact same degree. Moreover, it is almost entirely just by its being so quickly infused with that much heat that the entity once again comes to be in almost exactly the same state as just before the outset of the whole process. Beyond the loss and the gain of that heat, nothing worth mentioning happens to that entity. By contrast, in the recording and "dismantling" stage of the total process of taping with molecular restoration, there is nothing that closely parallels the gross physical difference that is the sheer loss of that much heat by the entity in question. And in the later restoration stage, there is nothing that closely mirrors the relevant gross physical opposite, the gaining of that much heat by that thing.

Gross and refined physical processes may be intermingled variously. Even so, we may often distinguish the one from the other. For example, to promote the occurrence of super freezing and super thawing, we might need to direct these processes by means of some refined devices and, thus, by way of some refined physical processes involving those directing devices. But the more refined directing physical processes are at a certain physical remove from the grosser processes directed. For that reason, they will not detract at all from the gross character of the freezing and thawing process.

Supposing it to be a fact, it is a highly empirical and contingent fact that super thawing is a real physical complement of super freezing, that is, that this thawing so thoroughly reverses so many of the effects that this freezing imposes. My surviving the total process that they sequentially compose will depend upon the contingent fact of their complementarity: For a pretty extreme example, there might be some universal laws of nature that always prohibit an appropriate sort of thawing for people. After being deeply frozen, my brain always might thaw out in a quite thoroughly scrambled way. In such a world, even the most immaculate freezing will mean the loss of my mental capacities. Consequently, in such a world, super freezing will result in my termination.

In a wider range of logically possible situations, the contingent relations between the freezing and the thawing may be not so simply extreme, but may be rather more complex. Some technical expressions may help us roughly describe a certain order that may be present in these complex relations: A process, like super freezing, will have another process, like super thawing, as a physical complement to the extent that the second process is *readily available* to entities that have undergone the first process and, furthermore, to the extent that the available gross process is *sufficiently restorative* with respect to those entities. What does this mean? Roughly, the availability of the process concerns the variety of conditions in which the originally affected entity, me, for example, may actually become involved in the potentially restorative process; other things equal, the greater this variety, the more available is the gross physical process. Also roughly, the degree that the available process is restorative depends on two things: First, there is the variety of conditions in which, once involved in the process, the affected entity may once again assume states like those previously enjoyed and, second, there is the degree to which those later states are, overall, like those just before the onset of the first process. The greater the variety of these restorative conditions, and the greater the overall physical similarity of the initial and final states, the more highly restorative is the available gross physical process.

The points here are quite general, not limited to questions regarding the physical realization of psychology. Consider a particular television that is super frozen. Does the television still have its characteristic capacities, say, its capacity to produce or relay certain patterns of light and sound? That depends on what thawing processes, in the physical order, are available for that television. If there are highly restorative thawing processes that are readily available, then, after the TV has been involved in these gross processes, its capacities may be readily exercised. For example, after exposure to an available thawing process, in order to produce the appropriately patterned light and sound, the set may need only to be plugged in and turned on. If there are available processes like that, then, even when it is frozen, the television has the capacity to function in the noted ways. If all thawing processes result in much crumbling of the television's parts, however, so that no picture or sound can later be readily obtained from the set, then super freezing will have destroyed the noted capacity of the television.

As regards related matters of survival, the only difference between you and the television is this: With no good thawing processes ever available, the television will just be broken by having been super frozen, it will just have lost its main capacities. Still, the television will continue to exist. But you will not merely have lost your most central capacities. Because your central capacities are so crucial to your very existence, in such a circumstance, super freezing will make you cease to exist. Of course, this is just another application of a point that is by now rather familiar.

By now we should have a reasonably good understanding of what we mean by physical complementarity. With this understanding in hand, we move to consider a quite different sort of gross physical process: During much of the process of *gentle explosion and gentle implosion*, the ordinary entity affected has precious little constitutional cohesion.

We shall suppose, then, that a person, myself for example, may come within the range of a certain sort of physical field that will separate his particles one from the other. In a simple case of this sort, easy for us to visualize, the relative spatial arrangement of these gently exploded particles will be retained by the field. When the field ceases to affect this matter, the array of particles gently implodes. The particles are then joined just as they were right before the gentle explosion. The occurence is one specific instance of quite widespread physical tendencies: To an entity in the field that has been so exploded, there is readily available a highly restorative process of gentle implosion. And, when one of us is the entity to whom the total process occurs, the physical events of the emerging person's brain, and the many mental events supported thereby, proceed in the ordinary ways.

There is a further parallel between gentle explosion and gentle implosion on the one hand and, on the other, highly available and restorative super freezing and super thawing: Just as a super frozen entity loses almost all of its heat, so a gently exploded entity loses almost all of a parallel property that it originally has to a considerable degree. For example, this may be a certain sort of magnetism. As we may suppose it to have been discovered, when physical objects have even a moderate amount of this magnetism, their parts cohere very well. But when they lose almost all of it, as they may sometimes do to a certain sort of surrounding field, then their constituent particles become pretty widely scattered. When that much of that magnetism is restored to the array of scattered particles, then they resume their previous bonded arrangement.

Will I survive subjection to this gross physical process of gentle explosion and implosion? My dominant response is, quite clearly, that I will. Because this process lacks the spatial proximity and the continuous bonding typical of ordinary cases of my survival, this response is not as clear as can be. Just so, this reaction is not as clear as the strong positive response to the case of super freezing and thawing, where the gross process does involve those customary features. Nonetheless, the positive response to gentle explosion and implosion is pretty strong. And, when we apply the avoidance of future pain test, the response is confirmed.

As I hypothesize, these are the main lines of implicit reasoning that generate this strong response: True enough, as regards a salient aspect of physical continuity, constitutional cohesion, the case of gentle explosion and implosion may represent a severe negative departure from the ordinary cases of human survival. But, as regards another aspect, physical complementarity, the case is so rich that the example involves, overall, quite a lot of physical continuity for my brain and body. Moreover, owing to the way this continuity is achieved, my brain will continuously realize my basic mental capacities. Accordingly, the reasoning behind our response concludes, I will survive gentle explosion and implosion.

It is fun to imagine other sorts of gross physical processes that might provide a lot of physical complementarity. As in certain science fiction movies, physical forces may place constituents pretty much all in one warped plane, or even pretty much all in one line. Then complementary forces may flip them back again into the more customary arrangement. But there is little point, I believe, to our going through the details of this exotica.

At all events, as I said near the chapter's outset, even relative to the general truth of our world view, the physical approach is not a fully adequate treatment of our survival. Indeed, as we have formulated this position, the approach is too pure and simple to be even a terribly close approximation. But, of course, our somewhat more modest idea is that this physical approach, now reasonably well understood, may provide a good basis for a more complex, and a more complete, understanding of what is involved in our identity over time.[15]

---

15. Especially as regards the material of sections 2, 3 and 4, but, even as regards the chapter as a whole, it was John Carroll who, more than anyone else, helped me to bring some order out of much chaos.

5

A PHYSICALLY BASED APPROACH
TO OUR SURVIVAL

It is not my aim to provide a highly detailed account of our identity over time, not even one that is adequate only relative to the general truth of our accepted world view. Rather, I aim only to sketch the outlines of a realistic account of our survival. As I see it, the best attempt toward this more modest goal may begin with the physical approach to our survival. Then it may look for ways to refine this rather pure and simple approach. Because it will retain the main spirit of the physical approach all the while, it is appropriate to call the account that we will be working toward, but never fully reaching, a *physically based approach to our survival*.

We will begin by discussing a possible refinement that is both somewhat uncertain and, even if needed, is not so substantial: In our original formulation of it, the physical approach insists that core psychology counts for everything while, correlatively, distinctive psychology counts for nothing at all. This might be an exaggeration. If so, then, even relative to our world view, the simple physical approach will fail to provide a necessary condition for our survival. Because of this, we might need a modest refinement that allows for the indicated compensations.

A second refinement is both more certainly required and more substantial. The issue here concerns how, even relative to our world view, the simple physical approach may fail to articulate a sufficient condition of our survival. The deficiency concerns *factors of assimilation*. These are certain *historical* factors that can be important to our survival. Even this more significant refinement, however, will be fully rooted in the physically continuous realization of psychology.

1. Might Distinctive Psychology Be a Factor in Survival?

On the face of it, there seems to be the possibility of certain trade-offs, within a person's total psychology, that will allow her to survive even if she does not retain all of her core psychology. The continuous realization of *almost* all of core psychology along with a great deal of her distinctive psychology might well do as much to secure a person's survival as the retention of all of her core psychology alone. For example, the loss of a smidgen of reasoning ability, even from the already low level required for a full psychological core, might be offset by the continuous physical retention of very many personal memories.

As we will notice shortly, a diminution in one of a person's basic mental capacities, from an already low level, may put severe restrictions on the extent to which distinctive psychology can properly be ascribed to that person. Indeed, once a person's capacity for thinking, for example, is at the minimal level required for inclusion in a full psychological core, there may already be considerable limitations on how much distinctive psychology can still be ascribed to her. Nonetheless, although there may be much less room than first appears for trade-offs of the sort envisioned, it is likely, I imagine, that there will be some. It is within this area, however modest or restricted, that the loss of just a little core psychology might be offset by the continuous physical realization of a great deal of distinctive psychology.

If these thoughts are on the right track, they may move us from the simple physical approach to what we may call a *slightly modified physical approach to our survival*. How might we express this modified approach? In the direction of happily flexible vagueness, it may suffice to make only a fairly small change: First, we may say that one's core psychology is the *most central* part of a person's psychology. Second, we may say that certain parts of a person's distinctive psychology are *more central than* others. Finally, we may say that what is important for survival is that there be properly continued *enough of* a person's *central enough* dispositional psychology. So, still relative to the general truth of our general world view, we may offer the following as a rough statement of the slightly modified physical approach:

> The person X now is one and the same as the person Y at some time in the future if, and only if, (1) from the present physical realizer of X's psychology now to the physical realizer of Y's psychology at that future time, there is sufficiently continuous physical realization of enough central enough aspects of X's

present psychology and [probably] (2) {some clause suitable for ruling out unwanted cases of branching}.

This formulation is offered as sensitive to the fact that, between the present and the indicated time in the future, a brain may realize different psychological features at different times: For part of the time, for example, the brain may realize much distinctive psychology even while it does not realize all of the psychological core, so that the original person, X, will then lack the full complement of a core psychology. Later, the brain may realize enough core psychology so that the person again has a full complement. Later still, while there is still realized all of her psychological core, the brain may not realize any of the person's distinctive psychology. As long as enough of what is psychologically central is physically realized at any time, and causal factors of physical continuity underlie such mental changes as may occur for us to reckon, then, over time, there may be a certain amount of shuttling around of dispositional psychology. With that much shuttling, although not with more, each of us may survive.

Although this formulation makes no mention of distinctive psychology, it is of some interest only because distinctive psychology may be a part of what is central enough psychology. Unless there are certain trade-offs of (some) core psychology for (much) distinctive psychology, the formulation will be extensionally equivalent to the original statement of the simple physical approach. Because there may be some such trade-offs, there may be no such equivalence.

A few paragraphs back, I remarked that there may be rather little room for any trade-offs of retained distinctive psychology for lost core psychology: At least for the most part, a person's basic mental capacities are heavily integrated with each other and, as well, form an essential basis for the rest of the person's psychology. I shall now try to explain these remarks.

My explanation comprises two parts. The first part observes that the *more basic aspects* of a person's main mental capacities are *required for*, and so are not detachable from, whatever *other aspects* there may be to those abilities: A person's basic reasoning ability is not detachable from the rest of her reasoning ability. Nobody can make what are, even for her, only complex inferences, while failing to make any simple inferences. The same is true of a person's capacity to form and maintain beliefs, desires, hopes, fears, wishes, and other attitudes. Further, in a world of many people, nobody can have her own distinctive attitudes only, without also having many of the simpler attitudes that, in fact, she shares with many. So, nobody can believe that she is three years older than her dog unless she can believe that she is older than her dog; nor can anybody want an antique knife unless she can want a knife. The same holds, as well, for a person's capacity to undergo emotions. So, nobody can be elated with a new scientific discovery unless she has, more basically, the capacity to be happy; nor can someone be envious of her sister's beauty unless she can, more basically, be unhappy. In a world of many people, nobody can have her own distinctive emotional proclivities only, without also having the simpler emotional capacities that, in fact, she has in common with others.

Second, regarding any being to whom a genuine personal psychology can be ascribed, there must be many interconnections among the being's main mental capacities. For example, the capacity for reasoning must have some connections with capacities for the formation, the maintenance and the abandonment of beliefs and other attitudes: Genuine reasoning must, in some circumstances, lead to the formation of beliefs; in others, to their abandonment. At the same time, there must be certain relations between a person's desires and her reasoning. Although a person may have certain quite basic desires, many things are desired because, according to the person's beliefs, they are effective in obtaining other things. As are a person's beliefs, these instrumental desires must be connected with her reasoning; in suitable circumstances, her reasoning will lead to the formation of, or to the abandonment of, various of these secondary desires. By the same token, unlike mere tropisms and organic needs, genuine basic *desires* must connect *with* beliefs, *through* reasoning, *to* other desires. In other words, through reasoning about their connections with certain beliefs, basic desires must lead to the formation of instrumental desires, directed at ways for satisfying the more basic wants.

Connections between capacities for reasoning and capacities for action must also be part of any properly ascribed personal psychology. For example, relative to suitable conditions, thinking must lead from beliefs and desires to the formation of intentions. Under favorable conditions, these intentions, in turn, must lead to action. In these ways, capacities of reason must be linked to the capacities of the will. In related ways, both of these capacities must be linked to emotional capacities. But there is little point now in outlining more of the network of a person's required psychological interconnections.

These two parts combine to yield the wanted conclusion: In order for an entity to have any personal psychology at all, that entity must have much of what we have been calling core psychology. Because of this, there may be severe, even if vaguely framed, limits on how much core psychology may be lost while there still remains any person at all. Because of that, there may be severe limits on the amount of lost core psychology that, for a person's survival, can be compensated by (physically well-realized) distinctive psychology: If very much core psychology is lost, there will be no person there at all, neither the same nor any other. Thus, there will be no person with any distinctive psychology to compensate for anything.

But, even if all of this is true, something else also may be true: A certain amount of a person's core psychology may be lost even while the rest remains.

Within the range of loss vaguely allowed, there may be room for the noted trade-offs: Without the retention of much of her distinctive psychology, when a person loses even a fairly small amount of her core, that may put an end to her. But if a lot of her distinctive psychology continues to be realized physically, then she might lose that much of her core and still exist.

2. Can One Survive Without a Capacity for Consciousness?

Before going on to propose some much needed and rather substantial refinements, I would like to discuss some conceptual speculations that I find quite intriguing. To be sure, these ideas are very sketchy and uncertain. And, perhaps, they might even lapse into incoherence. Nevertheless, these peculiar speculations do concern topics that are very central to this book. And, further, even if there might be some deep incoherence in them, some of these thoughts may, nonetheless, prove helpful in certain later chapters, where certain questions about our values will be under discussion.

Now, as I gather from scientific texts, provided that there is at least a small portion of her higher brain in good working order, a person's brain stem, or lower brain, will support consciousness on her part. But, without the great majority of the lower brain, no amount of higher brain will provide someone with conscious experience. If only in a provisional way, let us accept this.

Having accepted this assumption, we proceed to consider the *case of the taped brain stem*: While a certain person's brain stem is being destroyed, extremely detailed information about its constitution is recorded on tape and stored for future use. At the same time, by the operation of life-support and stimulatory systems, the rest of the person keeps functioning at the highest level available for it, or for her. Later, by employing the information recorded from the old brain stem, a duplicate of it may be produced from new matter. This new brain stem may then be joined to what has been kept functioning so as to form what is clearly a normal person. She is a person who clearly has the capacity for consciousness and even is conscious; she is a person who is at least ever so like the person at the beginning. Is the conscious person now before us the same person as the one whose brain stem was destroyed?

We are in a very poor position to answer this question. Placing aside various empirical difficulties, our main problem, I think, is a conceptual one: Suppose that in the middle period there is no capacity for consciousness realized. Then we ask, "To what extent can there then be realized, anyway, the rest of a normal person's psychology?" Now, for all I really know about these difficult matters, the answer just might be: "To no extent at all; for, the capacity for conscious experience is so heavily intertwined with all other psycho-

logical powers that it makes no sense, really, to attribute any mentality at all
to a subject unless we grant, in the bargain, the capacity for consciousness."
Although this might possibly be the correct answer to our question, my hunch
is that it is not. In just a moment, I will try to supply some reason to take this
hunch seriously.

Right now, let me place before you this quite modest *conditional conjecture*:
If a person's capacity for conscious experience *is* logically detachable from
much of the rest of psychology, so that it is indeed coherent to suppose that
there is a person with a significant psychology but no capacity for consciousness, *then* we can survive the loss of this capacity and yet survive. In other
words, if there may be a process that destroys my capacity for conscious experience, but that keeps enough mentality for there to be someone physically
realized throughout, then that person will be me. Now, should this conditional hypothesis be true, the reason for its truth might be this: If there may
occur that loss in my core psychology without very much more loss in my
core, and without there being any very great loss of distinctive psychology,
then, as regards the question of my survival, the loss of this precious capacity
can be compensated by the continuous physical realization of so much of the
rest of psychology.

Provisionally accepting the assumption in favor of coherence, we may use
our case of the taped brain stem to support this modest conditional conjecture. We need only suppose, further, that separate capacities can be realized
in separate structures. If anything, the least of our problems will occur there.
Let us suppose, then, that except for the capacity for consciousness, which is
realized in a person's brain stem, all the rest of her core psychology, and all
of her distinctive psychology, may be realized in her upper brain.

Then the case of the taped brain stem may serve us well: With these suppositions still foremost in mind, we respond that the person will survive the
destruction of her brain stem. If the original subject is me, then, in the middle
period, although my life may hold precious little value for me, owing to my
complete lack of conscious experience, I will exist even at that time. At the
end, when there is again a person with the capacity to be conscious, it will be
I myself who will have that capacity. The avoidance of future pain test nicely
confirms this conditional result. So, as I think, our modest conditional conjecture is probably true: If in the absence of a capacity for consciousness
there will be any person at all, then one of us can lose this capacity and still
survive.

Is it conceptually coherent to speak of the presence of much personal psychology even in the absence of a capacity for consciousness? Let me now try
to give some life to the surmise that it is. First, I will speak of certain hypothetical neural considerations: In deepest sleep, between dreams, there might

be a complete absence of a certain sort of neural activity. As we are assuming, certain devices for exploring the brain's processes may enable us to know this assumed fact. Now, to a very high degree, this activity may be present in normal waking life, and also when we have vivid dreams. To a lesser degree, this activity may be present when we are in a stupor, and in certain sorts of fairly ordinary trances, and when we are just about to fall off to deep sleep, and when we are awakening from it. As might become reasonable to conclude, when there is none of this sort of activity at all, then there is no conscious thought or experience. Let us call this brain activity *Cons activity*.

A quite different sort of neural activity might be associated with thinking. When the two sorts of activity are both present, then, as may be reasonable to conclude, there is conscious thinking. When only Cons activity is present, then there might be thoughtless conscious sensation. When there is only the activity of this second sort, then there might be non-conscious, or unconscious, thinking. Let us call this second sort of brain activity *Thot activity*.

Often, when there is only Thot activity, there are interesting facts about productive intelligent behavior. So, neural considerations may dovetail with behavioral ones to give added life to the idea of non-conscious thinking: Before going to sleep, a novelist may have little idea of how to develop his next chapter. If there is little or no Thot activity, then when he awakens he will still have little idea. If there is much, then, as it happens, he can pen the next chapter directly upon arising. By contrast, it makes no difference to such behavior whether there has been much, little or even any Cons activity during his sleep. So, increasingly, Thot activity comes to seem the brain activity of thinking, whether conscious or non-conscious, while Cons activity appears to be the brain activity of consciousness, whether thoughtful or non-thoughtful.

Suppose that, in cases of taped brain stems, during the middle period subjects never have any Cons activity, but many subjects may have quite a lot of Thot activity. At the end, when there are again subjects complete with brain stems, many of them finish books quickly or, for the first time, have rather fully formed conceptions of a more practical nature. As it appears, during the middle period none of these subjects had even the capacity for consciousness. But all of them may have the capacity for thinking and many may have, quite unconsciously, exercised this capacity to a very considerable degree.

By considering a certain hypothetical substance, the *permanent Trancelife drug*, we can vividly expand on the role that, perhaps, behavioral considerations might coherently attain. As we shall suppose, this drug affects a person mainly by influencing her brain stem and, thus, by causing her to have no Cons activity at all. With this quite permanent drug, just one dose lasts for the *rest of a person's life*. Moreover, there is no antidote to it. Indeed, on any relevant reckoning, the effects of the drug are *irreversible*. So, rather than merely inhibiting the exercise of a person's capacity for consciousness, this drug destroys that capacity.

Perhaps we may coherently suppose that, in all respects save having conscious experience, and even as her behavior may show, a person under the influence of this drug may have a rich and varied mental life. For example, while affected by this drug for years, someone may be a greatly talented, prolific and enormously successful writer. At the same time, she may be a caring, active and greatly loved wife and mother. How might this be possible? Here are some suggestions.

First, it might be that our beliefs as to what experiences we have are, logically, completely distinct from those experiences themselves: Perhaps we might not only have experiences without having the belief that we are then having any experiences, but, as well, we might have beliefs to the effect that we are having experiences even while we are then having no conscious experiences at all. Now, except insofar as experiences may influence our propositional attitudes, and may thus indirectly cause our behavior, it is our beliefs, not the experiences themselves, that will be productive of our actions. And, in the cases under discussion, the lack of indirect causation by the experiences will not be missed. For, as we might assume, even as many of our beliefs themselves continually change quite directly to reflect changes in surrounding stimulation, we shall almost always be prepared to act adaptively without any need for experiential mediation. Perhaps, then, having ever so many false beliefs as to what experiences she is having, and recently has had, the imagined woman might unconsciously proceed through the world about as well as does any creative and caring person.

While I am inclined to believe in the coherence of the foregoing distinctness hypothesis, I might, I agree, be wrong in this proclivity: Perhaps, contrary to the previous suggestion, our experiences and our propositional attitudes cannot really be so completely distinct. So, *second,* here is another suggestion on which a wholly unconscious person might possibly engage in intelligent and successful behavior: The individual, we may note, is very puzzled by the fact that, as far as even she can tell, she is not having any conscious experience of any kind at all. Unlike during the time before she took the Trancelife drug, her life has no feeling or any tone to it. As she somehow knows, she confronts a variety of discriminably different situations and, somehow, acts in appropriately different ways. These actions are not always directly forthcoming, of course; rather, they often result from protracted reasoning and deliberation. But even these episodes of thinking are, she says, quite without conscious experience or feeling.[1] Both as she avows and as the

---

1. An actual phenomenon found in certain injured human beings is that of *blindsight.* An interesting and accessible discussion of this is provided by one of the phenomenon's leading investigators, Larry Weiskrantz, in "Neuropsychology and Consciousness," *Mindwaves,* C. Blakemore and S. Greenfield, eds., Basil Blackwell, 1987. On page 314, Weiskrantz says, "A similar kind of

absence of any Cons activity appears to confirm, she gets neither any real enjoyment out of life nor, on the other hand, any genuine unhappiness. As she says, except for the fact that she wants her family to live happily, and that she wants to complete her ambitious writing project, she sees no reason to stay alive and, for that matter, no reason not to live.

In our most recent move, it is true, we allowed for a lack of consciousness to mean a difference in behavior. But the behavior described was all, or it was almost all, verbal behavior. Is that sort of limited description really a coherent one, or must there also be, between the conscious agents and those who are wholly non-conscious, some pretty substantial differences in non-verbal behavior? Again, I am inclined to think that there is no need to satisfy the stronger condition; but, again, it might be that I am wrong in this inclination. So, put very sketchily, here is a *third* suggestion: To begin, we allow that, as regards successful adaptive behavior, the being on the Trancelife drug might be much worse off than us conscious folks. But perhaps the entity still might be successful enough that, in all propriety, we may attribute to it, or to her, a significant psychology. Indeed, there may be a substantial enough mentality for us properly to recognize a person to be there. Moreover, along with the Trancelife drug, the entity may have been given potions that greatly increased whatever other mental capacities she might have. In such an event, the being's behavior might, in a different way but to the same degree, be very successful activity. Indeed, perhaps there might now be a pattern of action that is, overall, even more successful than the pattern of behavior before all the drugs and potions were taken.

3. Survival and Assimilation

Even if we might survive the loss of the capacity for consciousness, such a fact will fall within the compass of the small refinement made when moving to the slightly modified physical approach to our survival. A more central refinement is needed to accommodate factors of *assimilation*. A few well-chosen cases may provide a pretty good idea of what I mean by this term.

In the preceding chapter, several of the examples involved the abrupt and rapid replacement of substantial parts of a person's brain. As a case in point, we may recall the replacement of (non-overlapping) quarters of my brain by precise duplicates, where one quarter is replaced every fifteen minutes, where

---

phenomenon has been reported with damage in another sensory system—the somatosensory system—which has been called 'blindtouch'." Roughly, what I have in mind is the limiting case of exceptionally accurate blindsight, blindtouch, blindhearing, and so on, coupled with no conscious experience of internal thought processes, mental images, emotional states, and so on.

each old brain-quarter is destroyed directly upon its removal, and where, for the sake of simple exposition, there is no replacement with regard to the rest of the original body. To ensure that, even pretty realistically, a person will always be in the situation, we specify that each quarterly replacement will not be made in a one-shot process, and will not otherwise be very abrupt. Instead, taking less than a minute apiece, each of the four replacements may itself involve a rapid sequence of comparatively small replacements: For example, a distinct one percent of a quarter may be replaced at each successive one-tenth of a second. In virtue of the evenly gradual nature of these quick quarterly replacements, at every moment there will be present at least ninety-nine and three-quarters percent of a whole brain. Thus, quite surely, there will be no troublesome interruption.

Notice well, however, that those replacements are only comparatively small: Each quarter of a percent of the brain is a complex structure composed of many millions of well-arranged neurons (and glia), each of which is itself a complex composed of billions of well-arranged atoms. Notice also that, because it has just my precise type of DNA, for example, each of my nerve cells is in fact distinctive of me among all actual human persons. So this procedure is a very far cry indeed from the rapid, person-preserving process, discussed in the previous chapter, wherein my individual undistinctive atoms, or elementary particles, are sequentially replaced.

As is intuitive, at the end of about an hour, or even about forty-five minutes, there is, composed of new matter, not me, but, instead, a numerically different person. As the previous chapter reminds us, all of this may happen after the original person is super frozen, but before any thawing. On the other hand, the replacements might have been made under conditions of normal temperature, with the cells kept alive throughout. Indeed, between each ten-second sequence of quarterly replacements, whoever is then in the situation may think and act in rather a normal way. No more will I survive in such a circumstance than with the temperature so much lower in the middle period, when the person at any stage is doing nothing whatsoever.

The question arises: What will happen to me if there is, between rapid, evenly gradual replacements, a lot more time than just a quarter of an hour? Suppose there is a year between any given changeover and the next one in the quarterly sequence. At the end of four years, or even three, will I be there? The answer depends on what goes on during the time in question. Here are two possibilities.

If I am super frozen and, without any thawing, one of my old brain quarters is replaced each year, then, intuitively, I will not survive. By itself, then, the greater temporal interval will make no difference. Perhaps, in order to secure my survival in these situations, there must occur, between the replacements, processes of change that involve the brain quarters, both older and newer, in suitable ways.

By contrast, in a case of *all sorts of ordinary assimilation* for new brain quarters, between operations the person then in the situation may roam around in an utterly normal manner. Most of the time, of course, this person will have conscious thought and experience. When in deep sleep between dreams, we may suppose, the person will have no conscious experience at all. (With this supposition, we exclude the potentially distorting thoughts that may be aroused by a focus on experience.) Toward this very different sort of replacement case, there is the rather strong intuition that I will survive.

In this assimilation case, my survival is in no way dependent on the assumed fact that the replacements are effected by intelligent agents or, indeed, by any causal processes: We may explicitly suppose that the replacements are each due just to a *statistical miracle of molecular arrangements*. As the odds against each replacement are incredibly long, the odds against the occurrence of them all, in a suitably timed sequence, is almost beyond comprehension. Even so, such an eventful happening is consistent with the general outlines of our world view. At all events, and as we strongly respond, in such an extraordinary circumstance it is just as clear that I survive as when the replacements are intentionally made by knowledgeable scientists.[2]

Whether the replacements occur randomly, whether as the outcome of intentional activity, or whatever, there is a great disparity between the super freezing replacement case, where I pass out of existence, and the case with normal living between replacements, where I clearly survive. Why is there this great difference? For most purposes, a quick and general answer will suffice: In the more normal case, there are all sorts of ordinary assimilation; but, in the super freezing case, there is no assimilation of any sort. For an increased understanding of our survival, however, we may want an answer that is more ambitious. Perhaps we might see how each of two salient factors contributes to the marked difference between the two cases.

During these years, each quarter introduced has a chance to contribute to the realization of, and to the causal support of, my mental life, that is, to the support of my thoughts, experiences, intentional activity, reasoned changes of attitude, and so on. For at least a year, each new quarter has a period of *psychological assimilation*. This contributes significantly to the noted difference.

Each new quarter also has a chance to get caught up in, and to contribute

---

2. I see this example as an improvement on one offered by Jim Stone in his fine, provocative paper, "Parfit and the Buddha: Why There Are No People," *Philosophy and Phenomenological Research*, 1988.

to, the biological life of the person involved: Blood flows into a quarter from the rest of the person then existing, and out of it to the rest of him. Foods that he eats get digested and, then, help to fuel a new brain-part's activity. At the same time, a new brain-quarter may help to direct these biological processes. But there is no need for many illustrative specifications; the point is that there is plenty of relevant biological interaction between each new quarter, the others there before it and, for good measure, the rest of the person. In other words, for at least a year (and usually more), each new quarter also has a period of *biological assimilation*. This other factor of assimilation might also contribute significantly to the noted difference.

Perhaps these two factors of assimilation even overdetermine that there be the marked difference between the case with super freezing and the case with normal living between replacements. If that is right, then, by itself, each factor should produce a difference from the super freezing replacement case. By looking at appropriate examples, we may see that, indeed, this is the situation.

We first look at a case with much mental assimilation but virtually none that is biological. From the preceding chapter, we recall the hypothetical case where all of my organic parts are replaced by inorganic bionic units. So, again, we will make the supposition that, without any relevant impairment, the various parts of my brain (and body) may be sequentially replaced by non-living bionic structures that, as regards the effective support of psychology, integrate well both with each other and also with such brain parts as may remain. Now, at the very beginning, as we may suppose, my brain will be placed in a new bionic body, my old body then being destroyed. Then, getting down to basics, the brain-quarters themselves are bionically replaced in sequence: With one, two or three bionic brain-quarters at work, the living brain tissue that still remains, we shall suppose, is kept alive and well by life support systems. As we are imagining them, these systems are constructed and configured in such a way that, in any relevant sense, they are all external to me and, so, are in no way parts of me. At all events, just like the bionic (rest of the) body, no bionic brain-quarter is involved in any biological assimilation. At the same time, each quarter is involved in a year or more of psychological assimilation. If all of this happened to me, then, as is intuitive, I will survive.

We want next to look at the opposite sort of case, where there is much biological assimilation available, but none that is psychological. This may be a case where, after total coma induction, a different one of the four originally demarcated brain-quarters is replaced every year in a completely comatose patient. As we specify for this case, at any time during the period of induced coma, the brain then present does not even support any thought that is unconscious, let alone any conscious mental activity. With no mental activity throughout this coma, there is only biological assimilation, none that is psychological. Yet, intuitively, at the end of the period, it is the same person whom we may awaken from the coma.

From a broadly conceptual perspective, much psychological assimilation will suffice for our survival. And, by itself, much biological assimilation also will suffice. While it is perhaps unproblematic that there should be the first of these two sufficient factors, it may seem puzzling that biological assimilation will suffice. After all, while continuous realization of psychology is necessary for our survival, continuous biology is not. Perhaps this mild discrepancy is so mild that it may be readily tolerated. In other words, perhaps, in its treatment of the factors of assimilation, our conception of our survival might be a somewhat liberal one.

The possibility of there being this liberalism may be more comprehensible if, even in the face of it, we may observe there to remain a certain priority for the psychological: Perhaps what is sufficient biological assimilation for a living person is relative to the time it takes that person, or a typical person of some privileged group to which that one belongs, to think his thoughts, to perform his intentional actions, or to have a suitably varied sequence of experiences. Consider, hypothetically, a species of people the members of which each require about a month of our time to think one simple thought, like "The cat is on the mat," or "I think; therefore, I am." Although their mental processes are very much slower than ours, the biological processes are not slower. So, during that month, even with no particular intention to do so, they ate many times; often digested much of what they ate many times; frequently excreted what they did not digest; inhaled and exhaled often; and so on. Perhaps an enormous amount of biological assimilation will be required, in the problematic situations, for the survival of one of these enormously slow-witted people. For example, if only a few months will suffice to assimilate a new brain-quarter into me even if I was in a total coma, then, by contrast, quite a few centuries might be required for one of them, whether or not the mental slowpoke was in a coma. If these speculations are on the right track, then the rates of mental activity may set the relevant clocks for biological assimilation.

In whatever way the temporal standards are set for psychological and for biological assimilation, both factors of assimilation require significant physical continuity: First, even when each brain-quarter is replaced one percent at a time, there is considerable physical continuity with respect to the big brain-part that is then being sequentially replaced. At the same time, there is, of course, even greater physical continuity for those three-quarters that are not then being replaced. All of this counts toward there being considerable phys-

ical continuity for the whole physical realizer. Second, by virtue of an appropriately sequential replacement of the physically continuous parts—only one-
quarter goes while three remain—there is considerable temporal overlap in
the replacement process. This also contributes to there being considerable
physical continuity for the whole physical realizer.

Although they presuppose, or require, quite a large degree of physical continuity, these factors of assimilation are not exhausted by considerations of
physical continuity, but, instead, go far beyond them: Because both "physical
continuity" and "assimilation" are technical terms, and we thus have some
freedom in giving sense to these expressions, this point cannot be obvious.
On the other hand, because some senses for a technical term may be much
more fruitful than others, this point can be correct: On a most fruitful understanding of "physical continuity," however much physical continuity a brain
has in any of the cases that feature one year intervals between the replacements of its original quarters, it will have exactly this much even in the case
where these intervals occur during a super freeze. The other variations with
year long intervals—normal living, total coma, and bionic transformation—
may involve a lot more in the way of certain *other* sorts of continuity, psychological, biological, or whatever. But, as it is best to say, they involve *no more*
in the way of *physical* continuity than what is present in the super freezing
variation. To understand "physical continuity" in a way that will falsify the
preceding several sentences will make the expression less fruitful for philosophical investigation. On the other side, and for similar reasons, on a fruitful
understanding of "assimilation," it is best to say this: While in the other variations, there will be varying amounts of different sorts of assimilation involving the original person, in the super freezing replacement case, by contrast,
there will be *no* assimilation of any sort involving that individual.

Relative to almost any fruitful understanding of "assimilation," certain
conditions will generally hold true. A few examples of these follow, none
more interesting than what may be expected: For me to survive their replacement, larger, more central parts of me will require more assimilation than
smaller, less central ones. More than this, a sequence wherein all my matter
changes over by several abrupt replacements of greater, more central parts
will demand more assimilation than a sequence where complete material
changeover is by way of the replacement of lesser, less central parts. For
example, a changeover of abruptly replaced brain quarters requires considerably more assimilation than a changeover, in several billion stages, of individual brain neurons. Perhaps the main reason for this might be that the former, more abrupt process involves less physical continuity than does the
latter, more gradual one.

4. Some Differences in Assimilation for
Some Different Kinds of Ordinary Individuals

As regards questions of identity over time, there are some interesting differences here between us and, in contrast, "functional artifacts," like ships and shirts. Now, as we have already noted in earlier chapters, in certain respects their survival requires less physical continuity than does ours. On the other hand, and as we may now observe, because they are not thinking or living beings, these artifacts cannot have their survival secured by factors of psychological or biological assimilation, whereas we, who are both thinking and living, can have our survival so secured. The interesting differences do not end here. At the least, a third contrast is also worth noticing. Unlike us, an artifact that is involved in certain rather "accidental," or rather "external," relations to sentient beings can, by virtue of those relations, have the prospects for its survival improved considerably. This wants some discussion.

We begin by noticing how, when left alone and in no interesting relations to any sentient beings, a ship that undergoes substantial abrupt replacements is, with respect to the question of its survival, much like a super frozen woman who undergoes parallel replacements: Think of a ship locked up in a warehouse, observed by nobody, for many years. Simpler than the famous ship of Theseus, this wooden ship, or boat, is composed of only four roughly equal wooden planks. By a certain statistical miracle involving many trillions of molecules, a certain plank is destroyed, with those molecules then coming to compose nothing more cohesive than some powder. By another statistical miracle, occurring a few minutes later, some other molecules come to acquire precisely the same place and arrangement. Or, alternatively, the miraculous replacement may occur sequentially, rather than abruptly; in that event, it will be extremely clear that, even at every moment, a ship is there. Either way, a year apart, three subsequent similar miracles lead to a replacement of all of the original ship's original matter. At the end of some years, there is a ship just like the original ship and, moreover, one that has a pretty fair degree of physical continuity with the original. But, intuitively, that is not the original ship.

Variations on the case, in which someone interacts with the ship, give an interestingly different result. Between miracles, the ship present at the time may be taken out of the warehouse and sailed around a bit. In that case, the ship just might survive the miraculous material replacements. Indeed, even if the ship is only put on display and observed at various boat shows, it might possibly survive. On the whole, our intuitions are now in favor of the ship's survival. But these questions are somewhat delicate; it is hard to tell what are the best answers to them. Perhaps it is not determinately true that even a sailed ship survives more than one or two replacements. But, then, it will not be determinately true, either, that the sailed ship fails to survive all four replacements.[3]

The situation with you and me is different. If you are continuously super frozen and your brain undergoes four such miraculous·replacements, then, in any case, you definitely will not survive. This will be determinately true no matter how much you, or your brain and body, or your peculiarly intimate descendants, are perceived, or are utilized, or are involved in still further "passive" interactions with sentient others.

The differences between us and these artifacts ramify further: Suppose that the ship's large parts are not replaced by statistical miracles, but are replaced by people who get new planks from a lumber yard. Between replacements the ship is sailed around. Owing to the intentional activity responsible for the replacements, it is clearer than in the previous case that there is the same ship throughout: In the previous case, perhaps this might not have been determinately true. However that may be, in this present example, more richly involved with purposeful interactions, it is determinately true that the ship survives. By contrast, when *I* am super frozen and skillful surgeons replace quarters of my brain, it is determinately true that I will *not* survive such a grossly disruptive procedure. So, by contrast with artifacts, our own survival is much more heavily involved with the sorts of processes that, naturally or normally, may occur in us, that is, with *internal processes*. By contrast with us, their survival is much less heavily involved with such internal processes and, correlatively, may be much more heavily involved with various sorts of more *external relations*.

Like so much of what I am saying, these remarks are offered on the assumption that, by and large, we have gotten things right about how the world is. If, contrary to all we believe about them, ships and shirts, tables and cars, *are* alive, or *are* thoughtful beings, then the preceding several paragraphs will be just so many words. So, what I am saying has relatively little to do with the meaning of "ship," "shirt," "table," "car" or, for that matter, even "artifact"; it has very much more to do with how matters in fact are with the entities to which these meaningful terms actually happen to refer.

Supposing that our relevant beliefs about them are correct, somewhat different remarks may apply to inanimate objects of nature, like rocks. Unthinking things that are alive, like living bushes, may require a still different treatment, perhaps one that is, in these present regards, much like that appropriate to thinking beings, like ourselves. Perhaps typically living parts of living beings, notably our brains, might require a treatment much like that

---

3. An engaging discussion of artifacts like ships may be found in Mark Johnston's stimulating paper, "Relativism and the Self," in *Relativism*, Michael Krausz, ed., University of Notre Dame Press, 1989.

given for living bushes. Yet again, a clearly dead bush, or at least a (dead) twig, perhaps might require a treatment much like that proper for rocks. Concerned, as we are, with the conditions of our own survival, we will not spend much effort investigating the many further matters in this area.

5. Assimilation and Disassimilation

Over enough time filled with suitable processes, central new parts may become assimilated into a person's life in such a way as to secure the person's survival. Might our conventions for individuating ourselves also assign a role to a sort of converse of this assimilation process? In other words, might a person's original central parts become so *disassimilated* away from him that, after this other process, they are no longer qualified to serve as parts of that very person? It is pretty clear, I think, that we must allow for this sort of gradual disqualification.

For the most impressive disassimilation of my main parts, these parts will be alloted to one or more other people. Over enough time, my original parts may get so caught up in *their* lives, so *assimilated with respect to them*, that, in the bargain, they are *disassimilated with respect to me*. To put some concrete flesh on the bare bones of these abstract remarks, let us generate a suitable variety of examples.

First, we consider an example with just one other person. One for one, my brain-quarters might be abruptly *exchanged* with corresponding quarters of my duplicate's brain. If this sequential exchange is done rapidly, then, by the end, I go over there. In the middle, I will be scattered, part here and part there. Because there has not been enough assimilation, all of the main parts that were mine stay mine. If the sequence occurs very slowly, however, with much assimilation between quarterly exchanges, then I will stay over here, and my duplicate will stay over there.

My acquisition of my duplicate's brain quarters requires a great deal of assimilation, more than does my surviving the destruction of my original brain-quarters and their replacement with newly created quarters. Closely related to each other, there are two reasons for this: First, in the process of exchange, there is already a prior claim on the replacing parts to the effect that these quarters are central parts only of someone else, namely, my duplicate. To override this claim on these quarters, there is needed much assimilation of them with respect to me; only in that way will there occur the required disassimilation of these quarters away from my duplicate. Second, there is another prior claim to be overcome, namely, the claim that, as against any potential competitors, my old brain-quarters are the true central parts of me. For this related claim to be overridden, there must be much disassimilation of these old brain-quarters away from me and, at the same time, much assimilation of the new quarters into my life.

As with brain-quarters, so with thousandths of the brain. In exchanges with a duplicate, these much lesser contributors to mental realization require more assimilation toward me than they require in processes where they are replaced in a more straightforward way, with no competing claims on old parts or new. (Whether with quarters or with thousandths, parallel questions arise with ships: Just as two identical ships each composed of four planks may, in just four steps, sequentially exchange their four main parts, so, of course, a ship made of a thousand planks may, in a thousand steps, be involved in a plank-by-plank exchange with its counterpart. As I see it, the parts of ships are more readily exchangeable than are the parts of our brains: If so, then disassimilation will play less of a role with ships than it does with us. But I will not discuss this matter in detail.)

As may ships, we may be involved in exchange sequences that feature, not just one duplicate, but several of them. Thus a second sort of case: I may first exchange one of my brain-quarters, call it TopRight, with duplicate number one. I may next exchange another quarter, TopLeft, with duplicate number two. Then BottomRight is exchanged with number three and, finally, BottomLeft is exchanged with number four. Done fast or done slow, the survival of each of these four duplicates of me is clear; each person stays where there is three-fourths of his original brain. By contrast, the question of my own survival is heavily involved with how much assimilation takes place.

If there is very much, then I, too, stay put. But, of course, there also may be very little assimilation. If there is very little, then I will not be where the exchanges have been made. Instead, I will become a scattered person, my main parts farmed out to four others. If my duplicates retain these parts for a goodly while, then those brain-quarters will be assimilated into them and, correlatively, disassimilated away from me. Eventually, I will cease to exist. If they do not have these parts for long, then the parts may be rejoined so that, once again, they constitute me in a manner conducive to my thinking.

6. Might We Survive Brain Replacements and even Brain Exchanges?

With these ideas pretty well in hand, I would like to discuss some fairly delicate subjects. These are the question of *brain replacement* and the related question of *personal brain exchange*. In order to have your brain merely replaced, or just exchanged *for* another one, you only need to get rid of your original brain and get a new one instead. It matters not where this new brain, or its parts, come from. In order to have your brain *exchanged with someone else's brain*, however, not only must all of that happen, but more must happen as well: Your new brain must come from someone else; before it is your brain, it must be hers. And, conversely, the brain that was yours must later be her brain. Finally, through all of this, both of you survive. On the face of it, then, exchanging brains with someone else, and surviving that episode, would seem much more difficult to accomplish. But, due to certain features of assimilation and disassimilation, that might not be so.

Here is a possible example of surviving a mere brain replacement: A duplicate of a certain hundredth of your brain comes into existence. Whether by an intentional operation, a statistical miracle, or whatever, the hundredth thus duplicated goes out of your head intact. After that, it may be super frozen or, on a more mundane variant, it may be placed in a pickle jar, to be observed by medical students. Anyway, after that the new hundredth goes into the precise place lately vacated. This whole business may take only a few minutes. Three days later, a duplicate of a second, non-overlapping hundredth comes into existence, replaces another original hundredth that *it* duplicates, while that second hundredth nicely joins up with the first displaced original part. By the end of the year, all of the new hundredths form a brain in your original head and all of the original hundredths form a dead brain in the jar or, on the colder version, they form a revivable brain in a chamber.

It is very clear that, never yourself being in any jar or chamber, you will survive this year. In either version, you will be the person who has gotten so many new brain-parts. Factors of assimilation explain this intuitive answer. But, of course, a second question arises. At the end of the year, where is your original brain?

Although this question is somewhat more delicate, the main intuition is that, in the mundane version, my original brain is dead in the pickle jar. And, in the colder version, it is in the super freezing chamber. Intuitively, the main response is that, in both versions, I have acquired a new brain.

In the super freezing version, my old brain may, after the year, be super thawed. Then it may be placed in a suitable body. Quite clearly, there is now a new person there, not me. There is the intuition that this new person will have the healthy brain that I once had. My account of our survival, which features assimilation differently in force for different sorts of entities, encourages this answer. Far more readily than they can be assimilated into my brain, the new brain-parts will be assimilated into me. This is another way, then, that my account differs from those that say, roughly, "Wherever there is this original brain, functioning well, there I will be."

As is obvious, a minor variant of this example allows for the replacement of my entire body along with, or including, my brain. While hundredths of my original brain are replaced, so, also, are hundredths of the rest of my body. In the frozen version, my original brain and body all will end up as the brain and body of someone else, while I have acquired a new body along with a new brain.

Proceeding along similar lines, there is a pretty good case of my surviving a brain exchange with another person, who also survives: For this case, we just imagine that when a certain hundredth of my brain is removed, so is the precisely similar hundredth of my duplicate, who developed independently. These two hundredths are switched. One by one, after a full year all of the hundredths are changed. The main intuitions are, first, I survive over here and he survives over there and, second, my original brain is now over there, supporting his mentality, while his original brain is now over here, supporting mine. Although the matter is somewhat delicate, it does appear that, each of us surviving, the two of us have switched brains. (And, on the obvious minor variant, the two of us will have switched bodies as well.) On my physically based account, the reason is this: A person's brain parts disassimilate quickly enough from the person himself, but do so only much more slowly, if at all, from the brain they serve to compose (and, similarly, for the parts of a person's body.) At the same time, brain-parts assimilate quickly enough into a new person, but do so only much more slowly, if at all, into a new brain (and, similarly, for the parts of a person's body.) At all events, both intuitively and explanatorily, this is a related way in which my position differs from the view, given roughly, "I go where my healthy enough brain goes."

Because some of the foregoing points are somewhat delicate, I shall not insist on this section's main conclusions. Rather, in a modestly tentative spirit, I shall contrast our most recent case with certain famous examples in the literature: First, of course, there is Locke's old case of the prince and the cobbler possibly exchanging bodies (and brains?) by the exchange of their souls: Understood in any strong sense, that case comports poorly with our world view, while the present case agrees quite well. Understood more charitably, we must, I think, say this about Locke's example: In relation to our system of beliefs, the case is much like the example of the amazing parrot that we entertained in the first chapter.[4] Because the prince and cobbler case is so lacking in relevant detail, if we are charitable, we will be involved in fruitless guessing games. By contrast, because our recent cases are rich enough in relevant realistic details, the worst sort of guessing games do not arise.

4. The example is found in Chapter 27 of Locke's *Essay Concerning Human Understanding*, and is reprinted in John Perry, ed., *Personal Identity*, on page 44. In the same selection, Locke also mentions what was alleged to be a very amazing parrot. In Perry, this aviary mention is made on page 38.

Second, there is the rather realistically detailed case of Shoemaker's, a version of which was presented in the first full section of Chapter 4, where there is a double brain transplant: Your brain goes into someone else's skull, his goes into that part of your original body.[5] Well described only as a case of two people exchanging their bodies and both surviving, this is not properly said to be a case of people exchanging brains.

Third, there is Bernard Williams' famous case in which two people simultaneously undergo a sort of bipolar brain-state transfer device procedure.[6] While core psychology is, presumably, physically realized throughout, the distinctive psychology of each is informationally imposed on the original brain of the other. As I have always responded to the example, and as is Williams' main response as well, that is just a case in which people exchange distinctive psychologies, so to speak, including personalities.[7] Surviving just where he began, each of the two original people retains his brain and the rest of his body. (If core psychology is *not* continuously realized in each brain, then, for there being a mindless middle period, neither of the original people survive anywhere.) By contrast to all three of these famous examples, in our featured case, even while both of them survive a reasonably realistic episode, perhaps two people really do exchange brains (and, in the case's suitable version, perhaps they exchange their bodies, too).

7. Disassimilation and Double Bisection

What I often find quite intriguing is an example that presents a peculiar combination of elements collectively found in some of our previous cases: The present example begins with the slicing of a whole person almost precisely down the middle, so that there is a left side of him separated from a right side. This may be done in any of a number of ways. Here is one of the simplest: First the person is super frozen. Only then is he sliced down the middle. At the same time that this slicing operation is performed on me, a *precisely similar operation* is performed on a precise duplicate of me. (Where did this

---

5. As remarked in an earlier chapter's notes, this case is presented in Shoemaker's *Self-Knowledge and Self-Identity*.

6. This example is the centerpiece of Williams' "The Self and the Future."

7. As is well known, Williams presents his case twice over. The first presentation is aimed at eliciting the response that the people do switch brains and bodies; the second is aimed at eliciting the response that they do not. But when first reading this excellent paper many years ago, I responded "Each man stays put" not only to the second presentation, but also to the first. For very long, it appears, I have been disposed to take toward philosophical essays a rather different mind-set than the one I take toward fiction. As I am rather confident, this pattern of proclivities has served me in good stead.

duplicate come from? That does not matter: My duplicate may have been manufactured via the informational taping process; or, quite by accident, he may have arrived from outer space.)

After these simultaneous and precisely similar slicing operations, there is, in addition to my left half, a precise duplicate of my left half and, of course, there is also a precise duplicate of my right half. None of these four entities is, or serves to constitute, any person, or even any thinking being at all. There is a realistic reason for this which, by emphatic stipulation, I will use to advantage: True enough, the upper brain may be easily divided into two halves, the hemispheres, each of which, in the absence of the other, may quite proficiently, and in pretty much the same way, continue to realize psychology. But the lower brain, or brain stem, cannot be so readily and happily divided. Rather, in order for there to be the realization of much psychology, there must be, along with other things, much more than just the left half of a human brain stem, and there must be much more than the just the right half. So, in the case that I am now specifying, the realistically inspired stipulation is that none of the envisioned halves of the original people will be, or will serve to constitute, any thinking being.

This point having been made clear, we now proceed with our outline of the example's imaginative manipulations: Each of the four salient entities, as we may imagine, will be placed in its own section of a vast super freeze chamber. There is then a suitable joining of *my left* half with the *duplicate right* half, and also a joining of my right half with the duplicate left.

After the new right and left partners are joined, the resulting wholes are allowed to be highly functional. In each of two fairly nearby regions, a whole new human body and brain may be super thawed. There are now two new people, each precisely similar to the other. Never communicating, these two people may be placed in extraordinarily similar environments. Perhaps this may be done by confining them to precisely similar rooms with no view; more kindly and more fantastically, it may be done by placing them on precisely similar planets in precisely similar galaxies, even while they both are prevented from seeing any terribly distant stars.

As is intuitively clear, neither of these people is me. Nor, of course, is either of them my original duplicate. Instead, there are two numerically new people now, each of them just like I used to be. So far, then, the case contains four people: only two at early stages, but two more at this later stage.

For several minutes, these two people may live precisely parallel lives in their precisely similar environments. Then the whole process may be relevantly reversed: After being super frozen again, they are sliced down the middle, left and right. Then the old left-right partners are rejoined, just as they were at the beginning. Finally, there will be super thawing. In this quick scenario, there will still be only four people all told. Because there has been so little disassimilation of our parts, my duplicate and I will survive the whole process. As reflection makes intuitive, in the middle period all four people will be there. There will be the two new individuals who think and experience for those few minutes; and there will also be me and my duplicate who, with our big parts "out on loan," are then much too badly scattered to think or feel.

Alternatively, in their precisely similar environments, the two newly formed people may live precisely parallel lives, not for a few minutes, but for years. Only then will the whole process be relevantly reversed, as in the manner indicated just above. In this much more protracted situation, what happens to the original people? Indeed, and as we might first inquire, what happened to the separated salient parts of them?

As regards the important underlying realities, each new left side is, even after these years, much the same as the old left side from which it developed: For example, as regards the nerve cells that partially compose one of these big parts, both in their individual identity and in their relative arrangement, there is little difference between a left side now and the left several years ago with which this present one is conspicuously continuous. And changes in constituting atoms, for example, will also be the result of quite ordinary, relevantly continuous transformations. So, as is clear enough, one of the new left parts *will be* one of the old left parts, and the other will be the other. Similarly, of course, for the right-side parts. Accordingly, as we may then say, each of the left sides is *rejoined* with the right side with which, before any slicing at all, it first was paired.

By a subsequent super thawing, the people made of these rejoined parts are rendered most highly functional. *Who are* these people that are now before us? Quite clearly, they are *not* the people who ran in parallel for a few years. Moreover, the strong impression is that they *also are not* the people who were, in the first place, sliced down the middle. Rather, these are two numerically *new* people. Intuitively, then, this case contains *six* people; the first two, the middle two, and this final pair.

Because these important parts of me became assimilated into the lives of the two middle people, they became unqualified for constituting me later. This happened during the middle years. At the beginning of these years, I still existed, but was scattered in two large parts. But, as time went on, my important constituents became progressively disassimilated from me so that, eventually, they became unqualified for constituting me. And, as our conventions might have it, the qualifications in question may be such that, once lost, they can never again be regained. (While there might be some indeterminacy regarding fine-grained temporal assignments, at least during that whole middle period I ceased to exist.) So, by the end, as there is nothing left that might ever again constitute me, I do not exist (and never again will exist).

Just as there are interesting differences between our assimilations and the assimilations of ships, so the differences regarding disassimilation may be even more striking. For a case in point, there may be no disassimilation at all in the example about ships most analogous to this protracted double bisection example about people: Cut both of two precisely similar ships right down the middle. As we specify, and as so often actually happens, none of the four entities thus made salient will be, or by itself will serve to constitute, any ship. Get each original ship's left side and join it to what was the right side of the other original ship. The two newly formed ships, produced by these joinings, are to be sailed around for years (with no repairs, or with only a few precisely similar minor repairs, for each). Slice both of these sailed ships down the middle. We still have before us the original halves of the original ships. Rejoin each left ship half with the right half with which, at the very beginning, it was first paired. We now have the original ships themselves back again. In this double bisection case with ships, there are only four ships in all, not six all told. This is a striking difference from what, in the parallel case, happens with people.

As I see it, like other disparities observed in this chapter, this striking difference is, in largest measure, a difference based in a difference of conventions. But, of course, the patterns of our attitudes and concerns might often follow the patterns of our conventions. Consequently, for us, a striking conventional difference might have some considerable importance.

8. Some Strange Doings with Ships

As regards survival, there are important differences between us and ships, but also some important similarities. Because there are these similarities, certain intriguing cases involving ships find analogues in some cases involving us people. Because there are these differences, there are certain interesting disanalogies between the cases, too. In all of this, perhaps there may be the basis for some philosophical illumination of our existence, our nature and our survival.

Some ancient Greeks were exercised by the old problem of the ship of Theseus: This ship, composed of many planks, sails around from port to port. When in each port, some few of its planks are replaced by highly similar planks. After they are replaced, nothing very interesting ever happens with any of the old planks; they might even be allowed to rot. By the end of a year, say, after calling on many ports, all of the original planks have been replaced. As our previous discussion indicates, even with all new planks and all new matter, it will be the same ship.

It was Hobbes, I think, who proposed a more difficult variation on this old and rather easy problem. On the variation, when a plank is replaced it is saved, perhaps by being put in a certain storehouse. At the end of the year, all of the original planks are in the storehouse. The planks may all have been tagged with numbers. Following the order of the numbers, these planks may be intentionally reassembled into their original arrangement. Then, just as at the beginning of the year, these planks certainly compose a ship. Do they compose the *original* ship? Or, do the planks that replaced them compose the original ship? Or, is neither of these the original ship, that ship having passed out of existence in favor of two intimate descendants, each with its own distinctive route of descent. Or, do none of the previous three questions have determinate answers?

Many people respond that only the sailed ship, with the planks replaced, is the original ship. Many others, myself included, have no very strong intuitions, one way or another. In line with this, there may be a variety of defensible positions in the matter, none of them being demonstrable: Perhaps it is defensible that the original ship is composed of the old planks, also that the original ship is the ship composed of the newer planks, also that the original is neither of these more recent ships, also that it is indeterminate whether the old ship is either of these later ships or even whether, at the end of the year, the original ship exists at all. Other positions might also deserve some notice. Concerned as it is with the survival of us people, it is not important for our investigation that we try to decide among the alternative responses to Hobbes's puzzle.

Whatever the best response to it, there is an interesting lesson to be learned from Hobbes's variation that is worth the notice of those concerned with personal identity: If the old planks are never reassembled, and especially if they are allowed to rot, then the way is clear for the newer planks to constitute the original ship, without any sort of uncertainty or indeterminacy in the matter. That is shown by the correct response to the old Greek "problem" or example. As if by magic, when Hobbes has them be stored and reassembled, the old planks might put up a sort of *logical obstacle* for the new planks, as regards how much they can do for the original ship's clear-cut survival. As my wording suggests, this can seem very strange. The appearance of strangeness, however, might be due only to some confusions we harbor about the nature of, and the power of, the conventions governing "ship" and related expressions.

This sort of apparent strangeness is pretty pervasive. By considering a third case, we may notice what may be a more blatant instance of it: Suppose that, instead of being put in the storehouse as a consequence of a *replacement* process, the original planks are put there as part of a gradual and protracted *dismantling* process. They are taken out of the arrangement in just the same order, at just the same times and in very much the same manner as in the previous two cases, but no new planks are ever put in their places. After about a year, there are several stacks of numbered planks in the storehouse. At the same time, of course, there is no ship that is descended from the original ship by a sequence of plank replacements. As in Hobbes's case, the old planks may then be reassembled in their original arrangement. When thus reassembled, those old planks will compose, not just a ship, but the one and only original ship. (So, in the middle period, that original ship is a more or less scattered entity: Part of it is not yet disassembled; in the storehouse, the rest is in the unshiplike form of stacks.)

When we compare this dismantling case with Hobbes's replacement example, we seem to get strong logical magic working in the other direction: By being sequentially inserted into the old planks' places after they have been removed, the *new* planks seem to erect a strong logical barrier against what the *old* planks can do for the original ship's clear survival. As my wording again suggests, this can seem very strange. As I suggest, this more glaring appearance of strangeness also may be due only to some confusions we harbor about the power of, and the character of, our conventions governing "ship" and related expressions.

9. Extrinsicness, Time and Identity

A fairly standard way of trying to articulate the appearance of strangeness is to say this: "The survival of an ordinary concrete individual, even a ship, should be wholly determined only by factors that are *intrinsic* to that ship, or to the history of its "original" constituents. In the cases concerning the different treatments of the planks, no matter which side we take as our main point of reference for what is intrinsic, something that happens "elsewhere," or something that is *extrinsic*, does much to determine the truth-value of a judgment regarding the original ship's identity or survival. But, according to deep intuition and reason, this should not be so; indeed, it cannot be so."

Quite a lot has been written along the lines of the preceding paragraph. Almost all of it, I believe, is badly counterintuitive, and much of it is downright confused.[8] Instead of entering into the details of those discussions, it will be far better, I believe, to expose ourselves to some related examples. Being relevantly simpler, these related cases may blow away most of the motivation behind those misguided efforts.

Let us consider, then, concrete ordinary individuals that, in relevant ways, may be so divided that further individuals of their salient kind are thus pro-

8. For a nice discussion of some of these confusions, see Brian Garrett's usefully clever paper, "Personal Identity and Extrinsicness," *Philosophical Studies*, forthcoming.

duced. Stones are very good examples of this and many bushes, even when alive, are other good examples. I suppose that there are a few exotic ships that may answer this description as well. But let's now look at the common clear cases. To begin, we may consider a rather ordinary rock, or stone.

In case one, starting from its leftmost edge and going to its "central plane," the left half of a certain stone is pretty quickly, but ever so gradually and evenly, ground into dust. That dust is scattered to the winds, and is never after rejoined in any interesting way. In case two, the matter of the left half is again separated from the very same matter on the right, but in a certain much more abrupt way: By means of a blow struck against a chisel, there is a quite sudden separation, from top to bottom along the central plane, of that same matter on the left from that same matter on the right. Forever after, the matter on the right, just like the matter on the left, is never interestingly joined to any other matter.

As is intuitively clear, and as is entirely unsurprising, in the first case, we are left with the original stone, made much smaller by the grinding. Also clear and unsurprising, in the second case, we are left only with two new stones; owing to that severe separation, the original stone has ceased to exist.

Viewed from the right-half's side, so to speak, in this simple pair of cases, there is as much extrinsicness here as there ever is: As regards the original constituents on the right, and all of their internal relations throughout, things may be precisely the same in the two cases. Even so, I do not find my responses to these cases to be surprising in the least. Sometimes, as with the trio of cases about ships, examples featuring extrinsicness and ordinary inanimate entities will occasion some surprise. Other times, as with these examples about stones, such examples will occasion no surprise. It is these latter, simpler examples, I believe, that provide the clearer lesson.

We should not be much bothered by the appearance of strangeness arising only from our encounter with the more complex examples. Instead, we should simply admit that, in relation to ideas about intrinsicness and extrinsicness, we had a somewhat confused preconception regarding our conventions for individuating such ordinary individuals as rocks and stones.

This lesson is not limited to ordinary inanimate things. As I recently suggested, living bushes provide good lessons, too: In case one, the left half of a bush may be ground into fine powder, forever dispersed. At the leftmost points of those cuttings, the branches may heal well. In this first case, reduced in size by half, the original bush continues to flourish on the right side. In case two, the bush is just severed down the middle. The left half is uprooted and replanted. The wounds on both sides heal well. Even as there are now flourishing plants on both sides, none of this plant material is ever interestingly rejoined. In this second case, there are two new bushes, and the original bush passes out of existence, completely and forever.

As regards the plant material on the right, in both of these cases, the intrinsic factors are all just the same. It is only some other factors, again call them *extrinsic*, if you will, that make a difference. To my mind, at least, all of this is intuitively compelling and, perhaps more important, none of it even appears to be surprising. In the light of this sort of exposure, we should let our false preconceptions wither away. After all, in advance, why should we expect ourselves to know so terribly much about the various conventions of individuation that we may implicitly maintain?

What shall we say, however, about thinking entities, just like ourselves, who have the capacity for conscious experience? Here it seems much harder to believe that extrinsic matters can make a difference for survival. Eventually, in Chapters 6 and 8, I shall argue that indeed they can make the difference, just as well as in the cases of living bushes and inanimate rocks. Before embarking on those endeavors, however, it will be useful to get a feeling for what we shall be up against. As a first step toward that, I turn to consider, in the next section, some cases about people that parallel the somewhat complex trio of examples that, in the just previous section, featured ships.

10. From Strange Ships to Puzzling People: The Hobbesian Personal Case

Each of those three cases about ships finds a close parallel in a case concerning people: Where a ship has a hundred roughly equal planks, we may treat roughly equivalent hundredths of a person's brain; where a ship has a thousand, we may consider thousandths. The old Greek case finds a parallel in an example where we sequentially replace, over considerable time, say, thousandths of a brain. The appropriate case about people will be a standard, full-blooded case of much assimilation: Just as none of the old Greek planks, once removed, ever did much later to constitute a ship, so none of the removed brain-parts ever again serves to do anything much toward constituting any person. Just as, between replacements, the ship then involved takes on cargo, sails, weighs anchor and floats, so also, between replacements, the person then involved walks, talks, thinks, feels and sleeps. Just as, at the end of the ancient year, it is clear that the original ship survives, so, at the end of the futuristic year, it is clear that the original person survives.

Second, to parallel Hobbes's with a case about people, we must take good care of the brain-parts that are replaced by their duplicates: After their removal, these complex parts may be kept alive in different vats. By way of their vats being marked, the brain-parts may be numbered. In order to be synchronized with parts later removed, while in its vat a part removed earlier may be put through an appropriate sequence of states. The induced sequence will parallel the more naturally caused progress of its replacement in the continuously functioning brain. At the end of the year, these synchronized old parts may be rejoined just as the numbering directs. They will then compose a brain that is qualitatively identical to the example's continuously intact brain. Both the brain they then cohesively compose and also the continuously intact brain may be placed in duplicates of the original body. Now there are two people in the situation.

Who, if anyone, is the original person? Unlike the possibly indeterminate situation with which Hobbes's two ships presented us, in this parallel personal case the correct answer is extremely clear: The original person is the person whose brain-parts were, over a year, sequentially assimilated; the person with the old brain-parts is someone else, perhaps an importantly interesting descendant of the original.

Just as well as they do in the first sort of parallel personal case, where no brain-parts are well preserved and later rejoined, the replacing brain-parts constitute the original person throughout this Hobbesian variation. Given ample assimilation for the newer parts, the preservation, synchronization and rejoining of the old brain-parts is completely powerless to undermine, even partially, what the replacing parts can accomplish in this regard. So, in one place where the Hobbesian nautical example gave an appearance of magic at work, in this *Hobbesian personal case*, by contrast, there is no suggestion of even a mild mystery.

In another place, however, there seems to be, in the Hobbesian personal case, a *more powerful* magic at work than there appeared in Hobbes's nautical example. This powerful magic concerns the relation of the Hobbesian personal case to a third sort of personal example. Presenting no potentially confusing competitors, this third case mirrors the third example in the nautical trio, the straightforward dismantling and reassembly of a ship's planks. This third personal case is, of course, a standard case of the separation and rejoining of a person's brain-parts. By a sequential process, someone's brain is separated into a hundred roughly equal parts. If these parts are well synchronized, so that they may be later rejoined just as well as at the outset, then the person will clearly survive.

This Hobbesian personal example presents a glaring appearance of strangeness: By coming into the situation as they do, the new brain-parts erect a terribly strong logical barrier against what the old brain-parts can do for the original person's survival. In two ways, the strangeness here is more striking than the apparent queerness in the analogous case with ships. First, in the Hobbesian personal example, it is very clear that only the person with the continuous assimilation is the original individual; intuitively, there is not even a suggestion of indeterminacy in this matter. Consequently, there appears an *enormously strong logical barrier* against what the old brain-parts can possibly do. Second, in an example concerning us people, who are subjects of conscious experience, the appearance of *any* logical obstacle along these lines, even a rather weak one, seems to be utterly bizarre. Putting these two points together, the present appearance of magic is all but shocking.

Why is there the appearance of this very great strangeness? In large measure, this appearance may stem from certain confusions we harbor. Some of these confusions might concern the nature of, and the power of, the conventions governing "person" and related expressions, such as "sentient being." How can our conventions be so peculiarly powerful that they can jump across gaps of space and time to *stop certain* small, simple things from constituting certain bigger, more complex ones? And, in the bargain, they *get other* small, simple things to constitute the very same complex entities! As sensible speakers of a sensible language, we may be somewhat given to think, we ought not to have conventions like that.

Whatever its precise nature, our confusion in this linguistic matter is of a piece with our confusion regarding the conventions for our artifact words, for "rock" and for "bush." In the previous section, we did a fair amount to expose this sort of confusion, and to weaken its hold on us. Yet, even as we there remarked, and as we now feel all the more forcefully, in the case of us people, the appearance of magic is very much greater. Considering the great discrepancy in apparent strangeness, it is likely, I suggest, that some further confusion is at work in the personal case, a confusion that was altogether absent from our thinking about the nautical examples, as well from our thinking about the examples of the bushes and the stones.

This other source of error might involve beliefs of ours that concern how we deeply differ from entities, like ships, and stones, and even bushes, that are not conscious beings. Perhaps this confusion involves certain false beliefs about ourselves that we harbor. These false beliefs do not determine our dominant responses to the noted examples, of course, which are instead determined by stronger, and more realistic, beliefs about ourselves. By contrast, this explanatory suggestion runs, the weaker beliefs about our nature may issue in a feeling of strangeness that the dominant responses should be as they are or, perhaps better, may issue in a great strengthening of such a feeling.

What are these rather weak but potentially confusing beliefs? One of the beliefs might be this: As conscious beings, we need no conventions to demarcate ourselves from anything else in the world. Nor can any mere conventions do much in that regard. Why might we harbor this false belief? A large part of the reason may be that we hold certain other weak beliefs about ourselves. Prominent among them may be our beliefs in the six metaphysical doctrines, noted in our second chapter. In particular, we might be here affected by a belief in the absoluteness of subjects of consciousness.

Perhaps these two sorts of confusions do not fit well with each other. The one concerns the character of the linguistic conventions governing the application of our words for demarcating ourselves. By contrast, the other is to the effect that our survival can't really have much to do with any conventions at all, no matter what their character. Even so, the badness of this fit need not detract from the total explanation suggested. After all, what we are attempting to explain is not why we hold one of our more accurate ideas, but why we are confused about certain matters. And, of course, when we are confused, we might well be much influenced by ideas that, in addition to being deficient individually, cohere poorly with each other. So, perhaps our explanatory remarks are well suited to accounting for this striking appearance of magical strangeness.

6

PHYSICALLY BASED SUBJECTS AND THEIR EXPERIENCES: AGAINST THE SIX METAPHYSICAL DOCTRINES

The best approach to our survival, I have been arguing, is one that is based on, or inspired by, the physical approach. For some of those who are philosophically most sensitive, however, all of this may have proceeded too fast. They may agree that, with mere ships, for instance, our conventions really are needed to discriminate them, one from the other and, indeed, each from the rest of the world. And this is how it is, too, they may agree, with ever so many other sorts of ordinary things: rocks, mountains, planets, bushes, brains, and so on. Moreover, they may also agree, an appropriate physically based account is just the ticket for understanding the survival of these non-conscious entities.

But *we subjects of experience*, they will insist, are radically different from these ordinary physical individuals. As regards our own survival, it will be objected, any mere conventions are entirely irrelevant. Rather, the fundamental facts of our nature, with no help from conventions, ensure that each of us is, completely and absolutely, individuated from everything else that there ever may be. It is just this, some will say, that is the true lesson of the extra verbal magic felt in our own case.

This line of disagreement is undeniably appealing. But what is it, we may ask, that is the source of its appeal? My diagnostic suggestion is that most of that source may lie with our inclinations to believe in the six metaphysical doctrines that we noted in our second chapter.

When thinking of ourselves *as being conscious*, it can appear that these six propositions, and not any physically oriented thoughts, represent our most deeply held view of our experiences and of ourselves. In this frame of mind, the thought occurs that we believe most deeply, not in an objective view of ourselves as structured complexes occupying regions of physical space and time, but, rather, we believe in one of the more subjectively flavored views: Perhaps, the thought occurs, we believe a hybrid view or, perhaps, we even accept the purely subjective view of ourselves.

On these alternative views, we are not susceptible to any conventional demarcation. Accordingly, we cannot be susceptible to involvement with any apparent verbal magic at all. Forsaking one's favored alternative conception, one may sometimes go along with a physically based account of ourselves. Then one may encounter such puzzle cases as that view allows to arise and, thus, there will be the appearance of much verbal magic. For those who profess a more subjectively flavored view of ourselves, the appearance of such magic only underscores the truth of the six metaphysical doctrines, and the truth of their endorsed alternative, with which those doctrines accord.

If this diagnosis is on the right track, then the appearance of great verbal magic indicates a need to join issue with the six metaphysical doctrines. Having postponed a thorough examination of them from the second chapter, it is, in any case, high time for us to expose these propositions to scrutiny.

Searching argument may reveal that, according to our deepest beliefs in the matter, these doctrines represent no metaphysical truths at all. If that is what searching arguments show, then we may hold that, despite its allowing for the appearance of so much "verbal magic," the physically based treatment we have offered may be a reasonably adequate account of our survival. It is the main aim of the present chapter to provide arguments to just this effect.

1. What Do the Six Doctrines Claim?

What sorts of claims are made by the six metaphysical doctrines? As a case in point, let us discuss the claim made by the doctrine of the privacy of experience. And, then, as another case in point, we may briefly discuss the doctrine of the indivisibility of subjects. From our discussion of these two instances, we may get a pretty good idea, I think, of the intended import of all six doctrines.

At the same time, but in two different rooms, two precisely similar people may have experiences that, like the subjects themselves, are just exactly alike. Yet we say that, not only *are* their experiences numerically distinct, but they *must* be distinct.

We may compare the experiences of these people with certain familiar physical conditions of theirs, say, with their colds: At the same time, these two people may have, not only precisely similar experiences as of having colds, but also may have precisely similar colds. As we say, however, even their colds themselves are distinct from each other: The one has her own cold, while the other has her qualitatively identical but numerically distinct cold. And this is not only the way these colds *do* occur, but the way they *must* occur.[1]

As I see it, these necessities are rooted in certain logical features of our language. These features underlie pervasive parallels: On each of two precisely similar bushes, there may be a crack in a certain branch, also precisely similar. Yet the one bush can have only its own crack, while the other must have its numerically different crack. So, too, with precisely similar stones and their exactly identical cracks, each crack necessarily occurring in only the very stone whose crack it must be.

There are figures of speech that might seem to break the parallel here: We say that one person "gives a cold" to another, and that the second then "catches the cold" or "gets the cold" from the first. But even the slightest logical pressure shows these mere figures to be quite superficial: If just the first person, for example, receives a remedy and gets well, her particular cold will then cease to exist. The other person, who remains ill, will still have her particular cold; this other cold will not have ceased to exist.

Just as me and my duplicate each can have only his own cold, so a certain bush and its duplicate, we may say, each can have only its own illness. The illness of the one plant may precisely parallel that of the other in every phase of every process and, in certain cases, the two may be identically brought on by the same common cause. In certain parallel cases, the same sort of thing may occur with us and our colds. By the same token, in certain other cases, just as, in a very innocuous sense, one person may "catch his cold from another" so, in a similarly innocuous sense, one bush may catch its illness from another.

But although there are these parallels, there also appears to be a deep difference between the privacy of one's experiences on the one hand and, on the other, the more superficial privacy of one's colds (and the superficial privacy of a particular bush's illnesses.) According to the metaphysical doctrine of the privacy of experience, there really is a deep difference. One way of indicating this difference, a friend of the doctrine may urge, is by noting certain epistemological relations: First, in some sense, only I can be directly aware of my physical colds, while you, by contrast, will be aware of them only indirectly. (But the difference here seems to be a matter of degree, not one of two radically different kinds of cognitive access to the state in question.)

1. An interesting discussion of the privacy of experience occurs in A. J. Ayer, *The Problem of Knowledge*, Penguin Books, 1956.

Second, if I have an experience, then I must be aware of the main features of the experience. (But, if my nerves are relevantly blocked, I may be entirely unaware of my cold, including its main features, even if I continue to have it in full measure.)

These epistemological differences may themselves derive from, and be indicative of, metaphysical differences between our experiences and the obviously physical conditions that are our colds: Although there is a *metaphysical* barrier to people having, or sharing, numerically the same experience, there is no such barrier to people having numerically the same cold. Against the sharing of colds, by contrast, there is only a conventional or a semantical barrier.

The fact of this metaphysical barrier, friends of the doctrine may continue, might be indicated perspicuously, if obliquely, by a reference to a certain deep difference between possible languages for us to employ: The privacy of our colds, unlike that of our experiences, is merely a product of the particular way in which we happen to speak about the colds that occur to people. If we were to speak slightly differently, then we would say that the two subjects have numerically the same cold. The linguistic difference here would be quite slight, and even superficial: If we spoke in this alternative way, we would not miss out on asserting anything significant about reality. By contrast, imagine that we spoke in a way that did not allow us to assert the numerical distinctness, not of any physical colds, but of two people's experiences. Then, according to the doctrine of experiential privacy, we would speak a philosophically inferior language: If we spoke in that way about our *experiences*, then we would miss out on asserting important facts about reality. A statement about the numerical distinctness of precisely similar colds, then, is based primarily in philosophically dispensable conventions of the language we happen to employ; not so with a statement about the numerical distinctness of experiences.

According to another of the six doctrines, experiential subjects are indivisible. One way in which the doctrine may be elaborated is this: By the division of their constituting matter, a subject's brain and body certainly may be divided in two. But, even if those divisions occur, the possibilities for the person himself will still be severely limited: Either he will go in the one direction, or he will go in the other or, finally, just when the division occurs, he will cease to exist.

Although this way of putting the matter can be useful in making the doctrine vivid, it can also give rise to some confusion concerning its import. After all, we may say much the same thing for a non-conscious bush: Suppose that the matter that constitutes a certain bush is divided nicely in half. Then, in many cases, the bush itself will be divided in half. And, in many of these many cases, having given rise to two new bushes, the original bush will cease to exist. The very matter that used to constitute just one bush now, after its division, comes instead to constitute two bushes. Yet we may still say this: Either the original bush will go in the one direction, or it will go in the other or, finally, and as is true in the case at hand, the original bush will cease to exist. So it is, too, even for such humble inanimate entities as rocks and stones.

The doctrine of the indivisibility of subjects is not confined to asserting any such logical, or semantical, or conventional points as hold for wholly unthinking bushes. To be sure, in certain cases there will be a semantical barrier against the continued existence of a severed bush: One original bush cannot, by dividing, *become two new bushes and still continue to exist*. But, of course, this has nothing at all to do with any deep question of metaphysical indivisibility. For one single bush cannot, simply or in any way at all, become two new bushes and still continue to exist. That is a semantical barrier, so to say, against the continued existence of a bush that would become other bushes. The doctrine about experiential subjects, by contrast, means to make a metaphysical point. Owing to our basic metaphysical nature, we subjects cannot divide at all. It is for this basic reason that, unlike non-conscious bushes, one of us cannot, by dividing, give rise to the existence of two new beings of her own predominant kind.

In addition to contrasting with claims that are based in semantics, the six metaphysical doctrines also contrast with statements that primarily concern matters of empirical fact or, perhaps better, natural fact. Now, just as there is a certain necessity attaching to semantical truths, there is another quite different sort of necessity attaching to many of these propositions of natural fact. For example, there is some minimum amount of oxygen that is necessary for any ordinary adult human being, like you or me, to survive for a full day. In just this amount, there may be oxygen in a certain sealed chamber. Then there is the *real possibility* of your going into that chamber and, after using up some of the oxygen, your coming out half a day later. But there is not any real possibility of your going into that chamber and surviving for two full days. Nor is there any real possibility of your going into that chamber and, sharing that oxygen with ten other normal human adults, your surviving. Rather, as a matter of natural necessity, when trying to share that little oxygen with that many people for anything like that length of time, then, like the others, you must die.

Again, it may be that there are some terribly tiny particles that, as a matter of natural fact, are indivisible. There will, in actual fact, be no real possibility of their division. Rather, as a matter of natural necessity, none of these particles will ever divide.

The necessity attaching to the six metaphysical doctrines is also meant to be a far deeper necessity than this necessity of certain natural facts. In comparison with the metaphysical necessity attaching to the privacy of experiences, and to the indivisibility of subjects, this natural necessity, like the aforementioned semantical necessity, is a superficial sort of thing. Or, such is the thought of the friends of the six metaphysical doctrines.

For my part, I am somewhat skeptical about whether concerning experiences, or whether concerning subjects, or whether concerning anything else in concrete reality, there is any such deep metaphysical necessity at all. For one thing, I am doubtful whether there is any necessity that, on the one hand, is as worldly and substantive as the necessity attaching to certain truths of natural fact and, at the same time and on the other hand, is as epistemically accessible and secure as that attaching to the most familiar and simple truths primarily based in convention or semantics. But, in this discussion, I will not dwell on any skeptical idea of such great generality. Rather, the position for which I will argue is much more modest: Even if there are some deep metaphysical truths, which have this double-level necessity, the six doctrines about ourselves and our experiences are not statements of that sort.

2. How Might These Doctrines Be Contested Persuasively?

How might a claim about the metaphysics of experience, or about the metaphysics of experiential subjects, be persuasively contested? It sometimes seems that, for anything very persuasive at all to be offered, an impossibly strong case against the claim must be provided. Thus it may seem that no adequate case can possibly be provided.

At times, for example, I have thought that, in order to have a really persuasive case of my sharing an experience, I must confront a situation in which it is apparent to me, by the very nature of my experience, that I am sharing an experience. Similarly, I have thought that, in order to have a good case of, say, my dividing while conscious, there must be, available for me, a distinctively revelatory experience of my consciously dividing. But, of course, there cannot be any such cases.

There cannot be experientially revealing cases of my sharing experience: I cannot have the experience of both being myself having a certain experience and also of being someone else having that experience. For I cannot have the experience of being someone else at all. Nor can there be experientially revealing cases of my conscious division: I cannot have an experience of first being one person who has a certain experience and then being two people each of whom continue to have that experience. For I cannot have the experience of being two people at all. So it has seemed to me, at times, that there cannot be any really persuasive case to bring against the idea that experience is absolutely private, or against the idea that a conscious subject is indivisible, or against any of the other metaphysical doctrines.

The apparent requirement of distinctively revealing experience might, however, be as unnecessary for our goals as it is impossible to satisfy. As far as their qualitative character goes, as far as any internal mark they might conceivably provide, there might be nothing especially interesting about the experiences of a subject who, while continuously conscious, comes to divide, or comes to share experience with another, or whatever. In their qualitative character, the experiences of such a person may not differ at all from experiences of people who never do divide, and who never come to share experience with others. The difference between conscious dividers, experiential sharers, and so on, on the one hand, and, on the other, people who live quite normal mental lives, might lie elsewhere.

Against the six metaphysical doctrines, certain cases may be highly persuasive even if they give us nothing in the way of novel, revelatory experience for the subject ever to have. The persuasive power may come, instead, from our being brought to focus on *causal conditions* that, according to our deepest beliefs in these matters, may provide for conscious personal divisions, or for sharing of experience, or for whatever. The right sort of causally focused cases might persuade us that, according to our deepest beliefs in these matters, there is no metaphysically significant separation between the most direct causal conditions of our experiences and those experiences themselves. As we may deeply believe, the former might be certain physical processes that immediately precede a person's experiences at any given time, while the person's experiences themselves might be certain directly subsequent objective processes, perhaps even certain physical processes.

Although it is not impossible to describe relevantly persuasive examples, it is not easy, either, to propose cases that will contest the metaphysical doctrines in a satisfactory way. For one thing, suitable cases must satisfy four conditions. First, because we try to expose what are our deepest beliefs about our actual nature and about the real character of our experiences, it is important that the cases be *reasonably realistic*. Second, because we want our physically oriented beliefs most directly to join issue with our inclinations toward the subjective doctrines, it is important that, at every crucial stage in our cases, there be *conscious experience present*. Third, because we do not want continuous consciousness unduly to influence our judgments of survival, it is important that, in our examples, the *causal ground* of our subjects' experiences is *highly conspicuous*, a safeguard recommended by our discussion of the second chapter. Fourth, to comport well with our investigations of the last three chapters, there should be, in each of our cases, at least a pretty fair degree of *physical continuity* for our central physical parts. In order that all four conditions be met, our examples must be rather elaborate.

3. Against the Metaphysical Privacy of Experiences

In arguing against the idea that experiences are metaphysically private, we shall consider two related cases. As with several cases that we will later employ in discussing some related topics, the most basic features of both of these examples derive from Arnold Zuboff's highly imaginative work.[2] The first case encourages the idea that, at a given time, two different people might have numerically the same experience. The second motivates the idea that a particular experience may first be had only by one person and may later be had only by a quite different person. If both of these ideas are on the right track, or are derailed only by conventional considerations or by recalcitrant natural facts, then there will be little left to the metaphysical doctrine of experiential privacy.

Suppose that, because our brains are in states of precisely the same sort, both me and my identical double are simultaneously having experience of precisely the same rather simple sort. Secured so that I do not move at all, in one room, I look at a red circle on a blue background and listen to a mechanical piano play middle C. In an identical room across the hall, he has just the same sort of experience just then. To keep our two brains, and our two streams of total experience, running in perfect parallel, we may assume a strong form of causal determinism to hold, along with parallel particular conditions. Alternatively, we may assume a statistical miracle to hold, one that involves all of the parallels needed by the rest of our example. Either assumption is within the broad outlines of our objective view of the world.

Suppose that, while my brain is stimulated to support conscious experience throughout, the left and the right half of my brain are each fitted at their interface, slowly and gradually, with radio communicators, or transceivers. Not only are the brain halves, or half-brains, separated slowly and gradually, but, in line with that, the communicators are put in gradually: From top to bottom, my brain is very slowly severed. As the nerves connecting my half-brains are severed, a few at a time, more and more of the transceivers' parts are put in place. There is here what we may call a *zipper procedure*, or a *zip-*

2. The work in question, which forms the basis for about half of this chapter's discussion, is almost entirely unpublished. Most of the material of which I am aware, I heard on about a dozen casettes of taped lectures, which Zuboff kindly sent me a few years ago. The only published writing of his that directly pertains to these matters, so far as I know, is his brilliant but brief paper, "The Story of a Brain," in D. Hofstadter and D. Dennett, eds., *The Mind's I*, Bantam Books, 1982.

pering. At any time in the zippering, no more than a fraction of one percent of the original connections are broken and not yet replaced by transceiver connections. So, for example, halfway through the zippering, nearly fifty percent of the original connecting nerves are replaced by similarly communicating transceiver parts and nearly fifty percent of those nerves are still in place and still communicating between the half-brains. A zippering is also used to place transceivers between the half-brains and the adjacent parts of the (head of the) body to which they have been normally connected.

Because of the gradual character of this zippering, there is no time at all, no worrisome gap, during which communication between the half-brains is significantly reduced or altered. Because there is no gap, there is a continuous flow of conscious experience in our example. Gradual as the replacement process is, it comes to an end soon enough: The needed transceivers are completely implanted. In the other room, at the same time, my duplicate undergoes just the same operation.

These transceivers will at first be only a fancier, more indirect means of having my neural impulses proceed just as they normally would, without the presence of the devices. We may suppose that, though the total physical explanation is more complex, my mental processes will proceed just as they would normally.

We next separate each of the people into three spatially distant parts. During my separation, my three parts continue communicating in ways that are, in relevant respects, quite normal. Because of this, I continue to have the same conscious experience. At the end of the separation, I am in three rooms. My left half-brain is in a life supporting vat in one room, my right is in a vat in a second and, still in the original room, my debrained body sits with my eyes trained on the red circle. Because of the relevant normalcy of the communications, my three parts run in a suitable parallel; sequentially, they are in just the states in which they would be were they normally connected all in the original room. Because of this, I continue to have conscious experience of the red circle on the blue background, of middle C, and so on.

At the same time that I am being separated into three communicating pieces, my twin is divided in just the same tripartite manner. At every moment, each of us has precisely the same sort of total conscious experience as the other. By the end of the division process, the two of us are, collectively, scattered in six rooms.

Then a special switch is flicked. Thereupon, my duplicate's left-half brain communicates with my right-half brain, and with the rest of my body, in just the same way, and at just the same times, as does my own left half-brain. As we are supposing, there is, both causally and otherwise, perfect symmetry in these communications. Similarly, my own left half-brain communicates with his right half-brain, and with the rest of his body, in just the same way, at just the same times, as does his own. So, too, for communications of his right half-brain with my two obviously complementary parts and for my right with his left and his rest of body. So that we foster no jumbling, no left half-brain will communicate with the other left half-brain, of course, and neither right will do so with the other.

These communications continue for five minutes. Then another switch is thrown, whereupon all of the new communications cease while the old ones continue. During these five minutes, the two of us have, not merely qualitatively identical experience, but numerically one and the same conscious experience. Or, if we do not, or if the matter is indeterminate—both, by my lights, less favored descriptions, then any barrier to our sharing one experience is only semantical, conventional and superficial.

As Zuboff himself is well aware, having the rest of the bodies in play is not really essential to this thought experiment.[3] We may place the whole brains in vats near the outset, and may destroy the original bodies. Experience will then be provided by, say, electrode stimulations. My half-brains may generate experience by, first, communicating with each other and, second, each having suitable electrode stimulation for its part in optimally generative communications. It is just a nice bonus in the offered description of the example, then, to have the rest of the original people, the "whole bodies," also in play, with the qualitatively identical rooms more normally filling the causal roles that appropriate electrode devices might more directly fill. In the descriptions of the Zuboffian examples that follow, sometimes I will omit mention of the rest of the body, of the transceivers it might have, and of the communications it might then make with appropriate brain-parts. As context indicates, and if she so wishes, the reader may fill in these extra details.

In presenting this thought experiment, we have made several suppositions. Let us now observe what appear to be the most important of these. First, we have supposed that, without great detriment to its subsequent functioning, my brain may be divided in half, left and right. Now, in quite a few people, as is well known, the higher brain has in fact been divided, left and right, as a remedy for severe epilepsy. But no surgeon has come anywhere near being able to divide the lower brain. Can that be done, too? Parfit has written, "it seems likely that it would never be possible to divide the lower brain in a way that did not impair its function."[4] How serious an objection might there be here? For several reasons, I do not think that it can be very serious. For one

3. This awareness is made plain on the tapes cited in the just previous note. As Zuboff there acknowledges, his use of a debrained body (as something for the separated brain parts collectively to control, and as something from which they may receive stimulation) derives from Daniel Dennett's excellent paper, "Where Am I?," in The Mind's I.

4. Reasons and Persons, p. 255.

thing, there are possibilities and there are possibilities. It may be impossible for us mere humans, clumsy and stupid as we are, to generate a bio-technology that will support a really well-wrought bisection of the brain stem. But, so what? If we were very much more knowledgeable, intelligent and proficient, then there would be no obstacle.

For another thing, we can divide the brain in another way and, then, spell out the rest of our thought experiment accordingly. As with my duplicate, my brain may be divided, not left and right, but *higher* and *lower*, the cerebrum going one way, the brain stem and cerebellum the other. In this division, a zippering may be used. Then conscious experience will never cease. We then rewrite our example quite mechanically: Wherever we had my left half-brain, we now speak of my upper brain; wherever we had my right, we now speak of my lower brain; wherever there was my duplicate's left, there is now his upper brain, and so on. When the first switch is thrown, my higher brain communicates, as well, with his lower brain and rest of body, my lower brain, with his higher brain and rest of body, and so on. As should be obvious, there is nothing, in any of this, that requires a division between left and right. Providing that each of at least two brain parts is sufficiently important for generating experience, or at least for generating conscious experience of a particular character, any division will do.

A third reply is, by far, the most fundamental: Owing to various physical facts, it really may be impossible to generate conscious experience in anything relevantly like the way lately imagined. But if that is the only barrier to the generation of experience, then there is no deep metaphysical barrier. Further, suppose that the physical facts were different, so that experience could be generated along the imagined lines. Will the two subjects then share, for five minutes, one and the same experience? In such a different circumstance, it appears that they will. Unlikely though it is, let us suppose that this appearance is deceptive. But if even these optimally communicating subjects do not share experience, then that will be owing only to conventions that, even for their case, dictate an alternative description. This conventional prohibition against experiential sharing also will be no metaphysical barrier. So, in any case, there will be no metaphysical necessity in the idea that a subject always has only her very own experience. As the reader may bear in mind, this most basic reply pertains, just as well, to a discussion of our other suppositions.

Second, in describing our example, we have supposed that there need not be any problem of a time lag for communication between the somewhat distant members of the array of personal parts. This supposition is relevantly realistic: Signals between the rooms travel at the speed of light. That is very, very many times faster than the transmission of signals along our nerves. Playing into this fact, we may remove very short stretches of those nerves hooked up to transceivers. The time that it would have taken an impulse to travel one of these stretches will be the same as that required to trigger the supersensitive transceivers and for the signals to travel from room to room. Anyway, if there are any serious limitations here, they are all owing to what are merely physical facts.

Third, we have supposed that the imagined radio communications will, indirectly, be effective in continuing the realization of psychological capacities and processes. But perhaps the adjacent parts of our brains set up a field, for example, whose integrity and strength requires them to be adjacent? Then we might never in fact have an experiencer who is, at once, both conscious and spatially scattered. Although this may be a possibility, it is fair for us to make the contrary assumption. This assumption, after all, contradicts nothing in our deepest beliefs about ourselves. Indeed, as far as I can tell, the assumption is actually true. Anyway, if there are any serious limitations here, they are all owing to just so many merely physical facts.

Fourth, we have supposed that, in the middle period, when the personal parts were both spatially separated and mutually communicating, just the same two original people are still all of the subjects in the situation. Against this, some will object that, in this separated array, we have lost the original people altogether. Once the new communications begin, they will say, there is no reason to think there are two people anymore. Perhaps it would be better to say that, when this happens, there is just one person. Or, perhaps we might best say that it is then indeterminate how many people are in the situation. To this objection, there are a couple of replies.

On the one hand, suppose that, once the new communications join in, it is not definitely true that there are two people in the situation. Then that will be bad news, not good, for the six metaphysical doctrines. One piece of bad news concerns the doctrine of the separateness of subjects. According to that idea, there is a metaphysical barrier to the merging of two people. The people at the beginning of this case should, accordingly, neither merge into one being, nor come together into some indeterminate situation as to personal number, but should remain clearly separate throughout. Insofar as the present example might fail to strike a hard blow at the doctrine of the privacy of experiences, it will strike one at the parallel doctrine concerning the status of the subject of experiences. Friends of the six doctrines can't have it both ways.

More bad news is this: Whether the example primarily contravenes the privacy of experience or whether, by contrast, it primarily contravenes the separateness of subjects itself seems to be anything but a deep metaphysical matter. Rather, the considerations that would make one, rather than another, doctrine more vulnerable to the example seem to be largely conventional factors, even if these be well-entrenched conventions that are more natural for us than arbitrary. This suggests that friends of the subjective doctrines can't even have it either way.

On the other hand, the best description of the example, our strong intuitions urge, really is that there are the two people throughout. Even in the middle period, with much communication going, I will be just where my three original parts are. Indeed, at that time, if my original brain halves are destroyed, then I will be the only person then to cease existing. By contrast, if the other brain halves are destroyed, instead, then my twin would be the only person then to cease existing. My five minutes of communication with my twin won't alter the usual situation. In our theoretical terms, one reason for this is that, in the mere five minutes, there has been very little *assimilation* among my parts and my twin's parts. As is evident enough, our strong beliefs about ourselves favor this idea much more than they favor any competing subjective doctrines.

Fifth, we have presented an example that has these two salient features: On the one hand, the original people become spread out into parts that are, in substantial measure, *spatially separated*. On the other hand, not only is there still maintained the usual causal relations of these parts in generating experience, but there is imposed, on top of that, a symmetric absolute *causal redundancy* in the generation of experiences. For example, with regard to influencing anyone's right half-brain, and rest of body, each of two left half-brains plays a precisely identical causal role. It is the second of these salient features that is most important to the persuasive power of the examples.[5]

Although it is the feature of symmetric absolute causal redundancy that is most important to our example's wanted persuasive power, it is worth noting, I think, that the feature of substantial spatial separation provides, at the least, some psychologically useful assistance. For one tends to think of oneself as having one's experiences centered at a certain point, the seat or source of the experiences as well as the point of one's experiential perspective. We also

---

5. In "Causal Overdetermination," *The Journal of Philosophy*, 1979, Martin Bunzl raises doubts about how often there occur situations properly deserving that description. Perhaps, in the actual world, that might never happen. Can such doubts mean an objection to our example? For at least two reasons, they cannot.

First, when applied to our present example, the sorts of considerations that Bunzl adduces will mean, if anything, a *more* intimate causal relationship among the organic parts that, in perfect symmetry, play absolutely redundant causal roles. For the purposes of our argument, this causal redundancy certainly will be at least as good as any causal overdetermination.

A second reason is more fundamental: If anything does, what will mean little or no causal overdetermination in the actual world? It will be certain natural facts, even physical facts, of the actual world. Accordingly, we may stipulate an alternative possible world, or a counter-factual character for the actual cosmos, where there are no "troublesome" natural facts. By adding such a purified version of our example, we may achieve overkill in the topic area.

have more realistic tendencies that go in the other direction, but, usually, these latter are neither overwhelming nor entirely successful. So, we may vaguely think that a person's experience is *sort of* centered in a point in his head. This habitual tendency may help make us disinclined to allow that two people ever share experiences. For, as we may think to ourselves, the *one* person's experience is the particular experience that is centered just in *his* head, while the *other's* experience is the particular experience centered in his differently located, *other* head. Taking people's brains out of their heads and, most importantly, spreading out the extracted brains into roughly equal main parts, overcomes this habitual tendency.

On reflection, then, it appears that there is no metaphysical barrier against my sharing, at a particular time, a particular conscious experience with somebody else. There may be no more of a deep barrier to this than there is to my sharing, at a particular time, a particular cold with somebody else. Perhaps, just as our colds are physical conditions or processes, so our conscious experiences, too, may be physical.

Our second example, concerns the flowing of a single experience, over time, from one subject to another, rather than the sharing of an experience, at a given time, by two different subjects. The people in this example have their brains kept in such a boring sequence of states that, throughout, there is no change at all in the qualitative character of the experience that anyone ever has. For simplicity's sake, we suppose that this is just the experience of a homogeneous baby blue visual field.

The example begins with a zippering procedure that separates my two half-brains. Communicating all the while, they are placed in supportive vats, in different rooms; the left is in Room 1 and the right is in Room 2.

The plot thickens quickly. In Room 3, there is a duplicate of my left half-brain that, along with its transceiver and its supportive vat, has just recently come into existence. In Room 4, there is, similarly, a duplicate of my right half-brain. When a certain switch is flicked, the new left, in perfect parallel with my original left, also communicates with the right in Room 2. This lasts for one minute.

Then a second switch is thrown. When that happens my original left breaks off communications. For one minute, my old right communicates only with this new left. But then a third switch is thrown. When that happens, the new right, in perfect parallel with my old right, also communicates with the new left. This trio's communications proceed for a minute, when a fourth switch is thrown. At the flick of this switch, my old right breaks off communications. There is now in communication only the new brain halves, in Rooms 3 and 4.

In Room 50, there is a newly constructed body, a duplicate of my body.

Always communicating in the appropriate way, the new brain halves are both placed in this new body. By a very fine zippering, their transceiver connections are replaced by neural connections. After having the experience of baby blueness for ten minutes, the person composed of these new parts falls asleep. Similarly reconstructed in the interim, I am playing Ping-Pong in Room 100.

A particular experience of baby blue began as just my experience. This experience flowed through various combinations of half-brains, or through whatever they constituted, and it ended as the experience of a person quite distinct from me. In middle stages, it may be unclear exactly which subject, or subjects, are having this experience. If, as it seems, there is here this unclarity, then that is some bad news for the doctrine of experiential privacy. For, according to that doctrine, there never should be any unclarity about these matters. Moreover, even in the face of this unclarity, certain telling points remain quite clear: For one thing, at the beginning, I, and I alone, have this experience. And for another clear thing, near the end, right before he falls asleep, only somebody else has this very experience.

As just indicated, I think it is correct to say, or at the very least permissible to say, that a particular visual experience, one that lasts for quite a few minutes, began as just mine and ended as someone else's experience. Suppose, however, that this is not allowed. Do we believe that we cannot correctly say this because, in saying this thing, we would be contravening any deep fact about anything? That is not very credible. If there is any error here, in saying this thing, that can only be an error largely semantic in character, a mistake of going against certain conventions of our language. If there is any necessity to the privacy of my experience, and if this is not the natural necessity of certain physical laws and processes, then it is a necessity born of our linguistic conventions. There is no metaphysical barrier that keeps another person from having the particular experience that, in this case, begins as mine alone. There is no more of a deep barrier to this than there is to another person having a particular cold that, in a certain case, begins as mine alone. Again, it might be that, just as colds are physical conditions or processes, so our conscious experiences, too, are physical.

4. Against the Metaphysical Separateness of Subjects

In parallel with the doctrine of the privacy of experiences, there is the idea of the metaphysical separateness of subjects. On this doctrine, it is always a substantial error to think that two people fuse into one. When we think of ourselves as having conscious experience, friends of this doctrine may urge, we will not be prone to any such error.

In the previous section, when noting the various interpretations that might be offered for a certain intriguing Zuboffian case, we saw some difficulties for this doctrine. Now, another Zuboff-style case, more pointedly aimed at the doctrine of separateness itself, may more fully convince us that we do not, really, have any very strong belief in this metaphysical doctrine. The first stages of this new example are the same as those of the first case in the section just preceding. So, in this present case's middle stages, me and my duplicate, each scattered in three main parts, are communicating mutually from six different rooms. From this point, we move on to new material: First, our bodies may be destroyed, four sets of suitable electrodes taking up the stimulatory slack. Then the left half-brain from one of the original people is destroyed, say, my (old) left, even as the right half-brain from the other is simultaneously destroyed. These remaining two half-brains, my old right and his old left, are placed in a duplicate body, which is manufactured on the spot. By a zippering, their transceivers are removed. With consciousness still supported, there is now a normally constituted person in the situation. My duplicate and I have merged into one person.

In its most striking form, this example will include the supposition that each of the two half-brains are about equal in their psychological contribution to the person as a whole. Some might challenge this supposition. They may have in mind the fact that, for (almost) all of us, either one, or else the other, of our two cerebral hemispheres is *dominant*; usually it is the left hemisphere, the other then being non-dominant. Further, they might contend that, in actual cases, even as the half-brain that includes a person's dominant hemisphere is essential to his survival, so the other half-brain is of no more importance than is, say, the person's legs. While their original challenge to the supposition of near equality may have some merit, their subsequent contention is not just false, but is absurdly false.

First, to physicians and psychologists who encounter the relevant tumor patients, it appears quite obvious that a person may survive the loss of his dominant cerebral hemisphere.[6] Beginning almost immediately, and increasing with time, the non-dominant hemisphere subserves even the linguistic function of speech, a dispositional ability far too exalted to be part of core psychology. Second, the other half brain will include, not only the non-dominant cerebral hemispheres, but also half of the lower brain. And this half of the lower brain, just like the other half, will make a quite vital contribution

6. My textbook on the subject is Kevin Walsh, *Neuropsychology*, Churchill Livingstone, 1987, where the main evidence is cited on pages 296–97. But some material on page 293, I should point out, seems to leave the empirical issue in a somewhat cloudy state. As subsequent passages of the present work make clear, however, none of the empirical particularities matter much as regards the main philosophical issues.

to the final realization of total psychology. So, even for actual cases, denying the supposition of near equality will, at the very most, do nothing more than constrain the form in which our example is to be presented: Even if, for fairly realistic cases, we may not use our example in its very most striking form, we still can employ it in a form that is plenty striking enough.

Suppose that, contrary to fact, there was at least a fair amount of truth in the contention that the contribution made by one half of our brains simply overwhelms the piddling influx from the other half. And, suppose further, that, not just the upper brain, but the whole brain was relevantly divisible, so that one of us might survive with only half of his lower brain. Even if all of that were so, our example will provide an effectively persuasive argument against the metaphysical doctrine of separateness. This will be true for several reasons.

First, what sorts of considerations will mean some deficiency in the more realistic forms of the example? These will be only some uncooperative natural facts, in particular, some facts regarding the actual constitution of us human people by our various physical parts. In pretty mildly hypothetical variations of the original case, those uncooperative facts will be supplanted by more conducive propositions. In those variant examples, I will merge with my duplicate. So, even if the more realistic cases are extremely uncooperative, it will not be any deep metaphysical feature of my condition, as a subject of conscious experience, that stands in the way of my being able to fuse with a person who is relevantly like me.

Second, personal fusion may not require an equal, or even a nearly equal, contribution from each of the people who merge together, but will require only a sufficiently great contribution from each. So, in certain cases where there are (only) two contributors, the lesser might merge into the greater by way of making a somewhat minor, but still significant, contribution to the realization of the emerging person's total psychology. Now, in at least some cases of this sort, whatever the fate of the major contributor, the minor contributor will cease to exist. Yet, in many of these cases, the minor contributor will not have died, either, but will have ended in quite another way, having merged into a greater being.

Third, in cases where there are more than two contributors, merging may occur even when no one of them makes any very great contribution. Consider, for example, this variant case, in which we start with, not two, but four qualitatively identical people: Quarter-brains, not half-brains, communicate by transceivers in the appropriate combinations. If I am person A, then my quarters are A1, A2, A3 and A4. Another person's may be B1, B2, B3 and B4. In an appropriate combination of communication, A1 will communicate with B2, B3 and B4, as well as with its original partners, but not, of course, with B1, its twin or duplicate. Then all of the quarters are simultaneously destroyed except for, say, A1, B2, C3 and D4. In that way, even while conscious experience is flowing throughout the episode, a different sort of quarter will be contributed by each of the original people. Into a new duplicate body, these four quarters are then placed and, by zippering, they are neurally joined.

Even if someone's left half-brain might be highly dominant, none of his brain-quarters will, by itself, realize even (the minimum of) core psychology. So, in relevantly realistic versions of our example, none of the four original people survive. How did they come to an end? While most of each person was destroyed, enough of each suitably coalesced with enough from the others for there to be a fusion of all four into a single person.

As we most deeply believe, we are intricate physical complexes. And, as we also deeply believe, such great physical complexes may be, quite literally, taken apart and put together in a great number and variety of ways. With respect to a small minority of these ways, there will be, from each merger candidate, physical and psychological contributions that are sufficient for our merging together.

It is not very important, of course, whether I am right in offering what I take to be a correct description of this case. We recall our first line of reply: The important point is that there be no error in the descriptions of cases that stems from our defying a deep metaphysical truth about us conscious subjects. I submit that, in the claim of fusion for these cases, there is no error that is as fundamental as that.

5. Against the Indivisibility of Experiences and of Subjects

It is reasonable to infer that if subjects can fuse, then they also can fission. But, of course, the inference can work both ways: If personal division is impossible, as contrasted with the mere division of a person's brain and body, then people cannot really merge or fuse, either. It is important, then, that the argument against the separateness of subjects be complemented by a persuasive argument against the metaphysical idea that subjects are absolutely indivisible. In this section, we shall attempt to provide such a complementary argument.

If there is a deep block to our division, then it is one that is most clearly operative just when we are conscious: For one of us to divide when she is conscious, it is easy to think, that person's experience must divide. Otherwise, the thought may continue, the experiencing person will go whichever way the experience goes. Finally, perhaps, upon the division of her brain, a conscious subject's experience may suddenly cease altogether. Then, it appears, the conscious subject herself may also cease to exist. So, in order to convince ourselves that there is no metaphysical barrier to our division, we must convince ourselves, as well, that there is no such barrier to the division of our conscious experiences.

Although the interpretation of the experimental evidence is somewhat controversial, most commentators on actual "split-brain" patients consider these people to have, at least when they are in certain contrived surroundings, two separate streams of conscious experience.[7] Usually, that is how I myself interpret the situation.[8]

When I focus on my own experience intently, however, sometimes I wonder how that can possibly be so. What I then feel is that even if there should occur the severing of the main neural connections between my cerebral hemispheres, the effect of the procedure could not possibly be *that*. Rather, if the operation does anything very dramatic at all, then the slicing may, in a quite extraordinary way, put a sudden end to me and bring into being, directly upon my cessation, two new people, each with his own separate stream of consciousness. Usually, their two separate experiential streams will run in parallel. In suitably provocative experimental surrounds, however, there will occur a marked difference in the character of their two streams of experience.

When I feel friendly to the doctrine of the indivisibility of experience, it is to such extremes as this that I may be drawn. At other times, I feel confident that such a characterization is not just unduly convoluted and heroic, but is, indeed, quite ridiculous. So, all told, I have a certain ambivalence toward the situation. And this ambivalence, I feel sure, is not idiosyncratic. So, the question arises: How can we best convince ourselves that, according to our deepest beliefs, there really is no metaphysical fact that undermines the less extreme descriptions?

7. The great investigator of this domain is R. W. Sperry. A reasonably accessible paper of his is "Hemispheric Deconnection and Unity in Conscious Awareness," *American Psychologist*, 1968. Both lucidly and provocatively, Thomas Nagel provides a valuable philosophical commentary on this scientific research in his "Brain Bisection and the Unity of Consciousness," *Synthese*, 1971. Most reasonably, both authors hold that, in these cases, there is a division of conscious experience: At the same time, supported by what goes on in just one head, there are two separate streams of conscious experience. Despite some tantalizing suggestions from Nagel, it is also most reasonable to hold that, in these same cases, there is always one subject of experience, and one person, whose separate streams of experiences these two are. For some recent psychological research into the latter question, see Donald MacKay, "Divided Brains—Divided Minds?," in *Mindwaves*, C. Blakemore and S. Greenfield, eds., Basil Blackwell, 1987.

8. Both among philosophers and among scientists, there are some who deny that, in these cases, there are two separate streams of conscious experience. In his "Personal Identity and Survival," in addition to arguing for this position, the philosopher, John Robinson, cites some scientists of a similar persuasion, including a passage from MacKay. Still, this appears to be the minority view. At any rate, as the text will eventually show, these actual cases are far from being the clearest cases. To be met with shortly, what I care about are the clearer cases.

As a prelude to our discussion, we explicitly assume that we may speak sensibly, not only of various concrete *entities* dividing, but also of the division of certain *processes*, events, and whatever. This supposition seems justified. Natural physical processes like flashes of lightning seem appropriately described in this way. At all events, if there is only a semantic, conventional reason that conscious experiences cannot be correctly described as dividing, then the main lines of our argument will be sustained.

As with our other thought experiments, we look, first and foremost, to the causal basis and ground of experience, in fact, to a person's brain. Employing the familiar Zuboffian techniques, let us now introduce appropriate considerations of *gradualness*. The idea here is that the division of a conscious experience might be understood as proceeding in a relevantly gradual way.

A certain thousandth of a person's brain is duplicated twice over. One of the new thousandths is in Room A and the other is in Room B, while the original brain is in Room Z. Each duplicate thousandth may be placed in a vat, or else in a new duplicate body kept alive by suitable systems. Each new thousandth is fitted with transceivers. At the same time, by a zippering, the thousandth that they duplicate is also fitted, as is the rest of the brain. Continuing to communicate with the 999 thousandths of the brain that will still remain in Room Z, this single old thousandth is removed from the person's head, is taken out of Room Z, and, in Room T, is placed in a vat of its own. At the flick of a switch, the two new thousandths begin to communicate, in precisely the way that the old thousandth continues to do, with the occupant of Room Z. Then the old thousandth is destroyed. As should be clear, the new thousandth in Room A never communicates with the new thousandth in Room B, nor does anything else ever in one of those rooms communicate with anything in the other or with anything in Room T. Rather, the brain-part in A, as well as the brain-part in B, communicates only with what is in Room Z.

At the next step, a second, adjacent thousandth is copied twice over. After it communicates from Room T with what remains in Room Z, precisely paralleled by communications on the part of each of its two copies, this second original thousandth is destroyed. In a manner optimal for the generation of experience by the resulting wholes, each of its two duplicates is organically joined to the first duplicating thousandths. The transceivers serving the resulting little wholes are appropriately enlarged. Complementing that increase, there was an enlargement of the transceiver connected to what remains of the original brain, now 998 thousandths. On each side, a two thousandth part of a normal brain is in communication with what remains of the original brain.

Thousandth by thousandth, this continues down the whole of the original brain, with more and more of the work of supporting conscious experience being taken up by what is in Room A and by what is in Room B, less and less by what is in Room Z. When there remains only one last thousandth in Z, that is treated as were the previously isolated old thousandths in T. First, this last thousandth is joined, in its communications with A and B, by duplicates of itself. After being made causally redundant, it is destroyed.

At no time is there any interruption in the support of conscious experience. Moreover, there is never any change in the qualitative character of the quite simple conscious experience that is supported, say, just experience of a homogeneous blue visual field. By the end of the procedure, what happened to the original experience? The experience that started in the original person in Room Z divided into two experiences: one occurring in Room A and the other in Room B; each of these products of experiential division is the experience of a distinct new person.

A similar procedure can get an experience to divide into, say, five experiences. In addition to what happens in rooms A and B, exactly similar events may occur with the "growing of new brains" in other rooms, say, in rooms C, D and E. With such a five-fold process, a conscious experience may flow in five different directions rather than merely dividing in two. This may happen with a conscious experience just as it may happen with a piece of paper, which may be torn in five ways simultaneously, or with a flash of lightning, which might take a five-fold fork. Or, if we allow that this may happen with the paper, and with the lightning, but not with the experience, then that is only a matter of there being a difference in the conventions governing "paper" and "lightning" on the one hand and, on the other, those governing "experience." There is nothing in the metaphysics of experience that is an absolute barrier to the division of a particular conscious experience.

Once the key of gradualness has been employed, the door may be opened and we may observe some new terrain. So, as we will next bring ourselves to see, certain cases that do not feature gradualness may also be counted as cases where experience divides. Think of your brain-halves zippered with transceivers, and communicating at a distance from their separate vats. Each fitted with a suitable duplicate receiver, duplicates of each half may then come into being. Although we do not require it, we may allow that all of this may be a statistical miracle.

The push of a button then triggers a sequence in which two switches are flicked, the first flick occurring a billionth of a second after the other. Each flick of a switch has its own distinctive causal consequences. Now, the chief consequence of the first flicking is the introduction of *some new* communications: The new left communicates with the old right and the new right with the old left, even as the old brain-halves still communicate with each other. There is not, however, any communication between the new, duplicate brain-halves. A mere billionth of a second later, the second switch is thrown. (Such a short time interval is very far below the threshold of any noticeable occurrence in anyone's experience.) And, the chief consequence of the second flicking is the subsequent *cessation of some old* communications: Your old right ceases communicating with your old left. Thus your old right half-brain now communicates only with the new left, while your old left communicates only with the new right. It is in this very paragraph that the crux of our story is told.

After these distinctive happenings, the new partners, by a zipper procedure, have their transceivers removed and become neurally joined. Finally, each whole organic brain is placed in a new body, the two new bodies being identically updated duplicates of your old body. With conscious experience having been supported throughout, there are now, at the end of the case, two people who did not exist at the case's beginning.

As I see it, a correct description of this case is that a certain *conscious experience* quite suddenly divided in two. But, in all events, if there is a flaw in this description, that can only be due to the violation of some conventions governing some of its terms, not to any deep yet subtle facts about our experiences. So it seems, after all, that we do not very deeply believe in the metaphysical doctrine of the indivisibility of experience.[9]

Another correct description of this case is that, in it, a certain *person* divided in two. At the beginning, you are the only person in the case. At the end, there are two people, neither of them you. You have contributed much, and equally, to each of these two people: You have contributed half of your brain to each. Because the other half-brains just came into being, each independently of the other, nobody else contributed to these people in this peculiarly intimate way. So, in this case, you did not end by merging with anyone. Nor, of course, did you end by simply dying. Rather, it was by dividing in two that you came to an end. Or, if that is not quite how things happened, then the inadequacy of the description can be due only to the flouting of some convention of language. There was not any metaphysical barrier to your dividing. As our deepest beliefs in these matters run, just as with the doctrine of the indivisibility of experience, there is not much truth, either, in the metaphysical doctrine of the indivisibility of subjects.

6. Against the Absoluteness of Subjects: The Spectrum of Congenial Decomposition

With an eye toward undermining them, we turn to examine the two remaining metaphysical doctrines, those concerning the alleged absoluteness of ourselves and of our experiences. Toward this end, we will again consider our

9. A complementary example, which may be quite helpful to some readers, is Parfit's case of My Physics Exam, presented on pages 246–47 of his *Reasons and Persons*.

spectrum of congenial decomposition. Much as when it was first introduced, in Chapter 2, we will use this spectrum as the basis of an argument against the doctrine that our existence is metaphysically absolute.

Among other things, this spectrum provides a graphic way of showing ourselves the great strength of our belief that, even as conscious subjects, we really are complexes of many small constituents, no one of which is very much more important to our nature or survival than ever so many of the others. We are constituted of, and thus are most heavily dependent on, many tissues, which are constituted of many cells, which are constituted of many molecules, which are constituted of many atoms, which are constituted of many still smaller and simpler things. In generating the cases of this spectrum, we may focus on any even moderately low level of constitution. As before, we will focus on cells.

In a most innocuous manner, take away a least important cell from me, presumably any one of many tied billions, say, gently scrape a peripheral skin cell off my leg. Even after that cell is destroyed, as our procedure requires, there is no replacement of what is thus removed. Now, as it appears, no most innocuous cellular removal will mean the difference between me on the one side and, on the other, a situation where, in any sense or way, it is even the least bit problematic that I exist. Employing this highly appealing *principle of minute differences*, we may repeat this little procedure any number of times. But if we repeat too often, we obtain an absurd conclusion: With only one cell left, and even with no cells at all, it is perfectly clear that I will still be around. That is, indeed, absurdly false. Rather, without any cells in the situation, or even with only one cell, I will not be around. We have derived a contradiction. Perhaps the contradiction reflects badly on the supposition of my existence in the first place. Some years ago, I argued for that extremely radical position.[10] More likely, as we deeply believe, it reflects badly on that highly appealing principle of minute differences. This principle is, then, only approximately true; as a universal generalization, it is false. At certain points, the principle of minute differences fails to hold. But in what way does it fail?

Is the principle at fault due to anything of metaphysical significance? At first it might seem so. Perhaps at some precise point the removal of a cell suddenly killed me; I just couldn't take any more. I do not think that to be right, but it does have some plausibility. Rather than argue against the idea that there is a real fine line between the living and the non-living, let us *accommodate* the thought that there may be some such metaphysically significant line. We may do this by having all of our spectrum's cases be on the side of

10. Along this line, the main papers are "I Do Not Exist," in G. F. MacDonald, ed., *Perception and Identity*, Cornell University Press, 1979, and "Why There Are No People," *Midwest Studies in Philosophy*, 1979.

the living. In a manner that is only mildly hypothetical, we may provide an accommodation that is both simple and effective.

Well before any given biological danger occurs, we bring in life-support systems that will keep all of the remaining cells alive and, thus, will keep me alive. The components of these systems will be so arranged that they never become parts of me. So, at some middle stages, I will be hooked up to a machine that pumps my blood around, to another that manages to get needed oxygen absorbed into my bloodstream, to another that serves to remove my cellular wastes, and so on. At a fairly late stage, there will be only a brain floating in a vat. Then external systems will keep me well supplied not merely with whatever materials and processes are then needed to keep me barely alive, but with those needed to keep me functioning quite optimally. Now, this vat is not part of me, nor is the bath, nor the computers that are sending in the stimulations and supplies. Largely manufactured men there may well be, but this sort of case is not one that includes any: Rather, I am just that brain or, more precisely, I am then constituted of just that living brain.

In presenting this spectrum of cases, we have relied heavily on a certain supposition. This is an assumption that almost all of us do accept: Any of the processes going on in any (but the extremely minute) parts of me do not, in any very strong sense or way, causally require those parts to be surrounded by my other parts, nor by entities very like those parts of me. Processes going on in my liver, for example, can go on just as well under certain naturally possible conditions where that liver is not surrounded by my body, nor by an exact or near duplicate of my body. The liver may be placed in some suitable artificial surroundings, with quite artificial means of affecting it in all of the relevant ways that, more ordinarily, the rest of my body would do.

In *certain* of these cases, we must agree, the liver and what supports its continued functioning would form a notably organic whole, even if a whole most of whose parts were artificially produced and did not consist of protoplasm. But there are *other* such cases, we also believe, in which the liver does *not* combine with the rest to form any *organism* of any kind. Even in these latter cases, the liver won't "know or care" that what provides its supporting and stimulating input is not integrated with it in a way suitable for the unity characteristic of organisms. The rest of the world, by way of relevant parts thereof, will "fool" the liver into functioning just as it does now in my body. Whatever (non-relationally described) processes my liver is going through now in me, it could go through just as well as a sufficiently supported but quite isolated organ. We may call the proposition illustrated by this fact about my liver, the *principle of indifference to remote causes.*

The same considerations apply as well to my brain, and to any part of my brain composed of any large number of contiguous cells. Like the liver, my brain, or as much of it as any relevant situation contains, can be "fooled" into undergoing any of the processes it would undergo in the most ordinary surroundings. Even when it is quite isolated and not part of any very interesting organic whole, the brain, or any relevant part thereof, can be "fooled" into reacting just as if it were suitably attached to ever so many suitably arranged human cells. When thinking about our decomposition spectrum, we are employing the principle of indifference to remote causes. As does almost any very general contingent proposition, this principle of indifference may have some limitations. But those limits may not be reached, or even closely approached, by the cases in our spectrum of congenial decomposition. Because this is so, every case in our spectrum, from a whole human being down to a single neuron, will be on the side of the living, not on the side of the non-living.

Having accommodated the idea that there is a realistically significant line between the living and the non-living, let us now note that this accommodated thought is, to say the least, a rather dubious one: A century or two ago it was widely believed that there is a sharp metaphysical difference between the living and the non-living. Given the evidence available at that time, perhaps the belief might have been reasonable enough. But, at the present time, this belief is not so widely held and, more important, is not very reasonable. We know about viruses, for example, which defy clear classification in terms of such a dichotomy; we know about the ways in which even human death, or dying, is a *somewhat* gradual process.

Most of us are now pretty well beyond having any belief that there is a metaphysical break between the living and the non-living. But there is a related idea that we have not quite gotten behind us. This is the thought that there is a sharp metaphysical difference between the *conscious* and the *nonconscious*. It is this idea, I think, that lies behind so much of the appeal of the thought that our existence is always metaphysically determinate. Our spectrum allows us to *accommodate*, not only the idea that there might be an important break between the living and the non-living, but also this very influential parallel idea about the conscious and the non-conscious. The accommodation is made by our specifying that, in addition to bringing in life-support systems well before they are needed, we may connect the person to external stimulatory systems well before *they* are needed.

Without the help of such stimulatory systems, perhaps there might be a point where there would be a "catastrophe" for consciousness. This will be a point where, in the vat, there is a greatest brain-part that, for want of a single cell, clearly fails to support any consciousness at all. But, with one cell more, that brain-part would clearly support consciousness. The natural possibility of appropriate stimulatory systems will avert any such catastrophe as might occur without their employment.

With appropriate stimulatory systems in place, there may be consciousness continuously associated with what is, at any point in our spectrum, the "max-imal organic being" there present. Or, if the absoluteness of experiences is a false doctrine, there may be, associated with such a being, an uninterrupted, smooth gradation in the way of consciousness *and relevantly like processes*. But, as noted in our second chapter, the factual basis of this idea might be ques-tioned: Perhaps the progressively diminished entity needs to have some peri-ods of deep unconscious sleep, as we ordinary folks appear to require. This worry is also easy to accommodate: We may let there be such periods of sleep, perhaps occasioned when the stimulatory system is not working full blast. We need only say this about the relation of these rest periods to our spectrum: Never is a cell removed during these periods; but, once any such rest period is over, we resume our cell-by-cell removal procedure.

In our spectrum there is no consciousness at, or even near, the end: A single neuron is not conscious; nor does it constitute a unicellular being that is conscious. Indeed, that being does not even have the capacity for con-sciousness. But at the beginning there is a being that has a great capacity for consciousness and, as he actually is conscious, a being in whom that capacity is then being exercised. That being, of course, is nobody but me. In the pro-cess of cell-by-cell removal, when is there first no being with this capacity? Now, due to there being appropriate stimulation during each of the cellular removals, whatever capacity for consciousness is then present is being exer-cised. So, in context, our question about capacity reduces to this more straightforward query: In the process of the cell-by-cell removal, when is there first no being that actually is conscious?

Is there a definite answer to this question? Perhaps there is one. If there is, then that answer may be due primarily to the meaning of our term "con-scious," to conventions governing its proper application that we have implic-itly established and maintained. Alternatively, the definite answer may be due simply, or primarily, to purely non-conventional aspects of the world and, perhaps, it might even be due to the deep metaphysics of the situation. Or, as still others might maintain, there may be no definite answer at all. In dis-cussing the idea of the absoluteness of experiences, we must think about these questions with some care. But in the present context, where only the absoluteness of subjects is being challenged, those matters may be ignored. For, as is virtually certain, problems will occur for the original subject's exis-tence, for *my* existence, well before conscious experience gives out, indeed, well before conscious experience *even begins* to run up against any problems.

The reason for this is clear. Whether or not the continuous realization of a capacity for consciousness is necessary for my existence, it is far from being sufficient for my survival. For one thing, there is much to my core psychology besides this capacity. There is, for example, my capacity for reasoning. If too many cells gradually are taken away, then my reasoning ability gradually will fall to what are disastrously low levels, disastrous, that is, for my survival. When there is only a part of my brain left that, in addition to conscious experience, realizes only the reasoning ability of a *typical dog*, then *I* will no longer exist. There may then be a subject of experience in the situation, all right, a subject that is then and there even having conscious experience, but that will be a numerically different subject. As far as any non-conventional matters are concerned, the example's original subject of experience, me, will have gradually faded out of existence. A personal subject of experience will gradually have faded into, and will gradually have been replaced by, a very markedly sub-personal subject of experience.[11]

When reading the foregoing argument, some will focus on a proposition that, to my mind, is very plausible: Because I already am a person, for as long as I continue to exist I must always be a person. But, as is worth noting, the argument does not rely on this highly plausible proposition. Indeed, without using any term for any ordinary general category at all, I can conduct the argument directly upon myself as the starting subject. After a certain amount of congenial decomposition, it will be rather clear that I am no longer in the situation. Even so, there will exist a sentient being that, although enormously stupid, is having some conscious experience.

In presenting this spectrum, we have relied on certain contingent propositions about the natural processes in which we might become involved: For example, there is the principle of indifference to remote causes. There is also the idea that all of the underlying physical processes of these cases will have relevantly gradual relations, rather than there being, at one step in the sequence, a process that, no matter how congenial nature may try to be, must be abruptly catastrophic. And there is the related idea that psychological capacities will supervene on, or be supported by, these gradually differing physical processes in such a way that the relevant differences in them, too, will proceed, from step to step, in a gradual manner. As will be made even clearer in the next section, these are propositions that, although both contingent and about the natural processes of the world, are quite deeply believed. Beyond our deep belief in their truth, however, there is a still deeper, stronger belief that we have regarding their status.

If these propositions concerning relevant natural gradualness should,

---

11. As all the world knows, Descartes held that (non-human) animals have no conscious experience. In a very recent paper, "Brute Experience," *The Journal of Philosophy*, 1989, Peter Carruthers holds the same view, or a very similar view; he also holds that human infants, too, have no conscious experience. Not only are these views extremely implausible, but, insofar as I can tell, there are no good arguments for them. I place this note here only for the purposes of honesty and fairness: Not just long ago, but also nowadays, there are intelligent people who disagree with the position I endorse in the text.

against our belief, fail to be true, then that failure, we most deeply believe, will be due to some quirks in the natural character of concrete reality. In a counterfactual circumstance, where the natural propensities are more congenial than such quirky ones, I will, in the fashion envisioned, fade out of existence. So, even if there may be such surprising quirks of nature, they will not provide any metaphysical barrier to my fading gradually.

Moreover, although the appearance of such momentous natural quirks will come as a big surprise, that will not be nearly as surprising as this: What grounds the failure of even the most conducive attempt at getting me to fade is a deep metaphysical gap between two separate realms that, together, serve to compose a *relevantly disjoint* concrete reality: On this most surprising idea, there is, first, a physical realm, in which my brain and body have their existence, and in which those processes most crucial for their existence might happen in a relevantly gradual way. And, on this idea, there is, second, and quite separate from anything physical, a "purely mental" realm: As a matter of the deepest necessity, it is only in this second realm that I myself do exist. Moreover, any process that is crucial to my existence must happen only in this purely mental realm and, as such, must occur in an all-or-none fashion. So, it is because I must exist only in a realm of absolutely necessary abruptness that, unlike my brain and body, I myself am a being who is, quite essentially, absolute and all-or-none.

As our spectrum of congenial decomposition helps us to realize, we have a very deep belief that reality is not such a highly disjoint affair. Perhaps this is the main reason that, if we believe them at all, we believe only rather weakly in any contrary propositions. Accordingly, as we might now somewhat better understand, any belief that we have in the doctrine of the absoluteness of subjects is, by comparison, a rather weak belief.

7. Against the Absoluteness of Subjects: Spectra of Human Conception and Human Development

Even if they are only mildly hypothetical, the spectrum just considered does consist of cases that are hypothetical. In the course of normal human fetal development, there occurs a spectrum of actual cases that also bears on these issues, a *spectrum of normal human development*. Beginning with the zygote at conception, we can consider the developmental process as a series of one-second cases, or of one-trillionth-of-a-second cases. At the beginning there is no subject of experience. After forty years, if not nine months, there is a subject of experience. No significant metaphysical break occurs during any one second or, yet more certainly, during any one trillionth. The basic conditions of my existence, therefore, are gradual rather than absolute; it is our conventions for personal reference that draw the lines, not non-conventional reality.

Neither I nor any other subject of experience is ever a unicellular zygote. A human fertilized egg, it is true, has the potential to develop into a subject of experience and even into a person. But this truth about that potential entails that the fertilized egg is not itself a person or a subject of experience. For nothing has the potential to develop into what it already is. Noticing that there is this entailment, some few will retrace and deny that the zygote has ihe potential for that development. They will insist that, instead, the fertilized egg itself already is a subject of experience.

This absurdly false idea is to no avail. For the fertilization of the egg by the sperm is itself a gradual process, even if brief by ordinary temporal measures. If the time between contact and full penetration is, say, a thousandth of a second, we may take a time interval including the thousandth before, that thousandth, and the thousandth after. We may divide this interval into, say, trillionths. Then we have a new spectrum of a trillion cases, a *spectrum of normal human conception*. There is not present in any one of this spectrum's cases anything of much metaphysical significance that is not also present in the just earlier case. Yet no subject of experience is ever just an egg, or just a sperm, or exclusively related in some special way with just one of these. So, there is nothing metaphysically absolute about any subject of experience that I ever am.

These two *spectra of human reproduction* have one utterly obvious virtue. They are actual, not hypothetical. Because of this, regarding those questions that they cover adequately, they can give us more confidence than can even the most mildly hypothetical spectra. But this extra serving of confidence might be bought at a high price. Some might think that, although these actual spectra cover certain issues, they may not adequately cover the most central issues.

For the central issues to be well covered, it might be thought, it should be rather clear that the allegedly gradual subject be conscious for as long as he exists. Or perhaps even better, it should be clear that, like the subject himself, even his conscious experience should be gradual, not metaphysically absolute. Neither of the two spectra of human reproduction exhibits, in any very clear manner, either of these two features.

There is some justice to this complaint. Because there is, it is important for us not to rely solely on the actual spectra that normal human reproduction provides. That is a reason why we complement those actual spectra with our spectrum of congenial decomposition, wherein there is conscious experience (or perhaps a slightly lesser but relevantly similar process) in every case that merits serious consideration.

Once we have deployed a spectrum where experience goes on further than its original subject, as happens with congenial decomposition, we may have placed ourselves in a position to think rather boldly, and perhaps also rather clearly, about the cases in the spectrum of normal human development. As I said near the book's beginning, and now have some cause to reaffirm, there is much plausibility in the idea that, at one time, I might have been a tiny fetus only some few days, or some few weeks, removed from conception. At that time, I may have had no capacity for consciousness, nor any psychology at all. Perhaps, then, before ever I was a subject of consciousness, I existed without yet being such a subject. And, then, only gradually did I develop into the subject of conscious experience that, fortunately for me, I am today.

8. Against the Absoluteness of Experience: Congenial Decomposition Again

For the most subjectively oriented of philosophers, it will not be enough to argue against the absoluteness of subjects by way of a spectrum that keeps conscious experience going beyond the continued existence of the original subject of that experience. To be persuaded that we subjects are not absolute, these extremely demanding thinkers will accept nothing less than persuasive arguments that our conscious experience itself is gradual and not absolute. While I think that these demands are excessive, I will now try to satisfy them. At all events, we want to provide an argument against the doctrine of the absoluteness of experience. Toward this end, it is best to begin by turning again to our spectrum of congenial decomposition.

With enough of my brain in the vat, and with that smallish entity being optimally stimulated, there are processes going on that are correctly called conscious experiences. With only two neurons sending electric charges to each other, there are no such processes. About this we can be quite clear. Somewhere in between there are processes going on about which we cannot be so clear. Perhaps the semantics of our word, 'conscious,' is so sensitive as to rule decisively with respect to every one of these processes: If so, then, with respect to each case in the spectrum, it is either (fully) true that the case involves conscious experience or else it is (fully) true that it does not. Or, alternatively, perhaps there are processes for which our semantics provides no definite ruling. If so, then there will be cases with respect to which it is indeterminate whether they involve conscious experience. Because it is more a question of language than of anything else, this matter is one that we need not now discuss. For, however those conventional matters are treated, there will be no metaphysical break, anywhere in the spectrum, between the processes "of consciousness" and the other "lesser" processes. This may seem very surprising. But, upon pain of not doing full justice to our most deeply accepted beliefs, perhaps we must accept that it is so.

We do not have any clear conception as to the nature of any of the "highest" of these lesser processes, of those processes that barely fail to be (completely correctly called) processes of consciousness. There is nothing much that I can say to describe them positively and, at the present time, it is unlikely that anyone else can do a great deal better. Very unhelpfully, I might say that these barely failing processes are a little bit like the experiences I have just before nodding off to sleep. Perhaps better, but still none too good, these processes are to those pre-sleep experiences much as the latter are to the ordinary experiences of waking life. Perhaps those humble processes are too far down the relevant gradients to be correctly called *experiences* at all. On the other hand, if the phrase 'non-conscious experience' is coherent, perhaps at least some of these barely failing processes are non-conscious experiences.

What does this great difficulty of conception and description show? It may show very little about the processes themselves. It may show much more about our own impoverished understanding of them and, beyond that, about the limits of our imaginative powers. At any rate, although we cannot helpfully describe these lesser processes, it may be, as our spectrum appears to inform us, that we have a deep belief that they exist.

In certain ways, the matter here is like the matter of the gradualness of all phenomenal color. Spectra of color patches can convince us that, relative to our classification of colors, a standard question about what color is present must be, in a suitable sense, a matter of degree and even a matter of convention. There may be patches of color between clear orange and clear yellow for which we have no good word or words. But those patches do exist. Because such patches exist, there is a good deal of truth to a remark like this: In large measure, the "familiar" colors are conventional phenomena; there is not much "metaphysical reality" or metaphysical significance to red, orange, yellow, and so on. If anything in the neighborhood has metaphysical significance, it is the phenomenon of color as a whole, or the whole "modality" of color, including phenomenal black, phenomenal white, and other "non-spectral" colors. Perhaps there is some metaphysical significance, too, to each of the perhaps infinitely many absolutely specific shades of color. But between these two extremes, the whole of the modality and the absolutely specific shades, there may be nothing of any metaphysical significance.

There is, to be sure, this interesting disanalogy between consciousness and color: Poorly described colors, or regions of the modality of phenomenal color, are as clearly and easily experienced by us as is a paradigm patch of orange. But, almost by definition, we do *not experience the difference* between processes that barely qualify as conscious and those that barely fail. And, although we may very clearly experience very poorly described colors, we have no conscious experience of the processes that barely fail of consciousness. That is an interesting disanalogy between conscious experience and phenomenal color. But the interest of this disanalogy may be confined to logic and to epistemology. At any rate, as it appears, the noted difference will have no bearing on the questions of metaphysics itself, which are supposed to be more robustly realistic.

There is a related disanalogy between consciousness and other experiential phenomena. For example, consider felt pain. In a way, it is not hard for us to think that there is an absolute divide between feelings of pain and, on the other side, experiences that are not at all painful. But, even when thinking in this way, nobody thinks that there is here something of much metaphysical significance. For another example, consider our experiences as of *colored* transparent glass and, by contrast, our experiences as of *colorless* glass. Again, we can think of an absolute cut off, but do not think that there is one of any metaphysical moment. Why does it seem that there is so much more going on in the case of consciousness?

Perhaps much of the answer can be seen by looking in the opposite direction, *away from* the presumed threshold: Well *above* the threshold of felt pain, there is greater and greater felt pain. Even if there is an upper limit to this, before that limit, there is a vast range. And, well above the threshold of colored transparency, there is more and more intensely colored transparency. But, with the possible exception of a tiny range of "near sleep experiences," an exception that we may often deny altogether, above the threshold of consciousness there is not, in any clear sense, more and more highly conscious experience. Now, at certain moments, when meaning to contrast our unusual current mental state with our more ordinary mental states, we may sometimes speak of being intensely conscious. As it appears, however, we then have no very clear idea of what we are saying. Perhaps this is why it appears, to us, that there is such a great gulf between non-consciousness and consciousness: a difference between none at all and, on the other side, all that there can ever be.

This way of thinking about consciousness may be, not any road to metaphysical insight, but an artifact of superficial features of our language. In a way, we talk of consciousness as though it is a sort of space within which particular sorts of experiences may be instanced. Although someone's consciousness might be allowed to take on certain of the features of the particular experiences that occur to her, we do not allow it to take on features relating to magnitude or intensity. Or, if we do make some allowance, we only allow experience a very little power, freedom, or leeway in this regard.

We might, instead, speak differently of consciousness, so that we would allow it to take on these features. (There is, of course, an analogy here with recent treatments of physical space, as taking on certain quantitative features of the matter within it; this encourages an identification between the two.) If we spoke in this other way, then, when we felt very much more intense pain than we did just before, and in other ways our experience remained the same, we might say that we had very much more *intense* consciousness and, even, that we had very much *more consciousness*. When we had both visual and auditory experience throughout a certain minute, we might then say, not only that we had more sorts of conscious experience than if we had just one, but that, throughout that minute, we had more conscious experience. If we spoke in this other way, then perhaps we might be somewhat less confused. Perhaps quite rightly, there would not then seem, to us, to be a great gulf between conscious experience and, on the other side, all of the other processes that may occur in us.

When thinking of causes and their effects, we may be impressed by small causes that have very conspicuous effects. Impressed with these small causes, some might think that our spectrum is not persuasive about the gradualness of conscious experience. As they might think, perhaps the removal of a single cell will *cause a great change*. This huge change, triggered by this minute cause, might involve the difference between conscious experience and no consciousness. On this idea, the presence of experience may be a matter of much metaphysical significance.

On reflection, the plausibility of these causal suggestions seems rather superficial. True enough, a tiny part in a vast structure may be so centrally placed that its gentle removal causes the complete collapse of the entire structure. But, precisely because the decomposition involved really is so congenial for the maintenance of the person and all of the mentality that he ever has, it does not seem that anything like that is going on with adjacent cases of our spectrum. There is no big collapse of anything. Lacking only one peripheral neuron of many millions still at work, a neural structure that is ever so nearly as great and complex as that in the just previous case is involved in processes that, overall, are enormously like those in which the just slightly greater, just slightly more complex neural structure was involved.

Sometimes a small change in the balance of forces can cause a most notable result. As Roy Sorensen notes, a rocket may just barely have enough force from its fuel to achieve escape velocity from our planet's gravitational pull.[12] After take-off, it may begin to rain. A single raindrop may hit the rocket opposite to its direction of ascent. The tiny force of the one raindrop may tip the balance in favor of gravity. Because of this tiny cause, the rocket may never become a celestial body, returning to terra firma instead of journeying

12. This delightful observation is made in Sorensen's *Blindspots*, Oxford University Press, 1988.

to outer space. But nothing like this, it seems clear, is taking place between any adjacent cases of our spectrum. There is no force pushing toward the light of consciousness; nor is there another force pushing oppositely toward the darkness of non-consciousness. The removal of a cell does not, then, tip the scale slightly in favor of some such latter force, with the notable result that, for the first time in the sequence, the very different situation of non-consciousness obtains. To think otherwise is to deny that our spectrum really can be very congenial toward consciousness, which is not what we most deeply believe in the matter.

Now it is, of course, logically possible that there be some small cause, somewhere in this spectrum, which really does have some relevantly huge effect. We do not, however, have even the least inkling of how any such tiny cause might have this imagined effect. On the contrary, any intelligible models that we may bring to bear on behalf of this suggestion fail miserably. Moreover, as we become increasingly clear about the complete futility of those models, we increasingly realize that, for us, this is only a logical possibility. As we most deeply believe, with any one step between adjacent cases, there is never a significant non-conventional break of *any* sort in the life of the entity in question.

9. Against the Absoluteness of Experience: The Spectrum of Radio Communications

For many, the spectrum of congenial decomposition will be rather persuasive against the idea that, in its nature, conscious experience is absolute, or all-or-none. Still, that spectrum may be somewhat less persuasive in this regard than as an argument against the parallel idea that we subjects are absolute. After all, against the absoluteness of subjects, the spectrum works in two ways at once. Not only does it do something to undermine the absoluteness of experience, but it also suggests that, even as conscious experience continues fully, the original subject of that experience may, for example, have his reasoning powers so greatly reduced that he no longer exists. As that more intelligent subject fades out of existence, with the fading of those powers, his experience may perhaps be passed to progressively less intelligent sub-personal subjects. This might be just another case which shows that experiences are not metaphysically private to a single subject. Even if experiences are not metaphysically private, however, they might be metaphysically all-or-none.

As an argument against the absoluteness of consciousness, the spectrum of congenial decomposition might prove limited for another reason as well. We might harbor certain strange ideas about consciousness that are not addressed very squarely by this spectrum. Familiar from an earlier section, one of these is the idea that subjects of experience are each situated at a particular point, even if that be a vaguely conceived point. When we think this, we may also think that any particular conscious experience will be, if not situated at a particular point, then at least intimately associated with a point. Such a point, we might think, typically will be somewhere within someone's brain. Then we might think that, associated with a particular brain or large remaining part thereof, either there will be a point of conscious experience or else there will be the complete absence of that point. This tendency to "pointify" experience can aid our tendency to treat experience absolutely. This pointifying tendency is not addressed at all, much less is it countered, by the spectrum of congenial decomposition.

Along with the idea that consciousness occurs at a point, we have another idea. This is our idea that conscious experience conforms to a *dimming light model*.[13] Conscious experience can seem to be like a light that may get dimmer. At some points it may be extremely difficult, perhaps impossible, for us to *tell* whether the light is on or off. But there is a definite fact, nonetheless, as to when the light actually goes off. The light itself cannot really fade into darkness, which is the complete absence of light. As long as there is any light at all, there is not darkness.

In our spectrum of congenial decomposition, there is less and less happening toward the promotion of conscious experience at each progressively diminished stage. We might think that this is like there being less and less current flowing toward a certain light. When there is not quite enough current flowing, then, all of sudden, the light might not shine. There will then be real darkness, that is, the complete absence of light.

The spectrum of decomposition does quite a lot, I think, to help us realize that we do not really believe very deeply in this second conception. Yet it does not do as much in this regard as some may desire. Because it does not, we should like to complement the spectrum with another that is more effective in this way. So, there is this second motivation, too, for us to provide a suitably complementary spectrum.

Just as they helped us persuasively to counter other subjective metaphysical doctrines, perhaps examples in the style of Zuboff can be helpful here as well. In the present instance, as might be expected, we do not want just a few cleverly related examples of this sort. Rather, we want very many examples that, in a way that is more mechanically generated than cleverly arranged, form a relevant fine-grained spectrum.

This will be the *spectrum of radio communications*: The same sort of zippering procedure used to separate my brain can be used to separate the halves of my brain, or the resulting quarters of my brain. So, for example, just as

---

13. The discussion of this dimming light model derives from helpful correspondence with Mark Heller.

before happened with my brain as a whole, one of my half-brains may be gradually both bisected and fitted with radio transceivers at the opening interface. To get a very gradual spectrum, we may use this plodding procedure: At each stage, we always bisect just one largest brain-part of those then available in the situation. So, after we have half-brains, we will have one half-brain communicating with two quarter-brains. Then there will be four quarter-brains communicating; then two eighth-brains and three quarter-brains all communicating; then four eighth-brains and two quarter-brains, and so on, and so forth. This bisecting procedure can be repeated time and again, with arbitrary assignment to one side or the other in cases where the starting number of cells is odd, not cooperatively even. Eventually each neuron of my present brain will be in a supportive dish of its own, in splendid isolation from the others, while hooked up to an enormously complex device that is, among other things, a radio communicator.

At any stage in this spectrum of radio communications, each resulting brain-part may be moved so that it is a few miles from the others then maximally intact. For example, miles apart, each of four brain-quarters may then communicate with the others so that the appropriate quarter-brain states are consistently produced. Because communicating brain-parts can be moved miles apart, there will always be plenty of room for the two new brain-parts that each new step in the spectrum will generate.

When the smallest brain-parts are brain-quarters, then, as we may suppose, there will be, throughout, conscious thought and experience still generated. There need be nothing very fancy or controversial about this experience. As was the experience generated by the whole brain at the outset, the experience generated by these communicating quarters may be quite simple and minimal. It might, for example, be just experience as of a red circle on a blue background.

Eventually we get to the case where each nerve cell floats in a container of its own, hooked up to an enormously complex device. Will I exist in such a tremendously scattered condition as that? I think not. But that is not the important question for us now. Rather, the important question is this one: Will there be produced, in such an expansive situation as this, any conscious experience? I think not. Well, why not? The short answer may be this: There will be no subject in the situation, thus nobody to be the subject of any experience that might then be generated. And, even if experiences need not be private, there must be *at least one* subject for any particular experience. It is good, however, also to have a somewhat longer answer.

A significant part of a longer answer is this: Along the road of this separating procedure, the devices at the interfaces become significantly more complex, and more "intelligent," than mere communicators. The nature of their contribution to the causal processes becomes different. Progressively, they come to contribute "too much" to its being the case that the remaining groups of cells are, and continue to be, in the appropriate states. The groups of cells themselves, correspondingly, come to contribute too little. In the main and quite sketchily put, that is what goes wrong.[14] By the time we're down to scattered cells, the "communicators" are contributing almost everything, the original cells next to nothing. It is the communicators that are now doing almost everything in way of *coordinating* what is needed in the array of stimulations.

At all events, well after we have communicating brain quarters, but well before we have billions of individual neurons each in its own saucer, there will be a grey area as far as conscious experience is concerned. With the spreading of the brain, no tendency to pointify conscious experience, or subjects of such experience, will encourage us confusedly to deny this apparently quite evident grey area.

With so much radio communication even at late stages, the dimming light model, too, has little chance to gain a purchase. There will, it seems, always be plenty going on that might be needed to light any imagined lights. Indeed, at late stages, there is, in a way, *too much* current flowing about, or too much electronic guidance of communication, for experience to be generated.

Few will believe that, in this spectrum of radio communications, there is no grey area for consciousness. In this middle area, our conventions governing "conscious experience" will divide the better cases from the lesser ones. Except that they may be differently treated by our conventions, there will not be any noteworthy difference between two adjacent cases in this spectrum of billions of examples.

As do our other imaginative examples, the cases of this spectrum, too, rest on certain propositions of believed fact. Let us not once again tell a longish story about this situation. Rather, the upshot is that, as we most deeply believe, if there are any upsetting circumstances at all, then they will be owing to one or another quirk of, or breakdown in, the natural order; they will not be due to any deep metaphysical cleft between highly distinct realms. So, in any case, as we most deeply believe, there is little truth to the doctrine that conscious experience is all-or-none.

10. How One Person May Fade into Another

In the spectrum of congenial decomposition, and also in the spectrum of radio communications, a person fades out of existence. In the first of these spectra, this happens by having the original subject gradually fade into a

---

14. While I am very uncertain in the matter, perhaps this point is made by Daniel Dennett and Douglas Hofstadter in their Reflections on Zuboff's, "The Story of a Brain," in *The Mind's I*. As far as I can tell, the various other points made in those Reflections are much less convincing.

barely sub-personal subject of experience. (Later in the spectrum, a sub-personal being with experience fades into a "still lower" being with states that barely fail to be states of conscious experience.) In the second spectrum, it is less clear how to describe, in positive terms, what happens when the person fades out: Perhaps there is a direct fading out from a conscious person to no conscious subject at all, not even a sub-personal one, without the intermediate phases of a sub-personal subject with experience. In neither of these spectra, however, do we have exemplified what might be a third way in which a person might fade out of existence: The person may gradually cease by fading into another subject who is, just as clearly as is the first, another person. The provision of a spectrum that shows how one person may fade into another may round out, in a satisfying manner, our argument against the doctrine that we subjects are metaphysically all-or-none.

A certain modification of Parfit's Physical Spectrum will provide just what we want.[15] For, suitably modified, this spectrum provides not only a relevantly realistic sequence of cases, but one whose examples exhibit much good physical continuity. As originally presented, the spectrum is this: In the first ("active") case of the spectrum, a surgeon removes a few of the original person's cells and then, pretty much all at once, he replaces them with duplicate cells arranged in exactly the same way. In the next case, the surgeon removes, all at once, both the cells considered in the just prior case and also a few more of the patient's cells. Then, all at once, he replaces them with duplicates arranged in precisely the removed group's manner. In the last ("active") case, the surgeon replaces, at once, all but a few of the original cells. In each case, the removed cells are destroyed immediately upon their removal.

As presented by Parfit, this spectrum is aimed primarily at those who hold to the physical approach to our survival, or to some quite similar approach, such as our physically based approach. Relative to this aim, it is easy to see the need for modification: We need only ask, "In any given case in the Physical Spectrum, what or who is present during that time, however brief, *after* the removal and *before* the replacement?" There is just as much and just as little to the person in question, so to say, as in the corresponding case in the (somewhat finer-grained) spectrum of congenial decomposition, where just that many cells are likewise removed but are never replaced. In any given case in the Physical Spectrum, the person will survive if, and only if, the person survives in the corresponding case in our decomposition spectrum. Since we do not allow for a person to have interrupted existence, the later additions will do nothing to save him. Now, this argumentation may not be decisive. But, even if it is not, still, at the very least, the reasoning presents a good deal of trouble. Accordingly, to accommodate these considerations, a suitable modification is wanted.

15. The Physical Spectrum itself is presented on pages 234–36 of *Reasons and Persons*.

Here is the beginning of a nice modification: Each case in the Physical Spectrum must be made more complex. The surgeon will *not* remove the cells pretty much all at once, but, instead, he will very *gradually* remove however many cells a given case specifies. Moreover, after he removes a few cells, the surgeon *replaces those cells with duplicates before* any other cells are removed. Accordingly, at any time, there will be missing only a very few of the normal complement of cells for a healthy human being with a healthy brain functioning quite normally.[16]

The rest of the modification consists of specifying an assimilation constraint on the procedure of gradual cellular replacement: Although the replacements are made gradually, they are made very rapidly. Even in the most time-consuming of the operations, all the replacements may be made in, say, under an hour. In that way, there will not be enough time for any of the replacing cells to be assimilated into the original person.

As thus modified, the Physical Spectrum provides a complement to the spectrum of congenial decomposition. We have here a spectrum that we may use, very effectively, against those who hold to subjective, and to hybrid, views. First of all, in this Modified Physical Spectrum, as in the congenial decomposition spectrum, conscious experience may be continuously supported *beyond the points at which the original person fades out of existence*. But, second, unlike in that decomposition spectrum, where conscious experience itself eventually gives out, in this Modified Physical Spectrum there may be *full consciousness from the first case to the last*. For, at the lowest ebb for consciousness, there are only a very few brain cells that are missing, not yet replaced. And that is not a very low ebb at all.

Those who profess a (pure) physical approach to survival will not be very happy with this spectrum. For they will notice the high degree of physical continuity, throughout, for a continuously effective entity that they may identify as a persisting physical realizer of psychology. For them, this will mean one single person exists throughout the spectrum. After all, in their official position, they do not recognize that, for our survival, there may be a need for assimilation. In our fifth chapter, however, we argued that this pure physical approach is not plausible. To have a more credible view, these philosophers should move to our physically based approach to survival, where the intuitively evident factors of assimilation are given their just due. They may then be content to use this spectrum against subjectively inclined thinkers, who are friends of the metaphysical doctrine that subjects are all-or-none.

Those who hold to a version of the psychological approach also will not be very happy with this Modified Physical Spectrum. That is because, in this spectrum's cases, there are certain causal connections between the original

16. This modification was offered by Parfit in conversation.

brain and the replacing brain parts, which connections are responsible for the suitable character of the replacing brain parts. Because there are these causal relations, there will be many strong psychological connections between the original person and, on the other side, any person in the other cases of the spectrum. According to the psychological approach, these mental connections will ensure that every case in the spectrum involves nobody but the original person himself.[17] In our third chapter, we argued against the psychological approach, as well as kindred approaches. Consequently, we need not be much concerned, either, with this second source of discontent.

It may still be very well worth our noting that, quite directly, we can accommodate the concerns of those who were impressed with the psychological approach to our survival. Heaping one benefit upon another, we can, at the same time and just as directly, accommodate any remaining misgivings of those who were impressed with the (pure) physical approach. The key here is to consider this *physical spectrum of statistical miracles*: In this spectrum, each miracle involves the spontaneous destruction and removal of certain of my cells, the spontaneous agglomeration of atoms into precise duplicates of just those cells, and the insertion of the latter into precisely those places in the remaining arrangement lately vacated by the former. The spectrum might have a million alternative sequences of such miracles for us to consider; more manageably, it may have a hundred. In the first case in this spectrum with a hundred alternatives, there is the statistical miracle wherein, not all at once, but in the modification's highly gradual way, one percent of my cells are replaced by duplicate cells. In the next case, another one percent are so replaced and, then, miracle upon miracle, less than a minute later, yet another one percent are replaced. In the ninetieth case, a sequence of ninety miracles occurs.

In this physical spectrum of statistical miracles, there are no causal connections at all between my earlier states and the later states of the man with the newly arrived cells. Therefore, in the more radical cases of this spectrum, there are no causal connections that, on any form of the psychological approach, might secure my survival. Also, in those more radical cases, and as a proponent of the physical approach will notice, there will not be nearly enough physical continuity for my survival. Whether physically oriented, psychologically oriented, or whatever, on any sort of objective approach worth

---

17. In *Reasons and Persons* Parfit offers a Combined Spectrum on pages 236–41. Even if several needed modifications are made, this spectrum is less than optimally illuminating. But the Combined Spectrum is not as bad as I, along with others, have thought. As he has convinced me in correspondence, we were confused by Parfit's somewhat unclear, but easily improvable, presentation of that spectrum. When it is modified and presented clearly, then, the Combined Spectrum may be a useful complement to the cases presented in the text above.

serious consideration, this spectrum shows that, as we most deeply believe, my survival is a relevantly gradual affair.

In a variety of complementary ways, we have argued against all six of the metaphysical doctrines concerning conscious experience and the subjects of experience. By any reasonable standards, I submit, the arguments are convincing. As the arguments make clear to us, according to our deepest beliefs about ourselves and our experiences, these doctrines are false doctrines. What is true, we believe, is that, to the contrary, each of us is a highly complex entity, one who is at least very largely physical, constituted mainly, or perhaps even entirely, of many simpler physical entities. And our experiences, we believe, are each wholly objective processes, perhaps even physical processes, in which we are involved. Accordingly, as we most deeply believe, a physically based account of our survival may be a correct account of our survival.

7

WHAT MATTERS IN OUR SURVIVAL: DISTINCTIONS, COMPROMISES AND LIMITS

The current literature abounds with lively discussions of *what matters in our survival*. On one extreme, there are those who hold the *absolutely deflationary view of what matters in our survival*: Strict survival itself never really, or fundamentally, matters at all. Rather, what matters always might be, for example, the holding of certain continuities that, in favored cases, happen to underpin the truth of strict survival claims. Diametrically opposed to this, there are those who hold the *strict view of what matters*: All that ever matters in a given person's survival is the fact that the very person himself will still exist.

Unfortunately, discussions of this topic may be as confused as they are vigorous and stimulating. In the present chapter, we shall try to avoid most, if not all, of this confusion. When we are reasonably clear about what are the main issues of the topic, we may see our way to a complex position that lies between the two extremes, the *realistic compromise view of what matters*: First, we may hold that, in the most relevant uses of the terms, what matters in a given person's survival *basically* is only that the very person himself will still exist. But, second, other things, notably certain continuities, may matter *non*-basically, or *derivatively*. And, third, although these continuities may have only derivative importance, they may yet have *independent* importance: Regarding what matters in survival, certain cases without survival may be pretty nearly as good as certain cases of strict survival itself. Fourth, and finally, this derivative independent importance will never be as great as that basic importance: Regarding what matters in survival, no case that lacks strict

211

survival will be as good as any case in which the original person himself really does survive.

With many aspects to address, this question of what matters is really a very difficult one. Before we come even remotely close to a complete account of the matter, we will require the work of at least one further chapter. In such a place, we may treat those aspects that are directly involved in branching cases. In this present chapter, we place to the side examples in which branching occurs.

1. Survival as a Precondition of Broad Ego-centric Value

Philosophers sometimes speak of the *value of personal identity*, of *the value of survival*.[1] In certain contexts, remarks to this effect might not promote confusion. All too often, however, they appear to do just that. For this reason, although we will not always avoid speaking in that way, we will try to motivate, in addition, a more explicit, and a potentially less confusing, way of speaking. Accordingly, we will say that survival is a *precondition of* much of what we most value.

If I survive in a terminal coma, in fact never again enjoying any activity or experience, there is, for me, nothing worthwhile in that situation. If I survive only to be tortured, there may be lots of thought and experience on my part; but, unless we indulge ourselves in speaking of *negative value*, there is no value for me in that situation, either. By itself, then, my survival is of no value to me. Nor is my survival, by itself, of more general value, or of more objective value, as examples like these serve to make plain. Rather than thinking of a person's survival as *having value*, whether to that person or more generally, it may be better to think of the person's survival as being a *precondition of* certain things that, both to that person and more generally, have value.

Preconditions of what a person values may be, as well, necessary for related things that the person greatly *detests*. For example, as regards the future, my survival is as much a precondition of my being terribly tortured as it is of my being happy. While my survival is, thus, a precondition of certain of my *ego-centric values*, this fact is only one side of a more complete account. By way of some illustrative examples, these points may be clarified.

While I am still enjoying normal life, ten "duplicates" of me may be introduced. Perhaps these duplicates might have developed independently on distant planets. Or, they might have been produced by a taping process with physical temporal overlap. At any rate, we may compare two situations: In

---

1. In *Reasons and Persons*, Parfit seems to be subject to this confusion at a number of places. For example, see the discussion on pages 263–64.

the first, I am swiftly, suddenly and painlessly killed while each of my ten duplicates go on to lead a happy life for many years, none interfering with any other. This is bad for me and good for them. In the second situation, all of the duplicates are painlessly killed while I go on to lead a happy life for many years. This is bad for them and good for me.

By most reckonings of objective value, there may be more value in the first situation: There is one-tenth the number of killings and, for nice innocent people just like me, there is ten times the number of long happy lives. But *I* much prefer that the *second* situation obtain, where things are good for *me*. Reasonably enough, I most want it to be *me* who has a long and happy life.

Continuing with our illustrative cases, we may show how that is just one side of the story. In the first situation, where I am killed swiftly, suddenly and painlessly, suppose that, alternatively, each of the ten duplicates will be mercilessly tortured for years. Although they would like to end their lives, there is no way out for them. This is bad for me, but much worse for them. In the alternative second situation, it is they who are painlessly killed and I who am mercilessly tortured with no way out. This is bad for them, but much worse for me. Now, on most objective reckoning, the second situation is not as bad as the first. For only one person is relentlessly tortured instead of ten. But as I am not fanatically sympathetic, or anything of the like, I don't seriously evaluate the outcomes along those lines. Quite reasonably, *I* much prefer that it *not* be *me* who survives only to be so terribly tortured.

Before continuing with my main point here, let me try to be a little clearer about what I mean by my ego-centric values. Even while I have these values, I might also have certain ethical values that, in certain situations, can conflict with my ego-centric values: In certain cases, there might be a forced choice for me to make regarding which of the two situations will obtain and which will not obtain. (If I refuse to make the choice, then all eleven of us will be killed, and so none will have a long and happy life.) When I say that I prefer the second situation, where I alone survive to have a long and happy life, I do *not* mean that, according to my whole system of attitudes, when confronting such a forced choice, I should spare myself at the expense of the ten others. That is a quite separate issue. For, in confronting such a choice, I may have ethical values of impartiality that might prevail over my ego-centric values. Even if that is so, I will feel a conflict. At the least, that very conflict will indicate the presence of my ego-centric values.[2]

---

2. To be perfectly open in these matters, let me confess my suspicion that most of us, myself included, do not actually place a tremendously high priority on our impartial ethical ideals. True enough, many of us may care more about the masses than about the comforts of wealth; but, at the same time, we might care less about the masses than we do about those few whom we deeply love. Nor does this necessarily mean, I suspect, that we are bad people. Rather, for many good people, there might be a very important question of how, in the presence of a conflict between

Taking a complementary perspective on these matters may add some clarity: Suppose that there is no choice for me to make. The die has been cast by a super scientist, good or evil, who has already chosen. In that I have no choice in the matter, all I get to do now is to hear the news as to which choice he has made. Owing to my ego-centric values, I may be happier to hear that he has chosen to spare me and to kill the ten others; I may be unhappier to hear the opposite news.[3] Even if I myself were always to choose in favor of the ten, because of my ego-centric values, this may be the pattern of my more passive emotional reactions.

These evaluative attitudes, on which I am focusing, are *broadly* ego-centric. As such, no more than there need be anything unethical in these values, there need be nothing particularly selfish in them, either: Rationally, I prefer that my *son* have many future years of happiness rather than that I myself have many happy future years. But, as should be clear, a broad ego-centric attitude is, for all its breadth, an ego-centric attitude: I care as much as I do about my son, Andrew, a very great deal indeed, precisely because Andrew is *my* son, that is, just because he is related *to me* in certain ways, mainly personal and historical, rather than biological. Accordingly, and quite rationally, I may much prefer that there be many happy years left in store for Andrew than that there be many happy years left for each of ten duplicates of him.

Certainly, this third preference is a self-centered one, but is it also a badly selfish attitude? Perhaps, it is not. After all, there may be no more significant connections between me and these duplicate Andrews than, say, between me and ten randomly selected boys in Europe. Truth to tell, I do not really know these duplicate Andrews at all, but know only, even if quite thoroughly, those personal qualities that they happen also to possess. For I have no more *interacted with them*, in any personally significant ways, than I have with the ten boys in Europe.

Parallel broad ego-centric concerns occur on the other side of the ledger: Bad as it may be for Andrew, and for me, too, I prefer that my son die suddenly and painlessly than that he be relentlessly tortured for years, until his eventual demise. For that torture is far worse than that death. In line with this, I prefer that my son be killed and that I myself be thus tortured than the other way around. Finally, I prefer that Andrew be killed and his ten duplicates be thus tortured than the other way around.

---

our personal values and our impartial ethical ideals, we are to lead our lives. At all events, in the passage above, it suffices simply to distinguish between our broad ego-centric values and other of our main values, including our impartial ethical values. On all of these matters, I am much indebted to comments from Mark Johnston and Derek Parfit.

3. As I suppose, I owe the idea of looking at the matter in this way to Derek Parfit, although it was Frances Kamm who delivered the message when it was most needed.

There are many obvious differences between personal identity on the one hand and, on the other, conscious experience. But, as regards preconditions of what we value, there may be some illuminating analogies between survival and consciousness. Especially as regards how they may relate to our evaluative attitudes, noticing the analogies may help us to think more clearly about both consciousness and also survival.

Perhaps there might be people who do not care much about conscious experience. Perhaps they might have many goals that do not presuppose their ever having conscious experience. For example, one of them may be much concerned to write a great historical work, *whether or not* he is ever conscious. Another may be much concerned to climb a certain mountain, whether or not he ever has any conscious mental states. So, as we are supposing, these people care much only about having active lives that, *quite apart from any considerations of consciousness whatsoever*, are highly successful in the attainment of their goals. They may greatly prefer a life empty of conscious experiences but filled with such success to a life that, even while it is filled with conscious mental states, is only moderately successful as regards the attainment of those goals.[4]

For some of us, our discussion of Chapter 5 may encourage a more vivid idea about the (apparently) bizarre values of these people: Recall the permanent Trancelife drug. As we endeavored to explain coherently, this destroyed a person's very capacity for consciousness. This may have helped to raise some interesting questions about a person's survival. Alternatively, and raising no serious questions about survival, we may consider a drug that only inhibits, although it quite completely inhibits, a person's capacity for conscious experience. As we will call it, this is the *temporary Trancelife drug*. After taking such a drug, one will have no conscious mental states for about a month. But as with the permanent drug, during the month, one may engage in all of the ordinary forms of external behavior available to one without the drug. The temporary drug may be administered both successively and with temporal overlap for the rest of someone's life. (To underline the idea that, as compared with the permanent drug, the effects of this temporary potion are superficial, we may specify that, unlike with the permanent drug, there are antidotes to this temporary one. Although an antidote might be given at any time, allowing consciousness to return directly, no antidote ever is administered in the case now specified.) When all of this is done, then, even while she will never lose the capacity for consciousness, an actively successful person will never again have any conscious experience.

Provided that it did not interfere with the attainment of their goals, these

4. In these matters, I owe much to discussion with Stephen Schiffer.

super achievers will not mind taking this drug for the rest of their lives. Indeed, if this drug markedly increases various powers of those under its influence, thus making more likely the attainment of their goals, then the super achievers will actually prefer to spend the rest of their lives on the temporary Trancelife drug.

At all events, the people with these values may not particularly *mind* having conscious experience, so long as the experience does not interfere with the attainment of their goals. They might not mind this any more than I should mind having a duplicate of myself, so long as the duplicate does not interfere with my leading my own life as best I can. They are as indifferent toward their having conscious experience as I am toward there being duplicates of myself who roam freely on distant planets, or who are firmly ensconced on earth in most congenial experience inducers.

As regards evaluative attitudes, it is very clear that we are not much like these people. If one of *us* spent the rest of his life under the influence of the Trancelife drug, and having no more conscious experience, then the person's life will be of little or no direct value to him. Even if he unconsciously acts so as to fulfill ever so many of his ambitions, this will remain true.

Just as there might be people who did not care much for consciousness, so there might be people who do not care any more for themselves, or for their children, than for duplicates. But our own attitudes are not like that. We are no more like the people who are indifferent between themselves and their duplicates than we are like the people who are rather indifferent toward whether they ever have conscious experience.

Does this mean that, for us, consciousness has great value and that, after all, survival itself has value? If we like, we may speak in this way. But then we should be careful to avoid certain confusions. So, when clarity and explicitness are needed, it is better to say that, like survival, conscious experience is a *precondition of* there being much that we value. True enough, apart from whatever instrumental value it may happen to have, a life devoid of conscious experience will be no better, for me, than swift, sudden and painless ordinary death, or scarcely any better. But it will *also be no worse* than such painless ordinary death, or scarcely any worse. In short: If I have a life filled with much conscious thought and experience, then, from a logical point of view, this may as easily be a very bad deal for me as it may be very good. For, if my experience is all very painful, then I much prefer to have none. Quite rationally, I will prefer to cease existing, completely and forever. Just as consciousness is a *precondition* of our having lives that are *most worth living*, it is *also* a precondition of our having lives that are *least* worth living and, thus, that are most worth *ending*.

It is the *character of* our conscious experiences, and the *relations of* these experiences to the rest of our lives, that, for us, makes these experiences good, bad or indifferent. But, without our *having conscious experiences* that are, in this way, good, our lives themselves will be of little or no value to us. Similarly, it is the *character of* the later stages of our lives, and the *relations of* these stages to the rest of our lives, that makes them, for us, good, bad or indifferent. But, without there being later stages of *our* lives, without our *surviving*, the lives that, in the future, are lived will be of limited value to us. When we explicitly include, in the reference of the "our," the lives of all of those whom we actually know, and all of their children unto the sixth generation, we get pretty close to the full force of our broad ego-centric concern.

Because we are now clearer about these questions of what is directly valued on the one hand and, on the other, the preconditions of what is valued, we may speak more loosely, and more conveniently, without much fear of confusion. Safely enough, we may say that we value conscious experience, that we value our families much more than we value even perfectly similar perfect strangers, and that we value ourselves more than our duplicates. Clarity is to be valued; pedantry and prolixity are not.

2. The Spectrum of Congenial Decomposition with Reconstruction

Frequently, people undergo major surgery. During the hours of the surgery, the unconscious patients can do hardly anything at all. If all future hours were like these, few would opt for surgery. Few would do so even if, as in our imagined procedures, there was no danger at all to any patient's life itself. But a few hours like these are not so bad, provided that you can get through to the other side. On the other side, there should be many hours during which you can do very much more and, indeed, when, consciously experiencing a good deal of your activity, you actually do very much more.

Recall our spectrum of congenial decomposition. We may alter this spectrum systematically. After the low point reached when all of the earmarked cells have been removed, those cells are replaced by duplicates. In each case, first the removal, and then the replacement, may be effected almost all at once. In each case, at the end there is a person who is enormously like the original was upon entering the operation. On the other hand, there is very little assimilation time for the newly joined duplicate cells, perhaps well under five minutes. We may call this the *spectrum of congenial decomposition with reconstruction* or, for short, the *spectrum with reconstruction*.[5]

5. From the previous chapter, recall Parfit's Physical Spectrum. As actually presented in *Reasons and Persons*, this involves a hundred alternative operations, each one more radical than the previous procedures in the ordering. In each operation, a certain number of cells are removed and,

For our present discussion, there are several advantages to focusing on this spectrum rather than on the simpler spectrum of decomposition. First, with reconstruction, we may discount the loss of obviously desirable features of the person, such as his personal putative memories and his intelligence. With reconstruction, all of these are present in the emerging person, whomever that patient may be. Helping us avoid the misleading desirability use of the term, we are moved to focus on more relevant uses of "what matters in survival."

Second, in order to study the relation between survival and what matters, we will employ avoidance of future pain tests on the people emerging from operations. Consider cases just above the borderline for my survival. In the simpler spectrum, there may emerge from some of these cases a person who cannot feel pain that is comparable to the torture that a normal human person can feel. Basing his choice on that thought, a chooser might accept little pain beforehand in order to spare this future person pain, even if the chooser believes that this person will be nobody but him. As it is not relevant to our main topics, it is best to avoid this issue. By employing the spectrum with reconstruction, we avoid it entirely. For, in every case of this spectrum, there emerges a person capable of feeling any relevant pain, to wit, someone enormously like me now.

Third, we will also apply tests of selection between processes problematic for survival: Beforehand, how much pain will I endure to select one process rather than another? Unlike me, some of us will prefer to be terminated, swiftly and painlessly, rather than survive as just a brain in a vat, with an imbecilic mentality, even if they will then experience much pleasure. These rather high-minded people might think such an existence to be, say, too demeaning. Now, in the unadorned spectrum of congenial decomposition, interesting borderline cases might fall in such a region of diverse preference. Concerned as they are with demeaning conditions, the high-minded might prefer an operation which they do *not* survive over an operation which, just barely, they do survive. This may easily generate confusions.[6] By never leaving anyone in a state much different from his pre-operative state, the spectrum with reconstruction completely avoids these potential confusions.

In interesting cases, our spectrum with reconstruction does leave the orig-

---

a bit later, duplicates of those cells are all put in their places, pretty much all at once. In a finer grain, we may consider an ordering of operations that differ by just one cell. Then there will be billions of alternative operations, the longest of which, we may suppose, will take about two minutes. This will be (virtually) equivalent to the present spectrum with reconstruction.

6. If we have independent tests for who is high-minded, then the reverse preference of people who pass those tests may, in a nicely perverse sort of way, provide interesting confirmation of the more usual results. As indicated in the text, however, thinking a lot about these high-minded folks is, for most of us, more likely to produce confusion than illumination.

inal person in a pathetic state, but an unconscious one, for *some* period of time: the interval after removal but before reconstruction. But, like the time needed for removal, this period may be extremely brief. Scarcely anyone will abhor being severely attenuated for only a few seconds (or even for a few hours). Few indeed will prefer to end it all rather than undergo a debilitating operation with a reconstruction that is as swift, as certain and as complete as it is painless.

Various other spectra also have these advantages. Among these are *spectra of assimilation*. In the most basic ways, these other spectra are similar to the spectrum with reconstruction. But there are interesting differences, too. Near the chapter's end, we will outline a certain spectrum of assimilation. In that way, we will notice both the basic similarities and also some interesting differences. By so doing, we may do two things. On the one hand, we may confirm the most general points about the relations between our survival and what matters, first made with reference to the spectrum of reconstruction. On the other, we may notice special features of the reconstructive spectrum that do not readily generalize.

3. Three Shots at Survival: Easily Getting Through, Barely Getting Through and Barely Missing

In our spectrum of decomposition with reconstruction, a patient will *very easily get through* an operation where *only three* of his cerebral neurons are removed, are destroyed and, a bit later, are replaced by duplicates. But, with so little assimilation time, a patient will *not* survive an operation where *all but three* of his neurons are removed, destroyed and replaced by duplicates. Suppose that I am the prospective patient. How radical an operation can I survive, just barely getting through? We will not, of course, make any serious attempt to answer this question. But perhaps we may learn something from seriously thinking about the question.

In many severe cases of the spectrum, there will be a person even before cellular replacement. This may happen, for example, when there is only about a third of the higher brain remaining and almost all of the much smaller lower brain. Unlike the original person, whose general intelligence was pretty considerable, the person with this reduced brain may have the mentality of a moron. Yet it may be quite clear that this moron is me. In this case, where I am reduced to being a moron, it still may be that I will quite easily get through: Primarily because my core psychology is continuously realized by much of my appropriately structured brain, it is clear who is there.

In some other cases, with millions more neurons removed, I will *barely get through*. Although it will be *true* that the being at the end is me, it will, as we say, *barely* be true. These are the *bare survival cases*. Still further along, there will be the *near miss cases*, in which it is *not true*, not even barely true, that I survive.

In just a moment, I will try to make some points that, given our beliefs about this spectrum, represent what is, to my mind at least, clear logical thinking about these cases. According to these points, there will be, in this spectrum, a single first near miss case. Along with an uncontroversial simplifying assumption, to be introduced just a bit later, this idea of *the first* near miss case will allow a discussion of my concern, for the people in this spectrum's cases, to proceed in a very crisp and clean manner. Now, some philosophers may resist the logical points that I am about to offer. Let me reassure them, in advance, that the more substantive points do not depend upon (what I take to be) these points of philosophical logic: There will be available to them, in any case, less crisp discussions of those more substantive points. And the results of those more relaxed discussions will be essentially the same.

Right now, let's take a close look at some logical features of this spectrum with reconstruction: First, as we believe, very near the top end there is *nothing problematic whatsoever* about my surviving: When there are *removed* only three neurons, *it simply is true* that I survive. And, as we also believe, very near the bottom end there is *nothing problematic whatsoever* with the idea that I do not survive: When there *remain* only three neurons, *it simply is true* that I do *not* survive.[7] Further, as regards there emerging someone with good qualifications for being me, we believe that, in this spectrum of cases, there is a *general decrease*, starting from the top end and proceeding toward the bottom end. Finally, as we believe, there is not only a *finite number* of cases in this spectrum, but there is also a *greatest lower bound* on the relevant decrements. *Given that these beliefs are correct*, it is a matter of mathematics and logic that there is, in the spectrum, a *first* case where it is *not true* that I survive.

---

7. In many conversations over several years, David Lewis has consistently advocated an opposing view: In at least some senses, or suitable interpretations, there really is something problematic about whether I will survive the loss of a single nerve cell. Moreover, and according to the same underlying reasoning, in at least some such senses, the idea that a water molecule is a piece of ravioli is *less problematic* than the idea that a mere hydrogen atom is a piece of ravioli. Just so, the idea that a water molecule is *not* a piece of ravioli is *not* an idea about which (with quantifiers completely unrestricted) there is, in every sense, nothing problematic whatsoever. Against this, I believe that, in every possible sense and way, there is *nothing* problematic in the idea that a water molecule is not a piece of ravioli. So, although the details underlying Lewis's position may be very ingenious, the whole business strikes me as implausible in the extreme. (Of course, the main thrust of his ideas is an attempt to solve the sorites paradox, and even the most credible of such attempts will be, by any usual standards of plausibility, a very implausible piece of business. But, as I see it, even going by this exceptionally generous standard, this line of Lewis's is exceptionally implausible.)

Why do I make these remarks here now? Honesty compels me to state that a proposition that I endorse in the text, and that I heavily rely on, is actually denied by able and intelligent philosophers; indeed, it is denied by at least one truly brilliant philosopher.

The points just made do not require, it should be noted, the somewhat questionable assumption that every removal of a neuron, even every most congenially chosen and executed removal, will mean a loss as regards qualifications for being me. Sometimes there might be no loss in psychological realization and, thus, no loss of qualifications. Perhaps due to a slight lessening in potential for neural interference, sometimes there might even be a slight gain. (However, as we are taking a route of removal that is *most congenial* for my survival, out of very many trillions available, that appears doubtful.) Lapses in correlation, of either sort, are quite irrelevant to the main point here: Because sufficiently long stretches of neural removals are associated with losses in qualifications, as in fact they surely must be, there will be a first near miss case.

Once we are clear on this main point, we may, in order to aid exposition, make a simplifying assumption: In any interesting range of our spectrum, whenever there is a neural decrement from a higher to a lower case, there is also, before reconstruction, a small decrement of psychological realization. With this supposition, and owing to the same sort of logical points lately presented to disclose the first near miss case, we may conveniently spot a second conspicuous case: The bare survival case that is right before the first near miss case will then be the *last (bare) survival case*. In much of what follows, we will be discussing these two adjacent cases.

The points just made also do not require, it should be noted, that we subscribe to a classical logic, complete with both a law of excluded middle and the two traditional truth-values: true and, alternatively, false. Now, given our noted beliefs, we may further notice, there must *also be a first case* where it is *true* that I do *not* survive. Even this further point, while it perfectly agrees with the classical approach, does not actually require that pristine treatment of logic. Rather, on the classical view, there will simply be an identity of the two salient first cases: The first case where it is not true that I do survive will be one and the same as the first case where it is true that I do not survive. On non-classical approaches, by contrast, there will be two different first cases here: Between these two cases, there will be cases where one or another non-classical truth-value will be assigned, such as indeterminacy or perhaps some fractional degree of truth. Or, on some treatments, no truth-value at all will be assigned for these cases. As regards the main points we are now attending, however, the difference between classical and non-classical approaches is irrelevant: It is irrelevant whether there is just one first case, twice characterized, or whether there are two different first cases. Having made these points for clarity, we return to the main thread of our discussion.

From the perspective of my self-centered concerns, or a small extension thereof, what do we think of the first near miss case? In ordinary cases, of course, it will be very bad for me when it is not true that I survive. But in the first near miss case, although it is not true that I survive, how bad for me can that be? How much worse can this case be than the case just before it, with one more neuron remaining at the lowest point, where it *is true* that I survive? As many will agree, it may be *somewhat* worse and, perhaps, it might even be slightly but significantly worse. But few will believe that the one adjacent case is very much worse than the other. Rather, in the first near miss case, although there is "not all that matters in my survival," there is "much of what matters in my survival." Vague as their expression may be, most of us have rather strong intuitions to this effect.

By speaking of the first near miss case, and by speaking of the last bare survival case, we provided a particularly crisp and clean way of noting our vague but strong intuitions about some close cases in our spectrum. But even with a more relaxed indication of relevantly close cases, these intuitions may be easy enough to notice. For those who resist what I consider to be points of clear logical thinking about these matters, this more relaxed mode of indication will be particularly welcome.

The resisters will think that, even in our spectrum, there is no first case where it is not true that I survive (and no first case where it is true that I do not survive). Instead, they may hold that, as we vaguely run out of cases where it is true that I survive, we vaguely come upon cases where it is indeterminate whether, and so not true that, I survive. But, even as these thinkers will agree, before we run out of good survival cases, there will be *some* cases, maybe indefinitely many of them, where I *just barely* survive, that is, where it is *just barely true* that I survive. In *these* cases, of course, it is true that I survive. And, as even the resisters will also concur, a little ways further along, although perhaps indefinitely few cases further, there will be *some other* cases where that is not so. In these other, nearby cases, even as it is *just barely indeterminate* whether I survive, it is *just barely not true* that I survive. So, of course, in these very nearby cases, which will differ from those bare survival cases by only (an indefinitely) very few neurons, it is not true that I survive.

How do we feel about these two groups of cases? As regards the question of my survival, the cases where it is just barely true that I survive are, of course, better than those where it is just barely not true. But they are not enormously much better. It is not as though all of the cases in the just barely higher group are extremely good, and equally good, whereas all of the cases in the just barely lower group are, as regards what matters in my survival, worth nothing. Rather, differing by only a very few contributing neurons from the nearby higher cases, the barely lower cases will contain some of, and perhaps even quite a lot of, what matters in my survival.

Related to each other, there are many relaxed ways for us to notice our intuitions about these cases. Here is another: Instead of speaking of the first near miss case, we might speak of *a* case where, *just barely*, it is *indeterminate* whether I survive and, so, just barely, it is *not true* that I survive. And, instead of speaking of the last survival case, we might speak of *another* case that is *only a very few* cases closer to the top end. In this *other* case, it *is true*, just barely, that I survive. So, while it *is* true that the very slightly higher case is a case of my survival, it is *not* true that the very slightly lower case is a case of my survival. But, intuitively, as regards *questions relating to* my survival, the very slightly higher case is not enormously much better for me. Rather, even in the slightly lower case, there is at least a significant amount of, and perhaps there is even quite a lot of, what matters in my survival.[8]

4. The Prudential Use of "What Matters," Tests for What Matters and Highly Prudential Occasions

Whether we point them out quite cleanly, as I prefer to do, or whether in one or another more relaxed fashion, we have strong intuitions that, as regards what matters in survival, there is not a very great difference between a certain case and a very slightly lower case. Rather than explain them away, we shall try to explain these strong intuitions of ours.

Before we attempt an explanation, however, it will be well to confirm these intuitions and, perhaps, to get a clearer idea of what substance they may have. For a responsible attempt in this direction, we should spend some time discussing several topics that, for convenience of exposition, we have pretty much ignored. This discussion will occupy us during this present section and the section directly following. In pursuing it, we will find a rather fortunate result: The cases we are presently considering may be safely explored using even rather liberal methods. In coming to this result, we shall better appreciate the need, by contrast, for the rather stricter methods employed before this juncture. Moreover, we shall learn about some shortcomings of those stricter methods, as they have so far been articulated and employed. Finally, and as is important for those times when they really are needed, we shall learn how our more stringent methods might be improved.

In some important use, or uses, of the term, "what matters in my survival," the first near miss case preserves much of what matters in my survival even though it fails to secure my survival itself. Now, as will be recalled, in the third chapter there were distinguished three main uses of the term. One of them was the constitutive use. When understood as involving this use, there will be nothing but truth in our statement about that near miss case and what matters: In the case of the person emerging from that highest near miss operation, there is much of what counts toward a person at a later time being iden-

---

8. In working out this section, I have been greatly helped by comments from Derek Parfit, Mark Johnston, Roy Sorensen and, above all, David Lewis.

tical with me. For example, even at the case's low point, there may be the
continuous realization of almost all of core psychology by much of the brain
originally mine. But, in that there is a near miss, there cannot, of course, be
all of what counts toward my survival. Although all of this may be quite correct, it should not be at the very center of our present discussion.

In the third chapter, we noted that, although the constitutive use is highly
relevant to questions of identity, it is not a use that is directly connected with
questions of motivation and choice. The desirability use, in stark contrast, is
very well connected with these motivational questions, but is not highly relevant to questions of identity. By contrast to both of those uses, it is the third
of our distinguished employments, the prudential use, that has both wanted
features at once: This use is directly connected with questions of choice and
it also is highly relevant to questions of our identity. Accordingly, in discussing the cases in our spectrum with reconstruction, we should focus on the
prudential use of 'what matters in survival.'

The prudential use was spelled out in this rough fashion: From the perspective of a person's concern for herself, or from a slight and rational extension of that perspective, what future being there is or, possibly, which future
beings there are, for whom this person rationally should be "intrinsically"
concerned, that is, for whom the person should be concerned even apart
from questions of whether or not the being, or beings, might advance the
person's projects. Now, as we recently noted, our intuition is that the last
bare survival case contains significantly more, but not enormously more, of
what matters in my survival. As is intuitive, this holds true even when we have
spelled out the prudential use of our terms: From the perspective of my concern for myself, or from a slight and rational extension thereof, I should be
significantly more concerned for the person in the last bare survival case, who
is (determinately) me, than for the person in the first near miss case, who is
not (determinately) me. But, at the same time, and even from such a perspective as that, I should *not* be *very much more* concerned for the last bare
survival person than for the first near miss person.

At least since Hume, the distinction between "is" and "ought," between
categorical fact and unconditional value, has been as prominent as any in
philosophy. This general distinction is, of course, instanced in our present
topic area: There is the distinction between who it is that, from a certain ego-
centric perspective, I *actually am* concerned for and, on the other hand, who
it is that, from that perspective, I *ought to be* concerned for. By using the
systematically ambiguous "should," in our characterization of the prudential
use of the term, we have deliberately bypassed this prominent distinction.

What reason can there be for this? There are several reasons. By itself, the
first reason is a weak one: With the three uses of 'what matters' so far distin-

guished, we already have plenty to keep in mind. Unless there is a real need to do so, I don't want to burden the reader, and myself, with still more. Of course, the first reason does not occur by itself.

Second, with regard to the distinction presently under discussion, the "ought" side itself issues in still further distinctions: On one hand, the "ought" might signal that a moral point of view be taken in assessing the suitability of what ought to be the objects of concern. (This might fit well with certain sorts of "agent-centered," or "agent-relative," moralities, in which our broad ego-centric concerns can figure prominently.) On the other hand, the perspective of rationality might be indicated. Further, and mixing metaphors, on one foot some might seek an "all-in" perspective, wherein the claims of morality and rationality will, somehow, both be given their due, a verdict about the proper objects of concern then being issued in light of an appropriate adjudication. And, on the other foot, some might favor, as the point of view signalled, still another ego-centric normative perspective. For my part, I take the most relevant normative perspective to be that of rationality. But, no doubt, there are others who see things differently. Thinking these differences unfruitful to pursue at this juncture, I prefer to avoid the potential controversies.

To me, my third reason is most important: Suppose that, as I propose, we take the "ought" to signal the norms of rationality. As I believe, our actual broad ego-centric concerns are quite rational concerns for us to have. For example, just as my actual concern for my son is an especially intense one, so just this intense concern for Andrew is the concern that is most rational for me. Although intuitively plausible, this claim can use some argument. It is my aim that, in the remainder of this book, some argument will be supplied.

What are our actual self-centered concerns? There are two main ways to test for the presence, in us, of these concerns: sacrifice for future well-being tests and process selection tests. In the first chapter, we presented these investigative tools as presumptive tests for our deep beliefs about our survival itself. And so they are. But that is not all that they are. Rather, and perhaps more directly, they are also tests for what (as we deeply believe) matters in our survival.

In applying a future well-being test, as will be recalled, I contemplate a process that, with no choice in the matter, I must undergo fairly soon. What I do have a choice about is this: I may make a certain early sacrifice, before the process takes place. If I do, then the being who emerges from the process will, from then on, be much better off than if I do not make that early sacrifice. In choosing whether to make the sacrifice, I am to proceed wholly from my concern for a particular being, in the simplest instance, from my concern for myself. Or, if that appears impossible, then, just insofar as it seems appropriate to me, I am to proceed from an attitude that is but a small and natural extension of that familiar self-centered concern.

As noted, the other main sort of test for what matters is the process selection test. As its name suggests, with this test there is not foisted on me any process that might be problematic for my survival. Rather, the situation is this: Only by making a sacrifice now can I ensure that, just a little later, I will undergo a certain one out of two considered processes; if I do not choose to make the sacrifice, I will undergo the other process instead.

Regarding questions of what matters in survival, just as regarding questions of survival itself, both sorts of tests are most reliable, and are certainly most riveting, when they take a *negative form*. First, we note that this is true with the sacrifice for well-being tests. Quite dramatically, the avoidance of future great pain test is much more riveting than tests, at the other extreme, where the sacrifice is aimed at future positive goods. For a point of reference, recall a benchmark case from our earlier discussions: A dastardly surgeon's operation greatly reduces both my personality and my intellect, and quite completely removes my personal memories. As a prelude to making some points about what matters, we rehearse some implications of this operation for questions of my survival itself: Even if my deep belief is that the cretin will be me, such a cretinous future may seem so repugnant that I may refuse the early sacrifice asked. By contrast, sweeping aside, as they do, any reluctance that may stem from my high-minded fancies, thoughts of excruciating pain speak more clearly, and more urgently, to the most relevant questions: Just so, I will make a considerable early sacrifice in order to spare that repugnant amnesiac cretin, who is me, terrible torture right after that horrible operation.

We may extend these ideas to questions of what matters in my survival: When the stakes are differences only in future positive goods, often there is the danger that I will conflate two different sorts of factors: Making for unwanted confusions, I might be affected, not only by the highly restricted factors relevant to the wanted prudential use, but also by the "more expansive" factors that are relevant even to the unwanted desirability use of 'what matters'.

Consider for a moment, not the spectrum with reconstruction, but the original spectrum of congenial decomposition, where there never is any reconstruction. In that spectrum, too, there will be a first near miss case, as well as a last bare survival case. Indeed, as a moment's reflection reveals, they will be the precise parallels of the cases that have those descriptions for the spectrum of reconstruction; there will just be missing the later reconstructive parts of those cases. We focus on the first near miss person of this simpler decomposition spectrum. Just barely, but nevertheless, it is not true that this forgetful near miss moron will be me. In this case, is there a fair amount of what matters in my survival?

We may employ a positive form of a future well-being test for what matters: Will I sacrifice much now so that, after he emerges, this near miss person may have great pleasure rather than only moderate pleasure? Even from any natural extension of an egoistic concern, I find that I will not. Perhaps, even, I might no more do so than I will sacrifice to benefit a mere duplicate of myself, say, someone who emerges from a taping process with physical temporal overlap. But this might indicate nothing about (my beliefs about) what prudentially matters. After all, whether he is me or not, how much can I really care about the shallow positive goods that such a forgetful moron may get out of his rather vacuous future life? To avoid this conflation and confusion, it is good for us to adhere, generally, to this obvious general rule: In choosing a sacrifice for well-being test, not only for questions of survival itself, but for questions of what matters, we employ the extremely negative test that focuses on the avoidance of great future pain.

The superiority of the negative form is even more dramatic in the case of the process selection tests: At least in the contemporary literature on these topics, it is standardly but unfortunately assumed that, whichever process I undergo, the person emerging therefrom will have a life that, even assessed relative to my own present values, will be a life well worth living. With this standard assumption of a good future life, we have a very positively oriented process selection test. With prospects positive, inquirers into what matters in survival may have a confused idea that I will sacrifice to select one process over another if the first does, but the second does not, secure (a lot of) what matters.

As noted in the first chapter, positive process selection tests, although commonly employed in the philosophical literature, can be very unreliable guides to (what are our deep beliefs about) when it is that we survive. Perhaps in an even more direct way, these tests can mislead us with regard to (our deep beliefs about) what matters in our survival: For example, I might sacrifice much to undergo a certain one process that, while otherwise just like a second, alone does not involve my coming to be amnesiac with regard to my past life. As is clear, but as is insufficiently noticed, this choice need not indicate that memories of one's past are factors that contribute much to one's survival or that, in the relevant prudential use of the term, contribute much to what matters in survival. Rather, the situation may simply be this: To someone with my values, the good of my retaining my memories, attained with the one process but not with the other, may be well worth the sacrifice. Because positive selection tests may often conflate such merely associated values as this with factors that are directly involved in my survival, these tests often may mislead us not only about questions of our survival itself, but also about questions of what, in the prudential use of the term, matters in our survival.

We need not make the standard assumption about the positive value of the emerging person's life. In a most marked contrast, we may suppose that this life will be, even according to my own present norms, a horrible life for the emerging person: For the many years until he expires, this person will be entirely consumed with excruciating pain. As will be recalled, when applying such a negative process selection test, my selection between two processes should proceed in the "opposite" direction. In other words, I should make a great early sacrifice so that I undergo the *more* problematic of the two considered processes. In ordinary cases, by making that sacrifice, I will bring about my termination and, in that way, I will ensure that I be spared these many years of excruciating pain.

In certain exotic cases, however, as a way of having little to do with horrible future tortures, although I will still make a *significant* early sacrifice, I will *not make as great a sacrifice as in the ordinary cases*. In the spectrum with reconstruction, this is what happens in the case of the intelligent, reconstructed first near miss person. And, in the original spectrum of congenial decomposition, this is what happens in the case of the moronic first near miss person. Now, whenever this happens, we may have an interesting indication: In the process that I select to undergo, although there is not all of what prudentially matters in my survival, there is quite a lot of what matters.

As we observed in our first chapter, both with future well-being tests and with process selection tests, the extreme negative forms are the best guides to (our deep beliefs about) our survival. And, as we have just lately observed, with both sorts of tests, these negative forms are the most riveting guides, as well, to (our deep beliefs about) what matters in our survival. But, as we have yet to observe, there is still another important point about these two sorts of tests: Regarding both our survival itself and also what matters, there are certain occasions for applying such tests when, against the general rule, there is no significant advantage to using a negative form.

At these times, there will not be operative any significant factors associated only with the desirability use, which may turn our focus away from purely prudential considerations. On such *highly prudential occasions*, as we will call them, such desirability factors have already been specified at such a high level that, regarding them, there is no further advantage to be achieved by making any early sacrifice. By default, the only advantage to be gained by an early sacrifice, then, will concern the more central prudential considerations. Each case in the spectrum with reconstruction presents a very highly prudential occasion. That is because, through the reconstructive part of each case, desirability factors have already been specified to obtain to a very high degree. By contrast, most of the cases of the simpler spectrum of congenial decomposition do not present such prudential occasions. In those cases, where there is no reconstructive replenishment of lost attributes, there may be rather little of what, in the desirability use, matters in survival.

Using our convenient terms, we may express this important third point as follows: First, there are many highly prudential occasions, most of them easy to recognize for what they are. And, second, whenever there is such an occasion, there is no significant advantage in using an extreme negative form of either of our tests, rather than even a quite positive form. Finally, this is true not only for questions of survival itself, but also for questions of what matters in our survival.

This third point is well illustrated by the two salient adjacent cases in our spectrum with reconstruction: First, to these two cases, we apply process selection tests. To begin, we apply a severe negative form: We assume that whether the last bare survival person is chosen to emerge or whether it is the first near miss person, the emerging person will, after full reconstruction, go on to lead a horribly painful life. How much pain will I take on, beforehand, so that it be the near miss person, rather than the bare survival person, who leads this horrible life? I will take on some significant early pain, but I will not endure very great pain. To conclude, we employ a positive form of the test: Accordingly, we now assume, both for the bare survival person and also for the near miss person, a quite happy future. In advance, how much pain will I endure so that it be the last bare survival person, rather than the first near miss person, who emerges to lead a happy life? My response is in perfect parallel: I will take on some significant early pain, but I will not endure very great pain.

Second, to these same two cases, we apply sacrifice for well-being tests: In order to spare him frightful future torture, I will endure great pain for the last bare survival person, who is (determinately) me. In order to spare him the same (sort of) torture, I will endure great pain, too, for the first near miss person. However, for this near miss person, who is not (determinately) me, I will not take on quite so much great pain now, but will endure only significantly lesser great pain. From the negative direction, this indicates that, as I deeply believe, in the first near miss case, there is quite a lot of what matters, but not all of what matters, in my survival. This may also be indicated, about equally well, from the positive direction: In order to gain him future great positive goods, I will endure some considerable pain for the last bare survival person, who is (determinately) me. In order to gain him the same (sort of) great positive goods, I will endure some considerable pain, too, for the first near miss person. However, for this near miss person, who is not (determinately) me, I will take on only a significantly lesser great pain.

For all of its requisite complexity, this section's discussion has yielded results that can be stated very succinctly: Both of the tests, in both of their forms, confirm the somewhat vague intuitions recorded in the preceding section. What is more, they help give more clarity and substance to our intuitions in the area. Shortly, we shall begin to explain these responses.

Before we begin that explanatory project, we will address some important methodological questions first indicated in our first chapter. As I see it, even while conducting our investigation in a responsible manner, we have been able to circumvent these complex questions. But, with the discussion of this present section highlighting them for our attention, we really should, without further delay, address these issues directly.

5. How Presumptive Tests for Survival Beliefs May Be Improved

In the first chapter, we said that the avoidance of future great pain test is only a *strongly presumptive* test for (what we most deeply believe about) our survival. We may now see clearly that the presumption the test establishes sometimes fails to hold. In our spectrum with reconstruction, when we apply the test to a near miss case, we get the result of much antecedent sacrifice to spare the person at the end. So, the pain avoidance test establishes the presumption that the emerging person is me. But, as this is a near miss case, it is not true that he is me.

Why did the favorable presumption fail to hold? Well, as soon as I direct my attitude of self-concern toward the candidate entity, perhaps I might also direct toward him attitudes that I have, or that I immediately form, in the neighborhood of that intentionally directed attitude. I may thus direct toward that entity some such related attitude as this: a concern for anyone who is constituted of entities whose character, relations and histories are *at least very nearly* of the right sort for those entities to constitute me. Because it is a *relevantly inclusive* attitude, in the ordinary cases, as well as in many other cases, this concern will be directed at me myself; in some exotic cases, this same concern will be directed at someone who, although it is not absurdly false that he is me, neither is it true that he is me. Or, I may direct this related relevantly inclusive attitude: a concern for anyone in the future whose life stages are related to my present life stages, in *at least very much* the same ways and to *at least very nearly* the same degree, as someone's life stages should be related to mine now for that person, in the future, to be me.[9] Indeed, per-

---

9. When I talk of stages of a person's life, I don't mean to commit myself to a metaphysically rich time-slice view of reality, which might possibly be a distortion of reality. And I think that it is easy for me to avoid any such commitment. This is true for two reasons. First, my locutions provide what are, as I believe, perfectly ordinary descriptions. Second, even quite a few not so ordinary locutions may be perfectly harmless, provided, of course, that they are sensibly employed. For some discussions that encourage a friendly attitude toward this second proposition, see Chris Swoyer's "Causation and Identity," *Midwest Studies in Philosophy*, 1984 and Mark Johnston's "Is There a Problem About Persistence?," *Proceedings of the Aristotelian Society, Supplementary Volume*, 1987.

haps, both of these concerns may even operate together. But, of course, a joint operation is hardly required. For these ideas to be plausible, it is enough that one such related concern may motivate my choice to protect the near miss person.

In all ordinary cases, such related concerns will be satisfied when my basic concern for myself is satisfied. Only in some few sorts of exotic case will there be a difference in the satisfaction of the two sorts of concern. Because this is so, it is correct to say that this avoidance of future pain test establishes a strong presumption in favor of (what I believe to be) my survival: It is a presumption that fails to hold, after all, only in some few sorts of exotic case. Still, there certainly is room for improvement. How might we improve matters?

Even in a strongly negative form, the same sort of thing happens with a process selection test: Consider a near miss case, perhaps the first near miss case, and a case rather lower down in our spectrum with reconstruction. In advance, I may take on much pain so that I undergo the process of the lower case rather than the process of the near miss case. By considerations of self-interest, or relevantly similar attitudes, I am moved to get myself "as much as is possible" away from the horrible tortures that will fill the emerging person's life. By choosing that early pain, I establish a presumption that I am the near miss person. But, as this is a near *miss* case, that presumption fails.

To have a better test of our survival beliefs, it may be suggested, we might require that both of these tests be applied to a given puzzle case, and that both generate presumptions favorable to survival. When there is no limit on our time, space or energy, that might be, in any case, the most prudent methodology to follow. But being prudent, in that way, will not prevent many presumptions from failing. The reason for this is clear: First, generally, when either one of these tests establishes such a presumption, the other one does, too. And, second, when one of these presumptions fails, then, generally, so does the other. In our spectrum, this happens with some of the near miss cases.

As it appears, what both sorts of tests are best at disclosing is, not our deep beliefs about our survival, but our deep beliefs about what matters in our survival. Nevertheless, as our previous chapters indicate, they are quite useful for ascertaining our deep beliefs about our survival itself. Rather than abandon their use for that purpose, folly in any case, we should try to answer a slightly expanded form of our question: As indicators of our deep beliefs about our strict survival, how might these tests be improved?

We may improve either of these tests by using it in a *comparative* manner: First, we find a case to which I can apply one of the tests in a most reliable form, say, to which I can apply the avoidance of great future pain test. In the familiar, simple, and straightforward manner, I then apply just that (form of that) test. If we find that I choose to suffer no pain beforehand, then we have a very strong negative presumption. Almost invariably, that closes the issue: There is not survival. But, of course, I may choose, instead, to undergo significant early pain. Then there arises a positive presumption. That is where our problems have arisen.

So that is where we go comparative: Second, we look to find *another* case that, according to that same test, gives a still stronger result. Is there another case, where I will choose to endure *more* pain now to spare future torture for the person at its end? If there is, then the presumption of survival fails. But, if there is not, then it stands firm. So, too, we may use an extremely negative selection test comparatively: Is there *another* case, for which I will *sacrifice* so that I may select *it* over the case that won the first selection test contest? If there is, then the presumption in favor of that first winner fails. But, if there is not, then it stands. In practice, when employing these tests, we will operate in short steps. At each step, we compare one case with one other example. With enough successes at enough steps, we may build confidence that a given puzzle case is truly a case of survival.

In order for the comparative use of these tests to mean real improvement, it is required that a certain assumption, or background proposition, hold true: As far as my prudential concern extends, any genuine case of my strict survival is on a par, quite completely, with any other case of my survival. As long as I am around, the egoistically prudent thing for me to do is always, and is quite equally, to make sacrifices now in order that I avoid much greater pain a bit later. Although I believe that this proposition is true, the statement sometimes can seem paradoxical: In our spectrum with reconstruction, for example, should I really endure as much pain to spare the last bare survival person, who is me, as to spare a person emerging from an operation wherein *only one* of my neurons is ever destroyed and then is replaced? Yes; I should. But, won't the very big difference between those two cases, as regards their lowest points, ground at least some mild prudential force? As I will argue near the end of this chapter, the sensible answer is, after all, "No; it will not ground any." If that is right, then there is a solid background for the comparative use of our tests.

With this background in place, let us illustrate some of the main points regarding comparative employment. First, with a simple use of either test, there will arise a presumption that the person of the first near miss case is me. On the selection test: I do sacrifice to avoid that near miss case over avoiding cases significantly further down the spectrum. To me, it's worth the early pain to have some "significantly lower person" be the one who will endure the horribly painful life. On the pain avoidance test: I do accept significant pain now in order to spare from torture the person who, after reconstruction, emerges from the first near miss case. But, second, with either test, a comparative use undermines the presumption. On the selection test: Enduring some early pain for the purpose, I will avoid the last bare survival case rather than avoiding, instead, the first near miss case. A shift to a more ordinary perspective may be useful: Where the alternative to the near miss case is, instead of the exotic last bare survival case, the ordinary case of, say, my eating a bowl of tomato soup, I will sacrifice to avoid that ordinary case. In that way, I force the near miss person, instead of the soup eater, to endure the horrible future that lies in store. On the pain avoidance test: I will endure *more* pain to spare from torture the person who emerges from innocuously eating the tomato soup than I will to spare the person of the first near miss case. So, according to both tests, a comparative employment shows that near miss person is not me.

Except when they result in crashing failures, the comparative use of these tests is logically open-ended. As we face pairs of concrete examples, one pair after the next, the tests will never establish a positive presumption that both is usefully informative and also is impossible to override. Now, in some cases, like the tomato soup case, the tests might, for all I know, yield a result that simply cannot be overridden. But, if in some such cases the results are absolutely definitive, then, in just those case, the results also will be quite useless. For, if there are such definitive cases, then the tomato soup eating case will be a most typical one. And, as well as anything we will ever know about our survival beliefs, we know in advance, anyway, what we most deeply believe about typical cases of tomato soup ingestion: Quite beyond being merely minute, the changes brought about in me by the everyday processes involved in eating this soup are absolutely irrelevant to the question of who it is, at the end of the lunch, with the soup in his stomach.

In closing this section, let me provide some emotional relief. This relief should be most welcome: Among philosophical tools of thought, the extremely negative selection tests are about as grim as things ever get. Who wants to think about making a very painful sacrifice now only to get, as one's reward, a sudden and painless death soon? Not me and, I trust, not you, either. (In part, that is why, in previous chapters, we avoided process selection tests altogether. We relied, instead, on a severely negative form of sacrifice for well-being test—the avoidance of great pain test—a tool that is at least as reliable and that is a bit less grim. Now, those who can bear to do so may go back and, by running grim negative selection tests, they may check the results that we obtained in those chapters. As they will find, those results will stand up to that gruesome checking procedure.)

In much of what follows, by contrast, I will be much more cheerful. So, in the future, we will often use process selection tests, all right, but, in so doing, we will generally use them in a positive form. In part, this is allowed by the fact that, often, we will be dealing with highly prudential occasions, where the form employed makes little difference. And, the discussion of these last few sections, which has already alerted us to this cheerful form's potential dangers, also allows us to have this emotional lift.

6. Basic, Derivative and Independent Value

We will now begin an attempt to explain our strong intuitions about key cases in the spectrum with reconstruction. In our fourth chapter, we argued that, although physical continuity has *no basic* importance for our survival, it may have importance for our survival that is *derivative*. Moreover, as we also argued, the derivative importance of this continuity may be *very great*. Perhaps it will be useful to extend these distinctions, in certain ways, to our present topics. Or, much the same, perhaps we may find analogous distinctions that may be usefully applied to these topics.

My survival, we have agreed, is a precondition for there to obtain *certain* things that I greatly value, one of these being *my* living a long and happy life. We may now say that my survival is, in this way, a precondition for certain things that I *basically value*: I do not value my living a long and happy life only because, as I believe, my happy life will be related to certain other things in certain important ways. To be sure, it may be, in fact, so related to other things that I value. But that will only increase, not establish in the first place, the value that I place on my having a long and happy life.

There may be *certain other* things, very closely related to my living a happy life, that I *also* value, but for which my survival is *not* a precondition. And, I may value these other things, *precisely because*, as my deep beliefs have it, they are *so closely related*, in *such important ways*, to myself living a happy life. These other things are thus valued by me, not basically, but *derivatively*. As we may plausibly hypothesize, some of these derivatively valued things, not all of them, may be valued to a *very great* degree. As for values, so for related concerns.

Where there are derivative values and concerns, there must be a derivation from more basic values and concerns to those that are derivative. In the present instance, how does the derivation proceed? Well, I may have as a basic concern my concern for my son, Andrew: I am basically concerned about him, concerned for him to have a happy life, which state of affairs I basically value. In addition to this value, I have some rather basic beliefs about Andrew: I believe that he is a being, at least largely physical in nature, whose conditions of existence are highly gradual in a variety of ways.

Because my son is a highly gradual being, there will be certain situations where, just barely, it fails to be true that there are stages of a person's life that are stages of my son's life. In these situations, there will be, instead of future stages of my son's life, stages of the life of someone who, for want of a single nerve cell during a brief middle period, and for want of the small mental difference that will ensure, just barely falls on the "wrong" side of a certain conventional divide. My belief in this division, conventional though it be, will influence what concerns I have for such a near miss boy: I will be less concerned for him than for Andrew himself. But, on the other hand, my belief in this conventional division will *not* have a *very great* effect on my concerns in this neighborhood. My concern for the near miss boy will be only slightly less, not very much less, than my concern for my son. Why is that?

Here is a pretty plausible explanatory hypothesis: As a powerful valuational attitude, we have a general *concern for realistic congruence*. We are concerned that, overall and for the most part, our (more) particular concerns be congruent with the realities that, in terms of our own system of description and assessment, are most relevant to underlying the objects of our basic (more) particular concerns. As we believe, the underlying realities presently most relevant are highly gradual. So, according to our concern for realistic congruence, my particular personal concerns should be well proportioned with respect to these gradual realities. This being so, my concern for my son may *extend to* the future person who, for want of a single marginal neuron in a middle period, is not quite truly Andrew himself.

How might there occur a small extension of my basic concern to this precisely similar, but slightly more radically reconstructed, near miss boy? This is one way: There may develop, in me, a certain derivative concern that is directed *both* at Andrew and *also* at the near miss boy. This may be a concern for anyone in the future whose life stages are related to my son's present life stages in *at least* very much the same ways, and to *at least* very nearly the same degree, as someone's life stages *should be* related to Andrew's present stages for a person, in the future, to be my son himself. In outline, that is how there may derive, from my basic concern for Andrew, a valuational perspective that is but a rather small, natural and rational extension thereof.

As I have been describing these derivative values, they are well in place before we ever notice them. On this description, for many they may go unnoticed forever. Perhaps, however, this might not be the best description of these values. Maybe it is better to say that we form our derivative values, spontaneously, directly and also rationally, only upon our encountering certain peculiar cases. These cases are the examples where our salient basic values, from which the relevant derivations proceed, go unsatisfied, not simply or dramatically, of course, but with failures that are peculiarly like some successes. Actually, I am not sure that there is any substantive difference between these two forms of description. At all events, the reader may choose whichever form he prefers, casting the discussion in terms of that form. At least for those philosophical issues currently in focus, there will be no material difference.

In the ordinary cases, what I derivatively value will relevantly coincide with, and will be masked by, what I basically value. But, in certain exotic cases, including our near miss cases, it will not. In some of these exotic cases, the person emerging will *barely* fail to be continuous with me in *just the right ways*, or *to quite a high enough degree*. When this happens, then there may be *nothing* present that I *basically* value. And, largely for that reason, when this happens, there is nothing present that I value *as much as* I value *my* living a happy life. But it may sometimes happen, as in that near miss case, that there *is something* present that I value *pretty nearly* as much as my living a happy life. There may be present, for example, the happy life of a person whose life stages are related to my earlier life stages in very much the same ways, and to very nearly the same degree, as my own future life stages are, in certain cases, related to my earlier life stages. This person's happy life, that I value derivatively, may thus have, not basic value, of course, but *independent* value. At least for me, this future person's happy life, which has this independent derivative value, may have almost as much value as my own future happy life.

At this level of description, we may now usefully compare, and contrast, the difference between the two adjacent cases of our spectrum on the one hand and, on the other, the difference between ordinary survival and commonplace death: In the lesser of our two adjacent cases, there *will remain something* that, to me, has *quite great* value, even if derivative rather than basic value, namely, that happy, relevantly intimate continuer of me. So, as regards what I value, even if the difference between these two cases is significant, that difference may *not be very great*. By contrast, in the case of my ordinary death, as I deeply believe, there will *not remain anything* that, to me, is of great value. For, even as all of these cases drive home once again, my deep belief is that whatever will remain of me after my death, for example, my corpse, is neither anything I much value nor a precondition of any such thing. So, my deep belief is that, according to my values, the difference between common survival and ordinary death will be a very great difference indeed.

Perhaps we might gain perspective on the derivation of our extended concerns by making some quite opposite metaphysical assumptions. Supposing ourselves to have these quite different beliefs, we might see where there might fail to be any grounds, in us, for a derivation of such extended attitudes. With this aim, let us suppose that, as her only essential part, each of us has a distinct non-physical soul. Each soul is an utterly basic entity, not supervening on any reality that underlies it. Metaphysically, and not just logically, the conditions of a soul's existence are all-or-none.

On these suppositions, the spectrum of congenial decomposition with reconstruction may be entirely irrelevant to questions of what matters in my survival. We will suppose that, in our spectrum, after we pass through a certain range of cases, there are only cases where my soul is, at the least, no longer in the relevant situation. Perhaps my soul goes to a non-spatial heaven or, in a gloomier vein, perhaps it then ceases to exist, completely and forever. But, either way, it is no longer of this world and, so, neither am I. In this spectrum, there is a first case where this happens. In stark contrast, the case right before this will be the last case in which I emerge from the operation there performed. Now, between these adjacent cases, the *neural* difference will be very tiny and quite trivial. But, as regards whatever *souls* they may contain, the difference is absolute. Because of this, between these cases, there might be an absolute difference between the realization of much psychology and, on the other side, no realization of any psychology at all.

How will I select between *these* two adjacent cases? Trying to be upbeat, we will employ a selection test in a positive form: Well, as is quite the natural assumption to make, let us suppose that I very much want to remain here on earth, among familiar friends and family members. Then, in order to avoid the first of *these* failing cases, I will undergo not just some small significant pain, but very great pain. Moreover, if the alternative to remaining hereabout is not just a radical departure from everything physical and spatial, but is complete termination, then I may undergo even greater pain than that. For me, then, there is a quite radical difference, not merely a small but significant difference, in the choice between these adjacent cases. Why is there this radical discrepancy between these two differences?

With the slightly more extensive operation, my soul ceases to exist or, at the least, it ceases to be anywhere in this spatial world. If, after this, there is a person emerging from the reconstruction process, then, lacking my soul, that person will not be me. But that is only the beginning of the story. Closer to the heart of the matter is a point that we may put like this: In terms of all of the assumed non-conventional realities and, thus, overall, this person will *not come within light-years of being me*. On the contrary, there is *only a great gulf, not any relevant real connection*, between me and whoever may emerge from the reconstruction process.

Recall our concern for realistic congruence. Depending upon what are the realistic conditions of our existence, as we most strongly believe these to be, this general concern will, via these strong beliefs, issue in more particular concerns of ours. Suppose we strongly believe that each of us has a wholly distinct soul, quite separate from everything else in reality, that is absolutely essential to his very existence. Then, as this concern for realistic congruence directs us, each of us should have his concern for himself be quite separate from a concern for any other being. By parallel implicit reasoning, each should have his concern for each of his loved ones similarly be quite isolated and unextended. In stark contrast, suppose that we strongly believe, instead, that the conditions of our existence are not like that at all, but are quite thoroughly gradual. Then, as this same general concern directs us, our concerns for particular people should, instead, extend to other beings that, instead of those very people themselves, will supervene on the most relevant underlying realities.

As we have been arguing throughout this book, our deepest beliefs about ourselves are of the second sort, not the first. So, as it happens, our concern for realistic congruence directs us to have concerns that are certain extensions of our basic concerns. Because we have these extended personal concerns, we respond as we do to the near miss cases in our spectrum with reconstruction.

As far as it goes, this explanation of our strong intuitions is, I think, a rather good one. But it is of some importance that our explanation be taken a good deal further.

7. Underlying Realities and Conventional Separations

The explanations given in the preceding section lead us to further questions. By noticing these questions, we may uncover further explanations of our intuitions about the last bare survival case and the first near miss case. The first question is this: Am I, in fact, concerned about myself *significantly more than* I am about the person who emerges from the first near miss case? We may convince ourselves that this question receives an affirmative answer.

Recall the last bare survival case. Now consider, as well, the case that is, by just one neuron, just one step closer than that case to the spectrum's near end. This is the *next to last (bare) survival case*. These two cases, it should be clear, have some salient features in common: First, in *both* of these two cases, it is true that I will survive. And, second, as is true in all of this reconstructive spectrum's cases, both of these cases will end with a single person who is, overall, enormously like I am at the start. So, third, in both of these cases, it is true that *I* will be the single person at the end who is, overall, enormously like I am at the start. Now, suppose that I must undergo the operation of either the one or else the other of these two bare survival cases. With absolute certainty that no mistake in the surgery or cellular reckoning will be made, and assuming a normally happy life for the patient afterward, how much will I sacrifice to undergo the next to last rather than the last bare survival operation? At the very most, I will undergo scarcely any hardship at all. Indeed, perhaps I accept none whatsoever.

In our intuitive judgments, these two bare survival cases contrast strikingly with the "straddle" pair: Although there is no significant difference between the adjacent bare survival cases, there is a small but significant difference between the last bare survival case and the first of the near miss cases. This brings us to a second question: Why is that so? A good short answer is this: I will survive in both of the first two cases; but I will survive only in the higher of the last two cases; and I care about whether I will survive. But we want a longer answer as well.

Our longer answer must have something to do with our *conventions*. In particular, it must involve those conventions by means of which we individuate each one of us from the rest of the world. For the only significant difference between these two noted *pairs* of cases is this: Both cases of the first pair are on the favored side of a certain conventional line. But only one case of the second pair is on the favored side of that line, the other case being on the other side. Thus, there is a significant connection between certain of our conventions and (certain preconditions of) what we value. What is this connection? And, from where does it derive?

Quite basically, I am concerned for *my son*. Among my basic values is that Andrew himself have a long and happy life. Now, I have some strong beliefs about the general conditions of my son's existence. Like me, he is a complex, largely physical being, the conditions of whose existence are, in various ways, highly gradual conditions. Because this is so, certain of our conventions, call them *personal individuative conventions*, must separate him from the rest of the world. Now, as a matter of fact, these conventions *operate relative to certain underlying realities*, not other underlying realities or none at all. They do not, it is safe to say, operate with respect to an underlying reality of beans, or of diamonds, or of realistically possible arrangements of diamonds, or of stabs of pain, and so on. Rather, as a matter of fact, they do operate relative to an underlying reality of atoms, also an underlying reality of cells, also of ways in which cells actually can form complex neural structures, also of ways in which complex neural structures can realize various psychological features, and also relative to still other underlying realities.

Because all of this is so, as I strongly believe, in certain exotic but realistic situations, the difference between there being my son and otherwise—a descendant boy who is not Andrew, or some sort of indeterminacy, or whatever—may lie with a single neuron, or even with a single atom. In these situations, that tiny difference in the underlying realities will amount to there being fully satisfied in the one case, but not in the other, the very conventions according to which Andrew is distinguished from the rest of the world. But, this is just to say that, in these situations, my son's very survival amounts to the full satisfaction, by these underlying realities, of precisely those conventions of ours.

Well, if that is what *Andrew's survival* amounts to, then I am certainly concerned, derivatively but nonetheless quite strongly, about the full satisfaction of those very conventions. Of course, this concern generalizes. Consequently, in addition to my more basic concern about the survival of certain people, I have this general derivative concern: With regard to any of those people, there should be the full satisfaction, by the relevant underlying realities, of the individuative conventions directly relevant to the person's survival; moreover, as regards the concern for this person's survival, the underlying realities are important *only* insofar as they contribute to the *full* satisfaction of those very conventions. This derivative concern may be called our *concern for the full satisfaction of personal individuative conventions* or, for short, our concern for *conventional satisfaction*.

8. Striking a Compromise Between Two Conflicting Concerns

According to the concern for conventional satisfaction, we should *not* be concerned about the underlying realities *except* insofar as those realities serve fully to satisfy the conventions that distinguish certain people from the rest of the world. Consequently, the concern for conventional satisfaction will often conflict with the concern for realistic congruence.

Again consider the last bare survival case and the first near miss case. As regards questions of what matters in survival, the concern for realistic congruence urges that we treat these two cases as being scarcely any different at all. By contrast, the concern for conventional satisfaction urges us to treat these cases as enormously different. Perhaps we may strike a compromise between these two concerns of ours. How might we do this?

As we noted, I will undergo some small but significant pain for the last bare survival case rather than the first near miss case. But, why won't I undergo enormous pain? Don't I care about my own life? Of course, I care. But in this situation, as regards all relevant underlying realities, the difference between my survival and otherwise is an extremely small difference. As our concern for realistic congruence urges, this tiny difference should count for scarcely anything at all. At least somewhat affected by this concern, I will not undergo enormous pain to select the higher of these two cases.

As the concern for realistic congruence urges, that is only the bare beginning of what is required and, so, I should go very much further in this direction: The difference between these two conventionally conspicuous cases should count for *no more than* the difference between *very many other* pairs of adjacent cases in our spectrum. In particular, it should count for no more than the difference between the first near miss case and the case right *after* that, the second near miss case. To be sure, in *both* of these cases, it is *not true* that I survive. But, our concern for realistic congruence urges, that should not matter at all. For another comparison, consider the pair of cases just on the *other* side: the last bare survival case and, one step higher, the second to the last. In both of *these* cases, it *is true* that I survive. But, as our concern for congruence urges, that should not matter, either.

With the addition of these two flanking pairs, we are now considering three pairs altogether. In terms of the underlying realities, in each pair the higher case differs from the lower in very much the same ways as in each of the others. That is why, according to our concern for realistic congruence, the selection between each of the three pairs should be treated equally, or very nearly equally. Rather, in each of the three choice situations, I should undergo, say, a barely noticeable, exceedingly brief pain to get the slightly higher case of the pair. The fact that the two cases of just one of these three adjacent, or overlapping, pairs straddles a certain conventional line should not count for anything at all. According to the concern for congruence, we should *not* undergo significant pain to select within only just *this* pair, while undergoing scarcely any pain to select within the pairs that overlap it.

Our concern for conventional satisfaction urges us to proceed in a very different way. First of all, above the noted line, the underlying differences count for nothing. For, above that line, as it is simply true that I survive; in every case the conventions are fully satisfied. So the concern for conventional satisfaction urges no sacrifice at all to select within a pair of survival cases. Secondly, below the line, the underlying differences also count for nothing. For, below the line, as it is not simply true that it is me, there is not full satisfaction of the conventions. So the concern for conventional satisfaction also urges no sacrifice to select within a pair of near miss cases. But, third, according to this concern, the small difference that straddles the line will count for everything. For just there is the difference between full conventional satisfaction and the failure to achieve it. So, as this concern urges, I should make an enormous sacrifice to get the higher case within just this pair.

According to our concern for realistic congruence, we are to give scarcely any weight at all to the difference between the last survival case and the first near miss case. But we do not do that. According to our concern for full conventional satisfaction, in stark contrast, we are to give this difference enormous weight. But we do not do that, either. Instead, we accord the difference between these cases some small, but still significant, weight. In this way, we strike a compromise between these two general concerns.

Although the compromise effected is between the choice points urged by the two conflicting concerns, it is not midway between them. Rather, the point reached by the compromise is much closer to the choice point urged by the concern for realistic congruence. Does this mean that our concern for congruence strongly dominates our concern for conventional satisfaction and, by implication, that it dominates the basic personal concerns which ground that derivative attitude? No; it does not. There are two reasons for this negative answer. First, as will be discussed later, our basic personal concerns may restrict the range in which the concern for realistic congruence operates or, at the least, in which it operates with any significant force. Second, there is a rather more limited reason that we may now treat within the compass of a brief discussion.

9. Moderating Concern Throughout a Middle Ground

In our spectrum with reconstruction, there is a *middle range* or, as we may say, a *middle ground* of cases. At the higher end of this middle ground, there will be the near miss cases. Further down will be cases where there are misses that are not near misses. At the lower end, there will be cases that, as far as my survival is concerned, are just a little better than out-and-out failures. To the various beings who emerge from the cases of this middle ground, how do I direct, or extend, my ego-centric concern?

At first glance, it might seem that the answer will depend upon what sort of approach we adopt toward logic. For, as is evident, different approaches will characterize this middle ground differently. Furthermore, it might seem that the single most salient approach, the classical approach to logic, will not allow there to be any relevant middle ground at all. But I think that these must be intellectual illusions.

On certain non-classical accounts, the various middle ground cases will be indeterminate in one or another way, or at one or another level. On certain other non-classical accounts, these cases will have some "degree of truth" assigned that is lower than simple truth, or truth in the highest degree, but is higher than the assignment associated with outright falsity.

Regarding cases near the center of the middle ground, a certain non-classical approach may say that it is indeterminate whether the person who emerges is me. Noting that the case is near the center of a reasonably extensive middle range, I may sacrifice a lot to get the first near miss case, many cases higher up, rather than this significantly lower case. But, on the other hand, I may sacrifice a lot to get this intermediate case rather than still another case, beyond the middle ground, where it is determinately false that the person at the end is me. For example, that intermediate case may be much preferred over a case in which, before reconstruction, there are only three neurons where a whole brain used to be.

On a classical approach, all of the middle ground cases will be assigned (determinate) falsity, just the same as the assignment to all the cases below the middle ground. Can a classical approach then allow there to be this reasonable preference profile? Yes; it can. First, what another approach calls determinately false, the classicist may call, not only (determinately) false, but *absurdly* false. Second, while the classicist regards the near miss cases as (determinately) false, he may note, emphatically, that they are *so far* from being absurdly false as to be just *barely* false. Having said these things, the classicist may then give a suitably forceful description of the case near the center of our middle ground. "Well," says the classicist, "it is of course (determinately) false that, in this case, I survive. But there is much more to say. First of all, it is quite far from being absurdly false that I survive. Second, it is also quite far from being barely false. And, in the third place, the statement that I survive in this case is about equally far from being the one as it is from being the other."

Relating to our motivating concerns, the points that the non-classicist makes with certain words are, as it seems, the same ones that the classicist makes with certain other words. This raises broad questions in the philosophy of logic, which I will not even begin to try to answer: Beyond the purely verbal differences, is there *any* difference between any other approach to logic and the classical approach? What sorts of differences might there be that, in *any* case, can lead us to significantly different choices for our lives?

However things may be with these broad questions, in the case at hand no significant difference will arise: Regardless of the approach one takes to logic, one may rather flexibly extend one's self-interested concerns to the cases of a relevant middle ground. Within this flexible framework, we might extend our concerns in some such fashion as this: First, the importance we place on the difference between any two adjacent cases within the middle ground may be very small compared to the importance we place on the difference between the first near miss case—our spectrum's first step into the middle ground— and the last survival case, where, even if just barely, my strict survival is on solid ground. In striking a compromise between our conflicting attitudes, this is a fairly large concession to our concern for conventional satisfaction.

But, second, within the middle ground itself, consider any two *pairs* of adjacent cases that are quite *near to each other*. We may sacrifice to select within the one pair neither significantly more than, nor significantly less than, what we sacrifice to select within the other pair. Why is that? Well, in terms of the underlying realities, the differences between the cases of the one pair will be pretty much the same, over all, as the differences between the other. So, in striking a compromise, there is here a concession, perhaps a fairly small one, to our concern for realistic congruence.

Third and finally, consider the *difference of the whole middle ground*. In classical terms, consider the difference between the first near miss case on the one side and, on the other, the last case for which the claim of my strict survival is not absurdly false. To be sure, in both of these middle ground cases, it is *not true* that I survive. Nevertheless, I will accept *very great pain* to get this highest, rather than this lowest, of the middle ground cases. Moreover, I maintain the attitude even in the light of this reminder: In order to get the last bare survival case, in which it is true that I survive, rather than the first near miss case, in which that is not true, I will accept, even if significant pain, *only rather slight pain.* In striking our compromise, this is a large concession to our concern for realistic congruence.

Perhaps this large concession may include the small concession, noted just above, in the same direction. If so, then the compromise that we strike between our two general concerns will be a little more even-handed. Still, even if so, the upper hand will remain with what we grant to the concern for congruence. But the whole story about this compromise is far from over: We have yet to discuss the (all but) untouchable domains that we reserve for our basic personal concerns and, derivatively, for our concern for full conventional satisfaction. To this part of the story, we now turn.

10. Restricted Ranges for the Relevance of Underlying Realities

In addition to the middle ground, our spectrum has two other ranges, one above and the other below. How do we treat the cases in these other ranges? First, we may examine the *high range.* Throughout this range, it is simply and clearly true that I survive. Since, in every case, it is clearly and simply true that the excellently reconstructed person is me, it is hard to see any significant advantage in selecting any one of the high range cases over any other. Is this just so much abstract talk?

Consider two cases that are near opposite extremes of this high range. In the first of these cases, only one of my cells is ever extracted and, later, it is of course replaced by a duplicate. We may call this the (first) *bare scratch case.* The second case will be the last bare survival case, where very many of my cells are extracted and, later, they are all replaced by duplicates. The difference between these two cases is the *difference of the whole high range.* How much of an early sacrifice will I make to select the first of my two options, the bare scratch case, rather than the second, the bare survival case?

Now, generally, I find it hard to accept our assumptions as being quite certainly reliable. So, generally, I will elect some pain to get the difference of the whole high range. But, because this choice might be so heavily influenced by irrelevant uncertainties, a choice of some pain might not indicate a difference as regards what (prudentially) matters in my survival. Moreover, *even with* these uncertainties, I will *not* accept any *great* pain in order to get the difference between these two cases, far apart though they be in terms of ever so many sorts of underlying realities. Rather, I will accept only some slight pain.

This appears puzzling. For, as we just noted, in terms of underlying realities, there is an enormous difference between (the low points of) the bare scratch case and the bare survival case.[10] Within the high range, our concern for realistic congruence is given very little weight indeed and, remembering the point about uncertainty, might be given no weight at all. How can this possibly be? There is a puzzle here; we may call it the *puzzle of the high range*.

This puzzle may emerge even more clearly when we apply the future pain avoidance test. Beforehand, how much pain will I undergo to avoid torture for the person emerging from the bare scratch case? A very great deal, of course. And, how much for the person emerging from the bare survival case, after full reconstruction there, too? Also, a very great deal. Indeed, as it appears, I may sacrifice *just as much* in the latter instance as in the former. As regards what matters in my survival, it seems that my concern for realistic congruence might carry no weight here at all. How can this possibly be so?

What is required for my survival is that *enough* of my *central enough* psychology be continuously realized by physical structures suitable for that realization. When *enough* psychology is continuously realized physically, then I get through. Any *more* psychology than that will be superfluous and, as such, its realization will be *irrelevant* to the question of my survival.

Between the bare survival case and the bare scratch case, there is, of course, a great difference in underlying realities. But, for my survival, the only relevant thing is that I *never get below a certain level* as regards how much (central enough) psychology is retained. Wherever it may be, this level is set by the conventions governing reference, with respect to the future, of the terms that most standardly refer to me, like 'me,' 'myself' and 'I.' Somehow or other, there are established for these terms conventions that do set such a level. How this happens is very hard to understand, of course, and does itself

---

10. It is interesting to play some games based on available empirical data. So, let's focus on the higher brain, which accounts for fully eighty-five percent of the entire brain mass. Well, people have survived operations where one of their cerebral hemispheres is removed, losing half of their upper brain. Looking at the cerebrum another way, the frontal lobe, half of it in each hemisphere, accounts for about forty percent of the upper brain. Well, people have survived serious frontal lobectomies, wherein (virtually all) the frontal lobe is removed, or at least is destroyed. With enough trials, surely we can get a patient who, for a few minutes at least, survives both operations. How much of his *whole* brain has he left? Only about forty percent. And, as several other diminutions are, even at this point, also biologically possible, we're just warming up. Using surgical techniques already available, a *very carefully selected* sequence of evil removals might well yield a pathetic survivor who then gets by, for at least a few minutes, with only a quarter of a brain.

Elsewhere in the book, when I talk about brain quarters, it is assumed, of course, that *those* quarters are selected in a quite *opposite* way: Because they are so *uncongenially* selected, none of the impotent parts chosen will, by itself, realize any psychology at all. Although this point is fairly obvious, overlooking it can lead to confusion. For the habitually confused, this advice may help: Generally, where in the text I speak of brain quarters, you should think of mere tenths of a brain.

present us with a great puzzle. But that great puzzle is an extremely broad problem: It pertains just as much to how a level for weight is set for the proper application of 'heavy adult squirrel' as to how a certain psychological level is set for the proper future application of 'me.' In the limited context of the present discussion, we may bypass that great and very broad problem.

Because there are established the relevant psychological levels for the proper reference of "I" with respect to the future, underlying realities will contribute to my survival *only insofar as* they serve to realize this required psychological minimum. Beyond their serving in this way, these realities are quite irrelevant to the question of whether a future being is me. These remarks should dispel some of the puzzle of the high range.

With this clarification, we may see our concern for realistic congruence in a new light. Considerations of relevance place a restriction on where this concern is permitted to operate at all. In this light, there is the appearance of some rather even-handed justice to the compromises that we strike for the cases of the middle ground and for their nearest neighbors. Holding absolute sway over the high range, our basic and our conventional concerns can afford to be somewhat generous in the middle range.

Coming from an opposite direction, some complementary remarks reinforce these ideas: Below the middle ground, there is a *low range* of cases. In each of these cases, it is absurdly false that I survive. At the high end of this low range, there is the *first* case where it is *absurdly* false that I survive, for short, the *first absurd falsity case*. At the low point of this case, there might exist only a rather small fraction of my brain. But, of course, by most relevant reckonings, even this will be a pretty complex structure of cells. By contrast, at the low end, there is the *unicellular neuron case*: During the brief period before reconstruction, there is only one of my nerve cells floating in a supportive vat. The difference between the first absurd falsity case and the unicellular case is the *difference of the whole low range*. In terms of underlying realities, this difference is quite substantial. But, how do we feel about the people emerging from these two cases?

From anything much like a perspective of self-interest, what will I sacrifice to protect the person emerging from the first absurd falsity case? I accept no pain at all, thus, no more than for the person at the end of the unicellular case. This may also appear puzzling. So there is also a *puzzle of the low range*. Some of the puzzle is quickly dispelled: In every case in this range, it is not just false, but is *absurdly false* that I survive the operation. Accordingly, in every one of these cases, the underlying realities are so meager as to be *beyond having any relevance* to the question of whether the person at the end is me. Because not even the highest case in this low range offers any realities of any relevance, throughout the range there is nothing either to prefer or to avoid.

By way of some quite general remarks, we have made some progress with the puzzle of the high range and the puzzle of the low range. But we would like to offer something deeper, and more satisfying, as regards these puzzles. To do that, we must go beyond these rather bare generalities about relevance, exploring one of the main normative notions that we implicitly maintain.

11. What Matters and the Minimal Conception of a Person

Although the matter of its determination is replete with vagueness, there is a certain minimum level of psychology realized in every case of a person's survival. What sets this level for psychological realization? The level may be set by a *minimal conception of a person* that we have. This notion itself is replete with vagueness. But there may be some order to the vagueness.

On our minimal conception, a person need not be a rational agent, let alone a morally responsible being. Far from that, we are here concerned with people, first of all, only as patients rather than as agents and, second, only as patients that may be effected in certain very basic ways, such as being caused severe pain by being made to feel worthless. Regarding this minimal conception, then, we are not interested in people as patients insofar as, for example, they may be given much pleasure by being exposed to the Meditations of Descartes.

Perhaps some thoughts about altruism may help us to articulate, roughly but usefully, this minimal conception of a person: Although few of us are highly altruistic, most of us quite fully understand a *perspective of personal altruism* that, to varying lesser degrees, we actually embrace. On our minimal conception, a person is a being that, from this perspective, is a *tied preeminent patient*. Let us say that even a highly intelligent rational agent who satisfies our minimal conception is, for that reason, and at the least, a *minimal person*. Then, from our perspective of altruism, all of the minimal people are equally *preeminent*, while none of the other entities is as eminent. What does any of this really mean?

Consider two human beings that are innocent of any wrongdoing. According to our noted altruistic perspective, so long as both of these human beings are *people*, then, at least assuming a reasonably long and happy future life for each if he is saved, each of the two has an equal claim to have his life be spared. Regarding the reasons that are generated by this perspective itself, it does not matter if one of these people is much more intelligent, and more talented, and more rational, and more likeable, and more ethical than is the other.

To be sure, the extra psychological endowment of the one over the other may give him many advantages toward living a most worthwhile life. And, further, this endowment may make this person better able, and more likely, to confer more future good on others. From other important perspectives, such further facts as these may also generate reasons for saving the more talented individual over the much less talented. And, in making a final judgment, it may be important to give some weight to these additional reasons, not just to our altruistic perspective. But, however that may be, none of it can cloud the present point, which clearly remains this: As regards our perspective of personal altruism itself, the extra endowment gives the more talented person no advantage whatsoever; rather, from this pure perspective itself, the two are *tied*. That is because, as is clearly and definitely true, both of these beings are minimal people.

(A quick detour: Perhaps these claims of people are only defeasible claims and, for example, may be forfeited by certain sorts of wrongdoing. In any case, this is irrelevant to the main distinction. So, as we assume, none of the patients now discussed has a claim that is defeated.)

If a dolphin, as we might discover, also came up to, or exceeded, this vaguely understood but crucial psychological level, then, according to the noted altruistic perspective, that dolphin will also have an equal claim to be saved. For, at least on our minimal conception, that dolphin will be a person. On the other hand, a typical dog might clearly fall below this rather low level. Then, although the dog may still have a claim to be spared, his claim will be *less than* that of the reasonable dolphin and, of course, less than yours and mine. That is just to say that, even on our minimal conception, this dog is not a person. As well, a biological human being might clearly fall below the minimum psychological level. Then his claim, too, will be less than that of the perceptive dolphin. Again, that is just to say that, even on our minimal conception, this human "vegetable" is not a person. While all of the people are (equally) preeminent—you, almost any human moron, that surprising dolphin—none of the others has such a high status.

As these remarks suggest, there is a strong evaluative aspect to this conception of a person: Providing that a certain minimum psychological level is realized, psychological considerations count for more than potentially competing factors, such as biological considerations. From our altruistic perspective, we should choose to save a rational dolphin over a biological human that, clearly enough, falls below a certain "mercifully low" psychological level. (But, as my initial remarks about altruism indicate, in one's actions, one might apply the favoring values implicit in this conception only to oneself, not caring a fig about any other person or, for that matter, about any other creature at all. In such an event, one will still be a person, all right, one will just be an extremely selfish person and, according to the values of most of us, one will be a very bad person.)

In any event, the evaluative aspects of this minimal conception may incorporate, or even contribute to, the logical order implicit in the vague notion: As regards the question of when an entity is a minimal person, there is a significant middle ground. Whatever logical approach is preferred, one should, and one can, recognize this middle ground. So, in the case of certain beings, it will just barely fail to be true that the entity is a person. In other cases, there will be greater failures. Now, according to a non-classical logic, only when there is a truly significant psychological deficit will it be (definitely) false that the entity is a person. According to a classical approach, by contrast, even a minute deficit will confer falsity. But, for the classicist, only with more substantial failures will it be *absurdly* false, or *wildly* false, that the entity in question is a person. And, when this is *not* absurdly false, then the entity may be in the middle ground. This suggests a close logical connection between the question of when a given person survives, on the one hand, and, on the other, the question of when an entity is a minimal person.

In light of these considerations, but still with no great confidence, I finally move to endorse a position that I first floated near the beginning of the book: In that I now am a person, from now on, at any time that I exist, I will be a person. Without great confidence, I do offer this as a necessary truth, but, even then, only if the remark is understood as meaning this: From now on, whenever I will exist, I will be, at the least, a minimal person.

We may now be able to provide a somewhat deeper resolution to the puzzle of the high range. First, both for the question of my survival and also for the question of when there is a minimal person, certain conventions of ours must draw lines with respect to the same relevant underlying realities. These underlying realities are, in both cases, the smoothly graduated psychological features that may be realized in the world and, derivatively, those physical structures that may realize these psychological features. True enough, the many particular psychological advances that take us from the bottom to the top of the middle range extrapolate rather smoothly through (at least much of) the high range. Beyond the middle range, and within the high range, how much attention do we pay to these underlying realities? Now, I will pay them *no more* heed for the question of whether I survive than for the question of whether a situation contains a minimal person, myself or any other. But, I will pay them no heed at all with regard to the question of when there is a minimal person. For that would mean discrimination in favor of the more intelligent, or the more rational, or the more creative among us, whereas, according to our perspective of personal altruism, no such discrimination is allowed. Therefore, above the middle range, I will pay no attention to differences in the underlying realities, either, as regards the various candidates for being me in the future. From the perspective of this altruism, or from a perfectly parallel perspective, neither is that sort of discrimination allowed.

What can we say about the puzzle of the low range? Below the entire middle range, it is absurdly false that there are even any minimal people and, so, it is simply true that there are none. As regards the relative claims of these completely non-personal entities, our altruistic perspective itself offers us no guidance at all. Accordingly, if we are to have any perspective on these situations, we must employ another perspective.

Some of us may adopt a point of view that extrapolates downward, preferring to spare a pig's life, smart as those animals are, than to spare a turtle's much longer life. Others will adopt a stance that accepts no such extrapolation and, thus, no discrimination based on mental capacities. They may choose to prevent a young turtle's death over preventing the death of a happy old monkey. The point is that our perspective of personal altruism itself does not so much as suggest a single best perspective for dealing with the many cases that, not just barely, but quite clearly fall outside its domain.

For a similar reason, below the middle range, our minimal conception of a person gives us no guidance in how to treat non-personal entities generated from ourselves. But we can rationally extend our concerns for ourselves only insofar as this conception gives us directives for so doing. For a moment, suppose that, at its lowest point, a certain case features an entity that, clearly, is not even a minimal person. And let us also suppose, most plausibly, that I will not have interrupted existence. Then just as my altruistic perspective offers me no guidance on how to treat a monkey, a pig and a turtle, so my self-interested concern will offer me no guidance on how to treat a person that, at a later time, may emerge from the fatally low situation. In sum: There is no more reason to think that my self-interested concerns should extend to the differential underlying realities of the low range than there is to think that, as our personal altruism itself directs, I should save a pig's life rather than a turtle's.

We have given an answer to the puzzle of the high range. The answer is, I think, a pretty good one. But, so far, we have given no answer at all to the puzzle of the low range. We may now give this related puzzle a certain answer, of course, simply by citing the force of symmetry. In that way, we may try to draw some strength from our answer to the high range puzzle: In order that our treatment of the whole reconstructive spectrum be well balanced, we should treat its low part just like we treat its high one. That is not a terrible answer to the low range puzzle; but, as well, it is not a very good answer. Now, for all I know, it might be impossible to get a better answer to the puzzle of the low range. But, as we shall observe in the next section, it might also be unnecessary.

12. A Spectrum of Assimilation:
Parallels, Differences and Questions

Toward the end of section 2, we indicated that, in addition to our spectrum with reconstruction, there are various other spectra that present cases for striking compromises. Among these are spectra of assimilation. Now, there are, of course, indefinitely many interesting spectra of assimilation: In each, there will be a certain fraction of the original person's whole brain that will be replaced at each stage of replacement. A replacement will be swift but it will also be very gradual, occurring in many small sequential steps. Because of that, it will be very clear that, at every moment, there is a person who is enormously like the original patient. Some further specifications: No brain part ever replaced will be overlapping with any other, nor with any part doing any replacing. And, directly upon removal, any part about to be replaced is destroyed.

The great variety in size of replaceable brain parts generates a great variety of spectra: At one extreme, a spectrum will feature halves replaced at each of two stages; quite far away, another spectrum may feature billionths replaced in a billion stages. Following a choice made in Chapter 5, we will focus on a spectrum where, in four stages, brain quarters are replaced. In order to elaborate effectively, we do need some stable point for focus, although we might as well have chosen hundredths as the quarters actually picked. At all events, between sequentially gradual replacement operations, the person then involved lives a rather normal life.[11] Because he leads a normal life, recently inserted parts will have as much assimilation as the alloted time will allow.

From one case to the next, we vary only the length of time between replacements, that is, the length of time alloted each brand new quarter to assimilate. Throughout a spectrum, each case will differ from adjacent ones by having intervals that are, by a certain fixed amount, either longer or else shorter. Although we might make other reasonable enough choices, we choose a fairly fine-grained spectrum, in which the cases differ by a second for each brain quarter.

In the first case of this spectrum, each quarter has ten years of exclusive assimilation time. In this first case, I will survive: With so much assimilation as that, it is simply and clearly true that, even by the end of the quarterly rotation, I will still exist. In the next case, each quarter will have one second less of exclusive assimilation. At the far end, a recently added quarter will

---

11. For good measure, after the forth quarter has been put in, there will also be a nice assimilation period, especially for it. That period, of course, is *not between* replacements.

have only a second to assimilate before we move on. In that distant case, I will *not* survive: With so little assimilation as that, it is simply and clearly true that, by the end of the quarterly rotation, if not before, I will cease to exist. We may call this our *spectrum of assimilation with reasonably chosen fixed parameters* or, for short, the *spectrum of assimilation.*

There are many parallels between this spectrum of assimilation and the familiar spectrum with reconstruction. Like that familiar spectrum, this present spectrum is relevant to our topics only because, as we deeply believe, the conditions of our existence are, in ever so many ways, highly gradual ones. If we have discrete immaterial souls as our essences, then, like the spectrum with reconstruction, this new spectrum will show us nothing about what matters in our survival.

Moreover, like that familiar reconstructive spectrum, this assimilation spectrum has three main ranges, mutually exclusive and jointly exhaustive of its cases: There is a high range, in all of whose cases I will survive. There is also a low range. In every case of the low range, it is not only false that I survive but, as a classical logician might say, it is wildly and absurdly false. Between these two ranges, there is an interesting middle range or, as we may say, a middle ground.

Going from longer to shorter assimilation times, at a certain number of seconds, we will have a first case where it is *not true* that I survive. In our new spectrum, this is the first near miss case. It is, of course, the highest case of the middle ground. Right before it, there is the last bare survival case, which is, of course, the lowest case in the high range. How do we feel about these adjacent cases? Assuming happiness for the emerging person afterwards, I will endure slight but significant pain, not great pain, to get this bare survival case instead of this near miss case. So, this near miss case has much of, but not all of, what matters in my survival.

Between the two brands of spectra, the parallels continue. Within a substantial middle ground, I will endure only very slight and brief pain to get one very nearby case rather than a lower one, significantly less than what I will endure to get the last survival case. But I will endure very great pain to get the highest case of this middle ground instead of the lowest, much more than I will endure to get the last survival case rather than the first near miss case. Within the high range, by contrast, there appears nothing at all to choose between any two cases, no matter how far apart. If I will survive with one year of quarterly assimilation, as I most certainly will, then I will not endure any pain at all to get ten years rather than just the one. Within the low range, too, there appears nothing to choose. If with ten thousand seconds of quarterly assimilation—under three hours—I will not survive, as I almost certainly will not, then I will not endure the least pain to get the ten thousand seconds instead of just one for each quarter. As with the spectrum with reconstruction, there are limits to the range of cases—the middle ground—in which what matters in my survival can, in any relevant way, come apart from my survival itself. There is a strong parallel between all of our intuitions about the spectrum with reconstruction, on the one hand, and, on the other, all of our intuitions about the spectrum of assimilation.

How are we to explain our responses to the cases of this new spectrum? As far as they go, our ideas about basic, derivative and independent (preconditions of) value will apply just as well here as in the explanations given before. That is helpful. But, as before, by themselves these ideas cannot take us very far. In giving our earlier explanations, we then moved to postulate certain general concerns that conflicted in the middle ground. As we explained, in this area of conflict, compromises are effected between these general attitudes. Similar explanatory moves might work well now.

On the one side, there is, in addition to our basic personal concerns, our concern for full conventional satisfaction. This will work as well now as it did before. What is on the other side of the conflict? Perhaps it may be, as it was before, a concern for realistic congruence. But, then, just what are the underlying realities in the present instances? In the most favorable cases, perhaps they are psychological episodes similar enough to those normally composing the living of a normal mental life, as well as the physical, and the biological, processes on which those episodes normally supervene. Within the middle range, will longer periods, which have more such episodes, provide more in the way of relevant underlying realities? Perhaps they may. If so, then, in the middle ground, a concern for realistic congruence may operate effectively. If all of this is on track, then an explanation in terms of the striking of familiar compromises will explain our responses to the middle ground cases of this spectrum of assimilation.

What, then, sets limits to the middle ground, to the range in which a concern for realistic congruence may exert any influence? Regarding our spectrum with reconstruction, we were able to cite certain important normative conceptions as grounding at least one of the two boundaries of its middle ground: our perspective of altruism and, closely related to it, our minimal conception of a person. But those conceptions will not explain why there are any limits with regard to the spectrum of assimilation. After all, at every moment, in every case of this spectrum, there is a person enormously like me right now. With all due modesty, this person is very far above any plausible psychological minimum for altruistically acceptable discrimination. In digging for deeper explanations, we have here hit on a very significant difference between our two spectra.

Our standard notion of altruism and our minimal conception of a person are, it seems clear, among our more important normative conceptions. Indeed, in a certain way, the importance of these conceptions is even underlined by the role they play in explaining our responses to many cases of the spectrum with reconstruction. In explaining our responses to many cases of the spectrum of assimilation, what conceptions of ours may play a similar role? Are there any comparably important conceptions at work in this present situation? Might there, indeed, be at work some conceptions whose importance, in our system of values, we normally overlook or, at least, greatly underestimate?

Although I wish I did, I do not really have good answers to these questions. Although I suspect that there are some good answers, perhaps there are none. But, even if there are none, the pattern of responses we display for the spectrum of assimilation can stem from attitudes that, for us, are quite rational. For, even if there is no deeper reason, we might rationally place limits on what are, in our lives, substantial enough involvements of our central parts. Provided that we have stable attitudes to this effect, and no comparably strong attitudes in conflict, we might be entirely rational in maintaining these limits. As with any reasons for anything, our own reasons in these present matters must come to an end somewhere or else, of course, be within some circle of justification, however large or small. There is only so much justification, and only so much insight, to be had.

How much insight is there to be had as regards what grounds the limits for the middle range of the Modified Physical Spectrum? And, if there is a middle range for the spectrum of separating and joining, as I believe there to be, how much insight can be had into attitudes that set the limits for that middle range? Although there must be limits on our insight into our attitudes, there may be no limit to the sorts of spectra that require conventionally maintained separations concerning our survival. If so, then many of those conventional separations will find no ground in any important conception of ours. For, by any reasonable reckoning of conceptions and of importance, there will be only a rather limited number of important conceptions that we actually maintain.

8

FISSION AND THE FOCUS
OF ONE'S LIFE

Especially through consideration of their middle ranges, many fine-grained spectra of cases can show us that, even in the prudential use of the term, what matters in survival sometimes comes apart from our survival itself. In the literature, there is a second main way of showing, or attempting to show, that the two sometimes come apart: These are the various sorts of branching cases, especially certain cases of fission. In the present chapter, we will focus on some of these cases and, inspired by them, on some new branching cases. Even if not before, now we can properly study these examples.

By focusing on certain fine-grained spectra, we learned certain things about what is important to us in our survival. By focusing on certain branching cases, we might learn certain other things about our values. Perhaps the most interesting of these factors is one that I shall call the *focus of a person's life*.

1. The Standard Fission Case and
the Standard One-sided Case

Many philosophers have made the assumption that a normal human person's mental life might be continued, quite well and quite (nearly) equally well, either by the right half or by the left half of that person's whole brain. Moved by this assumption, but moved by other thoughts as well, philosophers have

shown much interest in an example introduced by David Wiggins.[1] Susceptible of many variations, I will call this example *the standard fission case*. After
the fission occurs, this is a case that has, in a relevantly interesting sense, two
sides.

Much of the interest in the standard fission case stems from its relation to
another example, which I will call *the standard one-sided case*: After being
placed under a potent anesthetic, my brain is removed from my body and
that body is destroyed. Then, perhaps by being rapidly ground into brainburger, either the left half or else the right half of my brain is destroyed. On
the standard supposition regarding the proficiency of both halves, it matters
not which half this is. For specificity, we may say that the left half is thus
destroyed. Then the remaining right half brain is placed in (the suitable part
of the head of) a new duplicate of my body. The person with this right half-
brain and this new body then awakens. Given the standard suppositions, it is
quite clear that this person is me.

The standard fission case itself proceeds as follows. After being rendered
unconscious by a powerful anesthetic, my whole brain is extracted from my
body, whereupon my body is destroyed. Still supporting no consciousness at
all, my brain is then divided down the middle, the result being a left half-
brain and a right. The left half is then placed in (the head of) one duplicate
of my original body, while the right half is placed in another such duplicate.
As it is supposed, there are now two sides to the case: At the end of the procedure, there may awaken, in one room, someone with my left half-brain, and
there may awaken, in another room, someone with my right half-brain. In
either room, the person who is there will have a half-brain that continues my
core psychology and much of my distinctive psychology, with neither of the
half-brains continuing much more, or much less, than the other. Beyond this,
however, there is no more of a mental connection between whoever is in the
first room and whoever is in the second than there is between, say, you and
me right now. If the person in the first room experiences red, for example,
that will not induce whoever is in the other to experience red. To parallel the
one-sided case most completely, we explicitly add this supposition: There is
no later rejoining of any parts of anyone who is in the two rooms.

In the standard fission case, what happens to me? The main intuition is that
I am not a person who is in just one of the rooms, nor am I in both rooms at
once, nor am I somehow constituted of whatever is in these rooms, but,
rather, I have ceased to exist. Intuitively, in each of the two rooms there is,
not me, but an entirely new person, who is a terribly intimate descendant of

---

1. See *Identity and Spatio-Temporal Continuity*, Basil Blackwell, 1967, page 50. In "Personal Identity," note 2, Parfit traces the general class of cases back to Locke's *Essay*, Chapter 27, Section
18.

myself. If that intuition is accurate, then further questions become quite interesting: When these two people are brought into being, then, in the prudential use of the term, how much is there of what matters in my survival?

Suppose that, if I suffer nothing beforehand, then one of the two emerging people will get terrible torture. But if I suffer early pain, then neither of them will have any pain. From a perspective of self-concern, or a small extension thereof, I feel moved to make a considerable sacrifice to protect the endangered person, whichever of the two he may be. Even from a relevantly self-centered perspective, I will do more for either of these descendants than I will for a mere duplicate of myself, say, one who may have developed on another planet. I will not, however, make as great a sacrifice as I will, in the ordinary case, to protect myself from terrible torture. Nor, then, will I do as much for either of these fission products as for the person who emerges from the standard one-sided case; for, as he is me, I will do as much for him as I ever do to protect myself from such horrors.

Especially in the face of these responses, but even in any case, the juxtaposition of these two standard cases fairly propels us to compare them: First, as we cannot help but notice, regarding anything beyond certain conventional descriptions, *what happens on the right side is precisely the same in the two cases.* In the one-sided case, what happens on the *left* side, it is true, is the grinding of half a brain into brainburger. And, in the fission case, what happens to that same left half of the brain is no such messy grinding, but is, instead, a neat severing of exactly that same intact neural mass from its original partner on the right. Now, those differences, it should be clear, all concern only the underlying realities on the left, there being, between the two cases, no difference whatsoever regarding those on the right. Still and all, it is just in the one case that the real entities on the right side end up constituting me, so that I survive. In the other, those real entities, although remaining precisely the same, apparently are not allowed to count as constituting me. This might, of course, be the work of our conventions for individuating ourselves.

When we compare the standard one-sided case with the case of my standard fission, it can be quite easy for us to announce that, as regards questions of rational choice, there *cannot be any* difference between the two cases. Regarding my concern to protect the person on the *right* side, how can it make any difference what happens on the *left* side? Regarding how much I will endure for the sake of the right side person, how can it matter whether there was, on the opposite side, a messy meat grinding or whether an intact half-brain separated by a neat surgical division? Apparently, there is a powerful force urging us to treat the right-side person precisely the same in both cases.

This potent force may be our concern for realistic congruence. Regarding what happens on the right side, all of the underlying realities are precisely the same in the two cases. So, as our general concern for realistic congruence directs, in both of the cases, our attitude toward the person on this side should be precisely the same.

As we noted, however, our intuitions about the two cases were not so egalitarian. This indicates that, in our system of attitudes, there is also a potent force working in the other direction. This other force stems from my basic concern for myself and, at a remove, from my derivative concern for full conventional satisfaction. Consider the conventions according to which I am individuated from the rest of the world. To be fully satisfied, perhaps these conventions require that there *not* be two candidates that, while better than anything else around, are equally, or even are nearly equally, good candidates for being me. As others have held, it is my hypothesis that our conventions do constrain things in this way.

Now, in the standard fission case, there occur, on the left side, underlying processes that relevantly duplicate what happens on the right side. Grounded in these symmetrical realities, there are then two equally good candidates for being me. On my linguistic hypothesis, then, there is not full conventional satisfaction. And, because there is this failure of full satisfaction, there will be two other failures. First, of course, it will not be true that the person on the right side is me. And, second, although the two-sided case will secure much of what matters, it will not secure all of what matters in my survival.

In the spectra examined in the previous chapter, the concern for realistic congruence played a role not everywhere, but only in the middle range. Confined as its operations often are, will this concern be allowed to play a role, it might be asked, in the standard fission case? To our suggestion that congruence does play a role, this question raises no serious objection: First of all, even in a non-classical mode, we may say that, in this fission case, it will not be (determinately) true that I survive. As long as that is so, there is room for congruence to play a role. Moreover, we may even insist on a classical mode of description, for a suitably flexible one is available: In this fission case, although it is false that I survive, it may not be absurdly false, or wildly false. Although it *is false* to say so, it might *not* be *wildly* false to say, for example, that, in this case, I survive while scattered in two main parts. At all events, it is perfectly consistent with our position in the previous chapter that there be plenty of room here, too, for realistic congruence to play a major role.

By reference to our more general attitudes, we have provided a partial explanation of our intuitions about these cases. As far as it goes, this partial explanation is, I think, a rather good explanation. Moreover, as we noted in the previous chapter and now have cause to reaffirm, there seems nothing seriously wrong with these general attitudes of ours. Nor does there appear to be anything defective about the compromise that we spontaneously strike between them. Stemming, as they do, from an appropriately flexible compromise between our coherent attitudes, our responses to the standard fission case and to the standard one-sided case may be quite rational reactions.

While those new to the subject might pass directly to the next section, there are a few things that I should now say to more sophisticated readers. As many of them will have noticed, my presentation of these standard cases has been anything but standard. There is a good reason for this: By getting us distracted by irrelevant side-issues, the more usual presentations are not well geared to elicit the most telling responses.

The examples are most often presented in this way: In both of the cases, not just the fission case, the suitably divisible brain is first split down the middle. Then both halves are taken out of the original body. On some versions, one of these two is successfully transplanted into a new body, while the other is dropped on the floor in the operating room, perishing upon impact. In other versions, there is no dropping, and both halves are placed in new bodies. But, perhaps for intervention by a corrupt doctor, one of the two halves fails to take and, in a short time, perishes.[2] In whatever version, this is a confused and confusing piece of business.

There is one confusing aspect of this presentation that, although it is minor, can be highly distracting. This is the part about slicing the brain while it is still inside the (skull of the) original body. Implicitly, we are confronted with unwanted questions: Through parts of the original person that are external to the brain, can the two brain halves still communicate so that together they may realize a somewhat integrated psychology? Or, at another extreme, are there already two little isolated beings in the old head now, in no way able to communicate and, perhaps, each having its own capacity for self-reference and each having its own willful inclinations? By a rather simple alteration, we may move away from these unhelpful distractions: Before there is any division of the brain, we first remove the brain from the rest of the body and, in the bargain, destroy the rest of the body.

This having been stipulated, we are in a position to see just how bad is the main flaw in the usual presentation: As the offering would have it, even after an isolated brain has been fully separated in two, and there are two fully isolated and psychologically proficient brain halves, there will be the original person. Further, and here is the main rub, we are asked to entertain the idea that whether or not this person survives depends upon what *later* happens to those two halves as regards their *possible biological surroundings*. In what is to

2. A locus classicus for such unfortunate descriptions of fission is Richard Swinburne, "Personal Identity," *Proceedings of the Aristotelian Society*, 1973–74, page 237. But these offerings persist even to the present day. Indeed, even in such a generally excellent work as Ernest Sosa's recently penned, and as yet unpublished, "Surviving Matters," such a confused description is offered.

pass as the one-sided case, what later happens is: One of the halves, but not the other, is dropped on the floor, or it fails to take, or whatever. In what is to pass as the only fission case of the pair, what later happens is good biological news for both halves. Somehow, as we are asked to suppose, the disparity between these two sorts of later episodes is to mean the difference between whether or not there is a case of fission. This is, of course, implausible in the extreme. How will the later acquisition of surrounding healthy bodies, for example, affect the question of whether there is a case of fission? Given the suppositions that make any of these cases at all interesting, it will have no such effect. Rather, once there has been the complete division of the suitably isolated brain, there is a fission case and that is the end of that matter.

When we are confronted with any of the more usual presentations, we can easily become distracted and confused. Then we may think all sorts of unwarranted things: Maybe fission is really incoherent; or maybe it is coherent but, as it shows, survival itself cannot matter at all; or whatever. But, when we present the cases more correctly, then our thoughts may be on target: Intuitively, in the one-sided case I survive, but in the fission case that is not true. And as regards what matters in survival, in the crucial prudential use of those terms, there is a small difference between the two cases. Although small, this difference is no smaller than the difference, in our spectrum of assimilation, between the last bare survival case and the first near miss case.[3]

2. Might I Survive My Standard Fission?

While some philosophers will agree that I do not survive my standard fission, and they may even welcome the explanations just given for our responses,

---

3. Not only do the usual discussions of fission badly present the cases, but, on top of that, the more confusing sorts of tests are then employed for assessing whether, and how much, a case secures as regards what matters in survival. Beginning on page 119, consider Shoemaker's treatment in *Personal Identity*, Basil Blackwell, 1984. Although he misses the bit about taking the brain out before doing anything to it at all, he does get the important bit right about having the one-sided case proceed by way of something like grinding. So, Shoemaker's is one of the best presentations in the literature. How good are the best?

To test for how much of what matters is secured, Shoemaker employs a *positively* oriented *selection* test. Far better to employ a negatively oriented test, where the poignant issue is future pain. And, to keep things simple and clear, far better then to use, not any process selection test, but, rather, the avoidance of future pain test. Largely because he fails to do any of this, Shoemaker is then led to confuse the marginal desirability use of "what matters" for the crucial prudential use. Then, unwittingly, he becomes involved in difficult questions about what I call *the focus of one's life*, issues which we shall later explore in the text. On top of all of this, there seems to be no awareness of this following crucial distinction: First, there are things that, in a given respect, do matter but matter only a very little bit; and, second, there are things that, even in that respect, do not matter at all.

others will think that I do survive the standard fission case. Now, some of these disagreeing philosophers may accept some of, or even all of, the six metaphysical doctrines. Having already given them my all in Chapter 6, I have nothing more to say to these thinkers. Other friends of fission survival, by contrast, reject those doctrines and, in the bargain, maintain a wholly objective view of ourselves. My differences with these latter philosophers, I am sure, concern the correct assessment of our conventions for individuating ourselves. Although this disagreement may not concern the most profound sort of questions, it might still be the focus for some worthwhile discussion.

Some fully objective philosophers, such as Nozick, are much concerned about fissions where, after the division, one of the two branches is very short. For example, after I undergo standard fission, while the person on one branch may go on to lead a normal life for fifty years, the person on the other may be painlessly killed after happily listening to music for just one minute. Can it be, the worry goes, that just because there is this other branch for just this single minute, it will not be true that I will live for all those years? As it might appear, this is a large price to pay for a small slip. More justly, perhaps, there should be a large price only for a slip that is at least rather substantial.

At any rate, Nozick and others propound the view that, in this fission, I survive only as the person who goes on to live a long time.[4] The idea here is that, according to our conventions for demarcating ourselves, short branches following a fission may be ignored, although long ones may not. On the face of it, at least, this appears to be a misunderstanding of these conventions of ours. Rather, as it appears, these conventions are not retroactive: We do not have to determine how long a person on a certain branch lasts, only after that being able to determine whether a division of the original person resulted in his ceasing or whether it resulted, instead, in his being the person on the other branch.[5]

Unlike the case with rocks or bushes, what occurs at later times should not determine how many people there are, or who the people are, at a given earlier time. Like the idea that a person's existence should be without any interruption, perhaps this proposition might not have absolutely universal validity. But, like that earlier idea, at the least, this injunction against retroactivity will be a strong guideline for judging any approach to our identity over time. To the extent that an account of our survival agrees with this idea, so much the better for that account. To the extent that there is a failure of agreement, there will be strong marks against a wayward account.

4. See Nozick's *Philosophical Explanations*, pages 43–47. Also see Ernest Sosa's "Surviving Matters."

5. As regards the propriety of being skeptical towards retroactive offerings, I find congenial Mark Johnston's discussion in "Human Beings," pages 67–68.

As these general reflections make most unsurprising, problems multiply quickly for the view that I will survive only on branches where someone lives for long enough: Switching gears, let us suppose that, unless I elect to endure considerable pain in advance, just after the operation, the person on the short branch will have, during his single minute, excruciating torture. Judging from a perspective of self-interest, or from a small extension thereof, I do not treat this person as I would a mere duplicate. To the contrary, although I will not do as much for him as I will for myself, I will make a considerable sacrifice to spare this person the torture. Indeed, I will sacrifice nearly as much for him as I would to prevent a minute of such torture for the person on the much longer branch.

Why is there even a small difference in my prospective sacrifices for the two men? It is only that the person on the longer branch may have many painful memories, and perhaps other painful consequences. As suitable stipulations may accomplish, this may be entirely discounted. Once that is done, then, although I will do more for myself than for either of them, there is no difference at all between my prospective sacrifice for the man on the short branch and that for the man on the long one. The best explanation of this is very simple: First, as I deeply believe, neither of these men is me. And, second, as I also believe, in the case of each man, there is quite a lot, and equally much, of what matters in my survival.

Let us again alter our suppositions about what happens after the fission operation is performed. Suppose that, after a minute of normal life in his room, the man on the short branch does not die but is rendered deeply comatose, or even is super frozen, then having no thoughts or experiences at all. He remains in that state for fifty years. Then he is brought out of the coma, or out of the freeze. Consciously thinking and experiencing, the man spends another minute in the room, the last minute of his life. Only then does he cease to exist. Now this man's branch will be as long as the other's, or even a couple of minutes longer. As regards matters of strict survival, will this mean that matters are worse for the man on the other branch? Not at all. The best explanation of this is the simple one: Even with a short branch for his fission competitor, as in the original example, matters are already as bad as can be for the survival of the man on the much longer branch.

Rather than being bad, might matters be as *good* as can be for the survival of the man on the longer branch, and perhaps *also be extremely good* for the man on the much shorter branch? Worthy of some discussion, there are at least two different views according to which this, or something like this, will be the truth.

Lewis, Perry and others hold that, after the fission, although there will be different people on each of the two branches, there will be strict survival

along both branches.[6] What sort of thinking lies behind this apparently incoherent claim? One main idea here is that, before this fission operation, the
pronoun "I" and kindred terms, like "Peter Unger," referred ambiguously,
or indifferently, to two people. Another is that, before the fission, the two
Peter Ungers may have shared both a body and a mind; they may have shared
all of their thoughts, actions and experiences. Then the fission occurs. From
that point on, each of the people will be on his own: The Unger on each
branch will have thoughts that are his alone, not shared with the Peter with
whom he used to share all of his thoughts and experiences. Ingeniously mar-
shalled by Lewis and others, further unusual propositions serve to make this
approach logically consistent and quite comprehensive. But, as is evident, this
approach is very hard to believe: It seems doubtful that these philosophers
are giving us the straight dope on how our own actual conventions help to
define our existence.

Beyond the patent fact that it is not very credible, what else may be fairly
said against this position? For one thing, just as does the approach that would
discount short branches, this approach also attributes a strong retroactive
aspect to our conventions for individuating ourselves: Only after a fission has
occurred, or else has failed to occur, can it be determined how many people
wrote this very sentence. But there certainly does not seem to be any such
aspect to those conventions: It was easily determined a few seconds ago, when
that sentence was written, that precisely one person wrote it. Now perhaps
certain evidence that deceptions occurred a few seconds ago might upset this
judgment of a single writer. But no future fission process, however baffling
and exotic, will ever come back to upset the judgment.

Further, we must ask, again, what really is our prudential attitude toward
the people emerging from this fission case? From self-concern, or a small
extension thereof, I will *not* sacrifice as much for either of these emerging
people as I will, whether in an ordinary case or in the standard one-sided case,
to protect myself alone. Indeed, suppose that there is the prospect of future
torture for not just one, but for both of these emerging people. From self-
concern, I will sacrifice less to protect *both of them* than, in a case with just
one suitable survivor, I will endure to protect myself. And, of course, I will
do more to protect both of these two survivors than I will do to protect just
one of them. Consequently, from self-centered concerns, there is a *considerable disparity* between what I will do to protect the single future person who

6. For Perry's view, see "Can the Self Divide," *The Journal of Philosophy*, 1972. For Lewis's view,
along with a family quarrel he picks with Perry, see "Survival and Identity," *The Identities of Persons*, University of California Press, 1976. For others, see the stacks of journals in your nearby
university library.

is me and, in contrast, what I will do to protect, from precisely similar horrors, one of the two people who emerge from my standard fission.

Why is there this marked disparity? Is it because I will spite myself in circumstances where I will have been using "I" so ambiguously, or where too many will have been sharing thoughts? This may be said, of course, as may many other things. But, for most of us, little credence will attach to words like these. Rather, the best explanation of the differential in sacrifice is just this: First, in the fission case, although there *is much* of what (prudentially) matters in my survival, there is *not all* of what matters. And, second, it is because I do not survive that, in this fission case, there is not all of what matters in my survival.

On a second view, after my standard fission, there will still be just one person, who will survive along both branches. This is the view that, emerging from the fission, I will survive with a divided mind. My divided mind, and also I myself, will be supported by two half-brains in two different bodies. As it may appear, this view will receive some motivation from what we say about "split-brain" patients. In order to lessen his horrible epileptic fits, each of these patients has had his corpus callosum severed, thus losing the service of this neural structure that, normally, provides the main means of communication between the right and the left cerebral hemispheres. Now, first, as seems perfectly clear, after these connecting nerves are completely severed, the original patient does survive; his desire for relief from epilepsy has not lead the patient, not even unwittingly, to have his life terminated. And, second, as it appears to many interpretive observers, the patient then has two centers of consciousness, each supported by a different cerebral hemisphere. Or, as we might say, the patient then has a divided mind. As may be suggested, perhaps the standard fission case is just an extension of this sort of actual case, differing only in the number, the variety and the degree of the separations effected in the original person.

Now, like the two positions just previously discussed, this view, too, may have its drawbacks. But, as we should first notice, the present view does avoid one failing shared by the two previous positions: Unlike them, this present view does not require that our conventions for individuating ourselves be retroactive. On the other hand, it does share with the Lewis-style view another sort of drawback: On this divided mind view, as well, after my standard fission there is all of what matters in my survival. But, as our intuitions have it, on the crucial prudential use of the terms, there is, at most, only a very great deal of what matters, not all of what matters. For example, in the standard fission case, there is not more of what matters than, in the spectrum of assimilation, there is in the first near miss case.

The reason for the failure of this divided mind view must lie, I think, in the degree to which it underestimates the importance of certain differences.

Whatever their precise characterization, these are the differences between the case of the split-brain patients and, on the other hand, the standard case of true fission. Some of these differences make for some disturbing situations. After fission, the person on the left and the person on the right may go separate ways and, as a result of different activities in different surroundings, on each side there may occur very different experiences and memories. As a consequence, there may occur an increasingly great divergence between the goals, and the personalities, supported on the two sides.

Suppose that, as the years pass, the person on one side may have one sort of radical cosmetic surgery, while the person on the other side may have another sort of such surgery. As a result of all this, whoever is on either side may become wholly unable to recognize whoever is on the other. Is the person on the left really one and the same individual as the person on the right, a man who, from each of his wholly distinctive perspectives, is completely unable to recognize so much of himself? At least insofar as avoiding outright contradiction is concerned, this is, I suppose, a possible description for the case. But, as things appear, it is not a description that is most in keeping with the conventions for ourselves that we actually do have.

Suppose that, in a duel of honor, the person on one side kills the person on the other and, also, vice versa. Is this a case of a single person killing himself, perhaps by attacking himself from two sides at once? It is very hard to accept that description as being literally correct. As this difficulty suggests, although they may be right in thinking that our conventions for ourselves are not retroactive, those who hold the divided mind view may be wrong about certain other aspects of these conventions.

There are still other views that, even while being wholly objective, claim that I will survive my standard fission. Some of these are briefly discussed by Parfit.[7] Moved by some of the ideas in our fifth chapter, I have outlined, or contrived, another of these views.[8] To most of us, any of these further views is even less appealing. Most likely, our original intuition about the standard fission case is accurate: I will not survive my standard fission.

---

7. In *Reasons and Persons*, Parfit does this on pages 255–58.

8. Here is what I call the Trinity View, which might just be a physically based variant of Perry's view: After my fission, there is a new person on the right and another new person on the left. But, as well, I still exist: Even as I am constituted entirely of two big brain-parts, half of me is in the head of one of the new people, serving as his whole brain, and the other half of me is in the head of the other. Now, if much time should go by with no momentous happening, then disassimilation will, eventually, do me in. But, if my fusion will occur reasonably soon after the fission, then there will not be time for that to mean my termination. Indeed, in such a happy circumstance, not only will I continue to exist still longer, but, whole once again, I may once again engage in my own conscious thought about myself. Enjoying, as I do, puzzles with hidden pictures, I find the Trinity View pretty long on charm. But I do not find it very long on plausibility.

3. Fission Cases and Questions of Realism

The standard fission case may not be very realistic. In practice, there may be an insuperable obstacle to standard fission. What is this obstacle? It is the brain stem, or lower brain. On the standard conception of it, the brain has three main divisions: the cerebrum, or higher brain, accounting for about eighty-five percent of the whole brain mass; the small cerebellum; and the brain stem, or lower brain. As we noted in Chapter 6, not only have some people survived the loss of their non-dominant cerebral hemisphere, but others have survived the loss of all, or almost all, of their dominant hemisphere.[9] And, perhaps, either half of the cerebellum may also be lost without much of a catastrophe. By most ordinary standards for reckoning what is possible, however, the brain stem cannot be divided and apportioned, about equally and quite proficiently, to two human people. Not only will the original person fail to survive but, at the end, there will be no one at all in the situation.

Recently, some philosophers have complained that this lack of realism may frustrate any attempt to learn anything useful from fission cases, standard or otherwise.[10] For two reasons, these complaints are misplaced. The first reason, although less fundamental than the second, is worth some mention. If we are prepared to be much more elaborate in our cases than Wiggins first was, we can provide a pretty fair amount of realism. (In Chapter 6, we suggested a pretty mildly hypothetical way, but a quite elaborate way, of dividing, and of proficiently apportioning, the brain stem.[11]) In an appendix, we provide a rather detailed discussion of some mildly hypothetical, if rather elaborate, ways of doing this.[12] At all events, these elaborate examples provide us with a useful lesson: By standards for reckoning possibilities that are only somewhat more liberal than the most ordinary ones, the brain stem *can* be nicely bisected and apportioned to two people. Further, by these same standards, there can occur branching cases which do not even involve a division of the brain stem.

This leads us to the second, and the more fundamental, reason why much realism is not needed for fission cases to be philosophically useful. Going back to our methodological discussion in the first chapter, we recall that, from any of our examples, the main thing that we want is a useful indication of what

9. My nearby textbook, Walsh's *Neuropsychology*, seems to say this; but it is not clear enough on the issue. As regards the main philosophical points, none of this, as I argue in the text, really matters at all.

10. Two very recent examples are Kathleen Wilkes, *Real People*, Oxford University Press, 1988 and, perhaps not quite as insistent, John Robinson, "Personal Identity and Survival," *The Journal of Philosophy*, 1988.

11. This was presented near the end of the section, "Against the Indivisibility of Experiences and of Subjects."

12. This appendix directly follows the body of this chapter.

our deep beliefs and values are. The standard fission case, as well as various other sorts of branching case, are not so wildly unsettling that they can provide us with no useful guidance in these matters. Rather, the assumptions required by these cases are mild enough so that, even while we leave intact almost all of our system of beliefs and other attitudes, we may yet entertain them vividly.

To appreciate these points, it may help to consider a quite different sort of circumstance: We might suppose that, *even by rather liberal* standards for reckoning possibilities, we cannot apportion ourselves to two people: For example, as we might suppose, each of us is essentially an immaterial soul, and that is why we are so completely indivisible. Such an assumption very strongly contradicts our system of beliefs.

An assumption that so strongly contradicts the fabric of our beliefs will rarely be useful in the construction of telling philosophical examples. The reason is this: When a very central belief of ours is assumed to be false, then, in our suppositions, there will be many related beliefs that are dragged in its wake. If only suppositionally, we are thereby depriving ourselves of a solid, familiar framework of beliefs from which to judge the import of examples. When it gets us to lack this background of beliefs, an example may fail to draw any notable response from us. But, as our responses to it indicate clearly enough, this does not happen with the suppositions required by the standard fission case.

It may also be instructive for us to make some rather different sorts of only moderately realistic suppositions, as in this highly asymmetric case. A certain bisection of my brain has these results: Part A continues to realize physically all of core psychology, but *only a tiny bit* of my distinctive psychology, while not realizing any new psychology. The remainder of my brain, Part B, similarly continues to realize the core, but continues *all* of my distinctive psychology, while also not realizing any new psychology. Each part is then placed in its own duplicate of my body, the original body having been destroyed. Then two people awaken, experience and act. As is intuitively striking, I am just the person with Part B in his head. What this appears to show is that, as concerns the physically continuous realization of my whole dispositional mentality, when just one future candidate for being me far exceeds any other, then that one future person will be me.

Interestingly enough, those who wish to use the term "fission" quite strictly may deny that this is a case of fission, even while they allow that there are some cases of asymmetric fission. For these reasonable enough philosophers, there is, in the two parts resulting from this present bisection, *far too great* a relevant disparity for the term "fission" properly to apply. For them, even as I continue to exist throughout, a part of my brain is simply extracted with the result that there also exists, constituted of that brain-part, an entirely new and distinct person. Perhaps with equal justice, other philosophers may say that this case is, nonetheless, a case of fission, even if it is such a highly asymmetric fission that there is not even the beginning of any threat to the original person's strict survival. In our use of the technical term, "fission," there may be many unresolved areas of vagueness and ambiguity. As I see it, there is no great need for these areas to be resolved.

Even somewhat wilder hypothetical examples may yet be mild enough to be useful. For instance, consider the supposition that each of a *hundred* nonoverlapping parts of my brain will be, not only mutually redundant, but also very highly proficient psychologically, each as much so as any other. This supposition will encourage fission cases with anywhere from two branches to a hundred branches. With its hundred branches, a *century fission case* certainly will not be very realistic. Yet it may not be so terribly wild as to prove entirely uninstructive: After anesthesia has been applied, my brain is removed from my body, whereupon the latter is destroyed. All at once, my brain is divided into a hundred parts. Each of these small brain parts will continuously realize all of my psychology. Then each of these hundred parts is placed in a numerically different duplicate of my original body. Each being ever so much like me, all of these people may then awaken. What are my attitudes toward these hundred emerging people?

To avoid future torture for any of these people, I will make a sacrifice now, before any division occurs. But I will make only a comparatively small sacrifice: I will sacifice far less than I will for myself. And I will sacrifice significantly less than I will for each of the two people who emerge from the standard fission case. This might not be very interesting.

Here is something that is more interesting. Suppose that the alternative to my enduring pain beforehand is *not* that just *one* of the hundred will be greatly tortured later, but is that *all* of them will. How much pain will I then endure? From a perspective much like that of self-concern, I will endure quite considerable pain. But I will not endure as much pain for all of these hundred as, in a parallel choice for the standard two-branch fission case, I will endure to spare *both of my two* descendants from such torture. So, as it appears, we have this interesting double-barreled result: First, the greater the number of the people who are my fission descendants, the less there is of what matters in my survival. But, second, even when the number is quite great, there will be some of what matters.

4. The Focus of a Person's Life

In connection with fission cases, we have not yet employed any positively oriented process selection test for what matters. This omission has been intentional. The main reason for the omission is this. Although it is not obvious, nonetheless, with the fission cases as presented so far, we do not have highly prudential occasions for testing. Rather, with a happily positive assumption made about the life of anyone who emerges from the fission processes, a fission case will differ significantly from a case of true survival not only in prudentially relevant factors, but also in respect of a certain factor that, as things are going well, will make only for greater desirability. As it seems, we have no ready term for this factor. So, as I propose, we will call it the *focus of a person's life*. Now, I cannot provide this term with any useful verbal definition. But my hope is that, in the course of the discussion that follows, the main idea behind the expression will emerge.

When I fission into two people, each of these people may, at the same time, go on to have a different sort of demanding career that, according to my values, is both personally attractive and deeply worthwhile. But, even so, given our actual values, there may not be much value for me, who fissioned before that, in this whole situation. At first, this may not be very obvious. But it might become clearer when we consider the century fission case: When I fission into a hundred people, each of these hundred may, at the same time, have a different sort of demanding career, all of these careers also being highly worthwhile. When the person who fissions beforehand has values much like ours, then, no matter how pleasant and worthwhile are the hundred lives led after the fission, there will be a loss for the person who leads his life before. Most of this loss, or perhaps even all of it, will be the loss in the focus of the original person's life.

As I see it, most of the focus of my life may be lost even in the standard two-sided fission case. Between two branches and a hundred, the main difference concerns *not how much* of my life's focus is lost, but, rather, it concerns *how clear it is* that I have indeed lost much of the focus of my life. In other words, when the number of my descendants is just two, it may be easier for us to overlook the loss; but, when the number is a hundred, it is hard not to notice that there is a loss.

Although there are huge differences between the examples, there is a similarity worth noting between these present fission cases and the examples of purely informational taping processes discussed in our third chapter. In informational taping, there is no survival when the number of people emerging is only one. But when the number is one, it may be easy to overlook the fact that, in these purely informational processes, there is missing something that is crucial to our surviving. When the number of people simultaneously emerging is notably larger, say, two, or a hundred, then it is hard not to notice that something is missing. And, once the case with the larger number is before us, it is hard not to notice that this factor is missing even in the case where only one person emerges. As we noted in Chapter 3, we have the second-order intuition that, as regards survival, those cases are very much alike.

Somewhat similarly, when we think about the century fission case, it is hard not to notice that, even in the standard fission case, with only its two people emerging, there is missing something that is important to our values. As we now note, we have the second-order intuition that, as regards this important something, those cases are very much alike. It is this shared factor, common to both of those cases, that we are calling the focus of the original person's life.

In the actual world, different people have different numbers of children. A certain man may have only two children. Another man, perhaps a polyga-mous sultan, may have a hundred children. Perhaps the first man may take a much more intense interest in each of his two children than the second can take in each of his hundred, and the former can keep better track of what children he has. For reasons like this, it might be that the ordinary man may be more elated by the joy of one of his children than the sultan will be elated by the joy of one of his offspring. And the sadness caused by one child's sad-ness might also be greater in the more ordinary case. None of this, however, has much to do with, or is even closely analogous with, the focus of a person's life.

For those who want a sign that this is so, perhaps these following consid-erations will be helpful: Regarding one's concerned attention for one's chil-dren, there is a rather gradual fading out, starting with a small loss with the move from one child to two. When going from one to a hundred, almost all of the loss occurs between two and a hundred; indeed, most occurs between four and a hundred. By contrast, regarding the focus of one's own life, almost all of the loss already occurs with the jump from one, the person himself, to two, his smallest number of fission descendants. As recently noted, the fur-ther loss between two and a hundred really is not a great loss at all.

In the preceding chapter, we noted that it can be misleading to say that we value our survival itself, and that we value consciousness itself. More accu-rately, consciousness is a precondition of almost all of what we value, and our survival is a pre-condition of much of what we value. So, too, it can be mis-leading to speak of the focus of our lives as something that we value. So, too, it is more accurate to say that the focus of my life is a *precondition for certain things that I value*: Roughly, if other things will go well, either for me or for my fission descendants, then a highly focused life in the future will be, for me now, much better than a much less highly focused life. In particular, it will be best of all for me to survive. But, if those other things will go horribly badly, for me or for my fission descendants, then a future with much focus may be, for me now, worse than a future with little focus.

Suppose that, for anyone emerging from the considered processes, there will be a long future life filled with naught but great pain. Then, for me, it will be worse to survive than it will be to fission. And, for me, it will be worse to fission only two ways than to fission in a hundred directions. When things are going to be terrible, anyway, then, like a loss of survival itself, a loss of my life's focus will allow them to be less terrible for me. And, other things equal, the greater the loss of this focus, the less terrible for me will be that terrible future.

Thinking about horribly negative futures clarifies the idea that the focus of a person's life is a precondition of certain of our values. Once we appreciate the potential dangers in saying that the focus of our lives is itself one of the things we much value, then we may often speak, safely enough, about the value that we place on the focus of our lives. Just as it is convenient for us to say that our survival is something that we value, and that consciousness is something that we value, so we may conveniently say, too, that we value the focus of our lives. It is pedantic to insist that, instead, we always employ the wordy talk of preconditions.

The focus of my life is always forward-looking, or directed toward the future. Whenever I fission, there will be at least some loss in the focus of my life. But if my fission descendants themselves never become involved in any other branching processes, then there will never be any loss in the focus of any of their lives. Accordingly, when there is to be only great pain, then, as a way of making that future pain a less terrible thing from the perspective of my own ego-centric concerns, I may welcome fission shortly before the pain begins: The more branches to the fission, the more welcome it will be. But, from the perspectives of my fission descendants, the fission that already will have happened cannot make any pain that is yet to occur any less terrible. Having already fissioned, and lost much of my life's focus, I have already benefited, somewhat, as regards the awfulness of this pain that will soon occur. But, as each of their lives is fully focused, and will remain so, there is nothing here to reduce, for them, the awfulness of the protracted pain that soon will begin to occur.

A further source of clarification may come from certain temporal considerations: At the end of the standard fission operation, just one of my two fission products may be super frozen and may be kept in that state for fifty years. During those fifty years, the other person may lead a rather normal active life, enjoying his demanding career as a philosopher. Right after this philosopher dies, the super frozen man may be super thawed. Then he may go on to live, quite normally, for another fifty years, enjoying his rather different demanding career as an experimental psychologist.[13]

As compared with a case where there is no branching at all, even this "no

---

13. See Parfit's *Reasons and Persons*, page 264.

overlap of life case" will mean some loss of the focus of my life. But, because there is no temporal overlap in these people's lives, that is, in their activities and experiences, this strange sequential situation will not yield as great a loss of focus as did the fission cases previously considered. So, in this no overlap of life case, there will be less loss of focus than in the standard fission case where a philosopher lives for fifty years on one branch and, at the same time, a psychologist lives on the other. Along the same general lines, we may compare both of these cases with yet another. In this third case, things are just as in the no overlap case except for this difference: The impending psychologist is super thawed a day before the old philosopher's conscious life ends. In this day of overlap case, there is more loss of focus than in the no overlap case; but there is less loss than in the case where, quite completely, the two descendant lives run concurrently.

Near the end of this chapter, we will discuss how the lives of my fission descendants might run in parallel and, alternatively, how they might diverge to varying degrees. Especially as these lives may be quite long, these matters can become rather complex. But, at this earlier point, some brief remarks about two quite modest cases may, in still another way, help clarify what I mean by the focus of my life: After my standard fission, each of my two descendants may, for just five minutes, live very painfully before he is shot to death. On each branch, the man will be allowed no activity whatsoever, but will have his painful experience be provided wholly by an experience inducer. Now, in one case, the two experience inducers will provide my fission descendants with precisely the same sort of painful experience: As each seems to perceive, he is being horribly mauled, for five excruciating minutes, by a ferocious tiger. In a second case, just one of my two descendants will get experience of that sort. The other will get experience that, while just as terribly painful, is of a very different character: As he seems to perceive, by way of wires attached to his hands and to his feet, a mad scientist is giving him excruciating electric shocks. In the first case, the short horrible lives of my two descendants run in parallel. In the second, their equally short and equally horrible lives significantly diverge. When their lives run in parallel, there is less of a loss of focus of my life. In these two cases, the futures are quite horrible short futures. So, with a choice between just these two cases, it is somewhat better for me that the second example, with significant divergence and a greater loss of focus, be the case that obtains.

As I believe, the focus of one's life is a precondition of certain things that we pretty strongly value. Moreover, like my survival itself, the focus of my life is a basic precondition, not a derived one. Although basic for us, I do not claim that this is a precondition for any rational beings that there may be. In other galaxies, there may be people for whom this focus means nothing. And, there may be other distant people for whom this focus is a precondition only of what they very weakly value.[14]

5. The Focus of Life and Heavily Discounted Branches

The number of fission descendants is a significant factor in the loss of focus of my life. But, as suggested, it is not an enormously important factor. A more important factor is the extent to which various branches may be *heavily discounted*. When *all but one* branch may be *very* heavily discounted, then, even when I have many fission descendants, there may be little loss in the focus of my life. That is because, in such an event, most of the focus of my life may resolve on the single branch that has not been so discounted. But, then, when can a branch be heavily discounted?

As a prelude to some remarks on this topic, I should like to set many complexities to the side: When I fission, it is true, my direct descendants may themselves become involved in exotic processes that, all over again, effect the number of the branches. But, with a few exceptions, I do not think it very fruitful to dwell on complex sequences of fissions and kindred processes. At any rate, in what follows, when I speak of a person *ceasing*, or *expiring*, that person's cessation will be presumed to be a rather normal one, with *no* enormously intimate descendants left in existence.

There are several reasons why a branch might be heavily discounted. All of them, I think, can be understood as sharing fundamental features with the simplest reason for such discounting. The simplest reason is simply this: On that branch, the person may exist only for a very short time, after which he completely ceases, or expires. So, after I fission into a hundred people, all but one may expire after a minute, while that one lives normally for another fifty years. Especially if there is no pain for any of the short-lived people when that happens, then all but one of the branches may be heavily discounted. For the focus of my life, and so for me, this situation may be *almost* as good as when I do not fission at all. If all but *two* of the hundred should expire after a minute, however, and those two each live normally for fifty more years, then neither of those two branches may be heavily discounted. In such a case, the situation may not be enormously bad for me, but it will not be very good, either. To be sure, in such a case, the situation may be nearly as good for me as one where I fission into just two people. But even when I fission

14. In "Branching Self-Consciousness," forthcoming, Carol Rovane describes some folks who look forward to their fission. For them, focus might still be a precondition for some of what they value; it will just not be a precondition for so very much of what they value.

into just two people, there is much that is lost as concerns the focus of my life. So, unless all but *one* branch may be heavily discounted, typically a fission will be significantly worse for the focus of my life, and so for me, than when I do not fission at all.

In addition to the cases with very short branches, when else may branches be heavily discounted? Let us say that when a life is desirable for a person, or when that life is undesirable for the person, the life is, for that person, *personally significant*. Of course, this may be a matter of degree. Even so, the answer to our questions may be put like this: A branch may be discounted insofar as, and only insofar as, the branch does *not* contain the *preconditions* for the person on that branch to have a life that, from the relevant perspective, is personally significant for that person. If the life will never be at all significant, then it may be completely discounted; if the life will be only very mildly significant, then the branch may be discounted, not completely, but very heavily.

But what determines which perspective is the relevant one? This is determined by certain of the attitudes, before the fission occurs, of the person who enters the fission process. Roughly, these are the person's attitudes toward the *content* or the *character* of a life that he may lead, in contrast to the consequences, for people and things distinct from himself and his life, of his leading such a life. In jargon and also roughly, we want to consider the lives that, according to the person's own values, are *intrinsically*, rather than instrumentally, desirable or undesirable for him.

Given my relevant attitudes, a life with no conscious experience and no purposeful activity is never personally significant for me. Such a life is merely something that I will just live through. When there is a long branch that always contains just a person in a deep coma, having no experience and no activity, then this branch does not contain the preconditions for a personally significant life for me. Accordingly, I may heavily discount this branch. If I fission into a hundred people, and all but one are always in a deep coma, then, for me, there is little loss in the focus of my life. In such an event, the situation may be nearly as good, in these respects, as one in which I actually survive and never fission at all.

Given my attitudes, even if a life has purposeful activity, it will not be personally significant should it entirely lack conscious experience. So, if I am always on a Trancelife drug, I will be leading a life that, for me, is not personally significant at all. If this is right, then, in assessing my prospective fission, I should heavily discount branches with wholly non-conscious intentional activity: If all but one of my fission descendants are moving around in a creative trance, while only the one leads a normal conscious life, I will discount all of those other branches. When this is the fission situation, there will be only a small loss in the focus of my life.

According to slightly different attitudes, a life with much successful intentional activity, but with no conscious experience, may be mildly, but only mildly, desirable. And a non-conscious life with much frustrated intentional activity may be mildly undesirable. A person with these slightly different attitudes will not discount Trancelife branches quite so heavily as will I, but he will still discount them fairly heavily.

What do we think of a branch where there is much conscious experience but no intentional activity? This may occur when, from right after the fission until my eventual demise, my descendants are inactively under the influence of an experience inducer. Given my values, each of them may have a life that is mildly desirable. But, given these same values, each may have a life that is *highly undesirable*. For, if suitably stimulated by an inducer, each person may always be in very great pain. Because each person may have a highly undesirable life, each branch contains the preconditions of a life that is, for me, *highly personally significant*. Because this is so, this time *no* branch of my prospective fission will be heavily discounted.

That seems quite right. Suppose that I fission in two and, while the person on one branch always lives a normal life, the person on the other branch is always conscious in an inducer. This situation is certainly worse for me than ordinary survival, or than fission with one very short branch. Even if the man in the inducer never does feel any pain, the fact of his having experience means a substantial loss in the focus of my life. This loss is just as great, or is quite nearly as great, as the loss when the people on both branches lead normal, conscious, active lives. Consequently, if, by making a sacrifice before, I can avoid this fission with one person in the inducer, I will make a substantial sacrifice.

What is important is that, in every case but one, I avoid branches that contain the preconditions for lives that, from the perspective of my attitudes, are personally significant for the people on those branches. For when there are personally significant lives on more than one branch, there is a significant loss of the focus of my life. And when there is a significant loss of this focus, there is a loss that, for me, is a significant loss.

6. A Person's Singular Goods

In addition to loss of focus, there is another undesirable feature that typically attends cases of fission. For example, there is a single person who is my wife. That person is Susan. For me to have a most desirable life, I must spend a lot of my life with Susan engaged in certain sorts of activities. Moreover, it is also important to me that no other man, but only this one, spend much time with her and engage in all of those favored activities. When I fission, however, there will be at least two people who may compete for Susan's time, attention and affections. At the most, only one of my fission descendants can enjoy the importantly exclusive arrangement with that very woman. An undesirable feature of my fission, then, is that only one of my intimate descendants can have this *singular good of mine*.

In the next chapter, I will argue for the importance to our lives of our main singular goods. For the moment, I will simply present the view, in what I hope is an intuitively appealing fashion, that these singular goods are important: Suppose that, by a statistical miracle, by taping with temporal overlap, or whatever, there comes to be a precise duplicate of Susan, right down to the last molecule. I may be offered two options: Option One is the continuance of my life with Susan herself and the deportation to a near duplicate of earth, a planet just like ours except for its lacking a person just like Susan or, in other words, just like the duplicate of Susan. That is the end of what happens on Option One. Option Two is the continuance of my life with the duplicate instead of my wife, and the deportation of Susan to that near duplicate planet, with its slot for a person just like her. But that is not the end of what happens on Option Two. Rather, unlike One, on Two I get some "external" advantages. One of these advantages may be, for example, a hundred million dollars.

As would many in similar circumstances, I choose Option One. Evidently, I do not just care about the very many highly specific qualities my wife has, or just about there being only one woman on earth with just those qualities, or just about my spending much time, in exclusive arrangements, with the only woman on earth with just those specific qualities. Quite beyond any of that, I care about the one particular person who is my wife: I care about Susan and, as well, I care about the continuance of my particular relationship with her. Now, unlike myself and these many people, there are, I suppose, many others who do not care very much about their mates or their lovers. But many of them will, at the least, care about each of the individual children that he or she might have. At all events, notwithstanding wild and superficial beliefs to the contrary, almost all of us have *some* singular goods about which we care a great deal.

In any standard fission scenario, at most one of my fission descendants can have all, or even most, of my main singular goods. To have a life nearly as desirable as mine, he must have nearly all of them. Suppose that one of them does have all. Perhaps all of the others are placed in experience inducers; or perhaps they may be confined to many foreign countries, which they may then explore. Then all of the others will have lives that, from the relevant perspective, are less desirable than the life of the one descendant who gets to be with my wife and my son. A significant factor in the badness of my fission may be, then, the absence of my singular goods in the lives of my fission descendants.

The *focus means nothing view* is a position that is at odds with my view concerning the importance of the focus of a particular life: When fission occurs, the *only significant loss* is a loss concerning singular goods. When one descendant gets to be with Susan, the others must do without her. Because they must do without, these others will have less desirable lives than that one will have and, perforce, than the life I lead before the fission.

On the most plausible view of fission, for people with values like ours, fission will generally be a pretty bad thing. And when all the futures are positive even while several branches, or all, cannot be heavily discounted, then fission will almost always be a bad thing. As he should, the proponent of the focus means nothing view may grant all of this. Even so, he is still unimpressed with our view. But then how will he explain the badness, for us, that generally attends our fissioning?

That proponent might say this: In assessing how bad my fission is for me, we should average, in a most suitable fashion, the desirability and the undesirability of the lives of my fission descendants. When we average them appropriately, then the lives after the fission score lower, on average, than my life before the fission. It is because there is this low average of the lives afterwards that, for me, fission is a bad thing.

How will this focus means nothing view deal with the discounting of branches? On the face of it, that may be a problem for the view. After all, it would seem that a life in a deep coma, being pretty worthless, should get a score near zero. Then, if I fission in twenty ways, with nineteen descendants always in deep coma, the average of the later lives may be pretty near zero. On any usual averaging, then, such a fission will be very bad for me indeed. But, because the nineteen coma branches may be so heavily discounted, this fission is not so awful as that.

By giving it a suitable dressing, perhaps the focus means nothing view can be made to look pretty good: When a branch is very short, or otherwise lacks the preconditions for a personally significant life for me, perhaps we may give the score for that branch a *very low weighting* in our computation of the average. More than that, perhaps, in computing the average, we may give *all such branches together* a very low weighting. Here is a possible rationale for this maneuver: When branches lack the relevant preconditions, then it may not matter very much, to me, that the people on them miss out on my singular goods. After all, people in a deep coma, for example, cannot really appreciate those goods anyway. If this rationale is solid, and the special weighting it recommends is allowed, then we get a new perspective on why certain fissions are not very bad for me: On the sophisticated way of most appropriately averaging for those fission cases where all branches but one are heavily dis-counted as a group, the average of the lives of my fission descendants will be nearly as high as the score for my life before the fission.

Although it may now look pretty good, the focus means nothing view can-not be correct. For one thing, there are people who live quite apart from others and who, in general, have little attachment to any particulars. These "reclusive" people may have many goods, but they will have little in the way of important singular goods. They may, for example, like their plants and their televisions. But given their attitudes—and for the example to be rele-vant, their attitudes must be relevantly similar to yours and mine—the replacement of their plants with precise duplicates will mean only a minor loss. And the precise replacement of their televisions will mean scarcely any loss at all. Nonetheless, even for these people, it will be pretty bad to fission with many branches that cannot be discounted. For, just as with you and me, when such a fission happens to these people, they lose much of the focus of their lives.

A less central difficulty is also worth our consideration: In situation A, I fission in two. In situation B, I fission in twenty. In both situations, all but one of my descendants spend the many years of their entire lives pleasantly, but also inactively and deceptively, in experience inducers. The branches of these people cannot, of course, be discounted. In A, one of my two descen-dants is always in an inducer; in B, nineteen of my twenty descendants are always, in that way, without my main singular goods. In both situations, my single remaining descendant is positioned so that he may lead a life that is a most natural continuation of my present life. And, indeed, for many years, he alone does enjoy my main singular goods.

Intuitively, situation B is somewhat worse for me, but not very much worse, than situation A. This is the result given by a most plausible version of the view that, in assessing these matters, the focus of life is the dominant factor. On such a view, when I fission in two, I lose most of what there is to lose as regards the focus of my life. If loss of this focus is the dominant factor, and most of my loss is a loss of this focus, then, when I fission in two, I already lose most of what there ever is to lose simply as a direct result of my fissioning. Thus, for me, fissioning in twenty is not terribly much worse.

On a most plausible version of the focus means nothing view, by contrast, quite an opposite result is obtained. When I fission in twenty, the average of the later lives will be very little higher than the score given for a life in an experience inducer. For, even as none of the branches may be discounted, nineteen of twenty get this low score. So, on this sort of view, B is a whole lot worse for me than A. But, intuitively, although B is worse than A, it is not really all that much worse for me.

7. Three Ways for Singular Goods to Go Two Ways

Apart from what matters in my survival, in the prudential use of the term, when I fission, generally there will be two main sorts of loss. One will be a loss concerning the focus of my life and the other will be a loss concerning my singular goods. This being so, the following question takes on some considerable interest: How do these two factors interact, or compare, in situations where no branches can be heavily discounted? We already have some idea about the answer. For, when they standardly fission in two, things will be pretty bad even for very reclusive people with hardly any singular goods. Nonetheless, to understand these factors at all well, we must place them in a wider perspective. In that way, we do not confine our thinking to how we may compare with recluses. Rather, even in our own case, we may notice the differential operation of the two factors. Three complex cases may help us to gain a properly wide perspective on these matters.

Before introducing these three examples, I shall make some brief remarks about what are, for almost all of us, our main singular goods: Many of us place at least some slight special value, quite beyond mere financial considerations, on certain unique inanimate objects: a particular painting or sculpture, a wedding ring, a letter written by Abraham Lincoln, whatever. For us, no duplicate of the original, not even one that is exact down to the last molecule, will quite fill the bill. For a few of us, indeed, in some few of these cases, the replacement of the destroyed original by the precise duplicate is a disaster. But, for most of us, this difference does not really matter a very great deal. Unlike some exclusive aesthetes, for example, most of us are mainly concerned about people themselves, not about what they have made. And, for the most part, each of us is mainly concerned about those comparatively few people whom he actually knows quite well. For the most part, then, our main singular goods are certain particular people and, in addition, the enduring relationships that we have with them.

This being so, there will be some interest for us in the following *case of standard fission with one new solar system*: Suppose that, along with your own fissioning in two, all of the people you most care about also standardly fission in two, say, there is this fission all the way down to all of your uncles, and your cousins, and your hundredth best friend. In each case, half of the person's brain goes one way, into one new duplicate body, while the other half goes the other way, into another duplicate body. The original bodies are, of course, destroyed. Right after that, each of the two descendants is fully reconstructed, getting a duplicate of the missing half-brain. Minus duplicates of just yourself and your chosen people, far away a new solar system may be created that is qualitatively just like our own solar system. One of each fission descendant goes into its slot, into the vacancy awaiting it, in the newly created solar system. The other stays here. Partly because the newly created solar system is so very far away from this old one, there will be no communication, nor any other interesting causation, between the people in the two solar systems. At all events, all of the relevant people go on to lead rather normal lives for quite a few years. What shall we say about this grandiose example?

First, while it is true that, in certain ways, this case is quite unrealistic, it appears that the example is not disconcertingly unrealistic. Let us say that it is "moderately" realistic: True enough, unless we put everything on hold for a very long time, perhaps by way of some vast super freeze, the example includes travel, by half-brains at least, at speeds far greater than the speed of light. And that is hardly the only departure from realism that we are making. But, for purposes of confident relevant response to the case, and as will become clearer as we proceed, these departures do not seem to matter very much. Second, this present case is obviously asymmetric. One of my two fission descendants gets to stay in the old solar system while the other must get involved with all of those new individuals out there. Third, and finally, this example is not very disastrous; nobody is made to cease in anything like the ordinary, quite awful way. (In just a few moments, we will complement this example with two others: One will also be moderately realistic, but it will be both symmetric and disastrous. The other also will not be disastrous, but it will be symmetric and highly unrealistic. Yet I have some mercy: I will not bother to sketch a case that is, at once, symmetric and moderately realistic, but not very disastrous.)

How do you feel about this case of standard fission with one new solar system? First, you must feel bad about the loss in the focus of the lives of yourself and the other people who also fission. But, for the moment, let us place this undesirable feature to the side. Bracketing that loss of focus, how important a loss is there, for you, in the way of singular goods. First let us consider the loss in way of singular goods that are not personal.

When I think of myself as being the central character, it appears that, for me, there is some loss of this sort, but the loss is a pretty small one. Only one of my descendants, it is true, will have the advantage of being in contact with the familiar streets and buildings of New York itself, while the other will have to make do with perfect duplicates. Although this other descendant does not have it *quite* as good as the homebody descendant, the difference does not seem worth enduring any very significant pain. So, excepting such singular goods as are involved with people—and perhaps certain fissioned pets—there does not seem much of a loss here.

How much is lost in the way of personal singular goods? Only the homebody descendant gets to be with the people he never cared very much about anyway. The other makes do with duplicates of them. That is only a small loss on the side of the traveler descendant. But what about the chosen few, who are destined to fission? Before the fission I have a certain relationship with Susan, who is a particular person. After the fission, each of my two intimate descendants has a very highly similar relationship with just one of the two precisely similar intimate descendants of Susan. As regards my singular goods, there is a significant loss here. But although it is significant, the loss is not a truly terrible loss. In that very area, it is much less of a loss than others I might suffer. In particular, it is much less of a loss than will occur with the ordinary death of my wife and her replacement by a duplicate.

In this post-fission situation, there will be, of course, a certain complex of losses of focus of lives: There will be a loss of focus of my own life, a loss of focus of Susan's life, a loss of focus of Andrew's life, and so on. This raises an interesting question: As regards the loss of my main singular goods, is there, beyond the loss of focus to the lives of those dearest to me, any further loss? I suspect that there is. But, if there is, this further loss is quite hard to articulate in any helpfully illuminating way. Perhaps partly because it is hard to articulate, but only partly for that reason, this further loss may be a rather small one.

Second, we turn to look at the moderately realistic, but symmetric and disastrous, *case of standard fission with two new solar systems*: As in the case just before, you and yours fission in the standard way. But now much more than your old bodies are destroyed. Disastrously, everyone who is not among the chosen few is destroyed completely, along with the rest of our familiar solar system. On the other hand, minus the chosen few, two new solar systems are created, far away from each other, each being a precise duplicate of our present solar system minus the chosen few. Each fission descendant of a chosen person goes into an appropriate slot in one of the two duplicate solar systems. How do we feel about this related example?

We may take a broad ego-centric view toward this vast situation. True enough, the sudden death of the billions is a terribly bad thing and, in a way, it is even a terrible loss. But how great a loss is it for me, that is, for the one who chooses the few who are allowed to fission instead of die? From my broader self-interested concerns, the loss does not appear to be a terribly great one. We shall briefly examine this appearance.

For the moment, let us forget the peculiarities of fission. Now, assume that I must choose between the destruction of my original solar system, minus my chosen few, and, on the other side, the destruction of a precisely similar solar system, also already in existence for a very long time, minus duplicates of the chosen few. As we are supposing, either way, all of my chosen few will get to live for many years in a solar system that, at the very least, is just like my original so recently was. While I have a preference for saving my original system, the preference is not very great. I will not endure great pain to get the preferred alternative. Nor will I choose death, or great pain, for those dearest to me in order to get the preferred astronomical option.

Because we like our old bodies, our old artworks, our old acquaintances and other familiar points of contact, in the case of fission with two new solar systems there is *some* distinctive loss of singular goods. And, of course, in this present case, the loss of these goods occurs with respect to both branches equally. But, because a person's most important singular goods may, along with that person himself, fission quite effectively, the distinctive loss in way of singular goods may not be a terribly great loss for the person.

For some, a very wild example to the same general effect may prove useful. Our third and last case, the *case of the fission of our solar system* itself, is symmetric and not so very disastrous; but, of these three, it is perhaps the most unrealistic example. Still, it serves to provide a nice completion to the present group of examples: As we may imagine, an amoeba might divide symmetrically in two. Much more fantastically, everything in our solar system might symmetrically divide in two in such a way that there come to be two descendants each precisely similar to their mutual original just before its division. Very rapidly, both descendant solar systems may then be moved very far away from the locus of their mutual origin. After their relocation, there will be no interesting causation between them. How do we feel about this rather wild example? For what it is worth, my response to this case is quite in line with those elicited by the two previous examples.

Noting the consistent pattern of responses to these three cases, I offer this following vague, but perhaps distinctive, position: In cases of fission, when futures are positive and cannot be discounted, the loss in the focus of lives is a more "dominant" loss, or is a more "distinctive" loss, than is the loss in singular goods.

8. Branches that Run in Parallel and Branches that Diverge

The idea of the focus of a person's life is still quite a vague one. But, of course, I am claiming some considerable importance for the idea. Let me, then, have one last chance to clarify this conception a bit more. In the present section, I will try to do this by examining a certain class of examples, some quite simple instances of which were mentioned at the end of section 4. With this class of examples, we can highlight certain differences in what may happen after a fission: We compare cases where, in a variety of ways, the branches run in parallel and, in contrast, cases where, in all those ways, the branches diverge.

In principle, after a standard fission with reconstruction, my two descendants may be, not only just like I was right before, but, as a consequence, precisely like each other. Moreover, in principle, each descendant may be placed in an environment that is precisely like the other's. This is fairly easy to imagine. For example, both may be confined to identically similar, enormous, self-sufficient buildings, with no views, or other differential stimulation, coming to a person from outside a building. Each building may be about the size of, and be about as interesting as, the Greater New York Metropolitan Area. But, being self-sufficient, each will have, for example, its own continuing food production. In his own building, each of my descendants may work on his own projects, even if the work of one is precisely similar to that of the other. And, each may enjoy the company of an intimate descendant of each person who is, before the fission, someone for whom I care a great deal. As we are imagining the situation, each of my descendants is part of a distinct, but a precisely similar, closed physical system. At the time of their origin, the initial conditions of these systems are alike in every physically relevant respect. We are also making a further assumption: All other (non-relational) characteristics of these buildings and their inhabitants are fully grounded in, and are fully determined by, their physical characteristics. Because this is so, these two systems are also alike in every relevant non-physical respect.

Let us suppose, moreover, that a very strong form of determinism holds true. Because it does, and because of our previous assumptions, the lives of my two descendants will proceed in a precisely parallel fashion, until their eventual demise many years later. We are supposing that, for these reasons, both branches of my fission run in perfect parallel. How will I feel about my fission then?

In large part, a more definite response will depend on what is assumed to occur, after the time set for the fission, on the condition that, instead, I do not fission. For a most relevant assumption regarding this matter, we will suppose that, if I do not fission, then, along with my friends and family, I am confined to just such a building anyway. Moreover, as we shall assume, for the same deterministic reasons, my single life will proceed in a precise parallel to the descendant lives that will have developed if, instead of my one life continuing, there is my fission.

In such a circumstance, my fission does not seem much worse for me than my survival and confinement to the enormous building. Why is there such a small discrepancy between the two? Perhaps a small part of the reason is that, in the case presented, my survival itself does not seem so good. But this cannot be more than a very small part of the reason. For one thing, we may increase the closed system at will, so that confinement becomes scarcely any factor at all. The noted discrepancy remains just about as slight. As a negative point about even the survival situation, there remains to consider only the strict determinism that has been assumed.

Many of us occasionally think of our lives as completely determined in some such way as that described just above. When we think these thoughts, our lives may not seem quite so appealing as they usually do. Nonetheless, just as it still appears to us, they can still be pretty good lives to lead. If a completely determined life is filled with loving interpersonal relationships and the intentional attainment of many deeply valued goals, and if all of this is always clearly appreciated through conscious thought and experience of it, then that life may be quite an attractive one. Indeed, a fully determined life with these desirable features may be much *more* appealing than many reasonably nice lives that, while lacking in these features, are not so determined.

Having one's life determined by *certain sorts* of causes, it is true, might make for quite an unappealing existence. For example, few of us would like our brain states to be directly manipulated by a scientist, or even by a self-contained computer, that employs electrode stimulation directly toward that end. There is no surprise here. After all, full determination by *such causes as these* seems to leave no room at all for genuinely intentional action on our part. But being subject to the laws of a deterministic physics does not appear to be nearly as bad as that.

Let us suppose, then, that, in each of our deterministic fission examples, each of the descendant's lives flows from the least objectionable fully deterministic factors and, in general, each is about as appealing as a fully determined life can be. As we are assuming, both my own continued life, on the one hand, and also my fission descendants' lives, on the other, will be quite attractive lives. Even with such attractive lives assumed all around, the discrepancy in favor of the envisioned survival over the comparable fission still appears to be quite small.

Receiving so little of the answer from the denigration of the fully determined survival situation, we continue to explore our question: Why is there, between the fission with branches running in parallel and, on the other hand, a relevantly similar situation of strict survival, such a small difference in what we value? One way of putting most of the answer may be this: In fission with branches running in parallel, there is only a small loss of the focus of my life. Through my fission descendants, there are *no more real ways for any life to proceed* than there is for my life to proceed on its own. Because everything is so completely determined to run in parallel on both branches, even in the fission case there is only one (absolutely precise sort of) possibility that can ever be realized. To me, it matters only a little whether this possibility is realized only once, by me, or whether twice, by my enormously intimate descendants.

Most fission situations are not like this. Rather, in almost all, the lives on the different, non-discounted branches will diverge substantially. Even if a wholly complete determinism is true, this will be so: For one thing, in most fission situations, the initial states of my fission descendants will not be absolutely the same. At first, there may be only a quite minute difference between the two. But, over time, the effects of a minute difference may reverberate, so that large differences eventually occur. Further, in most fission situations, the physical systems of the different branches will not be completely closed systems. When through the window of an ordinary building one of my descendants sees a certain cloud formation, this will effect just his brain in a certain way. The other descendant, not seeing that cloud formation, and not having any compensating causal relationships, will then have a brain that is in a somewhat different state. Just as these small differences each may also produce an escalation in difference, given enough time, so also, over time, there will be further differences of stimulation for my two descendants. For example, a day later, just one of them may face a stiff wind, while the other faces only a gentle breeze. Working together, all of these factors will produce progressively greater divergence in the lives of my two descendants. In sum: In almost all fully deterministic scenarios, sooner or later my two fission descendants will live quite different lives.

If there is not full determinism, there may instead be (simple) indeterminism, or randomness, to one or another degree. Whatever the degree, truly random factors will, almost always, make for that much more divergence between the two branches. Can there be neither determinism, nor randomness, nor an exhaustive combination of the two? We now enter the difficult area of non-determined, non-random choice and action. If they occur at all, perhaps such choices and actions are more deeply free than any others can ever be.

The questions of this area are extremely puzzling to me and, unfortunately, I have nothing very illuminating to say about any of them. For present purposes, however, all that needs saying is something that is as simple as it is obvious: If this non-random, non-determined choice is still another real possibility, then, should my fission descendants realize it, their lives almost certainly will diverge. This will be an almost absolutely certain consequence of each of them making his own deeply free choices. While there is the logical possibility of the free choice of the one in every case precisely matching that of the other, the likelihood of such a match becomes minuscule as time, and the number of free choices, progresses.

Whether there is full determinism, whether there is some true randomness, whether there is deeply free choice that differs greatly from them both, there will almost always be a significant divergence in the lives of my two descendants. Insofar as there is this divergence, there will be, when I fission, a loss of focus of my life. As did many of my remarks in section 4, these statements partially define what I mean by the focus of a person's life.

In part, this idea of focus is a *modal* notion, concerned, as it is, with real possibilities for a person's life. Consider a situation where there is some indeterminism. Largely owing to chance, after I fission my two descendants may behave in precisely similar ways, they may have precisely similar thoughts and experiences, and they may be in precisely similar relations with all sorts of other things that are precisely similar. When all of this does occur, then, in a *weak sense* of the term, their branches *run in parallel*. But in a *strong sense* of the term, their branches do *not* run in parallel: At least at certain stages, regarding each branch, there is the *real possibility* for the life on that branch to proceed in any one of a number of different ways.

Other than the zero loss that strict survival means, the smallest loss of focus occurs when, first, there are fewest fission branches, that is, there are only two and, second, all but one branch may be very heavily discounted. But when two or more branches cannot be heavily discounted, and must be reckoned with quite fully, then the smallest possible loss of focus that can still be sustained occurs when, even in the strong sense, all of the non-discounted branches run in parallel.

When, after a person fissions, the resulting branches diverge even in the weak sense, then there is the greatest loss in the focus of that person's life. When the branches run in parallel in the weak sense, and diverge only in the strong sense, then there is a lesser, but still a significant, loss of focus. When there is a significant loss of the focus of my life, then, for me, my fission will mean a significant loss. By contrast with the foregoing remarks, this last statement is not a matter of definition at all; rather, it is an expression of my substantive view on a question of what are our actual values. Is this view on the right track? Well, assuming that you will have several fission descendants each leading a lengthy, conscious life that diverges significantly from the lives of the others, how do you feel about your impending fission? As I suspect, your values here are quite similar to mine: Even if it is not as bad as your ordinary cessation, in death, your fission will be, for you, a pretty unwelcome turn of events.

APPENDIX
Toward Greater Realism in Personal Branching

As we remarked in the body of Chapter 8, the standard fission case is only very moderately realistic: Because of the real relations between its structure and its functional power, the lower brain cannot actually be divided into halves that are both (even nearly) mutually redundant parts and also are highly proficient realizers of dispositional psychology. This being so, there is no straightforward bisection of the whole brain that yields an interesting case of personal branching that is even pretty realistic. As we also noted, the rather limited realism of the standard fission case, and of such related examples as the century fission case, will not be any great obstacle to using the example profitably in our inquiry into the question of our survival, or into the question of what matters in our survival or, we may add, into the question of the focus of our lives.

Nonetheless, it may be interesting to see how, in terms of ideas already developed in the book, we may specify personal branching cases that, requiring no straightforward bisection, are more realistic examples than the standard fission case. In this appendix, we will present two sorts of more realistic case. In the first part, we will present a couple of examples that, even in a rather strict use of the term, 'fission,' are cases where someone undergoes fission. In the second part, we will present cases of a sort that, even if they might not strictly count as a sort of fission, might yet be the more interesting type of personal branching examples.

A. How Assimilation May Allow for More Realistic Fission

Both of the cases under this present head utilize the Zuboffian techniques that were so useful in Chapter 6 along with the assimilation factors that were so prominent in Chapter 5.

In a *case of fission with assimilated lower brains*, we may have the simplest way of dealing with the problem posed by our recalcitrant brain stems for effective division and allocation: In the first step, perhaps by way of a zippering procedure, a person's brain is removed from his body and is divided into three parts: These are the right cerebral hemisphere, the left hemisphere, and the lower brain. (In order to be suitably cautious and conservative, throughout this example the lower brain will be taken to include the cerebellum.) Each of these three salient brain-parts, as well as the rest of the body, is fitted with transceivers that, quite directly, are pressed into service: At this point the person is scattered into four mutually communicating parts; of course, the most massive of these, by far, is all of his body excepting his brain.

In the second step, two new duplicates of the lower brain are introduced, each fitted with precisely similar transceivers. Once introduced, these new lower brains effect precisely the same sort of communications as are being made by the old lower brain. Now the person is composed of six appropriately communicating salient scattered parts: These parts include three lower brains, one old and two new, that are mutually redundant and that, in this set-up, never communicate with each other. This remains the situation for several months, during which time the person proceeds to live quite normally. Consequently, there is much assimilation time for both of the new lower brains.

Through assimilation alone, perhaps neither of the new lower brains will ever acquire quite the status, in relation to the person's survival, of the original brain-stem-cum-cerebellum. This potential embarrassment can easily be circumvented. In the third step, the old lower brain is simply destroyed. Thus the new lower brains will not have to compete with that previously established psychological contributor. Still, the original person survives, now in five main communicating parts. At this point, our subject is ready for relevantly realistic division.

In the fourth step, the body is destroyed. But, as regards questions of survival, that is the least of what happens. As well, the left hemisphere breaks off communications with one of the new lower brains, and the lower brain that was *not* then abandoned by the left then communicates *only* with the left hemisphere. Symmetrically enough, and at the same time, the right hemisphere begins to communicate only with the other new lower brain, which, for its part, makes no communications but with the right hemisphere.

In a fifth step, again several things happen: Perhaps by way of a reverse zippering procedure, the left hemisphere and its communication partner are placed in a duplicate of the old body; similarly, the right hemisphere and the other new lower brain are placed in another duplicate body. There are now two people. One of them has the mentality of a subject who has survived dominant hemispherectomy, and the other has the mentality of someone who has survived non-dominant hemispherectomy. At all events, neither of them is the original person. Further occurrences help to solidify this last judgment: The person missing a right hemisphere gets an updated duplicate of the right hemisphere; he now has a whole human brain. The other person gets an updated duplicate of the original left hemisphere; he now also has a whole human brain. Each complete, normally composed human being goes on to live normally for several more months, giving ample assimilation time to the new parts acquired earlier in this step. Accordingly, at the end of these months, if not before, there quite surely are two people in the situation, neither of them scattered and neither of them the original person. For his part, that original person has not only ceased existing, but has fissioned into two highly intimate descendants.

When I imagine this process happening to me, I do not regard the result as being much like my ordinary death. Rather, my attitudes of self-concern extend to both of the two realistically produced descendants of mine.

The case of fission with assimilated lower brains involves the continuous existence of the two old cerebral hemispheres and their allocation, one apiece, to the people emerging from the fission process. Because that is so, this case will always provide only a very limited number of fission descendants, namely, two. Nor can this sort of example be readily extended so as greatly to increase this minimal fission number.

With a *case of fission with assimilated half-brains*, we get much higher numbers. In the first step of this case, perhaps by way of a zippering, a person's whole brain is divided down the middle, say, left and right, while each of those two large brain-parts is fitted with appropriate transceivers. At the same time, there is a zippering with respect to the rest of the body. As the last part of this first step, these three main parts, always communicating by transceivers, are spatially separated. From our discussion in Chapter 6, all of this is quite familiar.

In the second step, many duplicates of the left half-brain are introduced, say, a hundred of them, along with appropriate transceivers. Also, just as many transceiverized duplicates of the right half-brain are introduced. At the flick of a switch, every right half-brain, the one old and the hundred new, communicates with each left and with the rest of the body; every left communicates with each right and with the body; of course, no left communicates with any other left and no right with any other right. The original person survives all of this; it is just that, in addition to his old parts, he now has two hundred salient new parts. At first, of course, these new parts are not assimilated. But after quite a few months of living with all of these brain-parts directing the mobile body, and receiving stimulation from it, the new brain-parts become quite fully assimilated.

Suppose that all the brain-parts are destroyed except for one new left and one new right. Then the original person will survive by way of these highly assimilated complementary half-brains. But this is not what happens. Alternatively, suppose that the old brain-halves break off communication with the new and, for the sake of simple exposition, the old body is destroyed. Then perhaps the original person will be just where the old brain-halves are. Although the assimilation of the new brain-halves may give them a certain *sufficiency* as regards the person's survival, the old brain-halves may retain a concomitant *priority* as regards his survival. But this, also, is not what happens. Instead, in the third step of the case, what happens is this: The old left and the old right are destroyed. Because of that, there is no established psychological contributor with which the new brain-halves need compete. At the same time, by way of these assimilated brain-parts, the original person does survive.

In a fourth step, each right hemisphere ceases communication with all but one of the new lefts. This occurs in such a way that, as a result, a different right now communicates with each of the different new lefts, no right communicates with more than one left and, of course, vice versa. There is thus established a one-to-one partnering of the new left and the new right brain halves. Then the old body is destroyed. The original person has now fissioned into as many people as there are pairs of communicating brain halves, that is, into a hundred new people.

A fifth and final step will nail down this description of the fission process: For each pair of assimilated brain-halves, a duplicate of the destroyed body is provided. With an inverse zippering, each right-left pair is organically joined and is placed, appropriately, in the (head of the) new body assigned to the pair. The hundred normal human beings thus produced each live normally, perhaps in precisely similar buildings, for several months. Quite clearly, there are now as many people as there are whole human brains in human bodies, namely, one hundred. None of these hundred people is the original person. Rather, because he has fissioned into them by way of an appropriate assimilation arrangement, all of these people are extraordinarily intimate descendants of him.

As in the case of fission with assimilated lower brains, in this related realistic case of fission there is not survival. But, also as in that previous case, there is at least a fair amount of what matters in survival.

B. Toward Greater Realism: The Hobbesian Personal Spectrum and the Hobbesian Personal Chain

From Chapter 5, recall the Hobbesian personal case. As originally presented, in that example a person's brain-quarters are sequentially replaced; one quick replacement is made every three months; and, after each replacement, the person undergoing the operations leads a normal life. Consequently, each new quarter has a substantial period of optimal assimilation. As was also supposed, each part replaced is kept alive in its own vat isolated from all of the others. In its vat each replaced part is so stimulated as to be precisely synchronized with the brain-part that replaced it, the latter now being, of course, part of a whole, well-functioning brain that is in my old head. In this way, the original brain-quarters are continuously updated. Being so thoroughly updated, at the end of the year, the original brain-quarters may be joined in precisely the same arrangement as their replacements then enjoy. When this is done, there are two precisely similar brains: the brain made of the replacements and the brain made of the original brain-parts. The latter is then placed in a body that is a precise duplicate of my original body. For its part, my original body now contains the brain composed of the four replacements. Call the side of this branching process where there is the assimilation and the old body *Side One* and call the other side, where the vats are, *Side Two*.

At the end of the year, I will be the person on Side One. At the same time, Side Two has pretty good qualifications for containing (what constitutes) me: Contrary to the specified example, suppose that, on Side One, instead of taking hold well and lasting, each newly inserted brain-part died a day after insertion; but, everything else on that side—the remaining parts of the original person—was kept alive with the aid of medical support systems. If the whole process had, in that way, failed to be a positive branching process, then *what constitutes* the reconstructed person, on Side Two, *would have constituted* me. The same point is made by contrasting this Hobbesian example with the correlative case of sequential separation and subsequent joining: In this contrasting case, on *all relevant levels of underlying reality*, what happens on Side Two is *precisely the same*. It is just that, *on Side One*, there *never are* any replacements made for brain parts removed. With no replacements made, I will end up on Side Two.

The replacement of brain-parts as large and important as quarters is quite useful. These great changes make it clear that the main points are quite free of any connection with slippery slopes, the sorites paradox, misleading tendencies to favor consciousness, and anything of that ilk. If the changeover of quarters is quite abrupt, however, then the replacement of such large, important parts may give rise to a certain worry: Between the removal of an old part and the insertion of a new duplicate, there will be a time when only three-quarters of a brain is on Side One. With three-quarters of a brain, we might not always have a well-functioning subject of consciousness, or a person, on Side One. This worry can easily be laid to rest: Rather than abruptly, each brain-quarter may be replaced by the serial replacement of one hundred of its roughly equal parts. In a sequence of a hundred steps, each taking only a few seconds, a new brain-quarter is placed in the head on Side One. (In this same sequence, in a vat on Side Two, there is quickly built up a brain-quarter that is precisely similar.) So, then, on Side One, there will always be, in addition to the rest of the body, at least 99.75% of a brain. So, on Side One, there will always be a person.

In any *Hobbesian personal spectrum*, all of the cases will have the same structure as the example just considered. To get a particular Hobbesian personal spectrum, we must specify several parameters. We will suppose that, first, the person at the start of each case in the spectrum is me and, second, that the parts of my brain sequentially replaced, and later reassembled elsewhere, are non-overlapping quarters of my brain. Third, we must choose a temporal parameter, and I will choose one second. As a choice of this parameter, any reasonably short period, such as two seconds or half a second, would have done just as well.

At all events, it is a variation with respect to the temporal parameter that provides the differences among the cases of the particular Hobbesian spectrum that we shall consider: From one case to the next, the total assimilation time decreases by precisely one second. (So, from one case to the next, each brain part will have a fraction of a second less of normal assimilation.) At the near end, the total time for all assimilation will be, by a neat arbitrary choice, four years. At the far end, the total time will be only one second. At all events, in each case of the spectrum, right after all of the assimilation there allowed, on Side Two the original brain-quarters are reassembled and, thus joined, are placed in a duplicate body.

By reasoning remembered from the previous chapter, in this spectrum there will be a first near miss case for the person on Side One, where the assimilation is going on. Right before this will be the last bare survival case. In that last survival case, the person on Side One will have credentials that, by a whisker, are sufficiently much better than those of the person on Side Two. In the first near miss case, of course, the credentials of the two future people will be a tiny bit more nearly equal. Because the credentials are a bit too nearly equal, in this near miss case it is not true that the person on Side One will be me.

But it is also not true that the person on Side Two will be me. Indeed, as is most likely, the qualifications of that person will *still be less good* than those of the person on Side One. It is just that, for the first time in our progression through this spectrum, the discrepancy in favor of Side One will not be sufficiently great for the person there to be a clear enough winner. In that it is not true that either of these people will be me, this case is in the middle ground of this Hobbesian personal spectrum. From the vantage point of Side One, so to say, it is the highest case in this middle ground. Many cases beyond this, there will be another logically interesting first case: With sufficiently little assimilation on Side One, there will be the first case where it is true that the person on Side Two is me. (For a classicist, this may also be the first case where it is *absurdly* false that the person on Side One is me.) Between the last bare survival case and this logically interesting case, there is the whole middle ground of this Hobbesian spectrum.

In every case in this middle ground, my attitudes of self-concern extend, sometimes more and sometimes less, to the people on each of the branches. How does that occur? Briefly, and in quite general terms, our answer is this: Because the concern for realistic congruence operates effectively with these examples, and our conventional concern pulls the other way, we must strike compromises for these cases. These compromises will be struck along the following lines: In the cases highest in the middle ground, while they extend at least somewhat to each of my two descendants, my attitudes of self-concern extend more to the person on Side One than they do to the person on Side Two. In the cases lowest in the middle ground, these attitudes extend more to the person on Side Two. In cases near to the center, the attitudes extend about equally to each of the two people. In *none* of these middle ground cases, of course, will my attitudes of self-concern be *fully* directed at, or be fully extended to, either of these people. For, as this is a middle ground, neither of these people will be me. In none of these middle ground cases will there be my survival. But, in all of these same cases, there will be, in the crucial prudential use of the term, at least some of what matters in my survival.

In the cases of this Hobbesian spectrum, there will be only two descendants of the original person. These are branching cases with just two branches. In a case of fission with assimilated half-brains, by contrast, we may have any number of branches. Are there any Hobbes-style cases that also allow for many more than two branches?

We find the desired cases when we consider what I call a *Hobbesian personal chain*. To produce such a chain, we may proceed as follows: First, we consider a case very near the middle of the Hobbesian spectrum's middle ground. In particular, we may consider the descendant on Side Two, the one with my old brain. All over again, and with just the same middle ground amount of assimilation time as occurred before, we perform the replacement operation with respect to this descendant person. This operation results in two people. Just as happened with the operation just before, both of *them* are highly intimate descendants of me. Remembering also the person on Side One of that just prior operation, altogether there are now, not two, but three intimate descendants that I have. My attitudes of self-concern extend, significantly and equally, to each of these three descendants.

Always focusing on the person with my original brain, who is on Side Two of each operation in the chain, we may extend the chain any number of times. If the assimilation needed for each new operation is a full year, then extending it so that there are twenty fairly compelling descendants may take twenty years. More plausibly, it may require less time.

There is no great scarcity of time in these matters; thus no reason for us to economize with it. Nonetheless, as may be worth noting, we can save time by having each and every descendant undergo a similar Hobbesian replacement operation. In that way, we may go directly from two to four, within the time required for the assimilation. Similarly, we may go from four to eight, from eight to sixteen, and so on. By foregoing an operation with regard to selected descendants, we can quickly arrive at numbers in between these doubles. For example, to get precisely five compelling descendants most rapidly, the standard two-fold operation is performed once, performed again on both of those resulting descendants—yielding four and, finally, performed on just one of those four descendants. This takes three times, rather than five times, the original assimilation period. When generating exactly one hundred compelling descendants, the savings in time will be far more dramatic.

Without requiring a great deal of time, we can obtain a Hobbesian century case for me. I will endure some significant pain so that, after the operations, all of these hundred descendants will be spared torture. But I will certainly not endure the sort of pain that I gladly face in order to spare myself such later torture. Nor will I, even, endure what I will face to spare both of my two descendants, in a most simple Hobbesian personal case, where two are all the descendants that I have.

9

THE APPRECIATION
OF OUR ACTUAL VALUES

Although your values are different from mine, there is a basic core of values that we share. People from radically different cultures and eras may share little of this valuational core; people from other galaxies may share scarcely any of it. But the lack of universality need not diminish the importance of our coming to understand more clearly what our own main values actually are. In this final chapter, we will take a few steps toward achieving this understanding. In so doing, we will embark on a study that I will call *the appreciation of our actual values*.[1]

In our earlier chapters, we have already laid some groundwork for developing an appreciation of our values. Beginning with the very first chapter, our imaginative encounter with experience inducers helped us see that, beyond the value we place on our having pleasant and varied experience, we greatly value certain realistic involvements with a world beyond our own minds. In the just previous chapter, with our investigation of the focus of a person's life and our discussion of a person's singular goods, we provided quite a few examples useful for furthering this appreciation. And, in the chapters in between, mention was made of other useful cases. This final chapter is a good place to bring all of this material together, to discuss its impli-

---

1. Within the domain of this study's concern, some of the central issues go back at least to Plato's *Philebus*.

cations concerning our actual values and, as opportunities arise, to provide
further material helpful for the appreciation of our values.

In working toward an appreciation of our actual values, we seek descriptions that clarify for us what are (some of) the main values that we actually
do have. Our study cannot show, more ambitiously, that there are just a few
rather simple things that we basically value, while all the other things we value
are just complexes of these. The reason for the limitation is not just that there
are many whole situations each of which we value far more than can be
accounted by any reasonable summing of what might reasonably be regarded
as the situation's parts. Quite beyond that, with many of these situations,
there are greatly valued parts that are themselves relations between other valued parts: These valued relations, or valued relational parts, will not even
obtain without there also existing those other valued parts that they serve to
relate in just the ways that we greatly value.

Toward an appreciation of our values, we try to describe, in an illuminating
way, what are these most highly valued whole situations. When these descriptions are pursued, we find that much of what we value is that our broad ego-
centric interests are satisfied rather fully. The full satisfaction of these interests requires that we ourselves, and those others that we care most about,
have lives that not only are quite long and full of much pleasant conscious
experience, but that involve a reality that extends beyond our experiences.

As do you, I place much value on living a long life in which, as time goes
on, I fulfill more and more of my aims or projects. These projects concern
my activities in a world beyond myself. For example, one of my aims is that,
along with my wife, I raise my son, Andrew, to become a good and happy
person. The fulfillment of this aim requires, in addition to my own existence,
the existence of two other entities that are relevantly independent of me,
namely, Susan and Andrew. Even when I do not experience them, each of
them still exists. Further, for this project to be fulfilled, there is required both
my own survival over time as well as the survival of these two other particular
people.

In at least three ways, as we can see, the survival of particular people is a
precondition for much of what I value. First, as is similarly true for you, it is
very important to me that I myself act to fulfill my aims and projects. And, it
is important that I myself consciously experience both this activity of mine
and, partial though they may be, also the various successes that it brings. For
me, it will be very much worse if, after some few years, I expire and, for many
remaining years, a mere duplicate, perhaps one produced by taping with
physical overlap, goes on to complete many of these projects.

True enough, expiring and having such a duplicate fulfill many of these
aims may be much better than expiring and having them all be entirely unful-
filled. But it is also much worse than my not expiring and, while I live, having

these goals be fulfilled by my own conscious intentional activity. And my continuing to live, while actively attaining my goals, is at least somewhat better than, for example, my fissioning and having, on the only long branch, an extremely intimate fission descendant who consciously achieves many of the aims that I myself first formed. So, unless the conditions of my survival are fulfilled, there will not obtain so very much of what I value; and, unless it is not wildly false that those conditions are fulfilled, there will obtain only a quite moderate amount of what I value.

Second, as is true for you, much of what I value involves particular people and their lives. It is very important to me, for example, that Andrew has a long life in which he forms, acts toward and fulfills various goals and projects of his own. In order for what I here value to obtain, it must be Andrew himself who lives to attain these goals and who consciously experiences it all. If part way through my son is replaced by a mere duplicate, who then goes on to attain many of the goals that my son himself first formed, then, as regards what I value, that is only a rather poor substitute. So, only to the extent that the conditions of certain other people's survival are fulfilled, Andrew's for example, will there obtain so very much of what I value.

Third, partly because it is required by certain of my projects, but partly quite beyond any of that, I greatly value continuing to be related, in certain ways, to certain particular people. To be sure, these relationships will be developmental, changing in certain ways as time goes on. It is very important to me that, in one case, it be me and my son whose relationship develops in these ways. If a duplicate of him takes his place in my vicinity, for example, while Andrew himself is banished to a (near) duplicate of this planet, then the valued relationship will no longer obtain. For that reason, yet again, there will not be so very much of what I value.

Among other things, in this chapter we shall offer further argument for the importance of these three factors. If these ideas are on the right track, as they do at least appear to be, then, for each of us, one's own survival, and also the survival of certain other particular people, are preconditions for much of what one values. In retrospect, it may now be said, it was largely in order better to understand these preconditions that we have been engaged in a our extensive, and intensive, inquiry.

In working toward an appreciation of our values, it will be useful to confront some confusions about what are, and what rationally ought to be, our values. After noticing the initial appeal of certain simplifying views, we may observe, by way of telling examples, that our strong values actually are quite the opposite of what these views direct. Furthermore, against the seductive views, we may fully espouse, and may partially elucidate, the rationality of our actual values.

Finally, let me make it very clear that, unlike Socrates, I am one who thinks that the unexamined life often may be well worth living. By my lights, even if ill understood and never investigated, a long life filled with much personal love, much vigorous activity and much sensual pleasure is far better than most sorts of very short lives that include, as a central part, much successful philosophical investigation. On the other hand, the appreciation of our actual values, which is a large part of what should come from the examination of our lives, is almost as worthwhile as it is difficult to achieve. With this in mind, and in the hope that they may prove stimulating, some half-baked suggestions will be made and quite a few loose ends will be left exposed. The point is, I suppose, that, in working toward an appreciation of our values, each of us can use all the help he or she can get. At all events, whether or not its author will be among those who continue to explore these issues, I emphatically repeat that this book's final chapter is meant to provide only the first few steps of a much fuller philosophical investigation.

1. The Phenomenalism and the Verificationism of Values: The Ego-centric Form

Usually, it is in the course of ordinary conscious perception that we enjoy the most vivid, most coherent conscious experience that we have. As when we see and hear a real bird, for example, this ordinary perception involves our having conscious experience *of* things whose existence is *independent* of the experience itself. But, as is familiar, we can have precisely similar experience without conscious perception of such independent entities. Very vivid dreams sometimes may include such experiences; hallucinatory drugs may produce them. At various points in the book, we imagined experience inducers. These hypothetical devices are only a most systematic means for producing in us experiences like these. Whether produced by the processes of ordinary perception of independent external objects, or whether produced in one of these less representative ways, in their *qualities* or in their *character*, the experiences will be precisely the same. It is only in respect of their causal origins that there is any difference in these experiences that we might have.

Regardless of its causal origins, we value conscious experience that is pleasant and varied. If suitably coherent within itself, and producing no severe clash with our beliefs about the world, a vivid pleasant dream may be, for us, at least a modestly good thing. It may not be very meaningful; but, absent any painful psychological conflict resulting therefrom, at least it will mean some fun. With the experience inducers, there are highly systematic ways for us to have this experientially direct sort of fun. At the same time, perhaps very much of this sort of fun might be, for us, no very good thing. In order to see this point, we may usefully remind ourselves of how these imaginary machines are supposed to work.

With its electrodes attached to your brain and a highly "realistic" and pleasurable program selected for you running at its core, an experience inducer may provide what you will take to be a very satisfying active life. If your main interest is classical music, for example, you may spend very many years in the inducer having just the sort of life experience you would have if, against the odds, you really were to become a brilliantly talented, enormously successful orchestra conductor. Once you are in an inducer, as you well know in advance, you will have *no memory* of the day you learned of the inducers, the day right before entering, but only of all your still earlier days. Accordingly, as you are antecedently well aware, life in the inducer will be, not only pleasurable in other ways, but quite *free of psychological conflict*. In every way, it will appear to you that you yourself are responsible for all of your apparently quite real artistic successes.

Suppose, further, that we can be sure that the machines are not addicting: We can go into an inducer for a relatively short time, as into a movie, or even as into a resort complex. After we come out, we will not be compelled to go back in soon. Before and after, there will be no difference in the likelihood of our spending very much time in the inducers, no more so than our spending so much time in movies, or in resorts.

For short periods, many of us will be happy to go into these machines. At the same time, few of us will choose to go into the inducers for many years. This is pretty interesting. But why is it interesting?

In some frames of mind, we think that we are *phenomenalists of value*.[2] Then we think that, whatever their causal origins, suitably varied pleasant runs of experience are the *only* thing that we value *intrinsically*, that is, the only thing that, quite apart from any valued consequences it may have, we value in and of itself. Anything else that we value, we then think, is valued *only instrumentally*, that is, we value it only insofar as, and only because, it helps to produce, or to further, such nice runs of experience. (So nice experiences that are themselves productive of further nice experiences are, on this view, the only things that we value both intrinsically and instrumentally.) The example of the experience inducers helps us to see that this value phenomenalism badly misrepresents what are our actual values. That is a main reason for the interest of that example.

Looking also for more positive lessons, we may ask: Why do we so abhor spending our lives, or even spending much of our lives, in these machines?

---

2. Perhaps the most prominent philosophical advocate of this sort of phenomenalism is Henry Sidgwick. See *The Methods of Ethics*, London, Macmillan, 1907, 7th edition.

In very general terms, the reason is this. There are things we greatly value that will be missing from a life that is spent mainly in an inducer. Here are a few of these favorite things: directly informative perception of a world beyond our minds, with other people in it; informed by that perception, thought about that world around us; based on that thought, effective action with respect to that world, including communication with some of those people; informative perception of the effects of our actions upon those external objects and on those other people. Perhaps it is a great loss when we give up any one of these things. Quite certainly, there is a great loss when they all are gone. Against the confusion of value phenomenalism, it is these things that are among our actual main values.

But why are we ever confused in the first place? Part of the reason is that, while some of us are much more so inclined than are others, each of us is at least somewhat susceptible to the appeal of a false view about the *rationality* of our values, which I will call the *verificationism of values*. In discussing our confused tendencies, it is useful to divide this verificationism into two main forms: the *ego-centric form* and, at an opposite extreme, the *universal form*. We will first concentrate on the ego-centric form of the view. In the next section, we will move to consider the universal form (and, by implication, intermediate forms of value verificationism.)

According to the ego-centric form of the verificationism of values, it is *rational* for one to value something only insofar as that thing will *make a difference to one's own experience*. Much of the appeal of this ego-centric view may come from thoughts like these: If something makes no difference to your experience, then you will never really know, anyway, whether or not it obtains. So even if it does not obtain, you will never really miss it. So it is not rational for you to care about whether it obtains or not. We may then combine these thoughts with an idea that, almost certainly, is quite unobjectionable: As regards their basic nature and direction, our actual values are rational for us. When taken together, these thoughts lead to the ego-centric form of the phenomenalism of values: Except insofar as something may have consequences for one's own experience, when it is therefore valued instrumentally, one values only (certain of) one's own experiences.

This ego-centric verificationism of values directs that, except insofar as certain differences in causal origins will mean a difference in the qualitative character of my experiences, it is not rational for me to care about the causal origins of my experiences. Accordingly, it is not rational to prefer having my experience be caused by perceptual involvement with an independent reality to having precisely the same sort of experience produced by an experience inducer. For, even if I am always in an inducer, I will never really miss the greater world beyond. But, as is unobjectionable, in these matters our values are rational for us. So I am an ego-centric phenomenalist about values: I do not really care whether I spend my life roaming about the world perceiving many things or whether I always lie idly in an experience inducer.

But, of course, this argument may be reversed. And it is the reversal that is, by far, the more compelling of the two arguments: Quite certainly, we do care a great deal that we not spend very much of our lives so passively in an inducer. So, the ego-centric phenomenalism of values, which denies this, must be false. Further, it is most likely that, in such a basic area as this one, we are rational in having the values that we actually do have. So, as is most likely, the ego-centric verificationism of values is also false.

Sensible reflection on our ordinary affairs confirms the contention that the ego-centric phenomenalism of values is a false view.[3] Consider life insurance. To be sure, some among the insured may strongly believe that, if they die before their dependents do, they will still observe their beloved dependents, perhaps from a heaven on high. But others among the insured have no significant belief to this effect. And, as this book has argued, few indeed have their dominant belief in this heavenly direction. Still, we all pay our premiums. In my case, that is because, even if I will never experience anything that happens to them, I still want things to go better, rather than worse, for my dependents. No doubt, I am rational in having this concern.

Even in the face of these facts, it might be objected that, after all, a phenomenalistic reason might really be the operative motivation: The insured might only care about promoting, in their beneficiaries, behavior that is less insecure than would otherwise obtain. The point here is, of course, that, in paying for their policies, the insured want only, or want primarily, to avoid witnessing their children, or their spouses, behaving insecurely. Being highly contrived, this objection fails to represent our real attitudes.

Against the objection, there are at least two pretty telling replies. First, we may reply that there are many insured people who not only lack spouses, or any adult dependents, but have only very young children as their beneficiaries. These very young children will not know anything about life insurance on their mother or their father. Whether a two-year old's spouseless parent is insured or not, the young child will act the same. Knowing all of this, the parent gladly pays. As is overwhelmingly likely, the main motivation of other insured people is not very different.

A second reply directly applies even to married parents of a savvy twelve-year old: The insured may as well lie to their putative beneficiaries and, for a small sum, may obtain impressive papers that only purport to be a genuine

3. In his paper, "Death," Thomas Nagel discusses a number of rather ordinary examples that are useful for our position here. Originally published in *Nous*, 1971, the paper is reprinted in his *Mortal Questions*, Cambridge University Press, 1979.

policy. To be sure, almost all of us who are insured would be psychologically
unable to do this effectively. But *why* are we unable? The reason is *not* that
we abhor lying so much. As psychological studies have shown, almost all of
us lie several times every week, and many are rather indiscriminate in the
matters their fabrications concern. The reason also is *not* that we fear that
our inexpensive pretenses will fail to hold up: Lying through their teeth,
many married people have extramarital affairs without ever being found out.
Along similar lines, many may be confident enough that, *if they strongly wanted
to try*, they could fool their families about whether they had real life insurance
policies that were fully paid to date. Rather, the reason is to be found in this
quite different direction: Most of us who are insured hope never even to want
to try to do any such thing; instead, we want to provide for our dependents
in the event of our death. What motivates us, of course, is our great concern
for our dependents' future, *whether we experience their future or not*. Moreover,
this value that we place on their having a better future is not only quite great
but, no doubt, is quite a rational value for us to have. So, like ego-centric
phenomenalism, the ego-centric verificationism of values is a false view.

2. The Universal Form of These Views

On the *universal form* of the verification theory of rational values, all that it
is rational for us to value intrinsically is the conscious experience of people
or, more universally still, of any sentient beings. On the universal form of the
phenomenalism of values, experiences are all that we ever do value. As I
understand these universal views, it is consistent with them that a given agent
care, not only actually but also rationally, much more about the experience
of certain sentient beings, such as himself and his children, than about the
experience of others, such as a stranger and the stranger's dog.

Although useful for arguing against the ego-centric form of value phenomenalism, ordinary considerations, like that of life insurance, do much less well
against the universal form of the view. As we rationally believe, when taking
out life insurance, we raise the likelihood that, in the future, our children will
have somewhat less painful experience. It is because we value, not our own
avoidance of pain, but *their* having experience that is not so painful, that it is
rational for us to pay for our policies. So, although our payments may not
make much sense from the perspective of ego-centric value phenomenalism,
those actions may agree well enough with the universal form of the view. The
rationality of these actions will, likewise, comport well enough with the universal form of value verificationism.

If universal phenomenalism of values possibly is correct, then, in all likelihood, the universal form of the verification theory of rational values will also

be correct. Is it really at all likely, though, that this value verificationism is correct? There are some seductive thoughts to the effect that this might be so: Even apart from experiencing animal denizens, many people value a beautiful wilderness. But what value can this wilderness have if it never makes any impact on experience, not even on the experience of an animal? Without any experience, what value can there be in the clean fresh air, in the pure water, and in the healthy trees? Unlike G. E. Moore, many of us will see no value in such an experientially barren situation.[4] So, for us, the only value in there being the beautiful wilderness is purely instrumental: Assuming that plants do not themselves have conscious experience, the trees are rationally valued only insofar as, and only because, they may contribute toward the generation of worthwhile experiences.

As many will object, the foregoing thoughts may incorporate certain fallacies: In particular, there may be at work a fallacy of identifying the value of a whole, here, the conscious appreciation of a beautiful wilderness that is itself devoid of experience, with the value of the sum of that whole's mutually independent parts. Even in the light of this truism, however, many of the central questions remain: For example, if the very valuable whole is the conscious appreciation *of* that wilderness, then exactly what are the less valuable independent parts that, together, exhaustively constitute that very valuable whole? As we will later observe more clearly, they cannot be just a certain sort of pleasant experience and, in addition, a beautiful natural world that is external to our minds. For these fine components to generate much value, for us, they must be *related* in some *appropriate* way. But what sort of way will be an appropriate one? Providing no illumination on this central issue, the truism about parts and wholes might not provide much light at all.

At all events, it is with the consideration of these universal views that examples of experience inducers can come into their own. For these examples can be as expansive as we please: We may imagine that, if you so choose, everyone will spend most of his life in a suitably deceptive inducer, with appropriately selected experience supplied for him. A few individuals, randomly selected, may spend some time making sure that the inducers are running all right. A few others may spend some time hooking up those people that have yet to be placed in inducers. A few others may oversee the sperm extraction, the impregnation and the fetal development needed to produce further genera-

---

4. Here I refer to Moore's "two world" thought experiment, presented in his *Principia Ethica*, Cambridge University Press, 1903. Extremely inconclusive, in my opinion, this imaginative gambit was used by Moore to argue against the value phenomenalism of Sidgwick. (See this chapter's second note.) There is a useful discussion of Moore's thought experiment in Roy Sorensen's *Blindspots*, Oxford University Press, 1988.

tions. But, after their tours of duty are over, even these randomly selected custodians will spend more time in inducers than ever they spent actively performing their duties. (For good measure, even most animals may spend most of their lives in inducers constructed just for them.)

In terms of experiences enjoyed, life in an inducer might be more pleasant, more varied and also lengthier than life outside. Even so, few would choose to have everyone spend so much time in the inducers. Unless they were perfectly clear in their demands to go into the inducers, you would no more make this choice for others than you would for yourself. Nor is this because you are reluctant to intervene in others' lives: We may suppose that there is a process *already* underway such that, if you do not intervene, almost everyone will go into inducers. If you press a certain button, however, then this process will be terminated and people will not end up in the inducers. Unless almost everyone made it perfectly clear that they welcomed the outcome of this process, you will push the button. To prevent something that, according to our actual values, is a very bad thing, you are quite ready to intervene. According to our actual values, a situation where almost everyone is in experience inducers is a very bad thing.

The value of leading a consciously active life does not lie in, or does not lie only in, the good of consciously pursuing knowledge of the world. A passive inducer life is just as bad for a hair stylist, or for an athlete, as it is for a scientist, or for an historian. Indeed, as I imagine, it will be a pretty bad thing if (almost) all goats spent (almost) all of their lives in pleasurable inducers built especially for them.

In the inducer examples so far discussed, the people in the inducers certainly do *not* have precisely the same sort of experience that they would have if left outside of those inducers. They do not even have pretty nearly the same sort of experience. Rather, as specified, each person has experience that, as regards its qualitative character, is *far more* pleasant, interesting and satisfactory to him than he would have if left outside. This supposition concerning far more pleasant experience in the inducer is relevantly parallel to the companion supposition that, by every measure, a person in an inducer will have a longer life than he would have if left outside.

The purpose of both of these assumptions is, of course, to make the inducer option more attractive than it would otherwise be. Even so, for most of us, spending (even most of) the rest of one's life in an inducer will not be a very attractive option. Thus the supposition of so much unusually pleasant experience in the inducer gives us an a fortiori argument against the phenomenalism of values. Although such an argument is most compelling, it is also somewhat indirect.

With a slight variant of the examples, we may provide a more direct argument: When in an inducer, each person might have the very same sort of experience that he would have if left outside. This might happen in different ways. We will consider only the simplest of these ways: The inducer might be programmed to duplicate, in the person to be stimulated, the precise sort of experience that the person would have if he was not placed in the inducer. Given a rather complete determinism, and given certain companion assumptions, it is easy to imagine how that sort of program might be provided.[5]

We proceed to complete this more direct argument: With relevantly ordinary programs running at their cores, most of us much prefer not to enter an inducer. And, most of us prefer that others do not enter the inducers. As we are now supposing, all of us will know full well that, inducer or no inducer, there will never be any difference at all in the experiential character of anyone's life. Now, it may be that a world in which things are heavily determined will allow less attractive lives for us than a world where things are not so heavily determined. But, even if things are completely determined, living an active life is, according to our actual values, much better than being for so long in an inducer.

We have now argued for our conclusion quite directly: Even if there will never be any difference in the character of anyone's experience, we each value our actively living in, and our rather accurately perceiving, a world comprising many independently existing people and other things. This present direct argument and the previous argument a fortiori serve to confirm each other: At least as applied to us, in each of its forms, the phenomenalism of values is false. Moreover, there is little doubt but that, for us, these main values are rational values. So, in each of its forms, the verificationism of values is also a false view.

3. The Value of Experience of External Reality

When we have conscious perception that is most valuable to us, then there must be present causal relations among certain basic aspects of our lives. One of these basic aspects is our conscious experience itself, understood without regard to its causes. Another is our realistic activity, wherein each of us is involved with various entities that are "external to one's own mind." For us, not only is it important that, in many of the events of our lives, both of these basic aspects be present together, but it is important, as well, that they be in

---

5. Some may find the deterministic assumptions that fill in the details of this case to be somewhat objectionable. Although they might possibly be objectionable relative to certain purposes, they are not objectionable relative to the purposes of these present arguments. Still, it is nice to note that, with the simple a fortiori argument that features extraordinarily pleasant experience for everybody, no deterministic assumptions are needed at all. That is just one more advantage of employing that sort of simple argument.

certain relations with each other, presumably certain causal relations, when they are jointly present in these events. Perhaps we may appreciate the import of these points by seeing how they help us to answer a little puzzle about our values.

For folks with our attitudes, there are three considerations of value that, taken together, constitute a small puzzle: First, without having an active life with successful realistic involvements, pleasant experience will be of some intrinsic value, but only of very limited value. Suitable examples of pleasant experience inducers show that this is so. Second, without our having conscious experience, an active life with successful realistic involvements will be of virtually no intrinsic value. As we may remember from Chapters 5 and 7, and as we will presently rehearse for ourselves, suitable examples of Trance-life drugs show that this is so. Third, when we have a life filled with pleasant conscious experience *of* our successful realistically involved activities, then we may have a life that, to us, is of very great intrinsic value. Ordinary examples of happy lives show that this, too, is so. Now, as it appears, this highly valued, third life just combines the main feature of the first slightly valued life with the main feature of the second, even more slightly valued life; as it appears, the highly valued life just combines much conscious experience with much realistic activity. So, just by combining these features, how can the third life, the ordinary happy life, be of so much value to us?

Many would answer that the ordinary life can be so valuable because, as very often happens, the value of a whole can greatly exceed the value of that whole's constituent parts. The ordinary happy life is just such a whole with transcendently high value. Is this happy life a whole whose value greatly exceeds the combined values of its constituent parts? There is some sense of the terms, I suppose, in which that is true. Even so, there might be no truth here that is any very illuminating truth.

If a life with pleasant conscious experience of our successful realistic activities is, for us, a very valuable whole, then this whole *cannot even exist*, let alone be highly valued, unless its salient aspects are in the right sort of causal relations. These causal relations are much less conspicuous aspects of such a whole, but they are just as crucial to the very existence of the whole as are the more salient aspects. If the requisite causal relations are not present, if the conspicuous aspects are not related in the right sorts of ways, then there will be, instead of any greatly valued situations, only a life that is, at best, scarcely any better than a life spent in a pleasant experience inducer. Why will that be so?

Some general formulae give the outline of an appropriate answer: Without the needed causal relations, our realistic activity is irrelevant to our conscious experience. And, conversely, our conscious experience is then irrelevant to our realistic involvements. We may encapsulate these ideas in a convenient expression: When these causal relations are absent from a subject's life, then, even if he has much pleasant consciousness and also much successful worldly involvement, the person will lead an *experientially irrelevant* life. What sort of life will this be?

In the experientially irrelevant life, there will be combined, in one or another *wrong* sort of way, the salient main features of a life in an experience inducer and those of a life lived under the influence of a Trancelife drug. In section 1, we rehearsed the salient features of a life in a pleasant experience inducer. Now, let us rehearse the main features of a successful Trancelife.

Suppose that you are now twenty-one years old and, when you are aged twenty-five, you will be given a temporary Trancelife drug. But, before the drug's effects wear off, you will always be given a further dose. Because of this, you will spend the rest of your life involved in much non-conscious thoughtful activity, but you will never again have conscious experience. At the same time that this drug deprives you of consciousness, the drug itself, or another drug that you are also given, may greatly increase many of your psychological powers. As a consequence, you may then successfully pursue a variety of protracted projects, perhaps winning one Nobel prize for your contributions to physics and another for your literary works. You may contribute greatly, as well, to the raising of your large and successful family. The salient cause of this is that, although your brain will be involved in a great deal of Thot activity, it will be involved in no Cons activity. Because they don't have the special equipment needed to get the tell-tale esoteric readings from your brain, not even your spouse and children will ever know.

In reasonably ordinary terms, all of this might be explicable enough: Although you have no conscious experience, for seventy more years you will be involved in much unconscious but informative perception of the world around you; perhaps you will have many true beliefs about all sorts of other things, including your immediate surroundings, but you will have no true beliefs to the effect that you are having conscious experience. Owing to this very accurate unconscious perception, and to the true beliefs caused in you thereby, you will be involved, as well, in much unconscious but rational thought about the world. Because of that, you will be involved in much unconscious but effective intentional action in the world, including communication with others. Because of that, you will be involved in much unconscious but informative perception of the effects of your actions, and so on.

In terms of our actual values, although you will be very successful in your activities, after age twenty-five your life will be of little intrinsic value to you. After all, given these values, if your life is to be of much value to you, then, through your conscious experience of it, you must appreciate much of your life. Indeed, even if you are allowed two years of consciousness at the end, when, through conscious remembrance, you might relish your past exploits at a remove, you will still get rather little out of such a successful life. Among those with values like ours, few indeed will choose to be given the Trancelife drug.

We may imagine the Trancelife drug to be universally administered. For people with our values, that will only make matters worse. The complete absence of all conscious experience will negate, largely or even entirely, all of the possible benefits that someone in a Trancelife might, through his activity, bestow on other beings.

According to some philosophers who are more behavioristic than I, the scenario of the Trancelife will be very deeply, but very unobviously, incoherent. My own belief is that, on the contrary, the scenario described is coherent. Still, I cannot be certain of this. Let us agree that, for all we know for certain, the Trancelife scenario might be incoherent. But, even if that should be so, most likely it will not matter. For, without having the appropriate (and as yet unknown) philosophical argument very squarely in mind, the scenario *often appears coherent* to us all, whatever one's more considered guess as to its logical status. Let each of us wait to be in a mood when, as happens to almost all of us, there is the appearance of coherence for this scenario. It is in just these moods that we shall attempt a value judgment concerning the offered example. Now, when we make this sort of judgment, in this sort of mood, usually we will respond very negatively to the (offered description of the) Trancelife. By making this aversive response to that appearance, we may show ourselves that, at least as it may occur in an ordinary happy life, we greatly value our having conscious experience.[6] For many of us, I imagine, this point may be so obvious, anyway, that it really doesn't need to be shown by any exotic scenario at all. But let us now proceed to a point that is less obvious.

As I believe, just as the scenario of the Trancelife drug is completely coherent, so the scenario of the experientially irrelevant life, next to be described, is also coherent. Still, for all I know, the scenario of the experientially irrelevant life is not really coherent. But, just as the real, as opposed to the appar-

---

6. Here is a point that may give further force to the ideas that, first, the Trancelife scenario is actually coherent and, second, we really do value conscious experience quite a lot: Against the doctrine of the absoluteness of experience, in Chapter 6 we argued for gradualness. If that argument is well placed, then, between clear cases of conscious experience and clear cases of no consciousness, there is a middle ground. Consider experience-like processes that are only about one-tenth of the way from the top to the bottom of this middle ground. Especially when other aspects of psychology are enhanced, these processes might do much to help mediate between veridical perception and successful action. Perhaps there may be an actively successful person, then, whose "most nearly conscious processes" are of this sort. Although our indication of it is vague, it appears likely, I think, that we are pointing to a case that is coherent, or is logically possible. Now, if the rest of my actively successful "waking" life were to be filled only with such mental processes as these, then how much direct value would there be, for me, in the rest of my life? As I see it, there would be little value.

ent, coherence of the Trancelife might not much matter for our inquiry into our values, so the question of the real coherence of the experientially irrelevant life also might not much matter.

How might someone lead a life that, although it is filled both with much conscious experience and also with much realistic activity, is an experientially irrelevant life? Described in terms that at least appear to be coherent, this is one way for that to happen: First, a person is given a potion whose effects are somewhat less severe than those of the Trancelife drug and, perhaps through further doses of the potion, the person always remains under the substance's influence. This other drug does *not* prevent the person from having conscious experience. Rather, the potion only prevents the character of the person's conscious experience from being at all affected by any of his perception of external objects. Under the influence of this new drug, any experience that the subject has will be causally isolated from any of his sense organs and, in that way, from any of his perception of his external world. Because the potion has these effects, we may appropriately label it the *experiential isolation drug*. Now, although his sensory perception will have no effect on his conscious experience, someone under the influence of the experiential isolation drug may accurately perceive external reality. Formed via information received through his perceptual mechanisms, he may have, for example, many accurate up-to-the-second unconscious beliefs about his immediate surroundings. In other words, this unconscious perception of his may provide him with much current information about his immediate external world. Just as well as if it were obtained in perception that was conscious, this detailed information may serve to guide the person's actions. As a consequence of this guidance, these actions may be highly successful.

Second, in addition always to being under the influence of the experiential isolation drug, the person will always wear a (receiver part of a) *portable* experience inducer. This inducer (or the part of it that the person wears) may be very small and unobtrusive. Except that they are portable, these inducers are just like the standard, more stable inducers. At all events, in accordance with a program previously constructed for him, the subject will be supplied by the inducer with very agreeable, and apparently very realistic, conscious experience. The portable inducer generates this experience in the subject by directly affecting his brain, thus bypassing certain of those less central neural parts of the man that are affected by the experiential isolation drug.

The man with this stimulating "hat" may lead a life that is at once actively realistic and filled with pleasant and varied conscious experience. But his realistic activity and his conscious experience will be causally irrelevant to each other. For example, guided by his non-conscious perception of his surroundings, the man may be involved in conducting importantly new experiments in biochemistry. But he will have no conscious experience of any of that.

Instead, he may have only induced conscious experience *as of* his conducting importantly new, but quite different, experiments in physics. Now, provided that he *consciously experiences* his actual scientific activity, it may be of great value to this versatile man to conduct important experiments in either field. And, provided that he actually performs the activities as the experience makes it appear, it may be of great value to him to have conscious experiences of either sort. But, *unless there is an appropriate connection between them*, there will be little value for the man in any of these conscious experiences or in any of these realistically successful activities.

In ordinary conscious perception, there is a certain "appropriate match" between the subject's conscious experience and, on the other side of the match, the external objects that he perceives. There is such an appropriate match whenever a subject's experience falls in a certain range, as regards its qualitative character, and the subject's external reality falls in another range. When an experience and an external situation are appropriately matched, then the experience provides, for the subject who is having the experience, a "good idea about" the external reality that the subject then confronts. None of this, it should be noted, requires that there then obtain any sort of causal relations between the external situation and the conscious experience. Just so, there may be an appropriate match even in cases where the experience is not an experience *of* the external situation that, for its subject, the experience matches.

In typical cases of hallucination, of course, there will not be anything like an appropriate match. When the versatile scientist is performing experiments in biochemistry and is having experience as of performing quite different experiments in physics, then, again, there will not be a very good match. Now, when there is not an appropriate match, then, among other things, the subject acquires, or tends to acquire, many false conscious beliefs about his life and situation. In our example, often these conscious beliefs will conflict with the unconscious beliefs that are formed by perceptually acquired information. In our example, as we are supposing, it is these unconscious beliefs that are, by far, the more efficacious on the man's actions and, as such, guide the man's adaptive behavior.

Is it the lack of an appropriate match, along with a concomitant prevalence of false belief, that makes the situation of so little value for the scientist with the portable inducer? No doubt, that is part of the story. But perhaps there is, in addition, much more to be said.

As a more searching example will make clear, considerations of this sort cannot really explain very much. Rather, when an appropriate match contributes greatly to a situation's value, as often it does, then, at a minimum, the subject's experience must be brought about by causal processes that, *through his conscious experience*, reliably inform the subject *of his external reality*.

Generally, when these reliable processes occur, not only is the subject's experience caused by those aspects of external reality that the experience then represents, but, further, the appropriate match between the experience and the reality is itself caused by those same processes that produce, in the subject, that representing experience.

A certain person may spend much, most or even all of his life wandering around under the combined influence of the experiential isolation drug and a portable experience inducer. To such a person, there may occur a "statistical miracle": Quite by chance, there may occur, in one small fraction of a second after another, a truly excellent match between the person's experience and the external reality that he then confronts. Quite by chance, it may happen that, time and time again, the precise sort of experience that this person does have is exactly the same as the precise sort of experience that he would have if, not overcome by these drugs and this gadgetry, he was left alone to lead a causally ordinary sort of life.

If left entirely to his own devices, this person would go around the world "along just the same path" as he does when multiply overcome. Indeed, as we are supposing, if left alone, he would *consciously perceive* just those things that are readily enough perceptible to someone who is just like him, in just that situation, at just those places on that path, and so on. So, either way, whether his conscious experience is induced by his "hat" or whether it is enjoyed in conscious perception of reality, the qualities of the person's experience will be precisely the same. And, as the surroundings are exactly the same on both alternatives, the "appropriateness of the match of experience with external reality" will be the same.

As I see it, the point made by this case is quite clear: For people with attitudes like ours, a life filled with these quite coincidental matches will be a life of rather limited value. Quite conspicuously, we have something that an experientially isolated happy wanderer does not: In our own case, at least for the most part, the appropriate matches that we enjoy do not arise coincidentally. To the contrary, they arise through the very causes that both produce our experiences themselves and connect those experiences with our external reality.

To assess the import of these considerations, we shall briefly consider a very complex artificial device: An *extremely selective experience inducer* has a stock of trillions upon trillions of exceedingly short programs. Each tiny program is geared to run for only a small fraction of a second, and will provide only the smidgeon of experience that, in such a brief period, is normally enjoyed by a human being. At any time, how is any one program selected from all of these very many trillions? The inducer is attached to, or has as a part, a sensor that provides just the information that, in the absence of the isolation drug, the human senses ordinarily provide to the brain. On a continuous basis, the sensor informs the main inducer about the character of the perceptible external surround. Based on information of a small fraction of a second before, the main inducer then runs a brief program that generates in the person, for a small fraction of a second, an experience that is appropriately matched to the external reality (as that reality was just a fraction of a second before). Consequently, except when he is in situations that would fool most normal human observers, the person always has, in an up-to-the-moment fashion, experience that is well matched to his external reality.

It is, of course, misleading to call this complex device an experience inducer. Rather, it is just an indirect sort of good artificial sensor. The reason the device is indirect is, of course, that it operates via the selection of the tiny programs. By way of selecting and then running one tiny program after another, there is an indirect provision of appropriate stimulation to the brain. But, to the active person who uses this extremely selective experience inducer, and who has values like ours, this indirectness does not matter. What matters, rather, is the enormous reliability of the causal processes according to which the device operates. Much as eyes and ears more ordinarily do, this complex artificial sensory system will enable a subject to appreciate, through his conscious perception of them, his involvements with external reality.

4. The Rationality of This Value

Thinking of it in isolation from all of the rest of our attitudes, we may feel puzzled about the value we place on our conscious perception of an independently existing reality. For what does this conscious perception of ours amount to, anyway? Perhaps it is, in actual fact, only our having conscious experience that is caused in certain ways, rather than in other ways, by certain parts of an independent reality: Those first ways may be just the ways that are favored by certain of our terms, such as "having conscious experience of that part of independent reality." When, and perhaps only when, one's experience is caused in one of those favored ways, then one has conscious experience *of* an independent reality.

Even if it is just those causes that are the ones favored by those expressions, we might ask: How can it be rational for us to care about our experience having just those causes? Why should the fact that these causes are favored by those particular expressions, with their quite particular conventional meaning, matter much to us? We should not be so stupidly narrow-minded about these large matters of the quality of our lives. If the resulting experience is *pleasanter*, why not prefer, over an experience whose cause is favored by, say, "experience of independent objects," an experience that is caused in some quite different way? Much the same, why not go into a very pleasant and very unselective experience inducer? Viewed in isolation from the rest of our attitudes, the value that we place on our having experiences that have just certain sorts of causes can appear quite bizarre and quirky. Worse than that, it might even appear to be downright irrational for us.

Often, a value that appears to be quite bizarre may, on a more searching observation, prove to be a quite rational value for us to have. The revealing search involves several things. First, it requires us to find a suitable redescription of the value in question. Sometimes no sufficiently suitable redescription is available, but sometimes, too, it is there to find. Second, the search requires us to find, in the person who has the value, certain other attitudes. Often, these other attitudes will include certain beliefs the person has that, in his psychology, coherently connect the value in question with certain of his other values. When things go very well, some of these other values will be deeper and more comprehensive than the value in question. These two points are not unconnected. For, third, the most suitable descriptions of a value are precisely those that, when their application really is proper, allow for just such connections as display great coherence of the one value with others that the person holds.

When very barely described and considered all by itself, *almost any* value aimed at concrete reality can seem to be quite peculiar and bizarre. For example, we may consider someone who values the activity of intentionally placing oily substances on pieces of cloth. When we present this value *under this unstimulating description*, then we are most likely to consider it *in isolation from* most of the other attitudes that the person has. With this presentation of it, this value may appear to be an attitude that, even if perhaps not downright irrational, is not a rational value, either, for many people much like ourselves. But when we *suitably redescribe* the value as one that is placed on the art of oil painting, then this value appears more rational. That is because, when the value is presented under this *more stimulating description*, we are directly reminded that many of those who value the oily activity do so *by reason of many other attitudes that they also have*. These other attitudes, as we quickly infer, *cohere well with* the value placed on the oily activity. We then easily see that, conversely, the value placed on that intentional activity coheres well with all of those attitudes of theirs. In that way, we may see that these people may be rational in valuing that oily activity and may be rational, too, in valuing many of the products of the activity wherein pieces of cloth are covered with those substances.

What are some of these other attitudes? Well, for one thing, painters and their admirers have many beliefs that may serve to connect their value for oil painting with other values that they have. So, they believe that, when the oils have been intentionally placed so as to form certain patterns on the cloth, then, for many civilized human observers, the painted cloth may *represent* certain parts, or aspects, of an independent reality. So, too, they may believe that, in the intentional production of some of these representational patterns, it may happen that, both with talent and intelligence, certain aspects of this reality may be ignored, certain others may be highlighted, and some aspects may be distorted. So, as is believed, often this activity is aimed successfully at presenting observers with certain quite *originally selective* representations. Now, these viewers have a rather comprehensive value that is both strong and deep: Whether the works are produced with oils and cloth or whether with other materials, for example, marbled stone, they greatly value such originally selective representations of an independent reality as are infused with great talent and intelligence and, just as truly, they value the activity that results in such original representations. By way of the indicated descriptions and beliefs, the value placed on the covering of cloth with oils coheres well with this more comprehensive value that these viewers have. This is one way in which the value placed on the oily activity may be, for many artists and their admirers, a rational value, rather than a value that is quite bizarre or, worse still, that is downright irrational for them.

Moreover, the successful production of these quite original representational paintings, it is commonly known, requires the artist to employ certain techniques, and to exploit certain conventions, both of them extremely hard to articulate at all well. By *intentionally departing from* these techniques and these conventions in certain ways, an artist may, in *other styles*, place other dabs of oily substances on other pieces of cloth. Owing in part to these very departures, certain *non*-representational paintings may be produced and may be greatly valued. Neither is this very quirky or bizarre. For the viewers may greatly value those very departures from stylistic traditions that manifest striking artistic originality. Again, as suitable redescription helps reveal, by way of various beliefs, there is a coherent connection between the value placed on the oily activity and a more comprehensive value. Of course, this is just the barest sketch of the other attitudes that many people clearly do have. Because they have all of these mutually coherent attitudes, the vast majority of them scarcely hinted at by these few sentences, these people may be entirely rational in valuing the activity of placing the oily substances on the pieces of cloth.[7]

Just as many of us may be rational in valuing the activity involving oily substances, even more of us may be rational in valuing conscious experience that has certain sorts of causes. Because it may cohere well with very many other

---

7. The queerness of saying that people value the activity of putting oily substances on pieces of cloth, it may be objected, should be explained by reference to (something like) Grice's maxims of conversation. But this is no objection. Such an explanation is completely compatible with, and may even logically presuppose, the position advocated in the text.

attitudes that we have, we may be rational in valuing experience that is caused by certain parts of an independent reality in just such ways that, in virtue of its being caused in just those ways, the experience is *experience of* those parts of reality. In very general or sketchy terms, some of the most central of the other attitudes are these: We greatly value living an *active life in relation* to other people, and in relation to a variety of other independent things. But we greatly value living such a life only if *through* our experience of independent entities, we *appreciate* much of that realistically involved life. Now, as we believe, there is only one way for us, through our conscious experience, to appreciate this life: Our experience must have just such causes as allow it to be rightly counted as *experience of* those very activities of ours. Further, as we also believe, this will happen, as a matter of fact, when our experience is normally caused via our sense organs; but it will not happen when our experience is caused, instead, by an unselective inducer. Indeed, in these matters we have a very particular factual belief: For most of us who now live without the benefit of extremely high technology, and perhaps for us all, this will happen, as a matter of fact, *only when* our experience is caused via the normal operation of our eyes, our ears and our other human sensory faculties. Because we have all of these attitudes, it may be rational for us greatly to value such a very particular sort of thing as even this: the causation of our conscious experience via the normal operation of our eyes, our ears and our other human sensory faculties.[8]

5. The Value of Particular People and of Relations with Them

In the previous chapter, I noted the importance, to me, of my continuing my relationship with Susan, the particular person who is in fact my wife. Even if there should never be any difference in my conscious experience, a super swift replacement of her by a precise duplicate will be, for me, a very bad thing. Almost all of us have similar values of this sort: Not only is it important to us that certain independent entities, who are people, continue to endure, but, in addition, it is important that we continue in certain relationships with these enduring entities.

Just as the great value we place on conscious perception of the external world can seem peculiar rather than rational, so this value of enduring rela-

8. Although I am very sympathetic to the attempt to provide a coherence theory of rational values, in the present work I do not go so far as to endorse such a theory; instead, I endorse no general account of these matters at all. For some very interesting suggestions on how such a coherentist view might best be developed, see Stephen White, "Self-Deception and Responsibility for the Self," in Brian McLaughlin and Amelie Rorty, eds., *Perspectives on Self-Deception*, University of California Press, 1988.

tionships with enduring independent entities can also seem beyond the pale. Remembering the main lines of value verificationism, the reason for the bad appearance may be very much the same in the two cases. Moreover, for most of us, unless there is a certain amount of continuity in our relationships with some such enduring particulars, our conscious experience of the world might itself be of very limited value. If there is a very great deal of disruptive chaos underlying, and causally responsible for, our apparently orderly experience of these particulars, then it might be as well, or perhaps even better, for us to go into pleasant experience inducers. Owing to these considerations, we do well now to explore, first, the value that we place on the enduring people to whom we are personally close and, second, the related, but distinct, value that we place on our continuing relations with these particular people.

Suppose that, in addition to your daughter, there now exists a recently constructed duplicate of her. You may now face a forced choice between two options: On the first option, your daughter will live and will continue to occupy her same place in your family, while the duplicate is destroyed. Further, on this option, after the duplicate is killed, you will suffer some considerable painful experience, produced by some electric shocks and, except for the stipulated fact regarding your daughter, you will get no reward. On the second option, the duplicate lives and occupies that role, while your daughter is destroyed. Further, after the switch, you will suffer no painful electric shocks and you will get a large reward. For example, in some apparently plausible way, such as the inheritance from your cousin of a patent that becomes very valuable only later, you will acquire a hundred million dollars.

Now, as you know full well beforehand, right after the choice is made—whether made by you or, if needs be, made by a randomly tossed coin—you will cease to have any memory, or any intimation at all, that there ever was such a choice, or even that any duplicate ever existed. Accordingly, right after the impending choice, a matter of only a few minutes, your experience will be entirely free of any guilt or conflict regarding any such choice. Moreover, as you well know, after the choice is made, the only difference between the two options as regards the qualitative character of your future experience is this: On the first option, you suffer considerable pain, while on the second you enjoy, in addition to your customary pleasures, those pleasures that, ordinarily and for the most part, are reserved for the very wealthy. Even though you are well aware of all this, however, you will choose the first option. Although you care about your pains and pleasures, there are, evidently, other things that you care about as well.

This choice situation leaves us with many loose ends: Perhaps you saved your daughter, not because you wanted so much to continue your relationship just with her, but rather, or mainly, because you felt it was your duty, as her parent, to choose in her favor and, as is typical of you, you very much wanted to do your duty. That certainly is possible. When we think hard about these loose ends, our thoughts move in two productive directions.

On the one hand, we are moved to recognize that we care about people quite beyond anything that they can do for the course of our experience and, indeed, quite beyond what they can do for our interest in the continuation of our relationships with them: Even if you faced a situation where the choice was not between your daughter and a duplicate of her, but was between your daughter and you yourself, you might choose in your daughter's favor. Now, it is true, no doubt, that you very much do want to continue your relationship with your daughter. But *that* deep desire *cannot* give you any reason at all to choose her life over your own. After all, if *you are dead*, then, just as much as if she is dead, your relationship with your daughter will *not* be continued. The continuation of that relationship requires your own continued existence (and thoughtful activity) just as much as it does hers. So, keeping her alive by dying cannot benefit you in any such way as that. Except insofar as you are interested in *her continuing to exist*, and perhaps even in her continuing to have at least a reasonably good life, your self-sacrifice will make little sense. But, of course, that interest directly involves one of your deepest and strongest broad ego-centric concerns. So, quite beyond any effect that she will ever have on your experience, and even quite beyond anything that she can do to satisfy your interest in having continuing relations with her, you care a great deal about your daughter.

On the other hand, we are moved to consider another example. In this other example, a choice in favor of your interests should never run counter to your daughter's interests. After all, we want a case where there will be no potentially confusing conflict between your interest and your duty. How shall we describe such a case?

From the previous chapter, we may recall a case of a nearly duplicate solar system, one just like ours but for its (initial) lack of a few people. In mild contrast, we shall now consider a case of two completely duplicate solar systems, our own and another just like it: Far away from each other, both may have been around for billions of years, the development of each precisely paralleling that of the other. With this situation providing the background, you face another forced choice: On Option One, your daughter will remain right where she is and her duplicate, in the other system, will also stay put. As before, on Option One there is also some fairly bad electric shock that you will later suffer. On Option Two, by contrast, your daughter gets whisked away to fill the other girl's slot over there, while the duplicate gets put in your daughter's slot right here. All of this will happen much too fast for anyone ever to notice. And, later, there will be no relevant causal interactions between the two solar systems. Now, as before, on this second option you get no electric shock and you do get a hundred million dollars. As before, whichever option is chosen, you will have no memory of any of this once the choice is made. So, after the next few minutes, you will have no painful conflicts of any kind.

Being a good parent, you will choose to keep your daughter here by your side. That means putting up with some pain, to be inflicted electrically in due course. And, it also means foregoing the hundred million and the attendant pleasures. But having your actual daughter around is worth all that. Is there here, once again, a question of duty? Very likely there is. But, in this present instance, your duty, which is to look after your daughter's interests, coincides with your interests.

In this situation, your relevant interest is in the continuation of your relationship with your daughter. What is her relevant interest? Well, if she gets whisked away to the duplicate planet, what will she then be missing? Everything there is just like things are here: First, the character of her experience will be just the same no matter in which of the precisely similar solar systems she lives. Secondly, the qualitative character of her external reality will be precisely the same. Third, excepting such relations as are logically rooted in other times, her relations to her external reality there will precisely parallel those relations that, on the other option, she will have to her external reality here. Excepting those logical relations regarding time, which include the identity of individuals over time, on both options your daughter will have the same sorts of relationships with the same sorts of enduring individuals.

For your daughter, the only crucial difference between these present two options is whether she will continue to be suitably related *to the very individuals to whom she is now so related.* Is a change in the numerical identity of the individuals a significant loss for her? It certainly does seem to be. But, then, there is a complementary situation that we must directly notice: If a change in the identity of the individuals is a loss for *her,* as it quite certainly does appear, then she suffers, only on a grander scale, the *same sort of loss* that, on a smaller scale, you yourself suffer when she goes away and a duplicate takes her place. So, in relevant respects, your daughter's interests really do coincide with your own interests: It is in both of your interests, we realize, to continue the important relationships of your lives with the same particular individuals to whom, each in her own way, each of you is now importantly related.[9]

---

9. As may be obvious, certain cases of fission will provide a pretty close second best as regards these values. Of course, this does not contradict the points recently made in the text. To the contrary, when they are combined with the main points of the previous two chapters, the text's most recent points actually support the claim that, for those who undergo them, these fissions will not be any terribly bad thing.

6. Two Forms of Flexibilism

Along with other general values that we have, the few that we have discussed may be understood as *norms* that we maintain for the aspects of our lives that we may then evaluate by reference to those norms. Thus, as one particular case in point, we may think of a norm *of* conscious *perception* that we maintain *for* our conscious *experience*: Other things equal, pleasant conscious experience will be *most worthwhile for us* only when the experience *occurs in* conscious perception of an external reality. Now, what generally happens is that our conscious experience actually does occur in conscious perception of an independent reality. Accordingly, it is only natural to ask: What is the relationship between this norm for our experience, on the one hand, and, on the other, our belief about what generally happens when we have conscious experience?

When a person's norms are *flexibly realistic*, then he will maintain and employ those norms only insofar as what is evaluated in terms of the norms generally does occur, according to his beliefs, in the ways that the norms prescribe. For example, if our norm of conscious perception is flexibly realistic, then we will assign our pleasant perceptual conscious experience greater value than pleasant inducer generated experience only insofar as, according to our beliefs, our experience actually is enjoyed in conscious perception. If our experience does not generally occur in perception, then, with a flexible norm, we will not insist on any such preference regarding its causation.

Flexibly realistic norms appear to have a happy rationality built right into them: Contrary to our settled beliefs, we may come to have experience indicating that we have labored under gross misconceptions. According to such revealing experience, almost everything will have happened very differently from the way we have believed things to have happened. But, as a very plausible line of thought directs, whatever the actual course of events should turn out to be, we should have norms that are flexible enough to allow a happy rapprochement with the actual eventualities. With such flexible norms, we will be prepared to assign a reasonably high value to those sorts of pleasant enough things that will have been the most usual sorts of things in our lives and that, in all likelihood, will continue to be the most usual sorts of things. Almost no matter how the world turns out, we will be in a fair position to assign a reasonably high value to the lives that we will have lead and to the lives that, in all likelihood, we will continue to lead.

These ideas lead to a view that we may call the *flexibilism of rational norms*: It is rational for us to have only such general values, or norms, as will allow us to have our more particular values be satisfied in a very wide variety of the situations that it is logically possible for us to encounter. Vague as this view is, it is not so unclear that we must fail to see its main thrust. As is also clear enough, this flexibilism of rationality may be coupled with an idea that is, by now, almost as familiar as it is unobjectionable: Our actual main values are rational values for us to have. Together, these two ideas yield a third, the *flexibilism of our actual norms*: We actually do have only such norms, or general values, as will allow us to have our more particular values be satisfied in a very wide variety of the situations that it is logically possible for us to encounter. Because we may be confident of the idea that our actual main values are rational for us, we may be confident that these two flexibilisms both stand, or else both fall, together.

However attractive these flexibilist views may appear, we must ask some questions about them: In particular, is the flexibilism of our actual norms actually a correct position? To answer this question, we must examine some of our actual norms. Conspicuous among them is the norm of conscious perception of reality that we maintain for our conscious experience. Is this norm of conscious perception a flexibly realistic norm? As I shall argue, it is not.

Contrary to what we deeply believe is the fact of the matter, we may imagine none of your conscious experience has been enjoyed in the course of conscious perception of any external reality. As we are supposing, there is plenty of external reality there for the conscious perceiving, all right; it is just that few of us humans ever perceive it. Rather, as we suppose, our experience is produced by unselective experience inducers. Because you have always been in such an uninformative inducer, you have never had the least intimation of any of this. All along, you will have believed, just as you now do in fact believe, that, very often, you consciously perceive a complex independent reality. This is what all of your experience has so strongly suggested. But, as we are imagining things, one day you may come to have an enlightened belief that, far from your having been in contact with any larger reality, all of your experiences have been artificially induced and, along with this, they have suggested very little of what your true situation always has been.

One day, as we may imagine, you are detached from your inducer. Some non-human scientists, who constructed the inducer and affixed it to you, provide a very convincing detailed explanation of how, before the detachment, your experience was always generated. Just as their further explanations are confirmed by your subsequent observations, so this explanation is confirmed by your detailed observations of so many humans in so many experience inducers. The scientists then explain how, almost as soon as a human animal, like you, comes into being, they affix an inducer to the sentient creature.

In one variant of this scenario, it might be correctly explained how the humans are produced directly from scattered molecules. However the correct explanation of your creation may run, once you have arrived there are no two ways about the situation: In the case of each human subject, as is clearly explained, the scientists run a program that, for the subject in that case, provides at least tolerably pleasant experience almost all of the time. As you are informed, hardly any human animals ever do perceive the real world at all, or ever know anything very specific about the world. Indeed, you are one of the chosen few who will ever get to have even this much of a sequence of genuinely informative experience.

Some humans, however, do have at least this much genuine conscious perception of the world and, as the scientists convincingly assure you, each of them may elect to stay outside any inducer and to have much more. In addition to the many millions of humans confined to inducers, there are in a few other places, as you are shown, small towns and villages. In these places, there are those humans who, when given the choice whether to live within or without an inducer, chose to stay outside. And, for the benefit of these who chose involvement with reality, there are some other human people, constructed for that purpose, whose main features are described to you. (A couple of paragraphs from now, I shall briefly elaborate on these constructed people.) Quite apart from any of these villagers, there are still other human people, you are assured, but never are told how many, who were given this same choice but chose to go back inside; these people are now among the many millions who are in inducers. At any event, as you learn, a human who chooses to remain outside will thereafter live actively in the towns and villages, consciously perceiving at least that much of the world for the rest of his life. Finally, the humans comprise the great majority of the intelligent beings that ever are in the universe, and the great majority of these beings are always in inducers.

You are confronted with a forced choice between these two options: First, you may go back into your inducer, to live the rest of your life with no stimulations but those received from the program preselected for you there. As you are assured, your experiences now will be just as "realistic" as before, with only the difference that, from now on, your program will be virtually all uphill, with pleasure exceeding pain by a margin that you thought you could only imagine. On this option, you will have no memory of the single week when you were allowed out of the inducer and learned of your true situation. Nor will there ever be any other such external source of psychic conflict for you.

Second, you may choose to remain outside any inducer, and may live out your days in the small human society. On this option, too, you have no memories of this revelatory week, and will never have any other source of conflict associated with your choice. In particular, you will never again find out anything about the scientists or the inducers, as the whole operation is effectively screened from any observation that, on their own initiative, any humans could ever achieve. On this second option, your experience will be, overall, slightly less pleasant than it was up until the recent time that you were first allowed to come out of your inducer. So, as you are well aware, on this second option your experience will be much less pleasant than on the first option.

Without having any future experience as of a person I spontaneously take to be my son, I may be badly deprived. If nothing is done about this, then the offered choice will be, for me, a painfully hard one. But recall the constructed villagers introduced just a couple of paragraphs ago. On Option Two, I am assured, fifty such people will be constructed, the likes of which will be chosen by me; I will indicate precisely what they will be like, easily enough, by reference to features of the induced experience that I have had. (In actuality, I am correctly told, there really are no people who are terribly like any of my prime candidates.) So, if I choose to be in the villages, then I might begin to have reasonably many emotionally salient, and utterly genuine, interpersonal relationships. Now that we are clearer about our example, the choice may not appear to be such a painfully hard decision.[10]

As I suspect, you find the choice quite easy to make: You will be glad for the chance really to live an active, consciously well-informed life; you will choose to live in the real villages. Even if the *usual* thing for us humans, and for all intelligent subjects, is to be stimulated only by inducers, that is *not* the sort of life that you will greatly value. So your norm for conscious experience is *not* a flexibly realistic norm.

There are readers who will object to this argument. They might say: "There is no point in trying to guess what sort of choice one will make if such a horrible revelation ever came to pass. After all, if one then has the cognitive wherewithal to choose at all, one will then make a choice in terms of the attitudes that one will have at that time. But, of course, the horrible revelation itself may greatly alter one's attitudes. Accordingly, one may then be choosing on the basis of attitudes that are quite different from one's current attitudes. We should not even try to make predictions about these matters. All of this is far too speculative and hypothetical."

Although this objection appears to be a sobering one, it is based on misunderstandings: In being asked to make this choice, you are *not* asked to make *any prediction*. In particular, you are not asked to make a prediction of what attitudes you *would* have in a situation where you first were confronted with the (at least appearing) discovery of such a horrifying explanation of all your past experience. Rather, as requested, you are *now* to make a choice between the two imagined options, a choice that is to be made *on the basis of your own present* attitudes toward those two options. Surely all of us can understand the difference between the two requests and, just as surely, we can sensibly comply with the one even while we may object to the folly implicit in the other. Indeed, there is some very strong evidence that, although you will forgo spec-

10. As regards these last points, I am indebted to discussion with Stephen White.

ulative predictions, you can readily, and reasonably, comply with the request to make the choice: Concerning the two options described, and with hardly any conflict at all, you do respond with a quite definite choice. Here and now, it is clear enough to you that the preferred course is an active life in the real towns and villages.

7. An Inflexible Aspect of Our Norms for Our Lives and for Our Personal Relations

As concerns perception and experience, our norm is not flexibly realistic. Rather, as we might say, our perceptual norm for our experience is *inflexible*. Perhaps the inflexible character of this norm is, in certain ways, limited or relative or incomplete. Very well; then this norm is, in some such limited, or relative, or incomplete fashion, an inflexible norm of ours.

It would be surprising if our perceptual norm for our experience was our only main value that was inflexible rather than flexibly realistic. But there is no surprise. We need only notice the other main norms that, in this chapter, we have been discussing. To begin, we will examine the value that each of us places on his leading a long life that, for about as long as he leads it, is at least a moderately desirable life for him.

In Chapter 4 we noticed that, for judging questions of our survival, we employ certain standards of physical continuity and a correlative standard of continuous realization of psychology. These standards are somewhat independent of our beliefs about how, in actual fact, the matters of their concern actually have developed: Suppose it is revealed to you that, in a taping process with physical temporal overlap, your brain and body were constructed this very morning and, shortly after their construction, the precisely similar earlier brain and body were destroyed. When your present brain and body were awakened, your brain provided you with a rich stock of ostensible personal memories that served you well. For a few hours, there was no source of conflict with these memories. After those few hours, however, you are now confronted with detailed revelations that make the whole horrifying business all too plain to you. As you are shown convincingly, except for your now encountering these very revelations themselves, this is how it has been for a long series of duplicated brains and bodies. Each existing for one day, these have succeeded each other right up until your present brain and body now. And, in the case of *almost* every human being now alive, if he is apparently more than a day old, then this is how it has been for him, too.[11]

---

11. According to Derek Parfit, the crux of this example is due to Thomas Nagel. Compare my discussion here with Parfit's in section 98 of *Reasons and Persons*.

Suppose that you believe all of this and, further, given the constraint of reasonably good coherence with these detailed beliefs, all of your other beliefs are as much like your present beliefs as is possible. Then you will believe that you have existed for only a fraction of one day, not for as long as the series culminating in you now, say, some forty years. And you will believe that, if you are treated now very much as the others in the series were treated before, then you, too, will last only for one day.

Acknowledging that these will be your beliefs about the matters of your past and future existence, we may yet ask about the related question of your evaluative norms. Suppose that your life will be one that is, for you, quite desirable for about as long as you shall live. Then, is your norm for the length of your life satisfied by your being only the latest, and presumably not the last, in such a series of people? In other words, is your norm for your life a flexibly realistic norm?

Relative to the assumption of such a revelation, you may contemplate this offer: If you will endure some fairly significant pain for the next hour, then you will never be duplicated and destroyed. Instead, with your present brain and body in continuous operation, you will continue to live for another fifty years. If you avoid this pain, then you will be duplicated and destroyed. As you learn, few humans are ever given this choice. But, when the choice is offered, as you are also absolutely convinced, then the offer is entirely on the up and up.[12]

You will choose to endure that pain and to be among the few who, according to your own standards for survival, really do have in store a future of many years. Now, if your norm for your life were flexibly realistic, then this would not be your choice. But your norm is an inflexible one.

The next day, after you have survived your first night, you are offered a second choice: If you will endure another hour of such pain, then the person whom you are prone to take as your daughter will get to live for many more years, too, not just a few more hours. On reflection, perhaps you will choose in favor of a long life for this girl. But why do you make this choice in *her* favor? Is the reason that you are greatly concerned for her and, as you (correctly) believe, you can so greatly benefit this girl only by enduring that pain?

I do not think that this is the reason. After all, as the revelations make you well aware, this girl is not really your daughter, but, like you were yesterday, is only a recent arrival on the scene. By way of a minor variant on the example, we may confirm this contention: If you do not endure this second pain, then, although this present girl will not be around tomorrow, the duplicate of her that is next in the series will stay around for many years. With this as your option to favoring the present girl, you will choose to avoid the pain and

12. Compare sections 88 and 89 of *Reasons and Persons*.

to wait for just a day. Evidently, as against any of the others, you do not care a great deal about any one of the many transient girls in this succession.

This contrasts markedly with your great concern for your actual daughter: Even should there be a taped duplicate to take her place, in order to keep your actual daughter alive for many years, you will elect very considerable pain. The main reason for your relative indifference to the girls in the series appears to be this: Unlike your actual daughter, none of these girls will have been around long enough for you to have formed a very meaningful personal relationship with her.

In the first version of the example of this series of girls, you need to keep the present girl around if there is ever to be any enduring girl much like that near you for much more than a single day. So, accepting some pain, you choose in favor of the present girl. As we just saw, you did not especially care about that lately arrived girl. So, why did you make that choice in her favor? Well, in that situation, your choice to keep the present girl alive provides your only chance of ever forming an enduring personal relationship with any girl much like those in "your daughter's series." Of course, it is just girls of this rather precise sort that, spontaneously but not inevitably, you are prone to take as your daughter. Now, whether enduring relationships are common for people or not, it may be of great value to you to have such a relationship with just one girl of just that sort. Perhaps, then, the main reason for your choice of the pain was that, by your so choosing, you could secure the opportunity to form, and to sustain, such an enduring personal relationship.

These ideas are confirmed by some further considerations: If both you and your actual daughter have been around for years, and if you have been closely related to each other personally, then you may even sacrifice your life itself for your daughter and, to spare her life, you will quite certainly go through an hour of fairly bad pain. But, second, if you have been around for only a few hours, as you correctly believe, and if you have just painfully secured your own survival for years, then you will not sacrifice your life to spare the life of a girl. And, third, it will not make much difference if that girl herself has already been around for years and, in addition, is of a precise sort such that, spontaneously but not inevitably, you are prone to think such a girl to be your daughter. Now, fourth, perhaps you may value such an enduring girl's continued existence over that of a duplicate of her who, starting tomorrow, may exist for just as long into the future. But, fifth, unlike the difference between your actual daughter and a recently arrived duplicate, for you, the value of this last difference is not very great.

The value that we place on (a reasonably desirable life for) particular people is determined by several different factors. But, as far as I can tell, none of these factors is flexibly realistic, at least not to any very great degree. More-over, just as we have inflexible norms for people and for their lives, so also do we have an inflexible norm for our personal relationships. The preceding examples already provide some evidence for this last contention.

In order to provide some further evidence, we turn to another example: But for your possible choice to the contrary, your actual daughter will soon be switched with a precisely similar girl, a "duplicate," who has been residing in a precisely similar solar system. We may usefully expand upon that example: Let us suppose that there are, not one or two, but there are many thousands of precisely similar solar systems. With so many of these similar solar systems, every night a different switch may swiftly occur. Now, as you may learn, you are one of the very few people who never has been, and who never will be, involved in any such switch. Luckily, your spouse is another of these stable people. Unfortunately, your biological daughter was one of the vast majority. In various places just like this, she long has been, and now is, very far away. There is nothing to be done about any of that. But, from now on, things can be different. If you undergo a sacrifice, then the girl that, right now, you spontaneously take to be your daughter will remain nearby for the many years of the rest of her life. If you do not make the sacrifice, and you let this chance slip by, then, at least for the rest of your long life, there will be very many switches of girls of just this precise sort.

To keep this present girl here by your side, you will make a significant sacrifice. Of course, this sacrifice is not nearly as great as the sacrifice that, in a related but different case, you will make to prevent your actual daughter, who has been here with you for a full ten years, from undergoing such an astronomical switch. Nonetheless, in this present example, in which you have not had any enduring relationship with a daughter, you will make *some* significant sacrifice: Because it is your only chance to keep nearby you someone of "your daughter's precise type," you will make a significant *minor* sacrifice to keep near you, for a long time, the lately arrived girl toward whom you are so favorably disposed. You do not want to pass up your only opportunity to have, from now on, an enduring relationship with a single person of that "peculiarly familiar" precise type. In our restricted sense of the term, your norm for personal relationships is an *inflexible* norm.

8. Two Extreme Claims

Although our norm for enduring people has a certain inflexible character, it is also true that this norm has been conditioned by our experience. As our experience has led us to believe, we are constituted wholly of physical items that, in character, number and identity, vary over time. Moreover, we strongly believe that we are beings whose conditions of existence are, in a variety of ways, both highly gradual and also heavily conventional. These experientially conditioned beliefs of ours help determine our norms for the lives of enduring people. Thus do they help to determine the character of our strong derivative concerns: When a person is specially concerned about his future, then he is concerned about the future of just one among the complex physical beings that are the actual people; and, when he is specially concerned about his daughter's future, then he is concerned about the future of another one of them.

For many years, as well as in these present times, philosophers have questioned the rationality, and even the possibility, of this sort of experientially conditioned concern. Quite directly, their questions have led them to deny either that we do have this sort of concern or, perhaps more often, that the concern can be a rational one for us to have. For the most part, it is true, their protests have been directed against such conditioned concerns as might flow from a psychological sort of approach to survival, classically exemplified by Locke. But the thrust of their objections readily generalizes to cover the physically based approach advocated in these pages.

As directed against our approach to our survival, the thrust of these objections runs like this: "Why should I especially care about what will befall the person tomorrow whose psychology will then be realized by, say, the only physical entity that realizes my psychology now and, from now until then, alone will continuously realize the psychology of a single person? How could it be rational for me to care so particularly about anything like *that*, which is both so completely objective and so specifically complex? The idea seems preposterous. If I am constituted of such objective things and events as *those*, and do realize this about myself, then, if I am rational in the matter, I cannot really be so especially concerned about my future."

In line with our previous distinctions, we may distinguish two positions here. First, there is suggested the view that, for one of us to be specially concerned about himself in the future, it is required that he be, or that he believe himself to be, a metaphysically proper subject, perhaps that he be a simple, subjective self. Second, there is suggested the view that, even if we might actually have personal concerns without our strongly believing ourselves to be metaphysically proper subjects, still, for us to be *rational* in having these concerns, we must believe that we are just such proper subjects.

This second view, about what is rational for us, is very similar to what Parfit calls the Extreme Claim.[13] This claim is, it seems, accepted not only by some historical philosophers, but also by some contemporary writers.[14] And

---

13. See section 102 of *Reasons and Persons*.

14. According to Parfit, at least, some of the philosophers who accept the Extreme Claim may be Joseph Butler, Geoffrey Madell, John Perry, and Milton Wachsberg. For references, see the notes to pages 307–308 of *Reasons and Persons*.

according to Parfit, although we may have no good reason to accept this Claim, neither is there a good reason for us to reject it. But, to my mind, that cannot be right.

Why is it wrong? Although I am confident that we have a good reason, I am less confident about how to characterize this reason that we have to be concerned about our own futures. Still, as seems quite likely, most of the reason can be articulated along some such lines as these: First, our basic personal concerns may be accounted among our quite basic main values. Among the things most important to me, for example, is that I, and those nearest and dearest to me, have reasonably long and happy lives, free from much pain in the future. Second, these personal concerns of ours will be rational for us if they do not cohere poorly with the other attitudes that we actually do have and, especially, if they even cohere well with these other attitudes. Third, as with our other main values, our actual concerns for ourselves to have happy futures actually cohere quite well with our other attitudes. So, our concerns for our happy futures are quite rational concerns for us to have. By the same token, because we have this coherent constellation of attitudes, it is irrational for us to be unconcerned about whether we have happy futures.

How might my concern for my future cohere well with my other attitudes? A few leading points mark the way: First, this concern is not dependent upon (my beliefs concerning) my metaphysical character, but only upon (my beliefs in) my existence and my being able to have a future: If I do indeed exist, and if I can indeed survive, then, according to my strongest values in the matter, I shall care about my future. My belief in my own existence, and in my survival from an earlier to a later time, is flexible enough to accommodate a wide variety of metaphysical conditions: If I should be a simple subjective self, perhaps one who satisfies the three doctrines about subjects of experience recalled from Chapters 2 and 6, then, that's fine and dandy; I will exist right now and, barring a causal catastrophe, I will endure. But, if I should be, instead, a complex objective being, who satisfies no such conditions at all, then that's all right, too; I will still exist right now and, barring a greater variety of causal catastrophes, I will still endure.

Second, via my strong beliefs about my nature, which do not upset my belief in my current existence or my belief in my likely survival, I will come to be derivatively concerned about the objective entity that I take myself to be. Because I may believe that, as a matter of fact, in a certain situation where a certain healthy brain will continue to realize central psychology, there I will exist, I may be concerned that, in that situation, that physical realizer serve centrally to constitute a being that does *not feel much pain*. The reason that I am concerned about this is, of course, that I *believe* that this physically constituted being will be *me*, and I am concerned that, in the future, *I* not feel much pain.

We do well to compare the Extreme Claim to a somewhat parallel view, suggested by Shoemaker, regarding rational concern and the metaphysical character of our *experience*.[15] Let us call this view the *Extreme Claim about Experience* or, more conveniently, the *Second Extreme Claim*: Unless our experience satisfies certain demanding metaphysical conditions, it is not rational for us to care about our experience, whether as regards its future existence, its duration, its character, whatever. The metaphysically demanding conditions might be, for example, that our experience satisfy, not the three doctrines about subjects of experience, of course, but, also recalled from Chapters 2 and 6, the three doctrines about experience itself.

Now, on our strongest beliefs in the matter, we never do have any experience that is as "metaphysically satisfactory" as all that. Even with these metaphysical "disappointments" about our experience, is it not still rational for us to care about the "more mundane" features of such experience as we actually do have? In other words, isn't the Second Extreme Claim a false view?

Without either of them having any very marvelous metaphysical character, you may have very painful experience or, alternatively, very pleasant experience. On a certain occasion, you might be faced with a choice between the one and the other. For example, you can pleasantly munch the sweet piece of apple pie before you or, on the other side, you can painfully munch the sharp metal knife just used to cut the pie. Other things even roughly equal, is it not rational for you greatly to prefer that you experience the pleasure rather than the severe pain? Even if, just as you might believe, all of your experiences are just some sort of physical processes, this may be eminently rational for you. It may be just as rational, indeed, as it will be on condition that, as you might otherwise believe, your experiences are non-physical processes that, perhaps, satisfy even the three doctrines about experience.

As you might believe, if it does occur, then your painful experience will be a *certain sort* of physical process, while, if it occurs instead, then your pleasurable experience will be a physical process of a quite *different* sort. Then, other things even roughly equal, you will be very rational in your concern to undergo just the physical process of the *second* sort, and *not* to undergo the physical process of the *first* sort. You will be just as rational as if you believed that these processes are not physical, or if you were entirely agnostic as concerns their metaphysical character.

On another occasion, you may face a different choice: As you may be aware, either you or else some stranger somewhere in Europe will have some very painful experience, while the other has very pleasant experience. Now, you might believe that you are just one of the many complex physical beings that think, while that stranger is a quite distinct complex physical thinking

15. See Shoemaker's critical notice of Parfit's *Reasons and Persons*, *Mind*, 1985.

being. Then you will be very rational in being concerned that the first of these physical entities will enjoy the second sort of physical process, the pleasure, while the first sort of physical process, the pain, will be endured only by the second complex physical entity, the one that is somewhere in Europe. As is clear, then, both Extreme Claims are badly false views.

9. These Extreme Claims and Three Demanding Views

It is interesting, I think, to discuss these Extreme Claims in relation to certain Demanding Views. First we comment on two such views that relate rather directly to the original Extreme Claim. Then we will discuss a third Demanding View, which relates more directly to the Second Extreme Claim.

On the *Demanding View of Personal Survival*, one of us will survive only if certain demanding conditions are met and, quite specifically, are met in the instance of the putative person in question. On the *Demanding View of Personal Existence*, none of us will even exist in the first place unless some such demanding conditions are met. For example, with either of these Views, it might be required that the candidate entity satisfy the three metaphysical doctrines for subjects of conscious experience. Suppose that this is so and suppose, further, that these conditions are not satisfied by any actual beings. On the implausible Demanding View of Personal Existence, it will follow that, if there has been reasoning at all, then, at the least, there has been no one who has been engaged in the reasoning. Then the metaphorical hands may be thrown up at the suggestion of any concern for oneself or for others.

According to one fairly plausible interpretation of his marvelously seminal writings, Hume suggests that none of us actually exists and, if any of us does, then none of us survives for more than a fleeting moment.[16] Drawing on different arguments, in some of my own early writings I made similar suggestions.[17] When there is a hope that such suggestions will be rationally influential, there is a gross underestimate of our deep attachment to our actual beliefs. Although there is, I suppose, a certain silliness in these hopes and suggestions, it might be a silliness with which there can be some bemused sympathy.

However incredible they may be, I find the Demanding Views to be emotionally less repugnant than the Extreme Claim. For on the Demanding View of Personal Survival, at least it will be allowed that *if I will survive*, then, what-

---

16. See the selections from Hume's *Treatise of Human Nature*, 1739, in John Perry, ed., *Personal Identity*, University of California Press, 1975.

17. The two most conspicuous examples are "I Do Not Exist" and "Why There Are No People."

ever this survival may amount to, it may be rational for me to care about my future. On views like the Extreme Claim, by contrast, it is held that, *even if I do exist*, and *even if* it will be *me* who exists later, still, if my survival amounts to nothing that is satisfactory from a pristine metaphysical perspective, then it is not rational to care about what will happen to me.

If my imperfect metaphysical nature disappoints certain of my high-minded preconceptions, then that might be a reason for some slight depression. But how can anything like that mean that I have no good reason for avoiding torture? It cannot. My reason for avoiding torture is grounded in my very strong, deep and basic concern that I not feel intense protracted pain. In me, this concern is much stronger and deeper than is any concern to this effect: Only those entities that are metaphysically perfect or pure, if any such things there be, should not feel great pain. Because these are the facts about my actual attitudes, I am very reasonable in caring a lot that, no matter what my metaphysical nature, I should not feel much severe pain.

Further, owing to these attitudes that I now do have, any merely metaphysical disappointments *cannot override* my reason for wanting to avoid torture, namely, that the torture will feel terrible to me. By contrast, relative to certain horrible hypothetical circumstances, I may have certain other attitudes that will override my reason: For example, I may strongly believe that only if I accept torture will Andrew be spared still greater torture. Should I have this belief, then I will have, in addition to my rather basic desire to protect my son, an instrumental desire to accept the torture. This instrumental desire may cohere well with the other attitudes that I have. In that way, my strong desire to protect my son may provide me with a reason that overrides my reason for wanting to avoid severe torture. But, given attitudes that are even roughly like those I actually do have, no disappointment over the metaphysics of my existence or survival will ever accomplish that much. Much less can any such metaphysical consideration lead me to be without any reason at all for wanting not to suffer greatly.

A third implausible position is the Demanding View of Experience. On this view, unless certain sorts of things, say, certain processes, satisfy some very strong requirements, there will be no experiences. For example, the demanding requirements might be the three metaphysical doctrines about experience. Perhaps another instance of this sort of view is the thesis, pursued variously by Richard Rorty and by Paul Feyerabend, that goes by the name of "eliminative materialism."[18]

---

18. For example, see Feyerabend's "Mental Events and the Brain," *The Journal of Philosophy*, 1963, and Rorty's "Mind-Body Identity, Privacy and Categories," *The Review of Metaphysics*, 1965.

Although we may find the Demanding View of Experience quite incredible, whatever its particular form, we will have more sympathy with it, I imagine, than we have for the Second Extreme Claim. For unlike this View, the correlative Claim holds that, *even if we do* have severely painful experience, it will *not* be rational to mind having this experience, and may even be *irrational* to mind, *unless* the painful experience satisfies certain very strong general conditions. And even if we may have, as well, very pleasurable experience, unless that also satisfies those strong conditions, it will not be rational for us to prefer having this pleasant experience to our having, instead, experience that is very painful. This Extreme Claim about Experience is, quite clearly, a wildly false and a harshly bizarre position. But, just as clearly, the original Extreme Claim is also wildly false and very harshly bizarre.

As I see them, the Demanding Views are best understood in this way: They are, or the offerings of them are, oblique calls for drastically revising our view of the world. Or, perhaps, they are even calls for there to be, for the first time, any genuine view of the world. In some of my early writing, I meant to call for, as well, the creation of a genuine language, in the absence of any yet developed here on earth, as a first step toward having a real view of the world.[19] Perhaps somewhat childishly, I had in mind both truly enormous logical and philosophical deficiencies and, so, extremely grand ends for much greater minds to pursue. Partly through my own confusion or cowardice, and partly through infelicitous choices of wording, this was often unclear to my readers. Nonetheless, as I now try to make very clear, from Parmenides to the present, those who profess the Demanding Views are best understood in that way: They are calling for the pursuit of some extremely radical philosophical goal or, perhaps as in Rorty's and Feyerabend's case, at least some fairly radical goal.

Perhaps, as well, those who advance the Extreme Claims are also calling for the pursuit of some radical philosophical enterprise. For my part, I have not been able to see things that way. But, if that is indeed the case, then, just as we should have a certain friendly interest in the offering of the Demanding Views, so we should also have such an interest in the offering of the Extreme Claims. At all events, of course, both the Views and the Claims will remain quite incredible and, almost certainly, will remain very wildly false. But so, too, are most of the main propositions offered in most of the greatest classics of philosophy.[20]

---

19. In retrospect, as I now see, this is the ultimate point of the papers cited in this chapter's sixteenth note. As with the work of the Eleatics and the Megarians, my papers, especially "Why There Are No People," should be viewed as a sort of negative Tractatus.

20. For starters, recall the work of Plato, Descartes, Berkeley, Hume, Kant, and Wittgenstein.

10. The Extreme Doctrine and Norms for Our Action

Philosophical discussions of our action can appear not only puzzling but also depressing. On the one hand, we may contemplate a deterministic scenario in which every last movement of even the tiniest of our constituents always has been, now is, and always will be completely inevitable. Then we appear to be like protoplasmic machines that ineluctably wend their way from conception to death. As it appears, in such a scenario we never really can perform any actions other than those that, at any particular time, we actually then do perform.

On the other hand, if even so much as an inch is taken from the domain of determinism, then, as it also appears, that inch must be given to the realm of randomness. And, where randomness reigns, there we do not really act at all. Rather, up until some moment in time, it really is open whether or not I move in a certain way. Then, at that time, the movement occurs, or else it does not. Whichever happens, the event takes place for no real reason at all. So, in the little area of that inch, if anything, matters might go from bad to worse.

Perhaps this dilemma can never be resolved. Or, perhaps there may be a resolution. If there is a satisfactory resolution, then, as many have suggested, it might proceed in some such terms as these: There is the logical possibility of our each having a Free Will. Rather than proceeding according to any general law of nature, one's own Free Will is, somehow, a law unto itself. In other words, one's Free Will completely transcends the natural order and, accordingly, is a *transcendental* faculty. When there is the free determination of motion, or of rest, by one's own Free Will, then one will perform actions that are freely chosen from among one's real options for action at the time.

Perhaps remarks about such a Free Will are not good indications of a genuine logical possibility, but are, instead, only just so much soothing verbal hand-waving. Along with so many others, I do not really know what to think. But even if there is some happy logical possibility vaguely indicated by some such words as those, still, it often seems doubtful that, in the actual world, there is any exercise of any transcendental Free Will. Just as it is with us all, the more details I learn about myself, and the more I learn about the rest of the world from which I am conventionally demarcated, the harder I find it to see any room, on my part, for any such wholly self-generated and metaphysically free activity.

In parallel with the Extreme Claim about survival, there may be proposed the Extreme Doctrine about Action: Suppose that it is true that, and I believe it to be true that, none of my actions ever flows from a Free Will. Then, according to this Extreme Doctrine, beyond hoping that more pleasure than pain will unavoidably occur along the way, it cannot be rational for me to care about whether my life progresses in one way or whether in another.

When discussions of our action are at their most depressing low points, then this Extreme Doctrine may appear to be correct. But like the Extreme Claim about survival, the Extreme Doctrine is nowhere near being correct. In brief, the reasons are these: Quite apart from any concerns I may have about the deep metaphysics of my actions, I am greatly concerned that, often enough, I perform my own intentional actions. Further, I am greatly concerned that, by performing these actions, I will often have a real effect on other people, and on other entities that are external to my own mind, real effects that are pretty much what I intend and expect. Especially if these strong concerns cohere well with my other attitudes, as I am confident that they do, then, quite apart from any large metaphysical considerations, I may be rational in greatly caring about the way that my life will progress.

As were many of our earlier contentions, perhaps these present propositions may be well served by an example. Toward this end, I consider the *case of the pleasant radio control*: As is now revealed to you by them, some alien super scientists have installed in your head a tiny device. By way of this device, which can receive radio signals from their other contraptions, the scientists can continuously alter the states of your brain. In that way, the scientists can, to an exceedingly great degree, control your behavior.

As the super scientists credibly assure you, right now they are not controlling you. But, unless you choose for the lack of control to continue, at the end of this day they will exercise control, in this quite complete way, for the rest of your many days. This sets the stage for a choice that these scientists pose for you.

On the first option, beginning tomorrow you will always be subject to their control. Now, if they do control you, then, as you are credibly assured, you will have a *much pleasanter* life than you will have otherwise. For, on this option, you will be manipulated so that, as it appears, you are extremely successful in many varied activities. For example, since you have great literary interests, and since the super scientists offering the choice know this, if you should choose their control, then they will manipulate you so that, as it happens, you will "write wonderful novels." As we are supposing, these books will be much better works than the merely pretty good novels that, if left alone, you yourself will really write. Further, owing to the outpouring of these excellent books, you will be greatly praised by many literary critics. When reading those wonderful works, the critics will, of course, have no knowledge of any controlling scientists and, as expected, they will believe the novels to have been produced only by your own creative efforts.

On the second option, you will be left to your own devices. Then you will really write some novels. As just noted, these novels will be inferior to those excellent works that, on the first option, the aliens will cause to flow from your hand. Consequently, if on your own, you will not get nearly so much literary praise. At least in terms of your experience, in this second option you will have a much less pleasant life.

Whichever choice you make, after this one day there will never be any psychological conflict for you to endure: At the end of this day, you will be caused to forget all of the days's events and, from then on, you will have no indication of their existence. And, even if you choose the first option, you will never have any other indication, either, that you are subject to any such external control. So, even if you choose the first option, and then are manipulated by the radio control, it will seem that, to the contrary, you yourself really are writing wonderful works.

If your actual values are much like mine, then you will choose the less pleasurable second option. The protection from future psychic conflict will mean no more to you in this case than, before, it meant to you when you chose a less pleasant life outside of an experience inducer over a more pleasant life inside. As regards this present choice concerning the radio control, the very pleasant first option is, for you, quite a poor alternative. Being always subject to the pleasant radio control is, I suggest, only modestly better than spending the rest of your life in a similarly pleasant experience inducer. And, as is by now familiar, being always in a pleasant inducer is quite an awful situation.

Bad as the radio control is, in a choice between the two of them, you will choose the pleasant control over an equally pleasant experience inducer. So, for you, the control really is at least a bit better than the inducer. The question is then worth asking: In *what* ways is the pleasant radio control *better* than the pleasant experience inducer? Here are some of the main advantages of the control over the inducer: With the control, but not with the inducer, your body is moving about and, largely for that reason, you are moving about in relation to independently existing people and other entities. At least in that modest sense, with the control you will have some behavior. And, with the control but not with the inducer, you will have conscious veridical perception of your moving body and, as well, of many independently existing entities. True enough, as regards the sources of your behavior, even with the control you will be greatly in error. But, about many other things, your experience will be relevantly revealing.

As regards our present topic, a related question is even more worth asking: In *what* ways is the pleasant radio control *no better* than the pleasant experience inducer? First, and most obviously, just as with the inducer, with the comprehensively effective radio control, you will never perform your own intentional actions. Moreover, just as with the inducer, when you are subject to the radio control, then relatively little of your life will be determined by, or will be an expression of, your own distinctive psychology: In the case of the experience inducer, your psychology provided the scientists only with general guidelines for, or general constraints on, a program to generate pleasant "realistic" experience. Ever so many of the details will be provided in some other way, not much related to your own nature. Similarly, in the case of the radio control, your psychology provides the scientists only with general guidelines for, or general constraints on, a program to generate "successful" behavior.

There is little doubt that, at least for these reasons, just as a choice against the pleasant inducer is rational for us, so is a choice against the pleasant radio control. Even for those of us who do not believe in a transcendental Free Will, this choice will be a rational selection. Because this choice is rational, the Extreme Doctrine must be false.

Just as the desirability of veridical conscious perception is relevantly inflexible, so the desirability of performing our own intentional actions also does not depend on what has been the usual situation, or on what we believe to have been the usual state of affairs. For example, we might discover that, before the day of choice, all of our behavior was determined by pleasant radio controls. Still, against such pleasant control in the future, we choose a situation where, even after the day of choice, we will not again be radio controlled and, on our own, we will lead somewhat less pleasant lives.

Confronting hypothetical choices can help to clarify what actually are our values. Once a certain amount of clarity has been gained in a certain area of values, then, in that area, further situations of choice may not be needed. So, consider a world where both we ourselves, as well as non-intelligent computer systems that pleasantly control us, came into being via a statistical miracle. For us, this world, too, presents a bad situation. So, even if there never has been anyone performing intentional actions, it will be of value to us that, in the future, we perform such actions.

As reasoning shows, this case of the pleasant radio control nicely complements, and is nicely complemented by, certain key cases from our previous sections: As we already noted, with the pleasant experience inducer, a subject will lack not only intentional action but also veridical conscious perception. So, as we may now note, it appears that the badness of the pleasant inducer is overdetermined. To my mind, the badness of the pleasant radio control confirms this appearance of overdetermination. For, with that radio control, although we still lack intentional action, we do have veridical conscious perception. Even with lots of pleasant experience enjoyed in veridical perception, this control provides us with a situation that is quite bad.

Have I been too hasty? Might this radio case show, instead, that, among these factors, it is *only* intentional action that we value? After all, as is evident, intentional action is missing both with the inducer and also with the radio control. No; I have not been too hasty. We need only recall the case of the pleasant portable inducer and the experiential isolation drug. In that example, there was plenty of conscious experience, all right, and plenty of successful intentional action, too. And, to boot, on top of all that, there was even plenty of (unconscious) veridical perception of the world that served to guide the successful action. But, still, that situation, too, was rather bad. The reason for that, as we recall, is that there was no *conscious* (veridical) perception of the world. Because all of this is so, there is strong confirmation for the idea that, in the case of the pleasant *non*-portable experience inducer, the badness of the situation really is overdetermined. Indeed, as the experiential isolation drug helps to show, not only do we greatly value our veridical conscious perception, and not only do we also greatly value our intentional action, but quite beyond any mere conjunction of those goods, we greatly value our veridical conscious perception *of* our intentional action.

Working toward an appreciation of our actual values is a complex and difficult project. Having taken only a few steps toward gaining this appreciation, I will now call a halt to this particular attempt. Backtracking just a bit, before I close perhaps I may emphasize some points about the Extreme Doctrine and, in our primary topic area, perhaps I may nail down a point about the Extreme Claim: First, quite apart from large metaphysical considerations, you are rational in valuing situations in which, often enough, you perform your own intentional actions. Moreover, quite apart from those large considerations, you rationally value situations in which, at least to a fairly large extent, your intentional performances are manifestations of your own rather distinctive psychology. Because these points hold true, this related point also holds true: Just as the Extreme Claim about survival is badly false, so the Extreme Doctrine about Action is also badly false.

Especially if this chapter's sections had been presented in a different order, but well enough in any case, we may put this last point with the focus reversed. In that way, the point will be focused on our primary topic area: Just as there is no truth in the Extreme Doctrine, so there is none, either, in the Extreme Claim about our survival over time. To the contrary, although we may be physically complex entities, and although we may be conventionally demarcated from the rest of reality, we are very rational in caring about ourselves and, often enough, in caring a great deal about the conventionally demarcated people whom we love.

BIBLIOGRAPHY

Ayer, A.J. *The Problem of Knowledge*, Penguin Books, 1956.

Blakemore, Colin and Susan Greenfield, eds., *Mindwaves*, Basil Blackwell, 1987.

Brennan, Andrew. *Conditions of Identity*, Oxford University Press, 1988.

Broad, C.D. *Examination of MacTaggart's Philosophy*, Volume I, Cambridge University Press, 1933.

Brody, Baruch. *Identity and Essence*, Princeton University Press, 1980.

Bunzl, Martin. "Causal Overdetermination," *Journal of Philosophy*, 1979.

Burke, Michael. "Cohabitation, Stuff and Intermittent Existence," *Mind*, 1980.

Butler, Joseph. "Of Personal Identity" (first appendix to *The Analogy of Religion*), 1736, reprinted in Perry (1).

Carroll, John. "The Humean Tradition," *Philosophical Review*, forthcoming.

————. *Laws of Nature*, forthcoming.

Carruthers, Peter. "Brute Experience," *Journal of Philosophy*, 1989.

Chisholm, Roderick. *Person and Object*, George Allen & Unwin, 1976.

Daniels, Charles. "Personal Identity," in C. Brown and P. French (eds.) *Puzzles, Paradoxes and Problems*, St. Martin's Press, 1987.

Dennett, Daniel. "Where Am I?," in Hofstadter and Dennett.

Dennett, Daniel and Douglas Hofstadter, "Reflections" (on Zuboff) in Hofstadter and Dennett.

Descartes, Rene. (1) *Meditations on First Philosophy*, 1641.

————. (2) "Reply to the Fifth Set of Objections," in E. Haldane and G. Ross, *Philosophical Works of Descartes*, Volume 2, Dover Publications, 1955.

Enc, Berent. "Numerical Identity and Objecthood," *Mind*, 1975.

Feyerabend, Paul. "Mental Events and the Brain," *Journal of Philosophy*, 1963, reprinted in Rosenthal.

339

Frankfurt, Harry. *The importance of what we care about,* Cambridge University Press, 1988.

Garrett, Brian. (1) "Personal Identity and Extrinsicness," *Philosophical Studies,* forthcoming.

————. (2) "Personal Identity and Reductionism," *Philosophy and Phenomenological Research,* forthcoming.

Gillet, Grant. "Brain Bisection and Personal Identity," *Mind,* 1986.

Goldman, Alvin. "A Causal Theory of Knowing," *Journal of Philosophy,* 1967.

Hirsch, Eli. *The Concept of Identity,* Oxford University Press, 1982.

Hofstadter, Douglas and Daniel Dennett. (eds.) *The Mind's I,* Bantam Books, 1982.

Hume, David. *Treatise of Human Nature,* 1739, partly reprinted in Perry (1).

Johnston, Mark. (1) "Human Beings," *Journal of Philosophy,* 1987.

————. (2) Review of Shoemaker and Swinburne's *Personal Identity, Philosophical Review,* 1987.

————. (3) "Is There a Problem About Persistence?," *Proceedings of the Aristotelian Society, Supplementary Volume,* 1987.

————. (4) "Relativism and the Self," in Michael Krausz, ed., *Relativism,* University of Notre Dame Press, 1989.

————. (5) "Fission and the Facts," *Philosophical Perspectives,* 1989.

————. (6) "Reasons and Reductionism," *Philosophical Review,* forthcoming.

Kolak, Daniel and Raymond Martin. "Personal Identity and Causality: Becoming Unglued," *American Philosophical Quarterly,* 1987.

Lewis, David. (1) "Survival and Identity," in A. Rorty, reprinted with postscripts in Lewis (3).

————. (2) "Scorekeeping in a Language Game," *Journal of Philosophical Logic,* 1979, reprinted with postscripts in Lewis (3).

————. (3) *Philosophical Papers,* Volume I, Oxford University Press, 1983.

Locke, John. *Essay Concerning Human Understanding,* 1694, partly reprinted in Perry (1).

MacDonald, G.F. (ed.) *Perception and Identity,* Cornell University Press, 1979.

Mackay, Donald. "Divided Brains—Divided Minds?," in C. Blakemore and S. Greenfield, eds., *Mindwaves.*

Mackie, John. *Problems from Locke,* Oxford University Press, 1976.

Madell, Geoffrey. (1) *The Identity of the Self,* Edinburgh University Press, 1981.

————. (2) "Derek Parfit and Greta Garbo," *Analysis,* 1985.

Martin, Raymond. (1) "Identity's Crisis," *Philosophical Studies,* 1988.

————. (2) "Identity and Survival: The Persons We Most Want to Be," in *The Experience of Philosophy,* D. Kolak and R. Martin (eds.), Wadsworth, forthcoming.

McGinn, Colin. *The Character of Mind,* Oxford University Press, 1982.

Moore, G.E. *Principia Ethica,* Cambridge University Press, 1903.

Nagel, Thomas. (1) "Death," *Nous,* 1970, reprinted in Nagel (3).

————. (2) "Brain Bisection and the Unity of Consciousness," *Synthese,* 1971, reprinted in Perry (1) and in Nagel (3).

————. (3) *Mortal Questions,* Cambridge University Press, 1979.

————. (4) *The View from Nowhere,* Oxford University Press, 1986.

Nozick, Robert. (1) *Anarchy, State and Utopia,* Basic Books, 1974.

————. (2) *Philosophical Explanations,* Harvard University Press, 1981.

Oderberg, David. "Johnston on Human Beings," *Journal of Philosophy,* 1989.

Parfit, Derek. (1) "Personal Identity," *Philosophical Review,* 1971, reprinted in Perry
(1).
————. (2) "On the Importance of Self-Identity," *Journal of Philosophy,* 1971.
————. (3) "Lewis, Perry and What Matters," in A. Rorty, ed., *The Identities of
Persons.*
————. (4) *Reasons and Persons,* Oxford University Press, 1984.
Perry, John. (1) (ed.) *Personal Identity,* University of California Press, 1975.
————. (2) "Can the Self Divide?," *Journal of Philosophy,* 1972.
————. (3) "The Importance of Being Identical," in A. Rorty.
Plato. *Philebus.*
Quine, W.V. Review of Milton K. Munitz, ed., *Identity and Individuation, Journal of
Philosophy,* 1972.
Quinton, Anthony. "The Soul," *Journal of Philosophy,* 1962, reprinted in Perry (1).
————. *The Nature of Things,* Routledge & Kegan Paul, 1973.
Reid, Thomas. "Of Memory," in *Essays on the Intellectual Powers of Man,* 1785,
reprinted in Perry (1).
Robinson, John. "Personal Identity and Survival," *Journal of Philosophy,* 1988.
Rorty, Amelie. (ed.) *The Identities of Persons,* University of California Press, 1976.
Rorty, Richard. "Mind-Body Identity, Privacy and Categories," *Review of Metaphysics,*
1965, reprinted in Rosenthal.
Rosenthal, David. (ed.) *Materialism and the Mind-Body Problem,* Prentice-Hall, 1971.
Rovane, Carol. "Branching Self-Consciousness," forthcoming.
Shoemaker, Sydney. (1) *Self-Knowledge and Self-Identity,* Cornell University Press,
1963.
————. (2) *Identity, Cause and Mind,* Cambridge University Press, 1984
————. (3) "Personal Identity: a Materialist's Account," in Shoemaker and
Swinburne.
————. (4) Critical notice of Parfit's *Reasons and Persons, Mind,* 1985.
Shoemaker, Sydney and Richard Swinburne, *Personal Identity,* Basil Blackwell, 1984.
Sidgwick, Henry. *The Methods of Ethics,* London, Macmillan, 1907, 7th edition.
Sorensen, Roy. (1) *Blindspots,* Oxford University Press, 1988.
————. (2) *Thought Experiments,* forthcoming.
Sosa, Ernest. (1) "Subjects Among Other Things," *Philosophical Perspectives,* 1987.
————. (2) "Surviving Matters," forthcoming.
Sperry, R.W. (1) "Brain Bisection and Mechanisms of Consciousness," in J. Eccles
(ed.), *Brain and Conscious Experience,* Springer-Verlag, 1966.
————. (2) "Hemispheric Deconnection and Unity in Conscious Awareness," *American Psychologist,* 1968.
Stone, Jim. (1) "Parfit and the Buddha: Why There Are No People," *Philosophy and
Phenomenological Research,* 1988.
————. (2) "Why Potentiality Matters," *Canadian Journal of Philosophy,* 1987.
Strawson, Peter. (1) *Individuals,* Methuen, 1959.
————. (2) "Self, Mind and Body," *Common Factor,* 1966.
Swinburne, Richard. (1) "Personal Identity," *Proceedings of the Aristotelian Society,*
1973–74.
————. (2) "Personal Identity: the Dualist Theory," in Shoemaker and Swinburne.
Swoyer, Chris. (1) "Causation and Identity," *Midwest Studies in Philosophy,* 1984.
————. (2) "Rival Claimants," unpublished.

Unger, Peter. (1) "An Analysis of Factual Knowledge," *Journal of Philosophy*, 1968.

————. (2) "I Do Not Exist," in G. F. MacDonald, *Perception and Identity*, Cornell University Press, 1979.

————. (3) "Why There Are No People," *Midwest Studies in Philosophy*, 1979.

————. (4) "The Causal Theory of Reference," *Philosophical Studies*, 1981.

————. (5) "Toward a Psychology of Common Sense," *American Philosophical Quarterly*, 1982.

————. (6) *Philosophical Relativity*, University of Minnesota Press, 1984.

————. (7) "Consciousness and Self-Identity," *Midwest Studies in Philosophy*, 1986.

————. (8) "Conscious Beings in a Gradual World," *Midwest Studies in Philosophy*, 1988.

Van Inwagen, Peter. *Material Beings*, Cornell University Press, forthcoming.

Wachsberg, Milton. "Personal Identity, The Nature of Persons, and Ethical Theory," Ph.D. diss., Princeton University, 1983.

Walsh, Kevin. *Neuropsychology*, Churchill Livingstone, 1987.

Weiskrantz, Larry. "Neuropsychology and the Nature of Consciousness," in C. Blakemore and S. Greenfield, eds., *Mindwaves*.

White, Stephen. (1) "What is it Like to be an Homunculus?," *Pacific Philosophical Quarterly*, 1987.

————. (2) "Self-Deception and Responsibility for the Self," in Brian McLaughlin and Amelie Rorty, eds., *Perspectives on Self-Deception*, University of California Press, 1988.

————. (3) "Metapsychological Relativism and the Self," *Journal of Philosophy*, 1989.

Wiggins, David. (1) *Identity and Spatio-Temporal Continuity*, Basil Blackwell, 1967.

————. (2) *Sameness and Substance*, Harvard University Press, 1980.

————. (3) "The Concern to Survive," *Midwest Studies in Philosophy*, 1979.

Wilkes, Kathleen V. *Real People*, Oxford University Press, 1988.

Williams, Bernard. (1) "The Self and the Future," *Philosophical Review*, 1970, reprinted in Williams (3) and in Perry (1).

————. (2) "Bodily Continuity and Personal Identity," *Analysis*, 1960, reprinted in Williams (3).

————. (3) *Problems of the Self*, Cambridge University Press, 1973.

Zemach, Eddy. "Looking Out for Number One," *Philosophy and Phenomenological Research*, 1987.

Zuboff, Arnold. (1) "The Story of a Brain," in Hofstadter and Dennett.

————. (2) Casette Recordings of Talks on Consciousness and Personal Identity, 1983 and 1984.

NAME INDEX